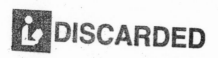

Theatre and Crisis
1632–1642

To JANE

Theatre and Crisis
1632–1642

MARTIN BUTLER

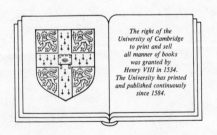

The right of the
University of Cambridge
to print and sell
all manner of books
was granted by
Henry VIII in 1534.
The University has printed
and published continuously
since 1584.

CAMBRIDGE UNIVERSITY PRESS

Cambridge

London   New York   New Rochelle
Melbourne   Sydney

Published by the Press Syndicate of the University of Cambridge
The Pitt Building, Trumpington Street, Cambridge CB2 1RP
32 East 57th Street, New York, NY 10022, USA
296 Beaconsfield Parade, Middle Park, Melbourne 3206, Australia

First published 1984

Printed in Great Britain by
the University Press, Cambridge

Library of Congress catalogue card number: 83–15250

British Library Cataloguing in Publication Data
Butler, Martin
Theatre and crisis, 1632–1642.
1. Theatre–England–History–17th century
I. Title
792'.0942   PN2592

ISBN 0 521 24632 6

UP

Contents

Illustrations

Nos 1, 2, 9, 10 and 11 are reproduced by permission of the
Trustees of the British Museum; nos 3, 4, 6, 7 and 8 by permission
of the British Library; and no. 5 by permission of the Syndics of
Cambridge University Library.

Tables

Preface

THIS BOOK is a study of the English theatre during the years immediately before the Civil War, focusing particularly on its treatment of political subjects and themes, its engagement with the issues of state, society and religion which were to generate the crisis of 1642. The character of this body of drama is revealed most fully and most significantly by an investigation of its political interests, and I believe that its modern critical devaluation has been due in considerable measure to persistent misconceptions about these concerns, and to a failure to recognize how frequently they were its leading preoccupations.

Moreover its historical placing, at the end of a long theatrical tradition and on the eve of a moment of major political upheaval, makes it a unique test case for examining certain basic assumptions which commonly surface in criticism of the whole seventy years or so of English Renaissance theatre. As I explain in my introduction, the wider implications of this study arise from the opportunity which it provides for verifying or qualifying what are broadly agreed to be the underlying social and political tendencies of the English Renaissance stage in general, the nature, extent and limitations of its sympathies, its prejudices and its allegiances. The belief that the Elizabethan and early Stuart theatre was eventually to turn into a Cavalier theatre has profoundly affected our conception of its history, for that history has implicitly been written very largely from the point of view that the situation of the drama was always fundamentally contingent on the situation of the court, that in the crisis of 1642 the drama would inevitably tend to come down firmly on the side of the monarchy and against its critics. This point has been crucial to our valuation of the later drama and to many interpretations of the greater drama which preceded it but on investigation it proves to be problematic and to leave much out of account – especially, I wish to suggest, those things which in the decade 1632–42 are of greatest interest and significance. This is the larger question which principally I am going to be addressing and challenging.

So I have adopted the chronological limits 1632–42 in the first instance for pragmatic reasons, that they denote a period of drama significant simply for having been neglected and misunderstood for so long, but also for their very considerable symbolic force, that they stand for the final decade of the Renaissance stage in England, supposedly the 'death' of the Elizabethan theatre, in which we might expect to find its characteristic strengths and weaknesses most fully manifested. In 1632 appeared the first of the new 'decadent' line of amateur courtier plays, Walter Montagu's *Shepherd's Paradise*, while simultaneously that notorious warning of the theatre's offensiveness to puritan sensibilities, William Prynne's massive attack on the stage, *Histriomastix*, was in the press. Ten years later parliament closed the playhouses virtually at the same moment as it took up arms against the king. In politics, the decade begins with Charles's experiment in personal rule at its most determined (William Noy was made Attorney-General in 1631, Wentworth was sent to Ireland in 1632, Laud became Archbishop of Canterbury in 1633); it closes with an unprecedented failure of confidence in the court, with political deadlock and civil war. Any drama is going to be judged in relation to the quality of its insight into the principal issues of its time, and this consideration impinges more closely on this decade than on most others. It has usually been felt that a drama which since the days of Elizabeth had been sponsored and protected by royalty went down in 1642 in the wake of the collapse of the court, but it may equally well be true that a theatre which had in the past been able to produce plays like *Tamburlaine* and *King Lear* was in 1642 involved in a political crisis which in important senses was partly of its own creation.

Preface

The preparation of this book has brought me many friendships and many debts. Heartfelt gratitude goes especially to Leo Salingar, who supervised this work when it was a PhD thesis with great kindness and care, and to Margot Heinemann who has been overwhelmingly generous with her ideas and her enthusiasm. Both will find much here that is more properly theirs. I am very grateful too to Marie Axton, Anne Barton, Professor Muriel Bradbrook, Derek Hirst and John Rathmell for reading and commenting on earlier drafts, and particularly to John Morrill for help and warm encouragement on the historical side, and to Peter Holland for friendly interest and criticism extending over a period of years. My unsolicited inquiries have been very kindly answered by Richard Luckett, Gill Spraggs, Lois Potter, Peter Salt, J. F. Fuggles, Susan Halpert, Geoffrey Trease, Ruth Spalding, Professor Jason P. Rosenblatt and Professor John Orrell. None of these however is responsible for any errors which I have introduced. The revision of this book was made possible by the generosity of the Master and Fellows of Trinity Hall, Cambridge, in awarding me a research fellowship, and made pleasant by the courteous efficiency which prevails at the Cambridge University Library. My family have been very good in moments of need and, above all, my wife has been constantly involved and has worked harder than any. If I say that we have learned the significance of the word crisis together, she will know exactly what I mean.

Note on procedures

I HAVE QUOTED Massinger from the edition of Philip Edwards and Colin Gibson (1976), Suckling from the edition of T. Clayton and L. A. Beaurline (1971), and Cartwright from the edition of G. B. Evans (1951). Elsewhere, in the absence of reliable modern comprehensive editions, I have quoted from the original texts, silently expanding speech-headings. The one exception is Brome, whose plays are difficult to obtain, and for convenience I have given page references to J. Pearson's three-volume reprint of 1873, but checking my texts against the originals. It should be noted that in volume 2 of Pearson's Brome *The Lovesick Court*, *Covent Garden Weeded* and *The Queen and Concubine* are paginated separately. Old-style dates have been altered to conform with the modern calendar, and to avoid confusion with the Cockpit-in-court I have referred throughout to the Drury Lane Cockpit by its alternative name, the Phoenix.

Some contentions

NO BODY OF English drama stands to gain more from the recent shifts in understanding the relationship between puritanism and theatre[1] than the drama of 1632–1642, since judgments of the quality of this drama depend crucially on beliefs about its responsiveness, or indifference, towards puritanism. The closure of the theatres in 1642 by a puritan-inspired parliament looks very much like the inevitable consequence of the rise of powerful new ideas, social attitudes and economic forces which puritanism broadly represented, a new order fundamentally opposed to the old, traditional ways for which the dramatists were the spokesmen and which puritanism quickly invalidated upon achieving power. The traditional view presents the drama of 1632–42 as unwilling to acknowledge these new threatening forces and withdrawing into a world of escapism, fantasy and romance, designed to divert its courtly auditors from the reality of their impending doom. By helping to foster the frivolous 'Cavalier mentality' the stage is held to have contributed to the national crisis and assured its own demise, as well as to have cut itself off from all that was serious or meaningful in contemporary experience;[2] already 'decadent', it was ripe for the cropping. Thus the decline and collapse of the theatre in this period has been seen as the unavoidable corollary of the simultaneous triumph of puritanism, but it is a picture which, we are gradually coming to see, simply will not square with the facts and often obscures them. I shall be contending that the drama of the 1630s, perhaps more than any earlier drama, did persistently engage in debating the political issues of its day, and repeatedly articulated attitudes which can only be labelled 'opposition' or 'puritan'. The political aspects of these plays frequently carry major levels of meaning, or even their primary meanings. To appreciate them fully it is necessary to attend continually to their political dimensions, but these have been hidden by misleading suppositions about their historical context and by insufficient concern for their sensitivity to 'opposition' points of view, tendencies which we are at last in a position to correct.

So this drama has great interest in its own right. While lacking that undergrowth of engaging minor talent which buttressed the theatre of earlier generations, it still produced several writers of distinction (notably Brome, Massinger and Shirley, on whom I shall chiefly be concentrating), and many plays of real, lasting merit. But it is also important for what it confirms or denies about the larger trends of the English theatre. As the last decade of the Renaissance stage in England, it presents the prime test case for many basic assumptions underlying our reading of the greater Elizabethan and Jacobean drama.

It is axiomatic in theatre studies that the drama was protected and fostered by the court, reflected its values, and always strove for closer identification with it; E. K. Chambers's monumental *Elizabethan Stage* opens with seven chapters headed 'The Court'. The dramatists have been repeatedly represented as inherently conservative and conformist, apologists for established hierarchies and degree and passive submission to the God-given ruler. Emotionally attached to a humane and ordered past, they had only hostility for the disruptive effects of the new science, commerce and mechanistic philosophy (Shakespeare has been seen as the great proponent of Tudor orthodoxy, and Jonson as the scourge of the rising acquisitive classes). To attack the stage, sustained as it was by royal prerogative, was, we are told, covertly to attack the monarchy,[3] so government critics drifted naturally into opposition to theatre; conversely, players ridiculed the puritans. Already in Shakespeare's lifetime, the theatre's national basis, on which the greatness of his plays was built, is supposed to have been disintegrating. The middle classes withdrew from the playhouses, audiences became progressively more elegant.

New dramatists preferred to write for the fashionable and restricted 'private' playhouses which rapidly developed into an exclusive Cavalier milieu, while the old-style open-air 'public' theatres faded into obscurity. As the drama reorganized on a class basis, it became the plaything of a dominant but unpopular elite. After the Restoration, it is the 'private' theatres, patronized by royalty, that alone survive.

These assumptions rest heavily – crucially – on the developments of 1632–42. This is regarded as the decade when the court finally 'invaded' the theatre.[4] Charles's queen took to acting in plays and even visited the Blackfriars playhouse; court masques became increasingly sumptuous; courtier-playwrights, perceiving dramatic authorship to be a new road to royal favour, appeared. Outside the court, the 'public' playhouses, only three of which now survived (the Globe, Fortune and Red Bull), scarcely saw a new play. The creative initiative seems to have fallen to the 'private' theatres (the Blackfriars, Phoenix and Salisbury Court), and their repertoire was becoming gradually dominated by court taste. The decade produced the first romantic–heroic plays of love and honour, and comedies of fashionable London life, the concerns and sentiments of which appear to be increasingly courtly. These look like decisive steps towards 1660, and indeed some critics have expressed an absence of surprise that when the puritan William Prynne thunderously criticized the stage the court responded as if to a personal attack, and that when parliament went to war on the king in 1642, the stage fell with the monarchy and remained inhibited until the court's return eighteen years later. The limits 1632–42 have been generally taken as marking the culminating steps in the underlying tendencies of the English Renaissance theatre: the stage's failure was a product of circumstance, but it was also a consummation which it had sought.

However, I wish to suggest that the evidence of this decade in fact calls these certainties into question. I shall argue that the best courtly plays were vehicles of criticism rather than compliment (chapters 3–4); that puritanism was often compatible with theatre-going (chapters 5–6); that the plays of the private theatres were engaged in debating serious and pressing issues (chapters 7 and 9); that all the life of the drama was not confined to the private playhouses but the popular theatre tradition still exerted a vital, formative influence (chapter 8). Most of all, we distort this drama fatally if we read it simply as a mouthpiece to the court, subservient, helplessly dependent, toadying. Rather, it seems to me strongest where it is most critical and questioning, scrutinizing received platitudes, proposing alternatives, engaging most closely with the contradictions inherent in living in a time of change and uncertainty. These qualities are surely common to all better drama, but in the 1630s it comes to mean increasingly that the stage is most exciting where it is most responsive to 'opposition' or 'puritan' feeling, and that the more purely courtly tradition, which has made all the running so far, is both the least interesting and least significant aspect of the period. The courtly stage is the modern annexe to the great cathedral of the professional theatre (with all its well established bourgeois and popular sympathies), not vice versa.

For this reason, I have made a major break in this study between chapters 4 and 5 to correspond to what I take to be this fundamental distinction in the theatres, between drama written principally for the court, and drama intended for other, wider audiences. These non-courtly stages – both 'public' and 'private' – were not sinking inexorably into a morbid condition of ever more intransigent Cavalierism, but inherited and continued to develop the rich, varied and essentially independent-minded tradition of the Elizabethan–Jacobean professional theatre. Their relatively free treatment of political subjects corresponds with their continued *detachment* from the court. As for court drama, that was another story entirely. The dramatists who wrote for Whitehall had a much narrower freedom of manoeuvre. They were limited in the material they could use, the diversity of opinion they could express, the range of conflicting or unresolved attitudes which they could incorporate into their plays. The assumptions underlying court drama are much more constricted, rigid and defined than are those which obtained on the non-courtly stage, and the non-courtly drama has been devalued exactly in proportion to the extent that it has been read as if subscribing to these alien assumptions.

So I wish to establish the importance and pervasiveness of un- and anti-courtly sentiment in this drama; and the continuing breadth and seriousness of the non-courtly drama. On the other hand, although the shift between courtly and non-courtly drama obviously has significance for the extent and freedom with which politics is discussed, I do not believe that we can make a simple correlation between courtly and non-courtly drama and courtly and non-courtly in politics (where this distinction is much harder to maintain consistently). The crisis of 1642 has been seen also as a cultural crisis in which the two nations that were England, one popish, cultivated and Italianate, the other puritan, iconoclastic and insular, achieved their inevitable collision.[5] But the lines of demarcation are much less absolute on the ground; Milton is only the most obvious example of someone who has affinities with both categories. 'Cavalier' and 'puritan', 'court' and 'country' were not fixed norms of sensibility or behaviour to one or other of which every individual conformed, but values in a continual state of flux or dialectic, each perpetually modifying and modified by the other as they issued into the experience of their time; nor can they be detached neatly, as a stereotyped pair of attitudes, from the confusions and complexity of the experience within which they were embodied and realized. Both exerted their claims simultaneously on all members of society, and they, subjected to many conflicting pressures, differed among themselves as variously, and contradicted themselves as often as we do now, so that the crisis not only divided men among themselves but caused a species of division in the minds of all. Variousness is something on which drama thrives, and in the 1630s the stage, rather than becoming the casualty of a cultural divide, was able to draw strength from the conflicting prejudices and aspirations still coexisting richly in its audience – the opposed tensions and tendencies within society which would ultimately fly apart but which at present still continued to overlap and interact. For example, Charles's court was by no means wholly in agreement with the way he was ruling and the best courtly drama is that which finds a voice for the dissent of those who are anxious about, or actively opposed to the tendencies of his government (chapters 3–4). Similarly, the non-courtly 'opposition' to Charles was not a uniform movement, but an alliance of opinion that cut broadly across the social spectrum and yoked many different kinds of discontent; nor were these people all looking for the same solutions to their grievances. The 'opposition' feeling which is expressed in 'private' theatre plays (chapters 7 and 9) often has a rather gentlemanly stamp; but the attitudes of the 'public' theatre drama (chapter 8) are altogether more violently plebeian, radical and levelling. There is here a society seriously at disagreement with itself; but the disagreements have not yet entirely polarized into mutually exclusive counter-cultures.

There was, of course, a well-oiled machine of censorship which exerted strong constraints on the players' freedom of expression, but this could be circumvented with caution in the non-courtly theatre, and even at court devices could be used which, without openly bringing political events and issues on stage, alluded to them obliquely. An unusually clear example is provided by a court play of 1620 'in which a king with his two sons has one of them put to death, simply upon suspicion that he wished to deprive him of his crown, and the other son actually did deprive him of it afterwards. This moved the king [James] in an extraordinary manner, both inwardly and outwardly'.[6] This corresponds with nothing in the immediate political situation (Prince Henry had been dead for seven years), and it has no obvious allegorical significance, yet James evidently saw something unpalatable here. Probably in these basic motifs of tyrannical kingship, misplaced trust and misused power he recognized a generalized but intended likeness to what were actually very real issues in contemporary politics. It was often in devices of this kind, that work not through direct statement or allegory but through analogy and oblique reflection – mirrors for magistrates, in fact – that dramatists reflected the political concerns of 1632–42.

6

2

Drama and the Caroline crisis

The '*ex post facto*' view

IF A PRINCIPAL PREOCCUPATION of this drama is politics, the
critical problem is one of historical perspective, and here there
exist widely-held preconceptions which pervasively distort and
predetermine discussion of the drama of the pre-revolutionary
period. These can be illustrated from Clifford Leech's essay 'The
Caroline audience'[1] which may be taken as representative of the
critical position (it is by no means an extreme example). To
Leech, the quality of this drama was entirely dictated by its
situation; its artistic inferiority he openly asserts was coded into
the historical processes of which it was a part. The basic
proposition is that 'Masques and plays were for these people a
way of escape from the unpleasantness of political circumstance
and a means of cultivating the graces ... It is difficult not to
take an *ex post facto* view, but the Caroline audience seems like a
community of people waiting for its own dissolution, sipping its
hemlock daintily.' A playwright could be good only 'in spite of
his time' (p. 161).

The concession to an *ex post facto* view, with its suggestion
that the decline of the drama in these last years was somehow
inevitable, is entirely characteristic. On the one hand, it reflects
the popular notion that this was the *decadence* of the drama, a term
surviving from late Victorian attempts to make literary criticism
scientific by appropriating Darwinian evolutionary language to
describe English Renaissance drama as a *species* which 'died' in
1642 (while the fitter strain, puritanism, survived). The fallacies
behind this have been exposed,[2] but *decadence* remains a
persistently-used term, with its pejorative implications for the

1630s that the stage was already in a state of irreversible organic decay. On the other hand, it also reflects Leech's nagging foreknowledge that the theatres were indeed shortly to be closed down, a foreknowledge which he implicitly attributes to the playwrights and their audiences themselves, characterizing their culture as one already in a process of retreat, narrow, isolated and toppling into imminent collapse. He continually berates the theatre-goers for their failure to come to terms with the coming nemesis, describing them as 'shallow', 'inattentive' and 'frivolous' (pp. 161, 168). Their palates were sick, for they lived a 'vicarious existence' and desired only dishes that pleased and were 'untroublesome to the jaded guest' (p. 178). The dramatists had to provide 'etiolated gracefulness' (p. 172), sophisticated bawdry (p. 177), 'a romantic escape into a world where there were none of the threats that they themselves knew but instead elegant menaces that were foreign to them' (p. 173). The one quality 'indispensable for success was some measure of withdrawal from the actual' (p. 178). A society of fashion and fickleness, they were ready to be swept away, and they knew it.

The effects of this perspective on criticism are really quite extraordinary, for at every point conceptions of what the drama ought to have been intervene to modify discussion of what it *was*. Leech feels that the playwrights must have falsified their perceptions to write as they did. He attributes 'unease' to Massinger, 'impatience' to Brome, 'compromises' to Davenant and 'discomfort' to Heywood (pp. 161, 173). Against their wills they tormented 'their natural bent of mind ... into the fashionable curve, but the continual modifications of this curve made them at times almost lose heart' (p. 181). The common feature of all these plays is their irony. No playwright dare speak of what he perceives, the complacency of each play is implicitly undermined by the 'realities' which surround it. Conversely, when a playwright does seem to be speaking out of turn, an *ex post facto* glance at his later career and opinions, or at the future history of the theatre, often suffices to discount the seriousness of his criticisms.[3]

Clearly, it is highly unsatisfactory that deep-rooted convictions about the inevitability of the decline of Caroline drama should interfere so radically with criticism of the plays (and even, in some text-book accounts, replace discussion of them altogether). I believe we are witnessing here a kind of critical Whiggery corresponding broadly with the Whiggish perspectives on the seventeenth century that have come under fire among historians in recent years,[4] since these critical judgments are couched so firmly in political terms. The drama is bad because its cause, inevitably, seems bad. Once the decline of the theatre is associated with the crisis of confidence in the court, the dramatists come to be castigated, with assurance born of wisdom after the event, for belonging to what always seems to have been the wrong side. Leech's *ex post facto* view involves a commitment (which can be matched in the comments of many other writers)[5] to a simplified view of the seventeenth-century crisis as one continuous move-ment, a two-handed struggle between parliamentary rule and royal absolutism in politics, and patriotic puritanism and hispano-phile crypto-Catholicism in religion, which begins at the acces-sion of James and accelerates in a uniform crescendo culminating inexorably in the execution of Charles in 1649. In this perspective, the 1630s stage seems involved in a systematic divide which already has several decades' history and is expanding rapidly and uncontrollably. Leech's backwards look onto the crisis reads 1632–42 as a 'high road to civil war',[6] fraught with difficulties that inevitably foreshadow the breakdowns of 1642 and 1649, and this superimposes the polarizations of subsequent conflicts, between 'Cavalier' and 'puritan', back onto earlier years. Hence the dramatists are discussed in terms suggesting that the nation was already irrevocably and decisively split, and that the only choice open to them was a single, simple one between court and parliament, and that a decision to write for the stage was equivalent to acceptance of a narrow and doomed set of attitudes. The standard book on the 1630s theatre (by Alfred Harbage) is called, simply, *Cavalier Drama*.

In the 1640s, Cavalier propagandists tried to suggest that this was indeed the case. In 1647, the royalist publisher Humphrey Moseley issued a collected edition of Beaumont and Fletcher's plays, prefacing them with thirty-seven sets of commendatory verses, many solicited from prominent Cavaliers such as the soldier Sir George Lisle (executed at Colchester, 1648) and the journalist Sir John Berkenhead. Four years later, a similar collection followed for the amateur dramatist William Cartwright, this time with fifty-three sets of verses! These were conscious acts of propaganda. The verses are arranged to give prominence to the well-known loyalists, and several versifiers, especially in the 1651 volume, can be shown to have been too young to have known the theatres before they closed in 1642, and they speak of 'reading' rather than 'seeing' the plays. They reflect the atmosphere of Civil War Oxford, not peace-time London, but it was very useful to Moseley to be able to suggest that such divisions between loyal and disloyal subjects had always been there, and that the Cavaliers were sensitive to the arts while their opponents were ignorant blockheads. By contrast, 'dammees' and sectaries appeared together on stage in one play of the 1630s, Brome's *Weeding of Covent Garden* (1632), but without any suggestion that there was a political divide between them, nor even that the audience should see themselves in the 'Dammees'.[7] England clearly did plunge into a tremendous crisis in 1642, one that had roots striking deep into the economic, social and religious changes that were profoundly transforming their society and the consequences of which may, in the last analysis, have been beyond the capacity of any but the most able and flexible government to overcome. But to infer that the nation was polarizing into two neatly opposed sides throughout the 1630s, and that any royal regime would inevitably have been swept towards a disastrous and unavoidable collapse is to attribute a purposiveness to events that is unwarranted and suspiciously teleological.

So it is necessary to look at the characteristics of politics in this period not only because this is a study of political drama, but because the prevailing *general* critical perspective here is determined entirely by presuppositions about the long-standing foreseeability of the failure of Charles's government and about the exclusiveness of the Cavalier–puritan divide. I have come to think that if there were 'Cavalier' plays in the 1630s they were only a minor factor, and represent the least significant tradition in their own time. Obviously there were 'Cavaliers' in the period, people who would have followed Charles into any wilderness without turning a hair. But equally, almost everyone was simultaneously trumpeting their devotion to the king, even (especially) those who would later fight him, something which has considerable importance for the way kings are treated in the drama and for the readiness with which we write off as 'merely Cavalier' plays in which strong statements of duty to princes exist alongside other, more disrespectful features. The following pages will survey the decade 1632–42 in order to provide a perspective within which its drama may once again become politically meaningful. I shall be arguing that the political possibilities of the period were much more various than the simple Cavalier–puritan polarization allows for, and that by trying to distinguish Cavaliers from Roundheads in the 1630s we are applying categories that will not fit, looking for the conflicts of the Civil War in a decade that was not yet fighting them. And we are missing the really interesting conflicts that actually *were* there.

Eleven years' tyranny and after

In no sense do I wish to minimize the seriousness of the conflicts of Charles's reign. His parliaments of 1625–29 demonstrated the existence of strong disagreements on fundamental issues of policy in church and state, and of shared concern for the survival of traditional rights and liberties. Some radical MPs of 1629 had already conceived a nightmare fear of a crypto-Catholic conspiracy in high places designing to subvert England's religion and government; for his part Charles held the radicals guilty of conspiring to undermine his government, dissolved parliament, and embarked on a personal rule which lasted eleven years.[8] However, it is doubtful whether this conflict could have *inevitably* produced a national breakdown or confrontation between king and parliament. Parliamentary protest alone did not amount to a challenge to royal authority, for parliament still lacked a continuous, fully institutional character. Contemporaries spoke not of 'Parliament' but of 'parliaments' that had different features, and they possessed little idea of, still less desire to see, parliament acting independently of the crown. Loyalty was due to the king-in-parliament, but theories of parliamentary sovereignty or resistance developed only belatedly and hurriedly in the 1640s. More widely held was a concept of parliament as the king's principal council, called by him to advise, and dignified by his presence. Even Charles's extremest critic, Sir John Eliot, thought parliament should counsel but not control the king, bringing 'preparation and maturity, but no further, the resolution and production resting wholly in the king'.[9] Restiveness did not necessarily indicate a desire for revolt, for a measure of protest and criticism was expected from parliaments. They were the national arena of complaint, and represented the people's grievances to the king, but this made them a place of reconciliation, 'an happy occasion and means to have united and settled the affections of Prince and people in a firm concord and correspondence', as much as of confrontation.[10] The notion that service to parliament might become radically incompatible with service to the king, that parliament was trying to take over the government and engaging in a life or death competition for power with the king which ultimately only one could win, would have been quite extraordinary at the time.[11] Rather, Charles began his reign by emphasizing his devotion to parliaments, and doggedly called four in five years. He certainly did have problems – inadequate finance, an antiquated administrative system, religious differences with his subjects – but of these his difficulties at Westminster were less a cause than a symptom. It has been tellingly observed that the important political events of these years occurred *outside* parliament.[12]

However, while lacking power, parliaments did have great influence and in the 1620s were coming to be seen as an important check on the crown. The electorate seems to have been growing and simultaneously demanding greater accountability from its MPs. Yet though this might limit Charles's freedom of manoeuvre, it could not produce out-and-out confrontation until he was in a position where his only option was to call parliament. As he reminded the MPs of 1626, 'Parliaments are altogether in my power for their calling, sitting, and dissolution; therefore, as I find the fruits of them good or evil, they are to continue, or not to be.'[13] Moreover, it is foolish to suppose that even a substantial group of these gentlemanly MPs wished to use parliament to create a national crisis which would be as catastrophic to their social dominance as to the king's. Sir Thomas Wentworth's rule, 'which I will never transgress', reflects the cautiousness of many – 'never to contend with the prerogative out of Parliament, nor yet to contest with a king but when I am constrained thereunto or else make shipwreck of my peace of conscience, which I trust God will ever bless me with, and with courage to preserve it'.[14] Probably most MPs of 1629 would have welcomed a less extreme leadership than that of Eliot (which ultimately broke the parliament). Nine years later, the firm Protestant and parliament-man Simonds D'Ewes lamented that 'most gloomy, sad, and dismal day' for 500 years on which 'divers fiery spirits' had deliberately disrupted a hopeful parliament, but he still felt the future prospects of co-operation were bright:[15]

An easy matter, indeed, it is for a King of England to gain the hearts of his subjects, if he oppress them not in their consciences and liberties; which blessing in my daily prayers I beg of God for our present sovereign, that so his reign over us may be long and happy, and his memory after his death dear and precious to posterity.

Clearly, the will to compromise was still there, and the 1630s continued to see expectations and rumours that Charles would return to a parliamentary way.

So although they might raise the question of the limits of his power, Charles's problems were essentially ones of government rather than authority, and he was still quite capable of governing. James had ruled alone (except for the nine-week Addled Parliament of 1614) for ten years, between 1611 and 1621, without provoking disaster; his son's personal rule was highly effective, the years to 1637 (at least) witnessing not mounting resistance but remarkable quiescence. In the 1620s, MPs had worried that parliaments were declining throughout Europe; in the 1630s Charles seemed indeed to be *en route* to an absolute monarchy on the continental model. The unparliamentary tax, Ship Money, was successfully collected until 1638; as yet, the gentry continued to co-operate with his needs in local government. By 1637, he thought himself 'the happiest Kinge or Prince in all Christendome'; some of the more puritanical nobility were considering emigration.[16] Ultimately, it needed the unusual circumstance of a Scots war to destabilize the personal rule. One observer thought in 1640 that 'with a little more continuance of those annuall charges . . . hee might have established his owne greatnes for ever'.[17]

It has been suggested that in this period future polarities of opinion were anticipated in a growing rift between 'court' and 'country',[18] and certainly the term 'country' had contemporary currency signifying an outlook or set of attitudes opposed to or critical of the 'court'. Country speech aspired to an honest yeomanly (or gentlemanly) bluntness like the 'plain country language, setting by all rhetorical affectations' spoken in 1626 'with excellent grace, boldness, and brave words' by Sir Dudley Digges, MP. It could be free and critical, yet was detached since uncompromised by ambition or interest. For example, Lucy Hutchinson described her father-in-law as 'such a defender of the country's interest, that without affecting it at all, he grew the most popular and most beloved man in the country, even to the envy of those prouder ones that despised the common interest' – his popularity was acceptable because it was unsought, and had no pretensions to faction.[19] Country feeling drew on patriotism and provincialism, concern for the good of the nation and of one's immediate locality. It was attached to traditional ways, order and stability, the importance of place, property and responsibility. These values the court, with its patronage, cultural elitism, administrative novelties and economic exploitation of the country for private ends, continually affronted.

Nevertheless, unlike the fully distinct country party of the Restoration, in an age when the only arena of national politics was still the court, the 'country' had no independent existence as a separate political entity (and the more merely localist, xenophobic levels of country feeling were anyway hostile to any political combination that went beyond their 'country' or county). Charles particularly weakened his 'country' critics by dismissing parliament altogether and so removing the only centre around which criticism could group and be sustained, and in the 1630s court and country cannot be kept distinct but continually interact. In the absence of parliament, Charles's prominent critics of the 1620s continued their political careers as equally prominent court office-holders (Wentworth became Lord Deputy of Ireland, Noy Attorney-General, Selden the apologist for the Ship Money fleet; even Pym held a Receiver-Generalship). Their behaviour does not indicate apostasy from earlier principles but an adjustment to the changing focus of political life. To be politically effective, 'country' figures needed to cultivate their court standing, and these links also reinforced their status back in the country. In 1636, Sir Christopher Wandesford advised his son against an exclusively country life, for 'that were to render you contemptible and unusefull at Home to your Neighbours', while in Somerset the erstwhile radical MP Sir Robert Phelips was said to be pursuing a 'double reputation', 'one above by pretending good affections to the [king's] service, another here by shewinge his dislikes against itt'.[20] In this way Charles's court, while narrower than those of James or Elizabeth, was never wholly monolithic but always included some divisions or dissenting opinion. Moreover, parliament was only the most effective of a number of ways of lobbying the king; we should perhaps see Charles's critics as wishing not to displace the court altogether, but to improve it by joining it. When Digges took office in 1629 he told Eliot, then in prison for his attack on the Speaker, that 'For the publick business, however our waies may seeme to differ, our ends agree; and I am not out of hope to see a happy issue one daie.'[21]

However, we may still conclude that the personal rule was *likely* to fail since Charles's resources were not unlimited and without the willing co-operation of the inferior magistrates in the provinces his government would be difficult if not unworkable; he needed to be able to retain widespread confidence among his people yet the tendency of his rule was such as to erode confidence rather than to inspire it. Financially he was sustained by fiscal devices which estranged those on whose support he was most dependent. Both his nobility and gentry were offended by prerogative schemes to squeeze money out of them (such as Ship Money, increased activity of the Court of Wards, and fines for failure to take up knighthood or for supposed, and often imaginary, encroachments on the royal forests). At London, commercial circles were upset by his discrimination in favour of preferred businessmen and by the proliferation of monopolies.[22] All men were disturbed by the ambiguous legality of his fiscal schemes, and by the use of the prerogative courts, Star Chamber and the church courts, to enforce political and religious conformity; a suspiciously pro-Spanish position in foreign affairs and an apparent rapprochement with Catholicism in the church sapped trust at a deep level. As soon as he ran into difficulties with the Scots he found the gentry unwilling to collect Ship Money and the city and even the court refusing him credit, and he was finally forced back onto parliament. There may not have been an 'opposition' in the 1630s but there still was opposition; once Charles ran out of options, the unpopularity he had earned placed him in a very weak position from which to bargain.

Nevertheless, although parliament in 1640–41 was determined not to lose the opportunity of bringing Charles to terms, it was still challenging his bankrupt policies rather than his authority. At this stage, parliament was not advocating radical change. Rather, Charles's rule was criticized precisely for its progressiveness, that it had introduced 'innovations' into church and state and depended on 'new ways' whose unwisdom was now patent, while parliament's platform was emphatically conservative, a return to old and tried paths, a reform of the constitution according to first principles variously enshrined in the common law, or the practice of Queen Elizabeth, or Magna Carta, or even in Saxon law. The brunt of parliament's attack was borne by the 'evil counsellors' who had subverted fundamental laws and misled the king, undermining his faith in his true subjects and blaming their own errors on him – Laud, Strafford, the bishops, monopolists and corrupt judges who were lampooned over and again in the pamphlets of 1640–41. By purging them, said Sir Benjamin Rudyerd, parliament would show Charles 'the real difference of better Counsels, the true solid grounds of raising and establishing his greatness, never to be brought again (by God's blessing) to such dangerous, such desperate perplexities',[23] and in these months the prospect of king and parliament, free from the interference of 'evil counsellors', returning to an idealized condition of traditional harmony and mutual assurance seemed a real possibility. Parliamentary counsel would *restore* to Charles's rule that dignity and authority it had lost through dependence on bad men, and a confirmation of parliamentary privilege would strengthen the royal prerogative for the two were necessarily interdependent, each sustained by and sustaining the other. Clarendon urged Charles to trust 'those persons who have been the severest assertors of the public liberties' for they 'value their own interests upon the preservation of your rights'.[24]

It must be emphasized that in 1640 there was no situation of confrontation between opposing camps. Rather than the personal rule witnessing a mounting divide between royalist and parliamentarian it produced demands for reform, not revolution. In 1640 Charles faced a nation which, far from preparing for war,[25] was strikingly united behind a programme of constitutional reform of which future royalists, such as Falkland and Clarendon, were among the strongest advocates – the replacement of bad counsellors with good, respect for the security of property, return to a parliamentary way instead of an arbitrary tyranny based on the king's prerogative powers. These were questions of government, not authority, and it looked like a return to a more generally acceptable working relationship between king and parliament; pamphlets and letters of 1640–41 are optimistic, encouraging them to 'go boldly on/To end the good worke, which they have begun'.[26] War was out of the question for Charles had no royalist party but, isolated, had thrown in his lot with reform. The development of a royalist party and the drift into war only became possible *subsequently* with the failure of king and parliament to reach quickly an acceptable compromise and with the appearance of more controversial issues (especially religion), which broke the Commons' unanimity, and of concern for the effect parliament's actions were having on the country at large, causing a regrouping of opinion during 1641–42. Royalism emerged partly as a party of order, its supporters not irresponsible Cavaliers unable to shake off their innate deference to authority, but men often sympathetic to reform and a parliamentary way yet who did not wish to allow the plebeian radicalism it carried in its wake and were shocked by the readiness of men like Pym to put pressure on Charles by mobilizing popular support.[27]

Even so, the conflict after 1642 was still not simply two-handed. Throughout the 1640s, parliament (and Charles's advisers) continued to include peace and war lobbies and more complex divisions besides. In the country, contemporaries, more conscious than we of the great similarities between opponents, divided only with extreme reluctance. Sir William Waller, a parliamentarian general, confessed, 'The great God who is the searcher of my heart, knows with what reluctance I go upon this service and with what perfect hatred I look upon a war without an enemy', while following the king Sir Edward Dering went 'out of my own house and from my own country the most unwilling man that ever went'.[28] Absolute commitment was only for the few, something which large generalizations about Cavalier and puritan disguise. Widespread and important was another phenomenon, 'neutralism', which from 1642 onwards spontaneously produced pacts of county neutrality, declarations of neighbourliness, local associations and even provincial armies of Clubmen who prevented depradation by restraining royalist and parliamentarian forces alike. On one level these are manifestations of 'localist' or 'county' feeling, a concern to preserve the integrity of the local community and minimize the effects of war, and reflect the intense introspection and deep attachment to traditional patterns of life so characteristic of provincial society at this period. On another, neutralist declarations that king and parliament are both 'soe rooted in our Loyall hearts that wee cannot disioynt them' indicate simple horror at the way alternatives had polarized, and express the perplexity of men faced with a simple political choice which few had imagined and in which still fewer found a solution answering to their hopes or expectations. More than merely passive, neutralism involved a positive wish for other options to be available besides king or parliament alone. So, for example, the Lincolnshire gentry who co-operated in 1642 agreed not 'to aid either side, but as much as in them lies, to endeavour accommodation', and the Wiltshire Clubmen of 1645 petitioned king and parliament to make a 'happy Accommodation of the present Differences'.[29] Clearly, this society was deeply divided, but there remained, equally deeply, fervent desires not only for peace but for alternative compromises within the traditional limits such as had failed to materialize (inexplicably, it seemed) in 1641.

The Caroline dilemma

Conrad Russell says, apropos of the imprisonment of Sir John Eliot in 1629, that the only place for an opponent of the king in this period was at the head of a rebel army or in the Tower.[30] His comment is useful for identifying the central dilemma of all those who felt alienated by the behaviour of the crown in an age which still expected to find in the monarchy the centre of society and the source of all power and authority – the dilemma of articulating criticism without placing one's self in a position of defiance of the ultimate authority of the powers-that-were. The age was still pre-political in the sense that it did not occur readily to men that society could tolerate dissenting opinion within itself as a matter of course. The unity of society was upheld by the fiction that all its members thought the same; even the men who continued to sit in parliament after 1642 were as deeply intolerant of a pluralist society as were the king's party. The problem of many who found themselves at odds with the crown in the 1630s was that it put them beyond society, that they had been conditioned to think of dissent as equivalent to rebellion. This tension between their alienation, and their need to limit the consequences of their own dissent emerges everywhere in the language of opposition to Charles.

Most obviously, there is parliament's perpetual and compulsive advertisement of its own loyalty, a theme to which Charles's early parliaments continually returned, reflecting their anxieties about the actual disharmony persisting in their relations with the king. In 1625, the suggestion that king and parliament might disagree was deemed 'scandalous and offensive', and when the 1629 assembly was accused of 'neglect of duty' William Coryton retorted, 'we know no such thing, nor yet what they mean'.[31] Advancing the country's grievances, said Eliot, must be to the king's advantage, since 'what is the country's is the king's good. Those that will distinguish or divide them . . . are neither good scholars nor good statesmen.' Rather, although MPs' complaints might make them appear 'anti-monarchically affected . . . such was, and ever had been their loyalty, that if they were to choose a government they would choose that monarchy of England above all governments in the world'.[32]

Then there is parliament's insistence that it attacked the king's servants, not the king himself whose authority they wished to rescue from those who had interfered with it. In 1629 Eliot asserted 'I have not the least suspicion of [Charles's] goodness, or the least diffidence of *him*'; rather, he wished to alert him to those parasites that 'have abused the King in his Customs and Revenue, and are the cause of the Stop of Trade'. Earlier, he claimed that 'If there were no false glasses between us and the King, our privileges and his prerogative would stand well together.'[33] The 1628 MPs declared, 'we do verily believe that all or most of these things we shall now present unto your majesty are either unknown unto you, or else by some of your Majesty's ministers offered under such specious pretences as may hide their own bad intentions'; Wentworth advised them that it is 'our greatest wisdom to show the King that nowhere is he to be so supplied and counseled as here'.[34] Identical sentiments that king and parliament were fighting a common enemy recurred in 1640. Pamphleteers warned the bishops that '*You cannot cheat the King if vve stand by.*/*Your Plots discry'd out*/*And [Treason's pried] out*/*Against the Honour of his Majesty*', while attacking the Ship Money judges in parliament Oliver St John purposefully emphasized that 'in these expressions there is no reflection upon his majesty; It is only that those judges would have forced upon the law an unnatural and contrary motion; his majesty's carriage in this business clears his justice'.[35]

Such criticism legitimized itself by reference to an ideal of traditional harmony between king and people which, however mythical or imaginary, had a theoretical validity which no one would challenge. Misgovernment upset this standard and hence was as harmful to king as to people; criticism which invoked it was acceptable since its purport ultimately was to restore harmony and thus *reinforce* the king's rule. For example, Isaac Penington, later a firm radical, deplored Ship Money but because it had caused 'much dejection among many good and loyal subjects'. Similarly, Simonds D'Ewes criticized Charles for overruling law with his personal will, but from the standpoint that it had reduced his subjects from freemen to mere slaves, and himself from a king ruling by love to a tyrant ruling by fear. Necessary obedience to an absolute will reduced the dignified king–subject relationship to a mere power relation, but it was 'the honour of a king to have his subjects rich, – nay, therein and in their affections consists his own safety and his kingdom's strength' (or, as Waller thought, 'Kings as well as subjects are involved in the confusion which necessity produceth').[36] This too, I take it, was one rationale behind the stance of country plainness which, by combining bluntness with a respect for authority, harmonized outspokenness with the claims of loyalty and duty, and just this combination of fierce criticism of the king with fierce devotion *to* him (as the idealized head of church and state) is also a recurrent, distinguishing characteristic of puritan polemic of the 1630s (see chapter 5 below).

It is tempting to dismiss such devices as merely devices, fictions which enabled men to imply indirectly what they could not say openly, but to do so not only underestimates the unwillingness of men to initiate change which might have unknown consequences, but diminishes the reality of the conflict in minds exposed for the first time to genuinely new ways of thinking. The same language continued to be used even when the need for such subterfuge had disappeared. The parliament that went to war in 1642 did so 'for the preservation of the true religion, laws, liberties, and peace of the Kingdom'. It was hard to believe that these could exist apart from the king, and in the same breath the MPs who took up arms against Charles took an oath 'for the safety of the King's person, [and] the defence of both Houses of Parliament'. One observer was relieved to find that parliament was fighting 'not against the kinge, happily nott against his person butt Crowne', and the moderate MP Denzil Holles truly believed parliament would 'most readily cast itself at the king's feet with all faithful and loyal submission upon the first appearance of change in His Majesty, that he will forsake those counsels which carry him on so high a dislike and opposition to their proceedings by mispossessing himself of them'.[37] It was possible for such men to hope that they could make war on the 'king' for the sake of the 'King', that they could bring Charles effectively to terms once he was separated from the popish and malignant party who had seduced him.

The unspoken assumption underlying these statements is the fundamental tenet of the modern nation-state, that the interests of ruler and people are (indeed, must be) the same, but in the Caroline period this was continually running up against the concrete fact that the two were not always compatible. The idea that king and people coexisted in a seamless, sacred relationship was built deeply into the fabric of society and exerted tremendous force; it was hard to imagine how society could ever be otherwise. But under Charles, with his insensitive and unpopular policies, it became increasingly difficult to hold the two sides of the equation together. Clearly, for the Caroline individual it was mind-wrenching to separate the two, something almost (literally) unthinkable, yet social and political pressures were insistently suggesting that this 'natural' relationship was no longer wholly satisfactory nor even acceptable. Phelips's *cri de coeur* of 1629, 'If it be a cryme to have loved his Majestie [too] well: we are criminous',[38] expresses the anguish of a man whose deepest political instincts are being contradicted by his experience, yet who is unable, or unwilling, to think in any other categories. Rather than watching the conflicts of the 1630s taking place between institutions, we are watching tensions pulling violently across the minds of every individual.

Caroline England was confronted by problems which, finally, it was unable satisfactorily to resolve. In his *Treatise of Monarchy* (1643), Philip Hunton said that sovereignty lay in king and parliament jointly, but its whereabouts if they fell out could not be determined. In those circumstances, the bonds of allegiance are dissolved and each man must act according to his conscience.[39] His solution openly acknowledges the real impossibility of the choice, that events had overtaken men's present capacities to deal with them. But if these problems proved insoluble to the politicians they were ones to which solutions could be propounded in fictional contexts, and the playwrights of 1632–42 repeatedly dramatized and explored versions of those accommodations which failed of achievement in practice. The decade's drama is replete with absolute kings tyrannizing over their realms, subjects trapped between their loyalty to the crown and their need to speak out, contrasts between government built on trust and enslavement built on fear, evil counsellors undergoing anatomization, bad kings reduced to penitence, courtiers and countrymen attempting different compromises or agreements. Naturally the dramatists were attracted to those aspects of life and experience which were most richly ambiguous and significant in their own times, and their preoccupations identify with greatest certainty the anxieties that exist in their society. They spoke to audiences in which the world-view of one man might not correspond at every point with that of the man sitting next to him, and they themselves were men gradually becoming aware that their received certainties were not being borne out by history. It is precisely in the drama that we might expect to find these tensions, and men's ambivalent and contradictory responses to them, receiving their fullest articulation.

Ultimately, the reforming conservatism of the Long Parliament would have revolutionary implications and, as the desire for change outran the desire to preserve, it proved impossible to restrain these adjustments within the customary limits. These were very complex events; the plays, like their auditors, were being pulled simultaneously in many opposing directions, between attachment to the *status quo*, alienation from it, anxiety for the effects of change and perhaps eventually conviction of its necessity. In responding to these contradictory impulses the drama was shaped by its society, but by encouraging its auditors to think critically, entertain alternatives, and explore the contradictions in their world, it was also helping to shape it; blocking change on one level, it was enabling it on another. And when it came to a divide, there were men who, despite their misgivings, believed that their interests were better served by parliament alone than with the king, and were prepared to take up arms and resist a bad ruler by force. It has become fashionable among historians to see the Civil War as the product as much of miscalculation, accident and circumstance as of design, but if we wish to see the readiness of those who *were* prepared to go to war as part of something much more deeply-rooted, then we may conclude that the drama too, by calling the old certainties into question and educating attitudes to them over a period of years, was in part responsible for creating the conditions in which men would have the capacity, and the will, to take such a step.

3

Court drama: the queen's circle
1632–37

Platonic politics

CHARLES NEVER ENJOYED the full confidence of his aristocracy. His court was boycotted altogether by the more avowedly 'country' peers who were out of favour or felt estranged from the general ambience of court life – by individuals such as the Earls of Bedford and Clare, but also by the immensely powerful Rich–Devereux clan in which, bound together by blood, marriage and outlook, were the Earls of Warwick (a notorious Ship Money opponent and patron of silenced ministers), Essex (who 'ever affected . . . a natural and just freedom of the subject [and] could not relish this growing way the cleargie had gotten'), Hertford and Viscount Mandeville; in the 1640s Essex and Mandeville would become generals and Warwick admiral for parliament.[1] Within the court were grandees like Arundel and Newcastle who, magnifying the prestige of the nobility and the important place due to them in government, resented the influence wielded by meanly-born upstarts, such as Archbishop Laud, who really made policy; these later remained firm to Charles. Between these two poles of aristocratic disaffection were men like Northumberland, Leicester, Pembroke and Salisbury, members of distinguished and important dynasties who often held high office yet who were outside the governing elite and while disapproving of the direction policies were taking were unable ever to challenge them effectively. Their connivance was a prime factor in emboldening the turbulence of Charles's early parliaments, and in the 1630s they continued to present a groundswell of sporadic aristocratic dissent from within the court; some even earned the label 'puritan'.[2] In 1640 they were widely expected to displace the old 'evil counsellors' and, with parliament's support, obtain influential positions in a reformed government. Charles, whose administration had always been bitterly divided anyway over questions of policy, fatally weakened his position in 1640–42 by failing to conciliate them and prevent them from moving into active partisanship for parliament.[3] In the 'official' culture which he sponsored, and especially in the masques of Inigo Jones, the court was depicted as happily and single-mindedly united behind royal leadership. However, contemporaries saw differently and often referred to the court as 'mainly factious and disordered', from the comment of 1630 that it 'was never so full of factions and enmities and emulations as it now is' to the record of 'great factions' at the Oxford court in 1643.[4]

Some cohesion was given to these factions by the behaviour of the queen, who was close to several courtiers who had connections with 'country' peers or themselves held mildly 'opposition' views. When Viscount Conway called Warwick 'the temporal head of the Puritans', he named his brother, Holland, as 'their spiritual head'. Holland was Henrietta Maria's steward and a leading court opponent of Lord Treasurer Weston, Lord Deputy Strafford and Archbishop Laud, with whom he was often at violent enmity and 'made a continual war upon . . . all others who were not gracious to the Queen, or desired not the increase of her authority'.[5] Like many other puritanical noblemen, he was interested in colonization and privateering, as was the queen's chamberlain, Dorset. A more courtly figure, Dorset nevertheless had urged English support for the Protestant cause in the European war, and been patron to the puritan polemicist John Reynolds.[6] Other friends included Henry Jermyn, the diplomat Walter Montagu (brother of Viscount Mandeville) and Henry Percy (an important link to his brother, Northumberland). While her courtiers never amounted to so much as a party, the queen does seem to have provided aristocratic discontent with a much-needed focus at court, and before 1637, when she came under the firmly Catholic sway of the papal agent, her French background and sympathies attuned her to the outlook of those protestant Englishmen hostile to the growth of the Spanish–Catholic power in Europe and to Charles's own instinctive leanings towards the Habsburg interest. Henrietta Maria was perhaps temperamentally inclined to political dabbling, and in the 1630s well-placed noblemen attempted discreetly to realize her potential as a lever through which pressure could be brought against Charles for alternative policies. At first acting as a counterbalance to Lord Treasurer Weston, by 1636 she was campaigning vigorously for a French alliance and an aggressive posture towards Spain. Such aristocratic lobbying served the interests of their more 'puritan' friends outside the court, for a Spanish war, besides fulfilling their patriotic and religious ambitions, would necessitate recalling parliament and returning to more popular forms of domestic government. Foreign ambassadors reported that 'the queen allies herself to the Puritans'; Essex's chaplain, Thomas Pestell, praised her for uniting court and country:[7]

> She was ordaind, for such a king
> That equall Virtues had-a,
> Which makes both Court & Contrie sing
> With hearts that be full glad-a[.]

The political scene at court was transformed drastically in the late 1630s when Henrietta Maria swung round into firm advocacy of the Spanish position, greatly limiting the court's receptivity to more 'puritanical' feeling. After the breakdown of 1642, Jermyn and Percy emerged among the ultra-royalists, but though Dorset joined Charles at Oxford he was consistently a leader of the peace party, and Holland, after helping parliament to destroy Strafford, alternated obsessively and hopelessly between Oxford and Westminster, unable to find with either side the compromise middle path which he desired to see.

The existence of these dissident voices within the court consensus reveals interesting possibilities for the criticism of court drama, especially since so many of these great men patronized the theatre. Outside the court, the radically-minded amateur dramatist Arthur Wilson was employed by Essex and Warwick; Pembroke financed Massinger; both Salisbury and Leicester evinced an interest in theatre.[8] Court drama itself centred on Henrietta Maria rather than Charles, and her courtiers followed her lead. Montagu wrote his *Shepherd's Paradise* (1632) for her. Dorset owned the rental of the Salisbury Court theatre and was involved in its affairs; he received the dedications of Davenant's *The Just Italian* (1629), Heywood's *Love's Mistress* (1634) and Rutter's *The Cid* (1637). Holland found employment for Thomas Randolph, helped the Blackfriars with the censor, and continued to sponsor private theatricals after the playhouses closed.[9] We might expect the factionalism of these people to have left marks on their private drama; for example, the joint apotheosis of king and queen which is the climax of Townshend's masque *Albion's Triumph* (1632) may complacently celebrate a political 'reality', but in a court where the queen is known to be an adversary of her husband's first minister, it may contain a significant burden of unspoken reproof.

Particularly associated with the queen was the 'platonic' drama of 1632–36. Romantic drama was not necessarily doomed to escapism. Romance and high politics are related activities; they share a vocabulary of 'courtship', 'intrigue' and 'service', and the romantic interests of the queen's circle always carried a strong political charge. Her courtiers were a virile group whom the Venetian ambassador called 'lively young men' that 'delight the queen very much, who as a young woman loves to hear lively stories and witticisms', and they flattered her as a 'mistress' in a sense ambiguously both personal and public (Holland was said to be never 'in better favour both with his master and mistress then at this hour').[10] Her political rival, the Countess of Carlisle, was also a witty woman surrounded by *literati* (Waller, Carew, Toby Mathew) who assured her that in her presence all men

> Ambition lose, and have no other scope,
> Save Carlisle's favour, to employ their hope . . .
> The gay, the wise, the gallant, and the grave,
> Subdued alike, all but one passion have . . .[11]

28

Here political and amorous rivalry entwined inextricably, for the feminine attractiveness of these women was for each a measure of their political authority. In these conditions, 'platonic' drama was a vehicle which would respond well to the needs of the queen's courtiers, for platonic love elevated women into the true objects of heroic action and, by not proceeding to physical consummation, had the character of a public devotion, binding together any number of admirers of a woman's beauty into a show of dependence on her, as servants or vassals. In Montagu's *Shepherd's Paradise* (London, 1659) it is the heroine's beauty that qualifies her to become queen for it is so widely admired that she is more like a monarch with her subjects than a private woman. Love, having 'such a soveraignity as to possesse all power, and fortune in it selfe' (p. 51), invests her in this state. Henrietta Maria herself took this role, the elaborate compliment implying that her authority derived not from her public position as Charles's queen but from her personal sway in the hearts of men, a sovereignty firmer – and so more powerful and valid – than any conferred merely by birth or place. Thus romantic motifs could act as devices to explore certain aspects of the relationship between ruler and people (the subject's public 'love') or, more narrowly, to indicate sympathy with the aims and outlook of the queen's circle. The court entertainments directly sponsored by the queen in the years of her freest political involvement, 1635–37, show that she did indeed endeavour to realize these significances.

Alone among court masques, Davenant's platonizing *Temple of Love* (London, 1634 [= 1635]) had four performances.[12] These repetitions reflect the importance it held for the queen who was emerging from a period of eclipse after the collapse of her intrigues against Weston in 1633. Late in 1634, Weston was dying and the prospect of renewed political ascendancy opening up, and with a view to her forthcoming masque, she began to cultivate her alliances. Lady Carlisle rebuffed her, refusing to take part ('I think they were afraid to ask and be refused, and she would not offer herself', said one commentator), and her brother, the queen's courtier Henry Percy, argued violently with her:

'what the Words were, I know not, but I conceive they were spoken on the Queen's side, where there will never be perfect Friendship. For my Lady of *Carlisle* . . . will not suffer herself to be beloved but of those that are her Servants.'[13]

Nevertheless the masque went forward, celebrating the glory of the queen (to whom nature and the ancient poets do homage), but also her particular power and influence. Its unusual feature was the inclusion of two groups of masquers, one male and one female, and its theme, expressed visually as the women led the men in dance, was the guidance of the masculine principle by the feminine in love. The men had been '*Seduc'd at first by false desire*' but the women '*kindle in their breasts a fire/Shall keepe Love warme, yet not enflame*' (sig.C4r). The queen's presence dispelled the mists of false love and would '*guide those Lovers that want sight,/To see and know what they should love*'; indeed, as '*the Mornings light*' she was herself the medium of love (sig.A4r). So the queen was saluted as the leader of all men's true affections, and as the male masquers submitted to feminine power, this idea of proper control was emblematized in a duet between the understanding and the will, the former masculine and the latter feminine. Normally the understanding guides the will, but, as Kenelm Digby's platonic letters explain, in love, the 'worthyest operation of a rationall creature', the purified will becomes superior and 'the understanding is but as the servant and as it were holdeth the candle to it'.[14] In the context of the revival of the queen's political activities, this statement of the deference due from the male to the female was tactful yet pointed, and in the final song Chaste Love recommended it as a precept to the chief spectator, wishing that this ideal fusion of '*perfect Will, and strengthned Reason*' would be epitomized in the loving understanding existing between king and queen:

> . . . *by a mixture thus made one,*
> *Y'are th'Embleme of my Deitie,*
> *And now you may in yonder Throne,*
> *The patterne of your Vnion see.* (sigs.D1r–v)

The rest of 1635 saw mounting pressure on Charles to recall

parliament and enter the European conflict. The queen consolidated her connections with interested courtiers, and Charles's German nephews, the Elector Palatine Charles Louis and his brother Rupert, protestant princes deprived of their inheritance by Spanish imperialism, arrived in England to importune military intervention in their behalf. They were just the types to attract the queen's attention (Rupert, for example, was 'full of spirit and action . . . observation and judgment' and would '*reussir un grand homme*, for in whatsoever he wills, he wills vehemently'),[15] and she embraced their cause. It was arranged that Charles Louis and the French ambassadors should meet 'in the queen's chamber, where they both have occasion to go almost every day', and newsletters reported that 'Comedies, festivities and balls are the order of the day here, and are indulged in every day at Court for the prince's sake, while all the greatest lords vie with each other in entertaining him at noble and sumptuous banquets.'[16] Charles Louis was presented with an anonymous 'Poem of Joy' which lamented Catholic atrocities abroad and reassured him that 'Heau'n and Earths Parlyment*es* can make ytt sure', while Thomas Heywood wrote a special prologue and epilogue for the court stage, welcoming the prince and admonishing the king of his obligations to his distressed relatives:[17]

> A numerous fruit, sprung from a golden Tree,
> Such (as old Atlas, was ne'er seene by thee
> In thy Hesperian orchard) long t'indure
> And prosper in the world: now growes mature.
> And the faire blossoms ready even to spread
> Their leaves abroad, and top the [imperial] *Eagles* Head . . .
> So may none issuing from King *Iames* his Stemme,
> But be thought fit to weare a Diadem . . .

In honour of the visit, the lawyers of the Middle Temple resurrected their old-style Christmas revels, electing a mock-prince who held his own sumptuous (and well-reported) court, and whose 'privy counsillors', under the safety of a festive game, publicly debated such sensitive questions as whether a prince could be content with losing his realm (like Charles Louis), and whether a prince was right to raise his finance through forced

loans in preference to a parliamentary grant (like King Charles).[18]
In February 1636, Charles Louis, the queen and her courtiers
were invited by the mock-prince to the Middle Temple masque,
Davenant's *Triumphs of the Prince d'Amour* (London, 1635), and,
as a mark of solidarity with the lawyers' venture, they arrived in
fancy dress: 'Thither came the Queen with three of her Ladies
disguised, all clad in the Attire of Citizens... My Lords of
Holland and *Goring* with *Henry Percy* and Mr. *Henry Jermyn* waited
on them somewhat disguised also.'[19] Charles Louis was met by
an ambassador sent from the mock-prince to assure him of the
lawyers' active support:

> *Thus whisper'd by my feares, I must impart*
> *For Ceremony now, what is his heart,*
> *Though with content of Truth, I may report*
> *You have a num'rous Faction in his Court.*
> *This palace where, by sword, then law maintain'd,*
> *His few, but mighty ancestors have reign'd,*
> *Is consecrated yours.*
>
> (p. 2)

Such an explicit gesture made the mock-court at the Temple
more than a merely playful counterpart to the real, hispaniolized
Whitehall.

In deference to the queen, the lawyers presented themselves as
servants of Mars and Venus; their masque emphasized aggression,
both in war and love. In the first dances, an antimasque of
ridiculous soldiers, including an 'old overgrown debaush'd
Cavalier' (p. 6), were displaced by masquers dressed as worthy
knights intended 'to imitate those heroique Knights Templers',
first inhabitants of the Temple (p. 8). After this declaration of
martial intent, the same knights, now dressed as a 'Troope of
noble Lovers', displaced an antimasque of foolish lovers. But
while the knights offered themselves to love, action was still the
keynote:

> *Breath then each others breath, and kisse*
> *Your soules to union:*
> *And whilst they shall injoy this blisse,*
> *Your bodies too are one.*
>
> (pp. 12–13)

Finally, Apollo promised the masquers success in all their designs, and, instructed to '*Expresse your [thankfulnesse] in active pleasure*', they presented the prince with a banquet 'which did declare them Labourers in a Fruitfull Soyle; and what they carried did demonstrate a Fruitfull Season' (pp. 14–15). The queen told the master of the revels that 'she liked it very well'.[20]

Three months later, as expectations of war continued to increase, Henrietta Maria took the prince to the Blackfriars to see *Alphonsus, Emperor of Germany*,[21] an Elizabethan melodrama which had probably been specially revived for him for it depicted the sufferings of Germany under a monstrous Spanish tyrant intent on destroying the electors, including the Elector Palatine, by violence and treachery. Alphonsus is opposed heroically by the valiant English noblemen Prince Edward (who marries a German princess) and Earl Richard (brother of Henry III), and in this fiercely patriotic and Protestant play Providence finally intervenes to strike down the wicked Spaniard and elevate the English into leaders of a new, purified Germany ('Was never Englishman yet Emperour,/Therefore to honour England and your self,/Let private sorrow yield to publike Fame,/That once an Englishman bore *Caesar's* name').[22] However, the king still failed to provide leadership of the kind this play demanded; in the summer, the court was entertained sumptuously by Laud at Oxford, but during its return an entertainment at Richmond (the crown prince's court) organized by the queen's chamberlain Dorset had more criticism for Charles. This was another martial masque, using many Spenserian echoes to evoke and hold up for imitation the ancient British military past. The crown prince appeared as the heroic British warrior, Britomart. The queen received many expressions of love; soldiers offered her their arms, and rustics (representatives of the 'country') brought presents. The king was rather pointedly ignored. For him there was only an attack on tyrannical government as an affront to the dignity of the subject:[23]

> if he heare vs, weele tell him,
> A certaine truth, that he which rules ore slaues
> Is not so great as he that's king of freemen:

O to command the wils of subjects, rather
Then bodies, is an Empire truely sacred,
And the next way to rule in heauen it selfe!

This is exactly the argument against unparliamentary rule which would be developed by Simonds D'Ewes (see p. 21 above).

In the event, nothing came of the queen's campaign. In December Rupert was 'amusing himself in the society of the ladies without any preoccupations besides what his own youthful inclinations at present supply', and by April 1637 the princes' plans had shifted to a suggestion that Rupert should lead a fleet to conquer Madagascar. Their aim was to establish a naval base which would be useful in a challenge to Spanish sea-power, but as their mother complained, 'as for Rupert's romance of Madagascar, it sounds like one of Don Quixote's conquests'.[24] Henrietta Maria lost interest; she came under the influence of the papal agent and, as the spate of scandalous court conversions began, her alliance with the 'country' peers dissolved. The only survival of the princes' hopes was Davenant's imaginative anticipation of Rupert's success, his heroic poem *Madagascar*, in which Rupert's foes fall overwhelmed before him, and the isle is conquered effortlessly by the miraculous power of British kingship:[25]

Sayles swell'd to make them comely more than swift:
And then I spi'd (as cause of this command)
Thy mighty Uncles Trident in thy hand . . .

But though unsuccessful, this campaign is significant for having existed at all, a challenge from within the court to the hegemony of Charles's 'official' culture and to the attitudes and policies it was designed to sanction. These entertainments were responding to, and helping to create, expectations of a kind which Charles preferred not to fulfil and which contributed materially to undermining trust in his regime. When in 1641 Milton called for a reformation in England, one motive was that 'Priestly policies' had left us 'naked of our firmest, & faithfullest neighbours abroad, by disparaging, and alienating from us all Protestant Princes, and Common-wealths'[26] – a prime instance of which was

Charles's apparent indifference to the Palatinate. Henrietta Maria's involvement with 'opposition' groupings helped to increase the court's receptiveness to ranges of opinion more normally regarded as un- or anti-courtly, and her politic use of romantic motifs enabled her private entertainments to participate in the debate of these issues. But the politicization of love opened up further possibilities for full-scale plays which stand independent of the queen, and I now wish to consider three plays from 1635–36 which I believe may be elucidated by reference to her intrigues in these years. They too use romantic motifs to raise questions of government, but they are able to pursue their themes with much greater rigour and completeness than was possible in the relatively circumscribed context of a court masque.

Choices of kings and queens

Richard Brome's *Queen and Concubine*, which I wish to suggest may well have been presented at court early in 1636, stands in that tradition deriving (by way of Massinger's romantic dramas) from old plays like *Friar Bacon and Friar Bungay* (1589), *Edward III* (1590) and *Locrine* (1591), which presented love and politics as two complementary spheres of action in which a man's behaviour in one illuminates his behaviour in the other. It has been called a 'long and confusing tragicomedy',[27] but in fact it is perfectly coherent, and recalls those Elizabethan dilemma dramas in which the spectator (usually the queen) was faced with a choice between two deities or dignitaries who represented alternative attitudes to government or courses of action.[28] Brome's Sicilian king sets his rightful queen aside and takes a mistress. This alone is a reprehensible deed, an 'error' (p. 112)[29] he will be forced to recant, but it also initiates an extended contrast between opposed styles of kingly government.

Alinda, the concubine, is ambition incarnate. Her overwhelming desire is to achieve 'the top of Soveraignty', the 'lofty height of towring Majesty' (pp. 19–20), in pursuit of which she will 'not regard upon whose Necks [she treads]' (p. 22). Her aim is absolute rule without control. Scorning her father's good counsel, she asserts 'Soveraignty you know, admits no Parentage./Honour, poor petty Honour forgets Descent' (p. 15), and once she has power over the king's 'dotage' (pp. 19, 98) she expects – in the language of Caroline personal government – 'by her Prerogative [to] take Heads,/Whose and as many as she listed' (p. 104). In making free with her, the king has (literally) embraced wilfulness. He tells *his* subjects he is 'Subject to this all-deserving Lady' (p. 25) and promises her 'all shall be/(Be thou but my *Alinda*) rul'd by thee' (p. 75). His acts, unjust in themselves, are those of an arbitrary monarch who elevates his will into law and overrides all constraints on his power. He demands unthinking obedience to his wishes, and though he calls a 'Parliament' (p. 23) of peers to ratify his divorce, it is an unfree assembly which he directs 'without all denial . . . [to] confirm what I will say' (p. 25). This is a travesty of parliamentary rule:

> KING. . . . do ye all approve it?
> OMNES. We do.
> LODOVICO [*aside*]. We must.   (p. 23)

Soon his subjects are complaining of 'oppression, Tyrannie indeed', for the new queen 'treads and tramples down the Government' (pp. 28, 30). But such absolutism is doomed to failure. Alinda, uncontrollable, runs mad with power, and the king, having estranged all his courtiers and provoked an army revolt, is reduced to impotence.

In the Sicilian subjects is played out that Caroline tension between alienation and conformity. From the 'old Courtier' Horatio the king receives absolute submission. Horatio is 'the onely man/That does the King that service, just to love/Or hate as the King does, so much and so long,/Just to a scruple or a minute . . . though he fear immediate death by it' (p. 10). He makes a parade of his loyalty, ventures no opinion until the king has shown his, and, in following the whims and caprices of the royal will, is led into ridiculous self-contradictions. He is the only courtier the king does not alienate, but as one who was ever just 'of your Majesties mind from my Nativitie' (p. 69) he is totally incapable of helping him when he runs into difficulties. Moreover,

neither he nor the king has any concept of responsible government, but both see sovereignty simply as the king's capacity to
act without control. Though knowing his injustices, Horatio
affirms that 'The Kings Power Warrants his Acts' (p. 28) and 'In
what you can command, I dare be Loyal' (p. 7). The royal will he
takes to be merely another personal will magnified and therefore
still subject to the same inconsistencies as any other: 'It must be
so, this is one of his un-to-be-examin'd hastie Humours, one of
his starts: these and a devillish gift He has in Venerie, are all his
faults. Well, I must go, and still be true to th'Crown' (p. 7). This
kind of absolutism is fundamentally weak for it reduces rule
simply to a wayward tyranny by one more powerful man over his
equals, and loyalty to a blind slavishness.

In her sufferings, the queen submits scrupulously to the king's
pleasure, but in lesser mortals passive obedience receives shorter
shrift. The better courtiers are genuinely distressed at the king's
behaviour and, while not openly opposing him, they are unwilling
to co-operate with his demands. Jealous of the good and popular
general Sforza, the king sends another soldier, Petruccio, to
execute him, but he decides instead 'for truth and Honours cause
[to] strain/A point of Loyaltie' (p. 43) and hides Sforza, pretending he is dead. Faced with revolt two acts later, the king
acknowledges his personal fallibility and that his absolute rule
has been built on weakness, not strength:

> Great Power, that knowest
> The subtletie of hearts, shew me some light
> Through these Cymmerian mists of doubts and fears,
> In which I am perplex'd even to distraction: ...   (p. 103)

The day is saved only by the return of Sforza, preserved by
Petruccio's act of disobedience, and the king admits that he is
indeed inferior as a man to the well-deserving subject:

> I am all wonder: now this man appears
> The Mansion and habitual Seat of Honour;
> Of which he seems so full, there cannot be
> An Angle in his breast to lodge so base
> An Inmate as disloyaltie ...   (p. 103)

Sforza's return shows that the king's power is firmest in the hearts of those whom he is most inclined to abuse, that their popularity or criticism does not compromise their loyalty but makes their support only more valuable. By contrast, Horatio's loyalty is comically shown to be powerless, as he invokes it unsuccessfully to exorcise the 'ghost' of the executed traitor Sforza.

Meanwhile the queen wanders the country in exile and is visited by a 'Genius' who gives her miraculous powers of healing and protection, powers she deserves not because she is a queen nor because she is loyal but, simply, because she is good. Brome makes it quite clear that divinity does *not* hedge a king, but protects that 'injur'd innocence' (p. 55) which royal injustice has abused. The queen tells a group of rustics who ascribe a curse on their country – her dowry – to her 'offence' against the king that it is the other way around:

it was th'injustice and the wrongs the innocent Queen hath suffer'd, that has brought sense of her injuries upon her Province . . . if she had died, her Dowrie here with her [would have] also suffered Death . . . to make it nothing to the King, as he made her. (p. 54)

Rather, those churchmen are irreligious who have used religion to justify royal tyrannies: 'Twas *everso*; Priests are but Apes to Kings,/And prostitute Religion to their ends' (p. 54). Concealing her identity, the queen earns by good deeds the love of the countryfolk who make her their May Lady and try to elect her as 'our Sacred Soveraign' (p. 86). This shocks her; she tells them they are endangering their allegiance and that (as a private person) she cannot be worthy to be queen for it is 'the Greatness of/The Person dignifies the [Title], not it the Person'. Their unanswerable reply is that 'in that, Madam, you are in your content/Above all Title's proper to great Princes' (p. 87). The queen's merit (like Sforza's) has made her worthy of that power which the king, through his unworthiness, has forfeited. Furthermore, she has earned a kingdom through her capacity to inspire love, a positive devotion untainted by compulsion unlike Horatio's barren subservience to an abstract idea, the crown. Her subjects cheerfully avow, 'if there be a Purgatorie on earth,/Ile venter through it for her, heigh, o, ho' (p. 56), thus proving the infinite superiority of a loyalty rooted in love to one built on mere duty.

Climaxing his play with a country festival, Brome evokes a nostalgic, Elizabethan idea of an organic community in which the members participate fully, and the political adjustments he has in mind are emblematized by the play's movement from court to country. This contrast Brome pursues in great detail. In the country, the queen has 'asmuch content/As ere I found in height of Government' (p. 77):

> all [the court's] happiness is but a dream,
> When mine is reall: nay, nay, I can prove it.
> Their costly fare breeds riot, mine content:
> Their rich Attire is but mere Pageantry . . .
> They boast of Honour and Gentilitie,
> For their Attendants then, when the chief Honour
> Of the best woman, meek obedience,
> Is my own handmaid; and my Patience
> A sweeter servant than Gentilitie . . .   (pp. 44–5)

Her faithful courtiers follow her into exile, leaving the court with only 'fine Lords' (p. 35), and when her good son, the prince, follows her, the court is resurrected in the country (p. 107). The countrymen with whom she consorts are attractively painted as energetic, downright and ruthlessly egalitarian common men. They hate courtiers and anyone with pretensions to birth – 'not a Gentleman,/Much less a Courtier dares breath amongst us,/But be as you pretend and write, but Yeoman' (pp. 62–3) – and they are incensed by Alinda's favourite Flavello who barely escapes their violence when he calls them 'Peasants' (p. 92). They resolve to form a 'Councel' (p. 90) to protect and advise the queen, and in the final act this council meets to try and punish the vicious courtier Flavello. He attempts to escape by appealing to the king, but they reassert the equality of all men before the law, avowing that common men can spy 'Great faults in Noble Coats' (p. 119). In their behaviour, Brome gestures towards the aims of those real 'countrymen' who desired a return to parliamentary govern-

39

ment. Significantly, the queen has become identified with 'Common Good' (p. 31) and in the rustics has earned 'the voice of the whole Countrey' (p. 77). Their council is a 'pettie Parliament' which will introduce a 'Reformation':

> Do not I understand the purpose of our meeting
> Here in our pettie Parliament, if I may so call it?
> Is it not for a Reformation, to pull down
> The Queens mercy, and set up our Justice?
> For the prevention of a superabundance of Treason
> Dayly practiced against her?   (p. 116)

The countrymen will 'make such a Reformation, that Treason shall not dare to peep over the Hedge of her Dominion' (p. 116). This 'pettie Parliament' would seem to act as a corrective to the king's original misuse of parliament, a restoration of free, non-arbitrary government, but with the significant difference that the ineffectual lords and bishops of Act II have been replaced by a vigorous 'hobnayl'd Common wealth' who are determined to stamp out the court fires (p. 120) and purge all those who like Flavello encumber and obstruct the state:

> Come all the Court in all your costly Braveries.
> And Treason in your Breech, we'll hang you for your Knaveries . . .
>   (pp. 119–20)

So the shift to the country is also a very definite one to more popular forms of government, and in the extraordinary finale the king abdicates in favour of the prince and queen who 'with these true/Statesmen [her faithful courtiers], will enable you to govern well' (p. 129).

The Queen and Concubine is clearly a thoroughly popular play, both stylistically and politically. Behind Brome's queen stands a long line of distressed dramatic heroines who carry the burden of complaint of an oppressed nation: the title character of *Godly Queen Hester* (1527), Widow England in Bale's *King Johan* (1538), Chastity in Lindsay's *Satire of the Three Estates* (1540) (which also has a crippled John the common-weal), Lady Verity who is despoiled in the morality fragment *Somebody, Avarice and Minister* (1550), Conscience reduced to selling brooms in Wilson's *Three*

Ladies of London (1588) or, more up-to-date, the genius of his country whom Antiochus imagines 'Wringinge her manacled hands' in Massinger's *Believe as you List* (I.i.51). The king's adultery is an immediately familiar emblem for the defilement of the purity of the state and the abdication of responsible government (the lustful king who neglects his country's good as he takes a mistress is a recurrent figure in the bourgeois historical chronicles of Speed and Holinshed; Foxe's *Acts and Monuments* recounts how the ungodly king Edward III was bewitched by a 'wicked harlot' who 'governed all and sate vpon causes her self').[30] Moreover, rather as the radical preachers of 1640 repeatedly exhorted England to cease '*a whoring*' after Babylonian impurity and to remain chaste to her 'marriage knot between God and his people',[31] there are suggestions of religious radicalism behind Brome's 'Reformation' too. When in 1634 a court preacher wished to complain of the state of the church, he personified her as 'distressed Religion' who comes 'with her face blubbered, and her garments rent, wringing her hands, and tearing her hair'; on the eve of the conflict, Milton declared that 'our deare Mother *England*' now dresses 'in a mourning weed, with ashes upon her head, and teares abundantly flowing from her eyes' for her church's wrongs.[32] Both writers were drawing on that powerful strain of Protestant polemic which had interpreted the conflict in Revelation between the Woman clothed with the Sun, driven out into the wilderness, and the Whore of Babylon as a foreshadowing of the struggle between the true reformed faith and the polluted Catholic church. The opposition of chaste Una and defiled Duessa had already been dramatized (in Latin) by the great martyrologist John Foxe whose *Christus Triumphans* (1556) depicted the whore Pornapolis setting herself up as the True Church but eventually deposed in favour of the persecuted Ecclesia who is decked for marriage with Christ, and the romish Whore had even appeared on the public stages as the supreme antagonist of that godly and virginal English queen Elizabeth in Dekker's *Whore of Babylon* (1606). It has been suggestively proposed that the fable of *Comus* (1634), in which a chaste and distressed lady falls into the clutches of the son of the witch Circe, was intended to connote the eschatological struggle of Ecclesia and the Whore.[33] Perhaps idealized reminiscences of Elizabeth's capable and godly rule, with which Charles's contrasted so abysmally, underlie Brome's saintly queen; it seems highly likely that many if not most of these allusions would have given force to his deeply felt and richly resonant play.

But it is plain too that *The Queen and Concubine* closely matches the outlook of the queen's courtiers in 1635–36. Its depiction of a good queen, capable of reforming bad courtiers, its mention of her province as '*The Paradice of Love*' (p. 52), its country setting and praise of parliaments would all have been highly complimentary to Henrietta Maria at this date. Nor are its attitudes merely popular and generic. Alinda is not just another 'evil counsellor' who may be replaced with good counsel, but functions more specifically to expose the nature of arbitrary, tyrannical government itself. The play's zealous frankness belongs clearly to the freer world of the professional theatre, but it could well have been performed at court under the queen's sponsorship, possibly among the three plays given at court by the King's Revels between October 1635 and February 1636.[34] If this was the case, then the queen's involvement in politics made it possible for the court stage to host one of the most openly radical, combative plays of the decade.

This is made more likely by the performance at court on 25 February 1636 of Shirley's *The Duke's Mistress* (pub. London, 1638) which is also a play in which a duke neglects his wife to pursue the affections of another. Like Brome, Shirley was a professional dramatist, but he had already written one play at the king's behest, in 1633,[35] so perhaps this too was a commissioned reply. Performed only one day after the queen took the Prince Elector to the Middle Temple, its subplot, in which a courtier pursues the ugliest woman he can find, looks like a deliberate parody of the romantic idealisms of the queen's circle (the courtier says 'Mine's a *Platonicke* love, give me the soule,/I care not what course flesh, and blood inshrine it' (sig.F1ʳ)). Shirley carefully rehabilitates faith in the integrity of the royal will. His duke does not consummate his lust but reforms and retains his place and power; the mistress, Ardelia, is a sympathetic figure who keeps her virtue untainted. Obedience to the duke is indeed questioned by a favourite who pities the forsaken duchess and by Ardelia's fiancé who protests he sees his 'treasure rifled, all my wealth tane from me' by an 'injurious power' he 'dare not question' (sig.E1ᵛ), but the former is undercut by his treachery (he too loves the duchess) and the latter by Ardelia's proof that the duke has not in fact violated his rights. Shirley's duke's actions never become real crimes, and so do not invalidate his authority. Attention shifts instead to the bad end of the favourite who has dared to challenge royal power.

The values of Shirley's play are carefully controlled by his language, which is one of deference, continually drawing attention to the correct social hierarchies. Ardelia's speech places a distance between herself and the duke:

> Never was subiect to a Prince more bound
> For free and bounteous graces, then *Ardelia*
> To your highnes, and with many lives to wast
> In service for them, I were still in debt to you. (sig.E2ᵛ)

Such language clearly separates 'subject' and 'prince'. By contrast, she allows her fiancé to approach closely to her:

> My dearest *Bentivolio*, why dost stand
> At so much gaze, and distance, as thou wod'st
> Teach love unkindnesse . . . (sig.D4ᵛ)

Her language preserves decorum, the distances and values established in the system. It is as a violator of 'place' that the favourite woos the Duchess.

> In vaine I still suppresse my darke thoughts Madam,
> Which in their mutiny to be reveal'd
> Have left a heape of ruines worth your pity. (sig.F2ʳ)

Ardelia is likewise outraged when a courtier tries to take advantage of what he takes to be her easy virtue:

> How dare you be thus insolent? though my person
> Move you to no regard, you shall finde one
> Will teach you manners. (sig.G4ʳ)

'Manners' are of the essence. Shirley does not question the system but insists that it is fixed. Subjects must know their place, and trust the duke (or king) to know his.

The Duke's Mistress is a conspicuous victim of that crucial divide between court and non-court drama. I shall later argue (chapter 6 below) that an upholding of 'place' and decorum was characteristic of 'gentry' attitudes to politics and was a very effective form of criticism when directed from those lower down in the hierarchy against those exceeding their 'place' above them (for example, in Shirley's own city comedies), but clearly this idea is not the same when advanced from above, in a court context, against critics from below, when it becomes merely a justification of the freedom of action of the constituted powers. This play must have seemed very unsatisfactory at Whitehall for its conspicuous failure to meet those criticisms which had been advanced so searchingly by Brome.

Six months later, during the visit to Oxford, the court was entertained by *The Royal Slave*, a romantic play by the academic dramatist William Cartwright. This was universally reported as a great success, but Laud recorded that it was specifically the queen who asked to have it repeated at Hampton Court,[36] and it is by no means clear that she was attracted by its spectacular scenery and music alone. Its setting was ancient Persia, and the slave, Cratander, is a Greek prisoner-of-war destined for sacrifice but permitted first to rule for three days as a mock king. His extraordinary reign raises all sorts of awkward questions about kingship, and presents a standard against which the capacities of non-fictional but less successful kings might readily be measured. It has been suggested that Charles might have found a curious and tantalizing self-image in Cratander. It seems much more likely to me that if any figure was meant for Charles, it was the Persian king, Arsamnes, himself, who continually finds himself outdone by the superior kingliness of the common slave.[37]

Cratander's elevation immediately initiates the inquiry, what makes a king? The Persian courtiers are divided over whether a private man could possibly fulfil the public role of king, and most believe worth is defined by social rank:[38]

                    the man lookes personable,
            And fit for Action, but he is a Slave.
            He may be noble, vertuous, generous, all,
            But he is still a Slave.
ORONTES.   As if the sullying
            Must turne all purer mettle into drosse;
            Or that a Jewell might not sometimes be
            In the possession of a private man.
MASISTES. What? you too for the rising Sun, my Lord,
            Though't be but a Meteor cast from the true one?   (l.213)

Cratander's capabilities threaten to show the 'true' sun is indeed only a meteor, that the 'conquer'd Hart' may 'lead the Lyon' (l.222). Arsamnes, now understandably nervous, sets out to prove him only a slave (l.337), but Cratander is a brilliantly successful ruler. In three days he reforms the court, negotiates a favourable peace for Greece, thwarts a slave revolt and earns the admiration of all.

Anne Barton says it is remarkable that Cartwright failed to make the 'orthodox discovery' that the slave really is a king in disguise.[39] King he is none, yet he bears a kingly mind, and rather as Henrietta Maria was flattered as deserving rule through her queenly beauty, so Cratander's bearing and virtues mark him out for majesty. He has 'A Kingdom in his looke; a kingdome that/Consists of beauty, seasoned with Discretion' (l.274), a nobleness beyond his outward fortunes (ll.528–9). Authority sits lightly on him ('I neither take/New courage from the Power, nor suffer new/Feares from the Death that waytes it' (l.184)). It is emphasized that Cratander is a philosopher (all part of his Greek background), and learning has made his desires kingly, his private affections public ('Bring me a Kingdome in one face, or shew me/A People in one body; then you might/Happily worke on mine Affections' (l.409)). Philosophy teaches him that monarchy is a state of mind; he has written 'a discourse o'th'Nature of the Soule;/That shewes the vitious Slaves, but the well inclin'd/Free, and their owne though conquer'd' (l.111), and he asserts kingliness resides not in the possession of power but the ability to use it for kingly ends:

45

> To offend
> Beyond the reach of Law without controule,
> Is not the Nature, but the vice of Pow'r;
> And he is only great, that dares be good. (l.351)

This is no mere unrealistic platitude, but a kind of philosophic Machiavellianism. Cratander perceives that power misused only makes a king a great slave, for victory must tend to the deserving man (l.123) and wisdom will always take 'the upper hand of Fate' (l.1136). His own superior intelligence enables him to overcome with ease the machinations of those who would depose him (IV.iii–iv), and as the man most able to rule himself and resist sensual music, women, drink and false appeals to patriotism (II.iii, II.vi, III.i), public rule comes naturally to him; by contrast, Arsamnes is subjected by his own jealousy and anger (III.v, V.ii). Cartwright's redefinition of the terms of rule shifts the onus of proof onto the king; the criterion of kingship has become not possession but desert. Piety demands that Cratander should be sacrificed, but in the play's final moments the gods intervene to prevent it. Arsamnes now invests him really as king of Greece, but the divine right of this king is one which, as the heavenly intervention shows, he has demonstrably earned, not, like Charles, merely claimed by descent.

The point is underlined by the behaviour of Arsamnes's queen, Atossa, who stands faced with a choice of kings (rather like Brome's king and his queens). Her approval of Cratander is central to validating his claims to kingship, since it is a direct challenge to Arsamnes on a personal level too, which is why he becomes so very jealous of her. It certainly looks at first as though she has fallen for Cratander; she gives him a golden chain, and he values it as a love token, though one of a superior kind:

> I can distinguish betwixt Love, and Love,
> 'Tweene Flames and good Intents, nay between Flames
> And Flames themselves: the grosser now fly up,
> And now fall downe againe, still cov'ting new
> Matter for food; consuming, and consum'd.
> But the pure clearer Flames, that shoot alwayes
> In one continued Pyramid of lustre,
> Know no commerce with Earth . . . (l. 939)

46

It is in fact a queen's love, a platonic love that feeds on 'refin'd Ideas,/That know no mixture or corruption', not on bodily parts (l.952). As Atossa tells Arsamnes (ll.1029–37) and later Cratander, she loves not Cratander's person but the goodness that is in him: 'I do't not to the Man, but to the Vertue' (l.1266), and so her favours are truly queenly, indicating the nobility of mind of both the lover and the person beloved (ll.901–9). Such pure love can only exist between people of equal and great worth. But the implications of this are far-reaching. It certainly demonstrates that Arsamnes does not have a monopoly of virtue and that in love the slave may really be the equal, if not the superior, of the king, something which Atossa tells Arsamnes in no uncertain terms:

> Doth not the Sun (the Sun, which yet you worship)
> Send beames to others than your selfe? yet those
> Which dwell on you loose neither light, nor heat,
> Comming not thence less vigorous, or lesse chast.
> Would you seale up a Fountaine? or confine
> The Ayre unto your walke? would you enjoyne
> The Flow'r to cast no smell, but as you passe?
> Love is as free as Fountaine, Aire or Flower.
> For't stands not in a poynt . . . (l.1003)

There are, then, surprisingly democratic implications in platonic love, which is free to choose rationally whom it will favour. Atossa's stridency recalls the courage of Perdita, defying the fury of Polixenes ('I was not much afeard; for once or twice/I was about to speak, and tell him plainly,/The selfsame sun that shines upon his court/Hides not his visage from our cottage, but/Looks on alike'), but unlike Perdita, Cratander really is the slave he seems to be.

The presence of the real king and queen would have given considerable bite to Atossa's defection. Moreover, while Cratander's success divides opinion at the Persian court, it becomes increasingly apparent that the lines of this division are the men versus the women. The question of the relative worths of male and female rule is first raised in the third scene, when in a wit-combat one of Atossa's ladies argues that the only difference of masculine government is that 'Your follies are more serious, your vanities/Stronger, and thick woven [than ours]' (l.254). An act later, Cratander gains the ladies' love by saving them from an attempted rape: 'though it be not/Reall as we could wish it, yet beleeve it/You hold a perfect Royalty in the hearts/Of those whose honours you have now preserv'd' (l.529). By contrast, the men regroup around the beleaguered Arsamnes, and this tactical divide issues into real action in Act IV when the women, under Atossa's leadership, take their own evasive measures against the impending slave revolt, in the hope that 'the Honour, as the Action,/Will be entirely ours ... our Husbands shall strew prayses in/Our wayes, which we will tread on, and contemne' (l.1065). The fifth act produces outright confrontation between Arsamnes and the men, and Cratander, Atossa and the women, but the women's strategies successfully vindicate them and Arsamnes is won over to Cratander's part by Atossa's pleadings and vows. The women have shown themselves to possess a heroism 'farre/Beyond the eager Valour of try'd Captaines' (l.1261), and the climax of the play at Oxford[40] was an Amazonian dance, the women in '*war-like habits*' (l.1496) clashing their swords and shields.

Clearly, all this had much relevance to the immediate concerns of 1636. Cartwright makes no reference to parliament; rather, Persia is a 'free Monarchy' (l.227) and Cratander's authority resides in his ability to rise above and regulate the passions of the 'vulgar' (l.348). But – surprisingly, in view of the military reputation of the Persians – all the energies of Cratander's rule are directed to toughening up a society gone to seed. He is a disciplinarian. Several times he is called 'serious', and he scorns 'big and pompous Luxury' as the delight of 'weaker mindes' (l.344). He sends whores to jail, prevents a rape, disapproves of lascivious music and would prefer some 'solemne Hymne' or song of valour (l.397). His critics say all his talk is 'of lying with surpriz'd Cities, and committing Fornication with Victory, and making Mars Pimpe for him' (l.784). He is incensed to find the other Grecians ignobly revelling and drinking in mock-martial 'postures' which parody the strategies of war:

> Doe but consider,
> (If that at least you can) how Greece it selfe
> Now suffers in you; thus, say they, the Grecians
> Do spend their Nights: Your vices are esteem'd
> The Rites and Customes of your Country, whiles
> The beastly Revelling of a Slave or two,
> Is made the Nations Infamy. Your wreathes
> Blush at your Ignominy: what prayse is't
> When't shall be said, *Philotas* stood up still
> After the hundreth Flagon; when 'tis knowne
> He did not so in warre?   (l.753)

Charles's court was chaste, but it also produced much that was trivial, superficial and frivolous; Thomas Carew urged a fellow courtier-poet to sing of revels and pleasures rather than heroics.[41] It is difficult not to conclude that Cratander, whose strenuous discipline contrasts so favourably with Charles's rather dreary and inglorious policy of 'Thorough', resembles the strong and serious leader who would have been much more acceptable to Charles's more puritanical subjects.

An outside view

These fine plays by Brome and Cartwright were performed at court, but are not limited by this fact. A knowledge of the queen's movements adds another dimension to their meaning, but is not essential. With or without Henrietta Maria, they are clearly extremely sceptical, unillusioned analyses of kingly government, its responsibilities and shortcomings. I wish finally to consider another play which, while dealing with the material of the queen's plays, does so from a standpoint now wholly outside the court. Massinger's *The Bashful Lover* (1636) also has a queen–mistress whose lovers fight battles over her, but it seems only to have been performed at Blackfriars. I shall suggest that this is because the play makes a critical tilt at the kind of romantic, factional politicking in which the queen and her circle were engaged.[42]

Massinger's Matilda is another political mistress like Henrietta Maria, adored from afar by the bashful lover Galeazzo. We later

learn he is a prince, but he woos as a subject, using masque
language that emphasizes Matilda's double nature, princess and
mistress ('As *Moors* salute/The rising Sun with joyful supersti-
tion,/I could fall down and worship' (I.i.149)), and his bashfulness
is proper to a subject. He dare not approach her, nor ask any
favour more than to kneel to her. His rival, though, is a prince,
Uberti, who is offended at his meanness, but Matilda defends her
admission of this love:

> I desire not
> The meanest Altar rais'd up to mine honor
> To be pull'd down; I can accept from you
> (Be your condition nere so far beneath me)
> One grain of incense with devotion offer'd
> Beyond all perfumes of Sabean spices
> By one that proudly thinks he merits in it ...   (I.i.288)

So she is loved as a queen who rewards desert, not birth, and
love of this sovereign beauty breeds public actions. Her father is
attacked by a third suitor, Prince Lorenzo, and the noble lovers
are roused into a defence of right. Matilda takes this as a
compliment to the public love she can inspire: 'love me ver-
tuously, such love may spur you/To noble undertakings' (I.i.295).
In fact, the whole country, moved by love for her, rises to her
defence. In such a cause the husbandman would leave the earth

> Untill'd, although a general dearth should follow:
> The Student would forswear his book; the Lawyer
> Put off his thriving gown, and without pay
> Conclude the case is to be fought, not pleaded;
> The women will turn *Amazons*, as their sex
> In her were wrong'd; and boys write down their names
> I'th'muster-book for soldiers.   (I.ii.81)

Matilda's beauty binds the country in a public devotion.

Love, then, is political currency. Matilda is fought over and
fought for, and the climax is her meeting with the aggressor,
Lorenzo, in Act IV. Her beauty has the force of armies and
conquers the conqueror. He at once regrets his actions, saying
had she been 'Imploy'd to mediate your Fathers cause ... your
demands had been/As soon as spoke, agreed to' (IV.i.175). He

kneels to her and relinquishes his power. The day becomes 'The triumph of your beauty' (IV.i.205), and Matilda appears in a chariot drawn by soldiers, leading a triumph closely recalling Henrietta Maria's masques:

> a wreath of Laurel on her head,
> Her robes majestical, their richness far
> Above all value, as the present age
> Contended that a womans pomp should dim
> The glittering triumphs of the Roman *Caesars*.   (IV.iii.59)

A brilliant *coup-de-théâtre*, Matilda's entry apotheosizes the political power of love.

However, in Acts II, III and V, Massinger subtly and cleverly undercuts the romantic assumptions of Acts I and IV. Most striking after the large claims of Act I for the power of public love is the abject failure of these noble lovers on the battlefield. They have all sorts of heroic personal combats, sacrificing themselves for friendship, or singling out from the enemy the inconstant lover Alonzo, but these remain essentially private quarrels – rescues and duels – rather than strategic action. Lorenzo's lower-class and lustful soldiers are pitted against an army of gallant aristocrats, yet he still sweeps the board, and Galeazzo, aware that his love has not performed what it promised, abjures public life altogether and retires to the woods as a hermit, seeking to die 'Loves martyr' (II.v.88). Lorenzo is first and foremost a soldier, and wins by dint of martial command. We see him urging his soldiers on and resolving their internal quarrels with an appeal to military discipline:

> shall division
> Oreturn what concord built? If you desire
> To bath your swords in blood, the enemy
> Still flies before you: Would you have spoil? The Country
> Lies open to you.   (II.viii.32)

It is this type of appeal that wins wars, not love.

Love's political effectiveness is qualified yet further in Act III, in which Matilda, flying from danger, is attacked by two soldiers, her rape, ironically, being inspired by the same beauty that raised heroics in others. Her pursuers express their lust, like her lovers, in terms of the masque:

> ALONZO. She cannot be far off; how gloriously
> She shew'd to us in the valley!
> PISANO.   In my thought
> Like to a blazing Comet.
> ALONZO.   Brighter far:
> Her beams of beauty made the hill all fire;
> From whence remov'd, 'tis cover'd with thick clouds.   (III.ii.28)

Thus Matilda's beauty has no intrinsic worth; its power is its reflection in others, and it continually inspires unwanted suitors and mutually contradictory courses of action. Uberti and Galeazzo are fighting for her, but so, ostensibly, is Lorenzo. Her involvement complicates, rather than clarifies political alignments, and the peace that she concludes in Act IV presents her with an impossible choice of rivals. This choice has a public character; she could choose Uberti, who offers alliance with Parma, or Lorenzo who offers a Tuscan alliance, or Galeazzo who as a private man brings no alliances. But these political claims are all irrelevant to the problem of who loves her best. Each insists that he loves her as much as the others; the sincerity of none can be contradicted. If politics becomes the competition of opposing groups for the same favours, it involves impossible decisions, for each group may 'love' the princess as highly as the next, and Matilda refuses to commit herself, admitting that 'all have deserv'd so well,/I know not where to fix my choice' (IV.iii.172). Politics and love are gradually being shown to be incompatible. Indeed, the two actively destroy each other, for the subplot deals with a courtier, Alonzo, who jilted his girl when her father Octavio fell from his place at court, and in Act V love makes the politician, Lorenzo, effeminate, turning him into a peevish, whining lover against his own better nature (V.i.170–4) and earning him the contempt of his captain Martino. Reduced to studying fashions, Lorenzo beats a doctor who dares to suggest Matilda may one day need such 'aids of art' (V.i.119). Massinger slyly hints that even sovereign beauties are not above the ravages of time.

It should be clear by now what decision Matilda must take. Throughout the play, love confuses public action but raises the private man to fine deeds. When war is declared, Galeazzo braves Prince Uberti and roundly tells him he will do actions as great as he, though he is a prince. Uberti is shocked at his contempt of place, but in Act II everyone praises Galeazzo's brilliance:

> Pay your thanks, *Farneze*,
> To this brave man, if I may call him so,
> Whose acts were more then humane: if thou art
> My better Angel, from my infancie
> Design'd to guard me, like thy self appear,
> For sure thou art more then mortal. (II.v.27)

In retirement, Galeazzo takes shepherd's weeds. It is as 'a rustick swain' (III.iii.93) that he rescues Matilda from her ravishers, and in token of his superiority the princess kneels to the shepherd. In the final scene, she takes the courage of her convictions and declares for Galeazzo, and it is emphasized that she loves him as a *private* man. In choosing love she relinquishes politics. She advises Lorenzo to return to his own sphere, the world of affairs:

> Remember sir, you were not
> Born only for your self; Heavens liberal hand
> Design'd you to command a potent Nation . . . (V.iii.110)

He will go off to war with Turkey, and leave her with her private love. Moreover, she chooses Galeazzo not for his martial deeds, but because he pleaded Lorenzo's public claim against his own, a great act of personal self-denial passing any public achievement or any claim to princely birth:

> Shall such piety
> Pass unrewarded? such a pure affection,
> For any ends of mine, be undervalu'd?
> Avert it Heaven! I will be thy *Matilda*,
> Or cease to be; No other heat but what
> Glows from thy purest flames, shal warm this bosom;
> Nor *Florence*, nor all Monarchs of the earth
> Shall keep thee from me. (V.iii.91)

Only now is Galeazzo's princely birth revealed; but the point is already made.

So Massinger seems to be criticizing the sort of political dabbling associated with Henrietta Maria as an unhelpful trifling with serious affairs. In this he may be reflecting the views of his patron Pembroke who, though a dissident lord at court and sympathetic to anti-Spanish, anti-Catholic policies, was certainly no friend of the queen. It may be he had Pembroke or the more thoroughly discourted peers in mind when in his otherwise irrelevant subplot he created Octavio, a nobleman whose banishment Matilda's father regrets, wishing he had his assistance. Octavio lives as a woodland hermit with an earthy rustic, Gothrio, who satirizes courts as places of forgetfulness. The country, though, is a place of charity, healing and restoration, Octavio recovering the wounded Alonzo even though he has wronged his daughter. In his shepherd's garb, Galeazzo is another such 'country' figure, and at the end Octavio is welcomed back to the court. With men of this stamp, rather than with the more courtly 'opposition' linked with the queen, does the good of the 'country' lie.

So the court stage, despite the narrow constraints under which it customarily operated, was still able to become the vehicle of that courtly feeling which was severely critical of official policies and to play host to plays by professional or academic dramatists that gave voice to radical attitudes with a freedom more native to the non-courtly theatre, during the period of greater court receptiveness to 'opposition' points of view caused by the queen's political intriguing. But we shall also find that neither under more normal conditions were the romantic plays of courtly, non-professional dramatists entirely politically innocent but provided them with a means of expressing their doubts about the unpopularity and inflexibility of Charles's government; and although the range of attitudes they were free to express was much more limited than that obtaining on the non-courtly stage, it was still more complex and varied than is suggested by the simple designation 'Cavalier'.

4

Lovers and tyrants: courtier plays
1637–42

Love's republic

DAVENANT'S *The Unfortunate Lovers* (1638; pub. London, 1643) opens with a revolt led by an enraged general who has returned home to find his beloved doing penance in a white sheet for an incontinence falsely laid to her charge by a royal favourite. His prince restores justice and order, but falls for the girl himself and tries to command her for his own use, unjustly imprisoning the general. Act III cuts this Gordian knot, for the prince changes his mind and subsequent events show love and right together being defended against a lustful invading tyrant. But the prince's injustice has provoked strong criticism ('False Prince, how cunning is thy crueltie?' (p. 19)), a dilemma of loyalty and the interesting reflection that his kingly authority has deferred to love's superior power:

> In this, Sir, you perceive the intricate
> Though powerfull influence of love, that doth
> Pervert most righteous natures to attempt
> Unjust designes, his Godhead [i.e. Love's] is not full knowne
> And's miseries have beene dully taught
> To men . . .   (p. 19)

It is difficult to know how seriously to read Davenant's intentions. Conflict between love and political power was the very stuff of courtly tragicomedies and they are full of hostility to kings. In the archetypal courtier play, Suckling's *Aglaura* (1637),[1] the political rivalry between king and prince is underscored throughout by their amorous rivalry for Aglaura, and the prince's political superiority is established by his greater love-worthiness; in finally relinquishing his tyrannies, Suckling's king is also purged of his adulterous lusts. A dimension of political criticism was always a strongly latent possibility, for love, the essence of which is equality, has a tendency to level down the distinction between king and subject. Monarchs must prove their worth in love, for it will not be commanded but must be granted freely, and to the person, not the place; the private sovereignty in love achieved by the virtuous prince in *Aglaura* exceeds any kingdom a mere hereditary monarch can rule ('come, to bed my Love!/ And we will there mock Tyrannie, and Fate' (III.ii.48)). Often romantic courtier-plays of these years derived a certain heady excitement from trespassing dangerously into sensitive and otherwise forbidden areas, and increasingly they seem to be doing this with deliberateness and purpose. Even though Davenant dismantled his general's dilemma after two acts he may have intended it to have some real, though temporary force, for after the Ship Money case and Scots revolt (1637), as Charles's government ran itself into ever-tighter corners, a number of dramatists followed Brome and Cartwright in employing romantic motifs less for their own sake than as vehicles for what were essentially political significances. In particular, plays about princes in love provided useful devices to enable discussion of the problem of a king whose resources and popularity were, in the late 1630s, coming to look increasingly limited; and a king, moreover, whose idea of government made little or no acknowledgment of any duty to consult the wishes of those over whom he ruled.

Charles's personal rule rested squarely on the concept of the king's intrinsic superiority, his freedom from accountability. He was generally recognized to have certain discretionary powers, his capacity to govern and make policy for the general benefit of his people but at his own discretion, and running deep in the period was a notion of constitutional balance, between the king's prerogatives and the subject's liberties and rights, each restraining and restrained by the other. This balance was preserved by the safeguards of the common law, but in the 1630s Charles went about to demonstrate the competency of his prerogative powers in the courts. While not putting him outside the state, his success at law enabled him to dispense with parliamentary counsel and to rule uncontrolled by any constraint save judicial decisions as to the legality or illegality of his acts, establishing him as the sole arbiter of the good of the commonwealth, the sovereign power who alone gave life to the realm; in the Ship Money case Justice Berkeley went so far as to assert that *Rex* was *Lex*, that all the king's acts were legal.[2] A lawyers' fiction located this intrinsic superiority in the king's 'public body', his sovereign and mystical identity as king of England, inherited from his predecessors, and which conferred authority on him, identified the country's will with his own, and made him a god among men. To Charles, his 'public body' was a tangible reality, and he prosecuted rivals who claimed to share his magical ability to cure the King's Evil. When in 1641 he agonized over the need to consent to Strafford's execution, Bishop Williams told him 'he had a public conscience, as well as a private' which would (neatly sophistical) 'not only permit him . . . but even oblige, and require him to do what his private conscience abhorred'. After the breakdown, Charles himself resorted to the use of the argument from balance in a mixed monarchy, but he never acknowledged the authority of the court that tried him in 1649, demanding instead 'what the Law is, if the Person condemned is without Peer? And if the Law seems to condemn him, by what Power shall judgment be given, and who shall give it?'[3]

Davenant's *The Fair Favourite* (1638; pub. in his *Works*, London, 1673) raises the highly relevant question of the difficulties of a ruler whose personal interests are diverging from those of his state. He does this by presenting a king whose public and private selves have, through love, become disjointed. Davenant's fictional king has married his queen for reasons of state, thinking his first love, Eumena, has died. In fact, before his marriage she had been secretly hidden by his councillors, but finding her to be alive he can neither love his queen nor fulfil his desires with Eumena. His dual identity, he complains, has made him a 'Monster' that 'beneath/Two bodies [groans], the Natural and the Politick . . ./By force compounded of most diff'rent things' (p. 89), and he asks his statesmen to unking him. This, they reply in horror, is 'treason 'gainst/Your self' (p. 89), but the play repeatedly demonstrates that he has already been 'depos'd by th'cruel tyranny of love' (pp. 107–8). Outwardly absolute, he is inwardly unfree (p. 88); love has made him equal with Eumena (she is a lady, but no princess), so 'how poor a thing/Is Majesty, compar'd to mighty love?' (p. 89). The king's experiences convince him of the thanklessness of kingship: 'who is so rash, that can/Desire to be a King? . . . I'm weary of it'. Rather, kingly rule is no power at all, for 'what a useless glory 'tis, to be the chief/Of Men, wanting the Charter to command/A tender Ladies love' (p. 105).

We are already familiar with motifs of this sort from *The Queen and Concubine*. Davenant's choice of a frustrated and frustrating king, whose private desires contradict his public imperatives, echoes the tensions of the time at which he wrote (November 1638) as Charles's relations with the Scots deteriorated towards war. But *The Fair Favourite* is a poorly constructed play and his overall intentions remain obscure (for example, the king's decision in the last scene to recompense his queen's undeserved sufferings is entirely arbitrary). However, some illumination may be provided by the verse letter which Davenant addressed to Henrietta Maria on the eve of the recall of parliament in 1640:[4]

> Madam, so much peculiar and alone
> Are Kings, so uncompanion'd in a Throne:
> That through the want of some equality
> (Familiar Guides, who lead them to comply)
> They may offend by being so sublime;
> As if to be a King might be a crime . . .

This view of kingly authority as powerful yet inscrutable matches the reaction of the subjects in the play, who are universally baffled and dismayed by their king's behaviour; for example Eumena's brother, in his confusion, describes the king's power as 'thy dark prerogative, which is/Divine indeed: For 'tis most fear'd, because/It least is understood' (p. 93). Davenant's purpose in the letter was to encourage Henrietta Maria to become the

'Peoples Advocate', an intermediary between Charles and his subjects, and to mollify Charles's 'high obnoxious singleness' by guiding his prerogative 'to a yieldingness/That shews it fine but makes it not weigh less'. This is exactly how Eumena acts in *The Fair Favourite*: respected by both ruler and ruled, she mediates between them, and the king recognizes that his power is made more acceptable to his people when moderated by her:

> Could every one that careless sits
> On his high Throne, depute his pow'r
> Where it might mingle with such innocence,
> Monarchal sway would be belov'd; For 'tis
> Our worst mistake, to think the Arts of Government
> So hard; since a perfection in the skill
> To rule, is less requir'd then perfect will.   (p. 96)

In 1641, Davenant would claim that he, Suckling and Jermyn bore no antipathy to parliamentary government but 'both in their writing, and speech have so often extold the naturall necessity of Parliaments here, with extreme scorne upon the incapacity of any that should perswade the King he could be fortunate without them'; furthermore, he himself 'not long since' had written 'to the Queenes Majesty in praise of her inclination to become this way the Peoples advocate, the which they presented to her'.[5] This obviously refers to the verse letter, but the evidence of *The Fair Favourite* suggests that Davenant was already moving towards an idea of the queen as a channel of communication between king and people, and supplying Charles's need for more moderate counsel, as early as 1638.

We are on much firmer ground with the translation of N. Desfontaines's *La Vraye Suite du Cid* (Paris, 1638) made by Joseph Rutter *c.* 1639. Rutter, a protégé of the queen's courtier Dorset, had already translated Corneille's *Le Cid*, and his version of Desfontaines's continuation was done at Charles's command.[6] It is easy to see why Charles liked the play, for it is the epitome of absolutist drama, its moral being 'A Kings entreaties must have no deniall' (*The Second Part of The Cid* (London, 1640), sig.C1ʳ). Desfontaines's king falls in love with the Cid's betrothed, Cimena, and his sister, the Infanta, falls for the Cid. In his king–subject conflict, Desfontaines carefully defends the king's interests, insisting that 'The wills of Kings can render all things lawfull' (Rutter, sig.A6ʳ) and arguing that as for Cimena's promised love to the Cid he has power

> T'absolve her of it; Princes render lawfull
> Whatever pleases them: respects become
> The people, not a King . . .   (sig.B6ᵛ)

Desfontaines's last act is an extended triumph for the king, who ties together all the subsidiary plots, joins lovers, reconciles brothers and sisters, restores kingdoms. The stage echoes with · his praise; more than a man, he works miracles:

> *Mais aussi n'est-ce pas vn songe qui m'abuse?*
> *Non, ie vielle, & ie vois mon frere devant moy*
> *Et ie ne puis douter des parolles d'vn Roy.*
> (Desfontaines, p. 85)

The Cid submits absolutely, offering Cimena to the king; his repeated line, '*Je ne suis qu'vn sujet, & vous estes vn Roy*' (p. 100), becomes a refrain. But the king's generosity outdoes all, and he forgoes Cimena, returning her to the Cid. More than just noble, he is the mainspring of the whole action. The characters' happiness and integrity are entirely dependent on him, and he wills them, '*Soyes tousiours Rodrigue, & vous tousiours Chymene*' (p. 104).

Significantly, Rutter changed all this. He restructured the plot to reduce the concentrated effect of these final moments and allow the Cid and Cimena to suffer more. Whereas Desfontaines, who made the Cid partly responsible for weakening his position with Cimena, did not bring them together in the last act, Rutter does, and shows that they love as strongly as ever, firmly incriminating the king. By bringing forward scenes in which Desfontaines unravelled his emotional tangle, Rutter makes the king and Infanta seem more perverse, and the play's whole weight now falls on the crisis at the end of the fourth act, where the king demands Cimena from the Cid and laments that love is subduing his kingly powers:

60

> Why . . . was I born a King then? if my quality
> Must crosse my dearest wishes, let me be
> A subject, any thing, so I have her:
> Some kinde fate rob me of my crown and scepter,
> And you shall see that I will blesse your rigour,
> If in exchange you'le give me but one heart,
> *Cimena* limits my ambition . . .   (sig.C4ʳ)

As in *The Fair Favourite*, love does not respect the quality of kings, but has an infuriating tendency to level ranks, and the king wishes to abdicate, finding his love compromised by his place. But Rutter's point is more daring than Davenant's, for love provides his king with no answering reassurance of his ultimate royal superiority. Though set apart by his public identity, in love's republic his kingly powers pass unacknowledged and he is rendered the equal of other men, and subject to the same passions, errors and shortcomings as they.

Rutter capitalizes on these changes in his dénouement, radically rewriting Desfontaines. Although the Cid (reluctantly) sacrifices his interest in Cimena, he admires her spirited resistance to the king and resolves to rebuff plans to marry him off to the Infanta:

> I ought him duty, and I have perform'd it.
> I've offerd with my life all my desires,
> Yet though I give I may refuse to take,
> He cannot force me to a new affection,
> Or make me love her lesse, then she does mee,
> In other things he rules, in this I'me free.   (sig.C6ʳ)

Here is the Caroline tension between defiance and duty; the Cid's vigorous truth to the freedom of his affections marks a significant limitation on the king's authority. But, crucially, Rutter transforms the foreign princess Seriffa, who in Desfontaines is attempting to wrest the Cid from Cimena, into a match for the king to whom his father contracted him years before, but whom he has neglected. Hence although all the characters' happiness does depend on the king, it is because his failure to acknowledge his duty to Seriffa is the root cause of their unhappiness, and he admits that although the public body confers authority on him, it does not enable him simply to act with impunity:

Must a Prince suffer violence? he must[,]
Or else imprison them that offer it,
(His wilde desires) there being no other course,
But to submit to reason or to force.   (sig.C8ᵛ)

Submitting to reason or to force is a good description of Charles's options at the end of the decade. Rutter's remotivation of the king's generosity turns it from an act of benevolence into a recognition of his obligations ('In justice sir, she is your wife, if contracts/Can stand in force with Princes' (sig.C8ʳ)); the king learns that the good ruler is the one who fulfils his responsibilities and duties to his subjects before his own desires or will:

come faire Princesse:
Y'are mine by a double tie of love and dutie.
Which I shall still preserve, since I am taught
To do not what I would; but what I ought.   (sig.C11ᵛ)

The Queen of Aragon: courtship, contracts and consent

In his purposeful recasting of his original, Rutter seized with some aplomb on the capacity of courtly tragicomedy to act as a vehicle for serious political statement, but we have to wait until William Habington's The Queen of Aragon (London, 1640) to find a courtly play of real poetic distinction and literary merit in which a political critique is comprehensively carried through. Habington was cousin to the Earl of Pembroke, and Pembroke evidently wished the play to attract notice for he arranged for two sumptuous Whitehall productions 'by my lords servants out of his own family, and [at] his charge in the cloathes and sceanes, which were very riche and curious'.[7] His sponsorship is a clue to the play's meaning, for in 1640 he was known as a favourer of accommodation with the Scots, an opponent of Strafford and a parliamentary magnate with several 'popular' MPs under his patronage; dismissed from his court post in 1641, he was a prominent peer at Westminster throughout the 1640s, was elected to the Commons in 1649 and earned a state funeral paid for by parliament. In several ways, Habington, who later praised Fletcher for having used the stage to teach kings 'how neere to God, while just they be:/But how dissolv'd stretcht forth to Tyrannie' and was himself said to have been 'not unknown to *Oliver* the *Usurper*',[8] was a dramatic heir of that other remarkable and politically unorthodox protégé of Pembroke, Massinger. His treatment of his story often resembles the strategies that Massinger employed in the 1620s for exploiting the political potential of romantic material, and his play suggests some of the directions in which Massinger might well have moved had he lived on into the greater crises of the 1640s.

The play concerns the courtship of the Aragonese queen Cleodora by Decastro, her late father's choice for her, and a trusted minister; but she really loves Florentio, a Castilian nobleman who has invaded Aragon to save her from Decastro's attentions. Florentio's military victory is made possible by the unexpected intervention of a third, anonymous man who afterwards pays court to Cleodora. Florentio challenges him to a duel, only to find that he is his own king, Ascanio, in disguise. This is interwoven with a comic subplot which debunks the pretensions of courtly love-making. A court lady is pestered for her favours by Sanmartino, a frivolous and disreputable nobleman, who is already married anyway. His behaviour generates ridicule of the pride and folly of the wealthy whose 'titular greatnesse' is 'th'envie but of fooles,/The wise mans pitty':

> [Once,] superstition
> Worship'd each Lord an idoll. Now we finde
> By sad experience, that you are meere men,
> If vice debauch you not to beasts. (sig.E2ʳ)

Instead the lady chooses a veritable puritan, a courtier noted for his soberness and seriousness, and tells Sanmartino to earn true honour in the wars. The social preferences established in the subplot alert the audience to the political preferences which the main plot will maintain.

Cleodora strongly recalls Massinger's Matilda. She is another queen–mistress whose beauty is praised in masque-language as sufficient to create a kingdom of admirers for her ('her beauty yet beares so much Majestie,/It could have forc't the World to throw it selfe,/A captive at her feete', says Ascanio (sig.D3ʳ)). Florentio's friends say that she 'By nature[']s seated and her high deserts' (sig.G1ʳ) and on this intrinsic worth her sway is founded. She rules with the imperiousness of a mistress; Florentio rebukes Decastro for attempting to overrule and restrain his queen exactly as an unfaithful lover:

> Where is then that humble zeale
> You owe a Mistresse; if you can throw off
> That duty which you owe her as your Queene? (sig.C1ʳ)

And Decastro acknowledges the force of this, explaining his acts as done in duty to the state, while reserving his love and loyalty to the queen's great person:

> Her beauty hath
> A power more Soveraigne, than th'Easterne slave
> Acknowledg'd ever in his Idoll King.
> To that I bowed a subject. But when I
> Discover'd that her fancie fixt upon
> *Florentio* (Generall now of th'enemies Armie)
> I let the people use their severe way:
> And they restrain'd her. (sig.B4ᵛ)

His language betrays a strain in reconciling love for the sovereign *person* of the queen with anxiety at the way she is wielding her sovereignty. First, her choice has fallen on a foreigner, an act which adulterates the integrity of the state. There is an illuminating parallel here with Brome's *The Queen's Exchange* (*c.* 1634–36?) in which the Saxon queen's councillor opposes her marriage with the Northumbrian king because

> I know, and you, if you knew anything
> Might know the difference twixt the Northumbrian lawes
> And ours: And sooner will their King pervert
> Your Priviledges and your Government,
> Then reduce his to yours . . . (p. 461)

As in Brome's play (and Stuart politics)[9] the sovereign's mis-marriage creates fears for the kingdom and the love that should exist between monarch and state; indeed, Cleodora has plunged her country into war, for Florentio's possession of her involves his (military) possession of her kingdom. Secondly, the importance of Decastro is that he is repeatedly emphasized to be the people's choice. Appointed regent by the queen's father, it is he whom 'The Kingdome judgeth fit to marry with' the queen (sig.B3ʳ) and he pleads

> since the vote of *Arragon* decrees
> That my long Service hath the justest claime
> To challenge her regard; Thus must I stand
> Arm'd to make good the title.   (sigs.B4ᵛ–C1ʳ)

He is attractive and sturdy, but never merely romantic, and the people are 'vowed to [his] devotion' (sig.I1ʳ).

Consequently Florentio and Decastro typify opposed views of kingly authority. Florentio submits scrupulously to Cleodora's will, yet even this can never deserve her love since, because of her public character, she is beyond all personal merit in a subject; he can only await a gracious and undeserved grant from her ('Like th'heavenly bounty/She may distribute favour: But 'tis sinne/To say our merits may pretend a title' (sig.C1ʳ)). He does ask her for a promise of love but even this she refuses:

> Upon
> My marriage day I have vowed to bring my selfe
> A free oblation to the holy Altar.
> Not like a fearefull debtor, tender love
> To save my bond. My Lord I must not heare
> One whisper of a promise.   (sig.E3ʳ)

Instead, she asserts, 'My resolution, grounded on his service,/ Ties more than formall contracts' (sig.G4ʳ), presenting her will as responsible yet entirely absolute, most free because not even formally acknowledging her commitments. Similarly, when Ascanio woos her she admits the great desert that he has displayed yet still denies that this exerts any claim on her liberty of choice. At the heart of this absolutism there is a deliberate capriciousness, that of a wayward mistress: the truly arbitrary royal will measures its freedom in terms of the obligations it *fails* to honour or even acknowledge, and the merit it *refuses* to reward.

Decastro, on the other hand, insists that desert must merit

reward, and endeavours to constrain Cleodora's will on just this basis:

> True, the Queene
> Stands now restrain'd: But tis by the decree
> Of the whole Kingdome, least her errour should
> Perswade her to some man lesse worthy . . .
> . . . than my selfe. For so they judge
> The proudest subject to a Forraigne Prince. (sig.C1^v)

Whereas to Florentio Cleodora is a 'Kingdome' in herself (sig.H3^r, H4^r), Decastro maintains a firm distinction between the person of the monarch and the greater public body which is the kingdom. He explains:

> Humbly have I labor'd
> To win her favour: and when that prevail'd not;
> The Kingdome, in my quarrell, vowed to emptie
> The veines of their great body. (sig.B4^r)

Cleodora denies the validity of any claim which her other 'public body' may make on her. When Decastro admonishes her for drawing 'into/The inward parts of this great state a most/ Contagious Feaver' she retorts, 'Pray no Metaphor' (sig.C4^v). But the following moments demonstrate conclusively that there is a rift in the community of interest between the body politic and body natural; as Decastro kneels to declare that he will not rise until Cleodora pities him, his dilemma between his courtship of her and equal love for the state is neatly encapsulated:

> *Alarum and Enter Ossuna*
> Ossuna. O my Lord!
> To arme, to arme. The enemie encouraged
> By a strange leader, wheel'd about the towne,
> And desperately surpris'd the carelesse guard.
> One gate's already theirs.
> Decastro. Have I your licence[?]
> Queene. To augment your owne command, and keepe me still
> An humble captive[?]
> Decastro. Madam! your disdaine
> Distracts me more, than all th'assaults of fortune.
> *Exeunt all but the Queene, Floriana, and Cleantha*
> (sig.D1^v)

That the interests of the monarch and the state are no longer identical could hardly be clearer; it is an astonishing incident to put onto the court stage in 1640.

Some of these perceptions have already rubbed off on Ascanio. Like Rutter's king and Massinger's Galeazzo he perceives that kingship discredits his love, and so fights and courts incognito that he may be loved for his person, not place:

> Consider
> In me nothing of fortune, onely looke
> On that, to which Love new created me.
> If once receiv'd your servant; what's *Castile*
> In the comparison? For Princes are
> Too bold, if they bring wealth and victory
> To enter competition with those treasures
> A Lover aimes at in his Mistresse favour.   (sig.G4^r)

He has learnt Simonds D'Ewes's lesson (p. 21 above) that a king's power to demand obedience automatically compromises that obedience. He may well have greatness of birth but 'without the/Merit' (sig.G3^r), and it is with an assertion of his merit that (still disguised) he woos the queen:

> The Starres shoote
> An equall influence on the open cottage,
> Where the poore sheepheards childe is rudely nurst,
> And on the cradle where the Prince is rockt
> With care and whisper . . .
>   . . . no distinction is 'tweene man and man,
> But as his vertues adde to him a glory,
> Or vices cloud him.   (sig.F1^r)

The romantic situation has enabled Habington to insert an extraordinary panegyric to the noble mind, against the claims of rank and birth; of course these levelling sentiments cut no ice with Cleodora. However, Ascanio offends against his own principles once he is unmasked. Florentio immediately relinquishes his love to his sovereign's superior interest, but once again it is because his public character has conferred priority on him ('What is an Armie of us/Exposed to certaine slaughter, if compared/To th'shortest moment that should serve your quiet' (sig.G3^r)).

Cleodora rebukes Ascanio that he had already (before having seen her) formally renounced any claim to her person, and that he is invading his subject's undoubted pre-existing right:

> promises of Princes must not be
> By after Arts evaded? Who dares punish
> The breach of oath in subjects; and yet slight
> The faith he hath made them?
>   Ascanio. But my *Florentio*
> Hath given me backe his [interest].
>   Queen. That gift
> Was like a vow extorted, which Religion
> Cancels, as forc't from Conscience.   (sig.G4ʳ)

Such a tangle of kingly privilege and violated private rights would have been entirely familiar to observers of the prerogative schemes used by Charles in the 1630s to finance his government without resorting to another parliament, and Cleodora's legal language emphasizes the inequity, and inequality, of Ascanio's actions. But the warning to Ascanio that he cannot exact from his subjects the obedience they have promised him if he himself breaks his promises to them is also a pointed moral for the politicians of 1640: princes must be made to keep their contracts or their power is mere naked tyranny, where all the promises are on the subjects' side, and none on the king's.

These difficulties are resolved in the fine closing scene. The three suitors meet again, and Ascanio attempts to intimidate Decastro by pulling rank, but Decastro fearlessly opposes him, proclaiming to his face that a private man may deserve as much as the greatest monarch:

> I will answer you
> (Proud Monarch of *Castile*) what mold
> Soever Nature casts me in, my mind
> Is vaster than your empire. And I can
> Love equally with him whose name did Conquer
> Kingdomes as large as yours.   (sig.H4ᵛ)

He reminds Cleodora that he brings a new army whose patriotism she ignores at her peril, confronting her, in effect, with her own 'public body':

> Cast but your eye on this vast body, which
> The Kingdome doth unite in my defence,
> And see how ruinous is your errour, that
> Must leane to forraigne succours! (sig.H4^r)

Ascanio and Florentio abuse him again, but at that moment the city rises in his support. He immediately sends word to protect the queen and her suitors, and the rivals marvel at this act of nobility ('This speakes him Noble, even to our envie' (sig.H4^v)). Greater generosity is to come. At this moment of victory Decastro submits to the queen, abandoning his suit and kneeling to her. Her amazement admits a telling reversal of opinion:

> Pray rise up my Lord,
> Would I could merit thus much favour; but [–]
> DECASTRO. Pardon I interupt you. But you cannot
> Finde love to answere mine . . . (sig.I1^r)

Cleodora admits that Decastro has done a greater act than she can do, and has more merit than even she can reward. So although he resigns, instructing his soldiers to return to obedience, Cleodora's acknowledgment of his superiority implicitly redefines her terms of rule. His submission is not necessitated, like that of the other lovers, but voluntary, and while it indicates a desire to find a solution by the noblest means, through generosity and self-denial, it also demonstrates that she cannot rule except by Decastro's consent. In recognizing his merit, she acknowledges that the love he offers – the love of all her people for her in her public character – is far in excess of her ability to requite it. She cannot possibly merit such trust, but the people choose to invest her in it. Her authority thus becomes something which is conferred on her, not something she naturally has; she rules by the people's *consent* (their love) rather than by her own innate power (her loveliness).

Habington is here arguing a radically new, and potentially revolutionary, understanding of the basis of government which anticipates (astonishingly) that distinction between *power* and *authority* which would enter the literature of political controversy only for the first time in the 1640s and, significantly, in the pamphlets of Massinger's friend Henry Parker.[10] The qualifications of rule do not inhere intrinsically in Habington's royal characters: whereas the king in *The Fair Favourite* (p. 100) could face a traitor unarmed (!), Ascanio, duelling with his subject Florentio, may exhibit a courage 'more than Mortall' (sig.G2^v) but no innate sovereign power protects him from being wounded, nor was his fighting in battle exceptional among soldiers of 'equall spirit' (sig.D4^v). Rather, the one principle that significantly interrelates the three problematic relationships of the play (Decastro–Cleodora, Cleodora–Ascanio, Ascanio–Florentio) is an emphasis on government as an agreement involving the *consent* of both ruler and ruled. As we have seen, Cleodora warns Ascanio that to command obedience from Florentio he must keep his own obligations to him. Similarly, in disguise Ascanio tries to urge his own claims to reward on Cleodora, but only succeeds in antagonizing her, by attributing the same foundations to *her* power:

> QUEEN. . . . heaven hath made
> Subordination, and degrees of men,
> And even religion doth authorize us
> To rule; and tells the subject tis a crime
> And shall meete death, if he disdaine obedience.
>   ASCANIO. Kinde heaven made us all equall, till rude strength
> Or wicked [policy] usurp'd a power,
> And for Religion, that exhorts t'obey
> Onely for its own ease.
>   QUEEN. I must not heare,
> Such insolence 'gainst Majestie . . .   (sig.F1^r)

Decastro too denies that 'Nature' placed him in 'low/Obedience' (sig.C1^r), asserting instead that kings rule Aragon 'but at the Courtesie of Time' (sig.C4^v) and that his own acts are warranted by 'The peoples suffrage, which inaugurats Princes' (sig.B4^r). Surely Habington laid his scene in Aragon because he knew of its semi-legendary history as a monarchy where the prince was answerable to the will of the people; the Aragonese were reputed to swear only conditional allegiance to their monarch, and had legal machinery to bring against an arbitrary ruler, and by which he could be abandoned and replaced. Certainly other men knew of this, for the president of Charles's judges cited the Aragonese example against the king when he sentenced him to death in 1649, and so too did Milton, defending the people's right of deposing a tyrant in *The Tenure of Kings and Magistrates*.[11] Within five years of *The Queen of Aragon*, events would have led Henry Parker, writing as the leading apologist for parliament's usurpation of Charles's authority, to formulate the view, entirely novel for England, that rulers hold their power only in trust from their people, which trust, if abused, might be revoked, and to elaborate it into a full theory of parliamentary sovereignty based on the principle of rule according to the good of the people, for this is 'the Paramount Law that shall give Law to all humane Laws whatsoever . . . The Law of Prerogative itself, it is subservient to this Law'.[12] The maxim so crucial to Parker's case against Charles – *salus populi suprema lex esto* – Habington himself put into the mouth of Decastro, to urge against *his* monarch: 'I must acquaint you that the supreme Law/Of Princes, is the peoples safety' (sig.C4^v). And in the restraint of Cleodora by her people, he demonstrates neatly but remorselessly the necessity of monarchs obtaining the consent of their people; Cleodora may have all the trappings of power, but without her people's obedience her authority is empty.

In effect, Habington's final scene shows this 'peoples suffrage' in action, actually re-enacting the original endowment of authority in the monarch. Decastro's generosity does not obscure this important emphasis on consent but it does meet the needs of 1640 by suggesting the spirit of accommodation in which it is offered. His generosity breeds answering generosity from the others, each graciously deferring to the wishes of each other. Ascanio states he 'will not be/Orecome in friendship' (sig.I2^r) and resigns his suit; and, in a highly suggestive action, Cleodora gives Decastro a blank paper on which to write any demands, but he, more generous still, returns it empty.

One would dearly like to know what this climactic, symbolic act suggested to its first audience. Probably they would have linked it with the charters in which royal grants or monopolies were recorded; possibly it would echo the writs for Ship Money. There is an interesting parallel to this scene in the speech of a king to his subjects in an otherwise lost play by Massinger from 1638, known only because Charles objected personally to its implications:

> Monys? Wee'le rayse supplies what ways we please,
> And force you to subscribe to blanks, in which
> We'le mulct you as wee shall thinke fitt. The Caesars
> In Rome were wise, acknowledging no lawes
> But what their swords did ratifye, the wives
> And daughters of the senators, bowinge to
> Their wills as deities . . .

Charles found this 'too insolent, and to bee changed'.[13] It is neatly inverted by Habington's blank on which the subject is invited to write the terms.

But in view of the issues of this last scene, the most likely analogue may well be Magna Carta itself, widely regarded as England's prime constitutional document, into which were written the liberties of the subject and by which England's freedom from royal tyranny was formally established. Laud damned Magna Carta as having 'an obscure birth from usurpation, and fostered and showed to the world by rebellion',[14] but to others it meant traditional, popular ways of government. Successive parliaments of the 1620s appealed to its authority in support of their grievances;[15] in 1641, before parliament was beginning to oppose the king outright, even the courtly playwright and future royalist John Denham concluded his *Cooper's Hill* with a eulogy of the Charter as encapsulating and protecting the balance of rights between king and subject:

> Faire Liberty pursu'd & meant a prey
> To Tyrany, here [at Runnymede] turn'd & stood at Bay . . .
> Which was or should at least have beene the last . . .
> There was that Charter Seal'd, where in the Crowne
> All marks of Arbitrary power layes down:
> Tyrant, & Slave, those names of hate & feare,
> The happier Stile of King, & Subiect beare . . .

This is the optimism of the early months of the Long Parliament; as in Habington's conclusion, the dignity of king and subject is mutually confirmed in an order founded on love, not fear.

Denham concludes with a statement of the constitutional balance Magna Carta guarantees, king and subject each strengthening the other in a relationship beneficial to both:[16]

> Therefore their boundles power lett princes draw
> Within the Chanell & the shoares of Lawe:
> And may that Law which teaches Kings to sway
> Their Septers, teach their subjects to obey.

A whole play on Magna Carta, Robert Davenport's *King John and Matilda* (c. 1634; pub. London, 1655) had been acted 'often before their Majesties' (sig.A1ᵛ). This is a boldly polemical, even puritanical play in the line descending from Bale's anti-papal *King Johan* (1534), firmly Protestant in its concern for the purity of religion and freedom of the state, and in its levelling attitude to personal morality. King John violates the Runnymede agreement and subjects himself and his people to the papal legate in order to have closer control over his unruly barons. The barons are spirited critics of John's absolutism, but they are true to England and rush to defend her when she is invaded, and they include one 'country' figure, a plain lord who demands 'plain dealing' (sig.B3ʳ) and weeps at John's infidelity to his trust. John and his queen are vicious and passionate and, in scenes of strong pathos, their minion kills two innocent women and a child from the rebels' families. John tries to rape Matilda, the daughter of the plain lord, and in his lusts he does not even spare religion but besieges the abbey where she has taken sanctuary:

> *Abbesse*, deliver *Matilda*
> Or with an Army fill'd with Ruffians, Ravishers,
> The very Sonnes of darkness, we will levell
> This building to the bottom. (sigs.H2ʳ⁻ᵛ)

The absolute ruler cannot even rule himself; the rape of Matilda is the private counterpart to his public defilement of church and state. His crimes derive directly from neglect of 'the seal'd Covenants' (sig.B4ᵛ) of 1215, and he only regains authority when he resolves to live and rule virtuously, in his penitence more like an ordinary man than a king. Living under another arbitrary king with papist leanings, Davenport wrote with no little urgency.

Habington draws on this highly politicized strain of imagery but in a more conciliatory manner than Davenport. Decastro's resignation is not an example of unrealistic wishful thinking, a courtly hope that the people, when they hold all the cards, might capitulate and solve Charles's problems. Rather, the exchange of the blank charter re-enacts the historical event, the granting of Magna Carta, recalling its principles but reinterpreting the understanding on which it is based. The charter of rule is reconfirmed, but on a basis of mutual love and trust, not force.

The prominence of Decastro is readily explained if we read the play against the sensitive moment of its first performance – 9 April 1640, four days before parliament reconvened after an eleven-year interval in which it had seemed that Charles might never rule with parliament again. Decastro's pleadings are those of all Charles's parliaments ('would your highnesse/Had lent a gentler eare to the safe counsell/Of him who had no crime but too much love' (sigs.H4^{r-v})); the new parliament might mean a new start, or repeat the deadlock of 1629. Observers of the Short Parliament all remarked on 'the temper and sobriety of that house', that they 'managed all their debates, and their whole behaviour, with wonderful order' and that even in the most heated debate 'there was not . . . an angry word spoken'.[17] Sir Benjamin Rudyerd spoke of moderation and co-operation, that parliament was 'the bedd of reconciliacion betwixt King and people And therefore it is fitt for us to lay aside all exasperacions and carry ourselves with humility'. He prayed this would be 'a breeding, teeming parliament' in which king and people collaborated, for 'As long as we have parliaments, wee shall know where to find our selves, when they are gone, wee are lost.' Pym too wished that 'the great Union and Love, which should be kept and communicated betwixt the King and his subjects' might be established firmly, for 'Where the intercourse betwixt the head and the members is hindred, the Body prospers not.'[18] The loss of this possibility of mutual understanding between king and parliament was most regretted at the Short Parliament's dissolution. 'It could never be hoped, that more sober and dispassionate men would ever meet together in that place, or fewer who brought ill purposes with them.'[19]

Habington's final scene catches brilliantly this balance between reform and restraint, remonstration and conciliation. The play resolves on the basis of concessions on all sides. Agreements are honoured, responsibilities acknowledged, failings forgiven, understandings made. The atmosphere of mutual trust would be highly pertinent to the eve of parliament. Ascanio's moral, that 'He doth live/Mighty indeed, w'hath power, and will, to give' (sig.I2^r), was admitted by Charles only a fortnight later when he assured parliament of his readiness to give in the hope of answering generosity. He insisted 'He would not be overcome with kindnes, but would be aforehand with them'; the people 'cannot expresse soe much, as he will requite'.[20]

This conclusion, with its respect for the feelings and honours of all the participants and for restraint, generosity and human dignity in politics, gestures towards important and strongly-held beliefs about the nature of political life, but it is rooted in the tensions of Habington's very specific historical situation. No doubt he knew that some people *did* desire change beyond the limits past which the Short Parliament did not wish to go; Oliver St John shocked Clarendon by his satisfaction at the Short Parliament's dissolution, telling him that 'this Parliament would never have done what was necessary to be done',[21] and his hopes were fulfilled by the greater resolution displayed by the new parliament six months later. Habington voices opposed impulses, for change and for conservatism, coexisting simultaneously and uneasily in his society – the desire to achieve one set of constitutional aims yet also the desire to preserve the fundamental balance of the constitution, the desire to bring Charles to an accommodation yet also to avoid pushing the state into social revolution in the process. The special excellence of his play is that at every point he faces the need to criticize and simultaneously to define the limits of that criticism; his extraordinary forthrightness about the realities of authority and degree is accompanied, nevertheless, with a clear conviction of the value and necessity of these things, and these tensions are felt with a vividness that gives the play's language its particular and fully dramatic edge. It seems to me easily the best of the courtly plays, and among the best of the decade in general, and its quality is directly related to Habington's penetration into the moment of crisis through which he is living: it measures the intensity of his engagement with the contradictions inherent, and finally unresolvable, in the politics of his time.

Alternative compromises

The courtier drama of the period concluded with two plays which present, in foreign settings, mirrors of England's political perplexities, and propound alternative strategies for resolving them. The aim of both playwrights, ultimately, is the re-establishment of Charles's authority on a firmer base, but, as I have been arguing, we need not ascribe this to an instinctive, reflex 'royalism'. Rather, before Charles's relations with parliament became decisively unworkable, it must have seemed that any number of different compromises might eventually be hammered out, and the solutions which these dramatists propose differ according to the different analyses they make of the causes underlying the failure of Charles's rule. To one, Charles has neglected the 'natural rulers'; to the other, a different kind of conciliation would be in order.

Suckling's *Brennoralt* probably belongs to summer 1640.[22] Its romantic story is set against the crushing of a revolt, and the rebels reflect both Suckling's Scottish experiences and Charles's English problems. Brennoralt, almost an *alter ego* for the author, is no simply loyal Cavalier, but a noble malcontent. To his soldiers, fighting a war they do not believe in, he is 'a discontent, but what of that? who is not?' (I.iii.58). His opening speech is an attack on the vanity and inefficiency of courtiers. The court is 'A most eternall place of low affronts,/And then as low submissions', run by 'A race of shallow, and unskilfull Pilots;/Which doe misguide the Ship even in the calme,/And in great stormes serve but as weight to sinke it' (I.i.9). The royal advisers are 'formall beards', men wise 'for themselves, not others' (I.i.26).

No flatterer, Brennoralt only fights when there is danger worth demonstrating his valour on; no party man, he praises valour even in an enemy.

The rebels see Brennoralt as a potential ally, and the scene in which they tempt him to avenge his neglect on the king probably recalls similar approaches the Scots made to English nobles at Berwick in 1639.[23] But Brennoralt is not flattered:

> How came it in thy heart to tempt my honour?
>> TROCKE. My Lord?
>> BRENNORALT. Do'st thinke 'cause I am angry
> With the King and State sometimes,
> I am fallen out with vertue, and my selfe?
> Draw, draw, or by goodnesse –
>> TROCKE. What means your Lordship?
>> BRENNORALT.   Draw I say.
> – He that would thinke me a villaine, is one:
> And I do weare this toy, to purge the world
> Of such.   (III.ii.36)

Trocke is saved only by the king's intervention. Brennoralt, though a malcontent, is sincere; by contrast, the integrity of the rebels, who voice the same grievances as the Scots and parliament, is suspect:

> Let all goe on still in the publique name,
> But keep an eare open to particular offers;
> Liberty and publique good are like great *Oleos*,
> Must have the upper end still of our tables,
> Though they are but for shew . . .
>   . . . Presse much religion . . .
> For things of faith are so abstruse, and nice,
> They will admit dispute eternally:
> So how so e're other demands appeare,
> These never can be prov'd unreasonable . . .   (II.iii.22)

This is not to say that Suckling denies these grievances. In a third-act council scene, the king is warned that 'though your Person in your Subjects hearts/Stands highly honour'd, and belov'd, yet are/There certain Acts of State, which men call grievances/Abroad' (III.ii.94). However, in the council scenes, the main contention is not the validity of the grievances but the

77

purely practical problem of the threat they pose to the public order. As the king says, 'Peace/And warre are in themselves indifferent,/And time doth stamp them either good or bad' (III.ii.147).

Although the king plumps for peace, the drift of the council scenes is to encourage him to firm, resolute action, and war if necessary – the sort of short, sharp incursion that Brennoralt himself later leads. Brennoralt calls on the king to take the initiative:

> Thinke you Rebellion and Loyalty
> Are empty names? and that in Subjects hearts
> They don't both give and take away the courage?
> Shall we beleeve there is no difference
> In good or bad? that there's no punishment,
> Or no protection? forbid it Heaven!
> If when great *Polands* honour, safety too,
> Hangs in dispute, we should not draw our Swords,
> Why were we ever taught to weare 'em Sir? (III.ii.60)

Resolution is needed because the rebels strengthen their position by obscuring the moral rights and wrongs of the case. When their demands are refused, they 'Exclaime against it loud,/Till the *Polonians* thinke it high injustice,/And wish [them] better yet', which makes them 'Admir'd, and flock't unto' by 'th'unknowing multitude', but once the people are involved in politics 'justnesse of Cause is nothing' (II.iii.53, III.ii.80, 85). Suckling is responding to the early fears generated by popular political activity, and his solution is quick action before events get out of hand by the natural rulers, king and aristocracy. His faith is in their effective leadership, and the stage king talks of advising with 'Our greater Counsell, which we now assemble' (III.ii.156). Presumably Suckling has in mind here the Council of Peers called at York in September 1640, rather than any sort of parliamentary action.

In January 1639, as Charles was preparing to make war on the Scots for the first time, Suckling's friend Thomas Carew, in a couplet of quite astounding ruthlessness, called on Janus to bless his campaign and 'Strew all the pavements, where he treads/With loyall hearts, or Rebels heads'.[24] After the humiliating failures of the next eighteen months, the sentiment remains the same, but its confidence has vanished and the strategies by which it is to be achieved have been modified. Brennoralt's arguments are those advanced by Suckling himself in his letter of November 1640 about the new parliament, in which he again criticized the courtiers for advising the king badly, only counselling 'as they believe the King [is] inclyn'd...which is a kinde of Settinge the Sun by the Diall'. The 'way to preserve [his] power' is 'to give it away', for instead of awaiting parliament's demands and thank-lessly doing 'nothinge, but what they have, or were petitioning for', Charles should 'doe somethinge extraordinary att this present' and promote his leadership and their goodwill by 'throwing away things they call not for, or giving things they expected not'.[25] When Charles dithered, Suckling, like Brennoralt, tried to take the lead himself and promoted the Army Plot of 1641. Ironically, this attempt to force the issue misfired disas-trously and was a major factor in the weakening of Charles's credibility with parliament.

Denham addressed the same problems in his *The Sophy* (London, 1642), but he was less inclined to trust Charles with unrestrained power (his father, a judge, had found against the Crown in the Ship Money case, as had judge Croke whom Denham praised in 1641 as 'the first who happily did sound/ Unfathomd Royalty and felt the Ground').[26] Laying his scene in Persia, he chose a setting popularly associated with tyrannical government, for the eastern monarchies had provided Charles's critics with a rich source of invective (most notoriously, one Richard Chambers was jailed for saying 'Merchants are in no part of the world so screwed and wrung as in England. In Turkey they have more encouragement').[27] Denham's opening action does indeed show the king, beset by poverty and war, pressuriz-ing his merchants for finance just as did Charles to support his Scottish campaigns:[28]

> KING. Let twenty thousand men be raised.
> Let fresh supplyes of victuals, and of money,
> Be sent with speed.
>   LORDS. Sir, your Treasures

> Are quite exhausted, the Exchequer's empty.
> KING. Talke not to me of Treasures, or Exchequers,
> Send for five hundred of the wealthiest Burgers,
> Their shops and ships are my Exchequer.
> ABDALL. 'Twere better you could say their hearts. [*Abd. aside.*]
> (pp. 3–4)

Denham's tale of revenge and violence – the king suspects his own son of treachery and destroys him, only to find that the favourite who advised him is the real traitor – is the vehicle for an account of the necessary weaknesses attending absolute government. The favourite, Haly, is able to make the prince's virtues – his courage, popularity and openness – appear his greatest threats to his jealous father. The court is full of useless and wicked advisers:

> Alas, they shew him nothing
> But in the glasse of flatterie, if any thing
> May beare a shew of glory, fame, or greatnesse,
> 'Tis multiplyed to an immense quantitie,
> And stretch't even to Divinitie:
> But if it tend to danger, or dishonour,
> They turne about the Perspective, and shew it
> So little, at such distance, so like nothing,
> That he can scarce discerne it. (p. 2)

Tyranny even corrupts religion. The Caliph is pressed into Haly's plots to 'set a grave religious face/Upon the businesse' (p. 15). The king makes him manufacture a divine revelation to justify his action against his son and delude the council. Demands of policy overcome the Caliph's scruples:

> do you thinke that Princes
> Will raise such men so neare themselves for nothing?
> We but advance you to advance our purposes:
> Nay, even in religions
> Their learnedst, and their seeming holiest men, but serve
> To worke their masters ends; and varnish o're
> Their actions, with some specious pious colour... (p. 18)

This portrait of the Caliph dramatizes the popular resentment at Laud and his use of the church courts to enforce political and religious conformity. In a long passage in Act IV, distinguished by being in couplets, two (reliable) courtiers comment unfavourably on the political involvement of religion:

> Even by these men, Religion, that should be
> The curbe, is made the spurre to tyrannie;
> They with their double key of conscience binde
> The Subjects soules, and leave Kings unconfin'd ... (p. 26)

But while disapproving of tyranny's use of religion, Denham equally condemns 'feign'd devotion' among tyranny's opponents, and worries that 'With popular rage, religion doth conspire' and that 'whatsoever change the State invades,/The pulpit either forces, or perswades' (p. 27). The consequences of extremism by either king or people are equally fearful.

So although Denham would emerge as a 'Cavalier' after the breakdown, he was by no means unsympathetic to the parliamentary position in late 1641–42. As he analyses it, the king's weakness is due to his isolation. In his council he insists on having his will unopposed and forbids even well-intentioned criticism, claiming

> Those Kings whom envy, or the peoples murmure
> Deterres from their owne purposes, deserve not,
> Nor know their owne greatnesse ... (p. 19)

The faithful councillors warn 'Crownes are not plac't so high,/ But vulgar hands may reach 'em', but his pride makes him scorn their advice (p. 19). The good courtiers flee and the king is left in the hands of Haly's faction. Haly arranges that 'no intelligence can be convey'd/But by my instruments' (p. 32), and when the king suddenly realizes he is alone and duped, Haly has him restrained and tells his men to 'let the people know/The King keeps state, and will not come in publike:/If any great affaires, or State addresses,/Bring 'em to me' (p. 42). Haly is defeated only by the restoration of the royal family to power by an army of the faithful people, whom the king should have trusted, headed by the good councillors. Haly protests, but is told 'Who dares dispute it? we have a powerfull argument/Of fortie thousand strong, that shall confute him' (p. 51). Paradoxically, Denham demonstrates that excessive claims for royal authority have subverted the true source of the king's strength, which lies in a loving amity with his people, and his solution is a rapprochement between king and subjects, based on the removal of those bad servants who have hindered or perverted the understanding which should prevail between them. This is to return to the idea of constitutional balance, a firm re-establishment of the ancient unity of the kingdom which provides for the interests of both ruler and ruled, and within which criticism of the king takes place yet without contradicting respect for his person. But if, as seems quite possible, Denham was still writing as Charles left London to set up a new court in the north, he may already have been too late. There is no evidence that *The Sophy* ever received its court hearing; the possibilities of it being seen at court, and of the compromise it was advocating being put into political practice, disappeared simultaneously.

We may agree, then, that the best courtier plays of 1632–42 show the stage acting not as an extravagant and narrowly 'Cavalier' plaything but as an important focus and voice for anxieties and dissent existing in tension within the court. The writers I have been discussing perceive the injustice, instability and unpopularity of Charles's regime with considerable clarity and concern. Their plays dramatize these weaknesses and flaws seriously, challenging the principles underlying the personal rule of the 1630s and propounding alternative styles of government which rest on wider or radically different bases. The best court play, *The Queen of Aragon*, is simply that which confronts the courtly complacency about rank and obedience most forcefully.

Of course the court drama was still a relatively restricted medium. Its evenness of tone, and the exclusiveness of the range of characters and situations which it dramatized indicate that the courtier-dramatists wrote within a firmly circumscribed context of shared assumptions and beliefs beyond which they were unwilling or unable to go. To take the most obvious example, in *The Queen of Aragon* Decastro's army appears on stage but the soldiers' voices, nevertheless, are unheard; the 'people' are spoken for by their aristocratic leader, but otherwise they must remain silent. If we wish to hear these alternative, humbler voices, for whom politics is more than merely a matter of kings and their courts, we must go beyond Whitehall to the richer and more vigorous world of London's professional theatres.

5

Puritanism and theatre

A MAJOR OBSTACLE to understanding the treatment of politics on the Caroline stage is the close identification which is supposed to have obtained between the professional theatres and the court. This has two aspects. One is the character of the theatre audiences, usually seen as a wholly courtly, 'Cavalier' body; this I discuss in the following chapter. The other is the question of the utter antipathy presumed to be prevailing mutually between puritanism and the drama in the 1630s, a hostility as much political as doctrinal. That enormous and notorious diatribe against plays, *Histriomastix*, and the savagery of the Star Chamber sentence on its author, William Prynne, appear to prove that the lines of battle between theatre-hating puritans and theatre-loving court were already drawn in 1632; that criticism of the court automatically meant opposition to the theatre, and that the authorities did indeed leap to the defence of the king's favourite pleasures. But in fact Prynne spread his fire far wider than the theatres. The famous reference to 'Women actors, notorious whores', taken as a slight on the queen, was only one out of nearly fifty exceptions raised against *Histriomastix*, and Prynne's judges specifically disavowed that it was 'the meaning of any of their [lordships], to appollogize for stage playes'.[1] Rather, Prynne had trodden on all sorts of sensitive toes (some observers believed his offence was ecclesiastical, for he had digressed frequently to discuss such anti-Laudian concerns as bowing to altars, candles and images in churches, non-resident clergy, and the observation of the Sabbath),[2] and he was condemned less for having attacked the stage than for his scandalously extravagant and inflammatory

84

language against virtually the entire social order: 'The truthe is, Mr. Pryn would have a newe churche, newe governmente, a newe kinge, for hee would make the people altogether offended with all thinges att the present'. The gentlemen of Lincoln's Inn repeated Lord Cottington's judgment when they expelled Prynne from their society in 1634.[3]

Prynne has gone down in literary history as the proto-revolutionary and arch-enemy of the court, but this is a caricature of his position. For his own part, he thought he was doing society a service, and *Histriomastix* repeatedly appealed to the civil powers to initiate the reforms he desired. Addressing himself to the 'religious vertuous Christian Prince and Magistrate', Prynne was close to those other godly men of substance of the 1620s and after who wished to see a national reformation, a tightening-up of society's manners and morals and a consolidation of the Tudor church reforms, the agent of which they expected to be the lawful constituted authorities, the godly magistrate wielding God's sword in a manner conforming to, and implementing, His Word.[4] The society they envisaged was not the riotous world of the plebeian sects but an environment firmly disciplined and institutionalized: Prynne's friend, the Presbyterian John Bastwick warned the oppressed saints not to 'take indirect courses of insurrections and tumultuation; this is a remedy worse then the disease, and more displeasing to God, and dishonourable to the subject: and deserues a greater yoke of seruitude'. The Grand Remonstrance (1641) declared 'it is far from our purpose or desire to let loose the golden reins of discipline and govern-ment in the Church'.[5]

So, without any intention of discounting the ultimately sub-versive tendencies of puritanism, we may note that recent historians have emphasized its widespread social entrenchment under the early Stuarts. In an important essay, Patrick Collinson has warned that it is impossible 'to distinguish absolutely between Puritanism and, so to speak, mere Protestantism', and argues against seeing puritanism simply as nonconformity, to be defined in opposition to the *status quo*, when that *status quo* was itself widely infiltrated with puritan feeling.[6] In so far as puritanism was carrying forward the continuing impetus of the initial impulse for a reformation, it embodied 'the mainstream of English Protestantism, to which some of the distinctive institutions of the established Church ... were not so much opposed as irrelevant'. If we interpret puritanism broadly, as that opinion which desired purification of the church from the taint of popery through close, or closer identification with the principles of the early reformers, we have a body of feeling which, while representing the militant tendency of protestantism, would not be significantly at odds with the fundamental doctrines of the established church and indeed would be chary of pursuing its aims in separation from the rest of England's godly. In a church as firmly Calvinist as England's undoubtedly was, 'what we take for Puritanism would have been widely equated with orthodoxy' rather than differentiating a distinct aberrancy,[7] and although it drew its strength from the middle rank of people, the merchants and substantial craftsmen, it would also have been sympathetically received across a wide and varied social range. Certainly the individualist, sceptical and levelling preferences of puritanism coexisted uneasily with Stuart absolutism, but puritan feeling was forced decisively into an alignment against the centre only in the 1620s when the centre itself, under the influence of Charles's favoured bishops, began to shift. Nor were Laud's opponents simply radicals and extremists, for the theology and sacramental practice of the Arminians whom he promoted (their rejection of predestination in favour of universal grace and free will, their ceremonialism and elevation of the altar over the pulpit) struck at the roots of basic tenets of Calvinism and were received as 'innovations' which were not only objectionable in themselves but deliberately sought to overturn and reverse the process of reformation. In 1640 Charles faced a nation widely convinced that he was trying to drag them back into the hated papist fold; one observer described the 'puritan faction' as 'most potent, consisting of some bishops, all the gentry and commonalty'.[8] For such men, 'puritanism' was not a blueprint for revolution but a desire to preserve and consolidate what had already been achieved, their religious radicalism enkindled in part as a reaction against the Arminian contamination which Charles himself was introducing and encouraging.

The violence of this reaction suggests the strength of the expectations which, had Charles been a different sort of king, might have helped to unify as much as to shatter the nation, for the Reformation, in replacing Pope with king as head of the faith, had fostered powerful emotional ties between the monarchy and the church and, subsequently, a strongly heroic and nationalistic idea of royal church-leadership which encouraged the godly to look instinctively towards the prince as their natural (even sacred) champion and defender. John Foxe's apology for the Elizabethan settlement, his astonishingly influential *Acts and Monuments*, explained the history of the English people as part of a universal struggle between Christ and Antichrist in which their destiny, as the Elect Nation, was to preserve the light of the gospel unstained, and depicted Elizabeth as the Christian Emperor, leading her people out of political and religious slavery under the corrupt Popes and towards the millennial consummation promised in Revelation.[9] Foxe elevated the sanctity of monarchy in order to depress the power of the Pope, and with prince and people identified in a common religious purpose the threat to kingly authority appeared overwhelmingly to be an external rather than an internal one, in the demands made by Popes on the obedience of other kings' subjects, and even on other kings themselves. Foxe and his followers dwelt with horror on the king-killing side of Catholicism and recounted the providential escapes of Elizabeth and, after the gunpowder treason, James, from papist plots; Catholicism was destructive of the subject's loyalty to his prince, and papists were supposed to connive in intrigues against protestant princes and even their depositions and murders. By contrast, leading 'puritan' clergy enthusiastically eulogized the monarch as a god on earth, invested with his power to fulfil God's purposes, and envisaged idealistically the godly prince and ministers of religion together promoting the interests of faith and nation at home and abroad in an irresistible combination.[10] For example, Samuel Ward, a minister later silenced by Laud, preached of how the 'soueraigne power' of the king could establish a godly discipline in England: 'verily next under the word of God which is omnipotent, how potent and wonder-working is the word of a King? when both shall meet as the Sun, & some good star in a benign communication, what enemy shall stand before the sword of God and *Gideon*? what vice so predominant which these subdue not'?[11] It is easy to see why the continental campaigns of King Gustavus of Sweden and Charles's brother-in-law, the Palatine Prince Frederick, against the Spanish–Catholic emperor excited so much interest (and why, twenty years before, the death of England's own promising Prince Henry had caused so much sorrow), for they were well-placed to be royal champions in the continual struggle against the Pope. But, equally, such hopes created expectations about the function of the godly ruler which exerted strong constraints on the freedom of action of these princes' successors, as may be gauged from this summary of England's history by William Gouge, minister of Blackfriars: 'King Henry VIII put downe the Popes authority, and began a reformation of Religion. Edward VI perfected that reformation. Queene Elizabeth restored it. King James and King Charles continued it. Thus by the divine providence this title *Defender of the Faith* is most justly put into our Kings stile. To this end, namely to defend the faith, maintaine religion, and advance piety, hath God given them that supreme authority which they have'.[12] James was flattered to be taken for the Christian Emperor,[13] but Charles's acts increasingly appeared to be violating this trust and when he assembled an army in 1642 it was hysterically rumoured to be composed of Jesuits and papists. His subjects had cast him in a role he did not want, but which he repudiated at his peril; the myth of the godly nation, designed to legitimize the monarch's power, finally turned against a king who seemed to be bent on becoming the enemy to his own nation's interests.

Consequently, we find as very characteristic of puritan polemic of the 1630s an almost contradictory yoking of fierce denuncia-tions of a debased church with extravagant expressions of devo-tion to the crown. The pamphlets of Prynne and his fellows, even as they fulminate against Charles's church, run thick with protestations of loyalty. There is a notable instance in *Histriomastix* which praises puritans for being great '*propugners of Monarchy, and Princes supremacy* ... none going so farre in suppressing the Popes usurped Authority, or enlarging the Kings and temporall Magistrates prerogatives and supremacy as they'; Prynne complained angrily to Laud that he detested the idea of deposing a prince as 'the doctrine of popish priests and jesuits', and 'impious, hereticall, and abominable'.[14] In his *Discourse Concerning Puritans* (London, 1641), Massinger's friend Parker asked rhetorically what motive the 'Nobility, Gentry, and Commonalty' in parliament, 'being wise and religious', could have for their actions besides 'the common good' (p. 49) and challenged their opponents to prove that puritanism involved denying the king's supremacy: 'I conceive there are not in all the Kings Dominions, three men, except Papists and Anabaptists, which hold it lawful to depose, or by any force to violate the persons of Kings, how ill soever' (p. 43). Rather, it is the bishops who are disparaging 'the common peoples loyalty' and arming 'the King against his Subjects and by consequence raising Subjects against the King', but they are foolish to 'pretend great danger to the King likely to ensue out of paper machinations such as these' (pp. 8, 14).

So there is a kind of emotional hiatus built into the language of these pamphlets. Prynne reiterated over and over again that his quarrel was with the bishops, not the king, whose power he wished to vindicate from those who were perverting it. The Laudians he identified as evil counsellors, the source of popish errors creeping back into the church and who, like the Pope, were attempting in a Counter-reformation to re-subordinate princely authority to renewed clerical control. In 1637 he defined puritans simply as 'those who maintain the Kings Ecclesiasticall Prerogative';[15] the previous year he accused the bishops of innovations 'point-blanke against the established doctrine of the Church of *England*, and his *Majesties pious Declarations*' even though the king 'hath so *oft protested against all innovations*'. By omitting the royal family from the collect for God's Elect, the bishops had shown their malice to the king ('O intolerable impietie, affront, and horrid Treason'); they 'dishonour his

Majestie, and grieve his peoples soules'. Their claim to hold episcopal office direct from God has 'pulled thy Crowne off thy Royal head, to set it on their owne trayterous ambitious pates, by exercising all ecclesiasticall power, yea Papall jurisdiction over thy subjects' and the king should 'hang up these Popelings' to defend his 'royall Prerogative against their Papall usurpations'.[16] A later diatribe attacked them for 'execrable Treasons, Conspiracies, Rebellions, Seditions, State-scisms, Contumacies, Oppressions, & Anti-monarchicall practices'.[17] The central maxim underpinning this view is 'fear God and honour the king' (1Pet. 2:17). The bishops do neither, but *Histriomastix* accounts as puritan those who 'both feare God and honour the King, though they oppugne the corruptions, sinnes, profanesse, and Popish and Pelagian errors of the times'.[18] Prynne's associate Henry Burton had a sermon called *For God and the King* (London, 1636) which accuses the bishops of treading *'upon the Kings Lawes, as the Pope did once on the Emperours neck, an Emblem of perpetuall servitude'* (p. 54) and of disobeying the king, which is to resist 'the Ordinance of God' (p. 37). Most remarkable of all, writing from the Tower in 1637 John Bastwick blamed his imprisonment on the bishops but praised the happy state of monarchical rule, declaring he would 'maintaine to the vttermost of my power the Kings supremacy' and would 'rather live with bread and water under [Charles's] regiment, then in all plenty under any Prince in the world'.[19] This extraordinary language presents an intensified version of that tension which I have termed the Caroline dilemma, as these men found themselves caught between their reverence for kingly authority, given by God to lead His people, and their perception that Charles was not conforming to type. In one sense, Prynne was more 'royalist' than even Charles wanted; his deeply ingrained and idealized notion of what the ruler should be was coming into continual conflict with the reality that Charles was, for Foxe had encouraged the godly to look for a reformation without providing for the possibility of a ruler who disregarded these expectations. In the headier atmosphere of the 1640s, these pressures produced demands for a reformation without tarrying for the magistrate, but within the concepts available to these men in the 1630s they generated a tension that was not resolvable; it could only be restated with increasing violence and frustration.

Hence we need not see puritanism as something which necessarily excluded or opposed those classes who went to the Caroline theatres. Both the Foxean version of English history and the frustration of the subject whose king repudiates the loyalty he offers were expressed from the stages in the 1630s (see chapter 8 below). Conversely, the godly divine Thomas Adams quoted from Webster's plays in his sermons, while a typical contemporary account book lists purchases of plays alongside pious tracts; in his *The Ordinary* (1634), William Cartwright supposes that sermons and devotional books might be on sale outside the playhouse entrances.[20] These are not freakish exceptions in a society for which puritanism was part of the experience of more than a resolutely committed minority. Henry Parker claimed that 'all the Commons in Parliament, and almost all the ancient impartiall temporall Nobility, and all such as favour or rellish the late proceedings of both the houses, which is the mayne body of the Realme, Papists, Prelates and Courtiers excepted . . . are Puritans' (*Discourse Concerning Puritans*, pp. 10–11), and the great names of parliamentary puritanism, the Hampdens and Cromwells, came from wealthy landed gentry families; the audience of Edmund Calamy's weekly lecture in 1639 included 'persons of the greatest quality'.[21] The blending of godliness with gentility is well shown in Samuel Clarke's *Lives of Sundry Eminent Persons* (London, 1683), a compilation of pious biographies of 'NOBILITY and GENTRY of both *Sexes*' (part 2, t.p.) that draws considerably on our period. Clarke's first example is that noble patriot Sir Philip Sidney. Later follows Mary Rich, Countess of Warwick (whose autobiography mentions theatre-going in the 1630s)[22] whom Clarke praises for devotion, humility, hospitality, self-mastery, wifeliness and above all courtesy of bearing: 'She made it her great design to represent Religion as amiable and taking, and free from Vulgar prejudice as possibly she might . . . she was affable, pleasant, of a free and obliging Conversation, unaffected; not sowre, morose, sad, dejected, melancholy deportment, which presents Religion most disadvantagiously' (p. 172). Another woman who made religion pleasant was the Earl of Holland's daughter, Susanna, who had a natural '*pleasantness* of *Behaviour*, and Civil *Urbanity*', 'affable and accessible to all'. Clarke apologizes for mentioning these traits 'which seem to be but Moral Vertues, if they had been indeed no more but meer Morality; but I am well assured they flowed from a gracious disposition in her . . . and we may well baptize them Christian Vertues in her' (p. 211). In his hands, godliness is becoming blurred into social respectability.

In the life of her husband, that godly lady Lucy Hutchinson described how her 'party' esteemed 'solid wisdom, piety, and courage, which brought [them] real aid and honour' without standing too prudishly on 'little formalities' and 'insignificant circumstances'. Her husband later signed the king's death warrant, but in Caroline London he wore his hair long and participated in fashionable society, exercising 'himself in those qualities as he had not such good opportunity for in the country, as dancing, fencing, and music . . . and entertaining the best tutors, was at some expense that way, and loth to leave them off before he had perfected himself'. He may have visited the theatres too, for Mrs Hutchinson alludes in passing to *Volpone*, and he is probably typical of many men of substance who could reconcile puritan belief with behaviour that was not precisely 'puritanical'.[23] To take another example, Bulstrode Whitelocke became parliament's ambassador to Sweden, acting Speaker (1657) and Lord President of the Council (1659), yet he had certainly visited the theatres for, as well as being Christmas Master of the Revels at the Middle Temple in 1628, he wrote music for Shirley's *Triumph of Peace* (1634) which became so popular that it was played whenever he appeared in the Blackfriars theatre as he did 'sometimes in those days'. Queen Christina said of his dancing that she had thought that 'all the *noblesse* of England were of the King's party, and none but mechanics of the Parliament party and not a gentleman among them . . . But I see that you are a gentleman and have been bred a gentleman'.[24]

Another play-going puritan was Sir Thomas Barrington of Hatfield, whose accounts include payments to jesters, wassailers, a lord of misrule and to Francis Quarles (his godson) 'concerning the Comedy'. His library included playbooks and his daughter visited the theatres; his wife was something of a society lady. Yet the Barrington family had a strong puritan tradition, both Sir Thomas and his father distinguishing themselves as supporters of radical clergy, and as prominent court critics in the parliaments of the 1620s and 1640s. Sir Thomas invested with other 'puritans' in the Providence Island Company; he opposed Ship Money and the forest law scheme; he was imprisoned as a forced-loan resister. A close associate of the puritan Earl of Warwick, Cromwell and Hampden were among his cousins; in 1630 he loaned Pym Barrington Hall. Another friend was John Maynard, later a leading Presbyterian MP but also the author of a masque.[25]

Then there was the MP Sir Thomas Lucy, whose funeral sermon, preached in 1641 by a leading puritan divine, praised his delight in '*Practicall Divinitie*, and unaffected *Preaching*' and 'his vehement expressions of the *base*, *base*, and more than *slavish flatteries* of some of our *Churchmen*'. Lucy's father's private tutor had been the martyrologist John Foxe himself, and his wife Alice was admired by Samuel Clarke as one who never 'removed out of one Room into another, but she used some short *Ejaculations*, with lifting up her Eyes and hands to God' (*Lives*, p. 141); nevertheless, players were entertained at the Lucy family home of Charlecote in 1633.[26] Brilliana Harley, who shared with Alice Lucy the dedication of John Ley's *Pattern of Piety* (1640), was another woman of zealous Calvinist belief, made famous by her heroic defence of her house against a royalist siege, yet her brother was Viscount Conway, a fashionable Caroline gentleman and patron of the London theatres; her husband, an MP and energetic iconoclast in the 1640s, was a friend of Donne and Herbert of Cherbury.[27] The Hastings family, Earls of Huntingdon, had a long and famous history of piety, yet playbooks were among the purchases of the fifth earl in 1638–40.[28] Even the strict Simonds D'Ewes came of a family that celebrated Christmas gaily (his stepmother told a friend in 1629 she had had 'much good company this Christmas; yet the halle is a great deale better filled than the parlour, among all which we still wanted your company, which would have been most acceptable'), and he was not above seeing plays at Westminster School and the Inns of Court and court masques.[29] And there are still more examples (see chapter 6 below).

Of course *Histriomastix* must have had an audience, but such evidence shows how false it is to conceive of puritan feeling as being in a state of intransigent hostility towards the theatres in the 1630s. Prynne did become a popular hero, but that was in 1637 when he suffered with Burton and Bastwick for his attacks on the bishops, not in 1634 for his opposition to the stage. Only the lawyers protested against his sentence for *Histriomastix*, and then solely because of the indignity it cast on their status. The ordinary citizens were much more taken by the show the lawyers staged through the London streets to *apologize* for Prynne:[30]

Their display at the palace with a numerous, stately and glittering cavalcade, by their dresses, liveries and devices, attracted a great crowd, exciting the curiosity and applause of all the people, and afforded particular gratification to their Majesties, so that they had to repeat their procession and representation.

It is a telling corrective to the usual assumptions to note that neither of Prynne's fellow-sufferers in 1637 disapproved of plays. Burton criticized the performance of Strode's *Floating Island* at Oxford in 1636, but his reasons were that it had caricatured Prynne and had been organized by the bishops. In the same tract he quoted with approval James I's declaration that '*Certaine dayes in the yeare would be appointed for delighting the people ... as in making playes, and lawfull games in May, &c. So that alwayes the Sabbaths be kept holy, & no unlawful pastimes be used*'. In another sermon he drew a moral from 'him in the Comedy, that lay stretching on the grasse, in harvest time, wishing [that] were to worke in Harvest'.[31] Similarly, Bastwick's *Litany* attacks prelates who fill 'their very pulpits with playes' against pious puritans, 'bringing into their deskes Christ and the King on the one side, and the Iewes and the Puritans on the other'. This he calls 'an interlude' and replies by making his pamphlet a 'play' of truth contrasting with theirs of falsehood: 'I hope it will deserue no blame, If I should play a little vpon them'. And he lives up to this claim, for a major

influence on his jovial, robust style is surely the theatre. Here is
Laud coming from Star Chamber:[32]

see what pompe grandeur and magnificence he goeth in; the whole multitude
standing bare where euer he passeth, hauing also a great number of Gentlemen,
and other seruants waiting on him, al vncouered, some of them cariyng vp his
tayle, for the better breaking and venting of his wind & easing of his holy body
(for it is full of holes) others going before him and calling to the folke before
them, to put off their hats and to giue place crying roome, roome, my Lords
grace is comming. tumbling downe a[n]d thrusting aside the little children a
playing there: flinging and tossing the poore costermongers and souce-wives
fruit and [puddings], baskets and all into the Thames (though they hindered not
their passage) to shew the greatnes of his state and the promptitude of their
service . . . one can scarce keep from laughter, to see the grollery of it . . .
hearing on the one side, the noyse of the Gentleme[n] crying roome, & cursing
all that meet them and that but seeme to hinder their passage & on the other
side seeing the wayling mourning and Lamentation the women make crying out
saue my puddings, save my codlings for the Lords sake, the poore tripes and
apples in the meane tyme swimming like frogs about the Thames making way
for his Grace to goe home againe.

Clearly, this vivid, scurrilous language owes a great deal to the
popular stages. Like the Martin Marprelate pamphlets before
him, Bastwick adopts a railing style that is highly dramatic, and
caricatures Laud with a theatrical verve designed to appeal to the
anti-clerical sympathies of a popular, plebeian audience accustomed to play-going. There is, of course, no reason to suppose
that the more lower-class, radical sects were opposed to the
theatre. We do not find anti-theatrical diatribes among their
literature; rather, the Presbyterian Thomas Edwards, in his
famous encyclopaedic attack on the sectaries *Gangraena* (1646),
reported that they would argue 'for a toleration of Stage-playes,
and that the Players might be set up again'.[33] Undoubtedly such
men would have been standing in the playhouse yards in the
1630s.

So although the closure of the playhouses clearly was gratifying
to disciplinarians of Prynne's stamp, what we must firmly dispose
of is the assumption that the theatres were swept aside in 1642 by
a tidal wave of puritan protest which had gradually been
gathering head throughout the 1630s. The notion that the decade

saw a sustained, accelerating moral and doctrinal attack on the playhouses is commonly repeated but is utterly misleading, for there is not a shred of support for it. *Histriomastix* did *not* initiate a new wholesale onslaught on the stage, for there were no more anti-dramatic treatises. It was, rather, the last of its kind, and the idea that it was followed by a continuous and unremitting campaign against the theatres cannot be upheld; quite simply, the evidence cannot be found. By comparison with the 1580s, for example, the 1630s was not a time of virulent puritan antagonism to the stage but, instead, one remarkable for its quiescence. Certainly troupes on tour met resistance from civic authorities in the provinces in this period, but in a brilliant study Leo Salingar has demonstrated that their hostility arose from fears of the disturbance to public order that visiting players provoked, rather than from any ethical or doctrinal disapproval, and he has related this to the economic distress of the country at large in the 1620s and 1630s.[34] Similarly, when the Blackfriars inhabitants complained against the theatre in 1626, 1631 and 1633, their grounds were exclusively fear of plague and public inconvenience (and traffic jams), rather than the immorality of playing, and these were problems experienced by all the 'liberties' (areas outside the jurisdiction of the proclamations against new building) of over-crowded Stuart London.[35] A similar complaint against the Black-friars theatre's hindrance to trade was briefly discussed in the Commons early in 1641, but the meeting of the Long Parliament did not produce a sudden upsurge of denunciation of the drama. Rather, I have found that on only two other occasions before the closing of the theatres (26 January and 4 February 1642) was the question of the playhouses raised in parliament, and one of these was in passing in a debate on the security of the kingdom after the Irish rebellion, the other followed the death of a man after a duel arising from a playhouse quarrel. Neither of these discussions got so far as to be mentioned in the Commons journal; the first was set aside by no less a person than the leader of the House, John Pym himself.[36] The Root and Branch petition of December 1640, speaking for 15,000 citizens who were its signatories and which soon became the prototype for many similar petitions from all over the country, did complain of the numbers of 'lascivious, idle, and unprofitable books and pamphlets, play-books and ballads' then current,[37] but it included no plays among the titles it listed by name, and made no demands that the theatres should be closed; nor was the drama even mentioned among the 204 articles of the Grand Remonstrance a year later. Such interference in its activities as the drama received in the 1630s came exclusively from the court (see chapters 6 and 8 below).

The reasons for the decline of puritan militancy against the stage are not far to seek. Although buttressed by disapproval of the hypocrisy of acting and by reference to the biblical prohibition against men dressing as women, the principal grounds of hostility had always been the social dangers the theatres posed and the fact that they did not observe the Sabbath. By the 1630s, both these complaints had largely been answered. With the rise to importance of the 'private' playhouses, theatre-going had become a much more respectable activity. Three 'public' stages still performed, but the theatres did not pose exactly the same social menace that they once had seemed to; Prynne was not attacking quite the same rowdy, volatile institution that Gosson and Stubbes had been. Secondly, when James had forbidden Sunday playing, and Charles confirmed his order,[38] a fundamental point of friction was at once removed, and to this we should probably ascribe much of the puritan acceptance of the theatres as a permanent element in weekday life. Significantly, it was precisely because the court still saw the occasional Sunday performance that it continued to provoke some criticism from the godly. Richard Baxter disapproved of the court's Sunday plays, and another godly lecturer wished in 1640 that 'the Parliament would reform two things: 1. The sitting of the Council on Sunday afternoon. 2. The having plays on Sunday night'.[39] The most telling comment was by the Long Parliament's official historian, Tom May: 'The example of the Court, where Playes were usually presented on Sundaies, did not so much draw the Country to imitation, as reflect with disadvantage upon the Court it selfe, and sowre those other Court pastimes and jollities, which would have relished better without that, in the eyes of all the people, as things ever allowed to the delights of great Princes.'[40] May's implication is unavoidable: their plays would have been acceptable to parliament had they abstained from them on Sundays.

Moreover, the possibility of establishing a godly reformed stage does seem to have been in the air. Prynne entertained it, only to reject it:

> I take it for my own part; that Christians should rather argue thus; [They] are onely reduceable to good, and lawfull ends, but they are not yet reduced: their abuses may be reformed, but as yet they are not corrected: therefore *wee must* take them as we finde them now, vnpurged, vncorrected; and so we must *needes avoyde them* . . .

Nevertheless he admits that it may be 'lawfull to read Playes or Comedies now and then for recreation sake' and when faced with plays which do have godly purposes, such as Bale's and Skelton's, he can find no objection to them and even praises them. The crucial element in his disapproval is the performance of plays on stage; if a play's matter is good, he grudgingly allows that it may be read, and even *recited*.[41] More suggestive is the case of Milton who, as is well known, was deeply influenced by the drama and whose first elegy shows that when in London he, like other prosperous citizens' sons, visited the theatres; his first published poem was in the Shakespeare second folio. *His* view of a reformation in 1641 included the suggestion that

> it were happy for the Common wealth, if our Magistrates, as in those famous governments of old, would take into their care, not only the deciding of our contentious Law cases and brawls, but the managing of our publick sports, and festival pastimes, that they might . . . civilize, adorn and make discreet our minds by the learned and affable meetings of frequent Academies, and the procurement of wise and artfull recitations sweetned with eloquent and gracefull enticements to the love and practice of justice, temperance and fortitude, instructing and bettering the Nation at all opportunities, that the call of wisdom and vertu may be heard every where . . .

This noble ideal he would have had instituted 'at set and solemn Paneguries, in Theaters, porches, or what other place, may most win upon the people to receiv at once both recreation, & instruction'.[42] As I have already suggested, *Comus* gives a suggestive idea of what such a reformed drama might well have been like. Another possibility is the pamphlet-play *Tyrannical Government Anatomized* (1643), a blank verse tragedy on the arrest and death of John the Baptist translated, perhaps by Milton himself, from George Buchanan's *Baptistes Sive Calumnia* (1541). This does indeed speak feelingly of the 'love and practice of justice, temperance and fortitude'. John is a godly preacher, boldly admonishing his king of his faults, but Herod is an uxorious tyrant and his queen another bloodthirsty Henrietta Maria who goads him to suppress his religious critics and rule by fear; the chorus appeals to God to vindicate His people's sufferings. Parliament ordered its publication and might perhaps have approved of a theatre performing plays as stately and high-minded as this; a decade later Cromwell rediscovered the usefulness of the drama for entertaining visiting dignitaries and celebrating special occasions in his family, while Davenant obtained the establishment of his opera on the understanding that it would show 'morall representations . . . without obscenenesse, profanenesse, and scandall' and propagandize usefully on behalf of government policies.[43] If the examples of *Comus* and *Tyrannical Government Anatomized* may be trusted, such a reformed stage, within its necessary limits, would have been far from contemptible. For the reasons for its failure to materialize, and for the eventual closure of the theatres in spite of the general decline in militancy among their critics, I suggest we must look elsewhere than puritanism, the importance of which as an anti-theatrical force in this last decade has been greatly exaggerated. At least as important were the nature and social composition of the theatre audiences themselves.

6

The Caroline audience

THE OTHER SIDE of the identification of the professional theatres with the court is the question of the Caroline audience. Although the old-style 'public' playhouses are recognized still to have been attracting a heterogeneous audience in 1632–42, the more expensive Blackfriars, Phoenix and Salisbury Court are commonly represented as moving into an exclusive association with the court, performing before a plush-and-velvet clientele for whom playgoing was only an extension of the normal courtly round, almost as outhouses to Whitehall in the city. Clearly, if we regard the 'private' theatres as entirely dependent, economically and socially, on court patronage, we impose radical limitations on their treatment of political subjects, but (I intend to argue) we are unwarranted in doing so. It is, therefore, fundamentally necessary to explode the myth of the 'Cavalier audience', and to do this I shall have to describe in detail the social round to which the theatres belonged, which will take me some little way from my main theme. However, I shall go on to suggest that the social developments to which I am about to turn had political consequences of their own of which Charles was extremely wary, and which are under discussion in the Caroline comedies of manners that set out to reflect the social life of the drama's patrons in London (chapter 7 below); for the theatre audiences, while not lacking strong links with the court, were themselves drawn from those same parliamentary classes from which the political challenge to Charles in 1640 would come.

A related problem is that the players are frequently described as royal servants which, for the purposes of regulation and censorship, they were indeed. But it is misleading to think of the companies as tied and shackled to Whitehall for they had an independent, autonomous life of their own in comparison with which their dependence on the court was merely irregular. When Brome, in the epilogue to the *Court Beggar* (1640), invited the Phoenix audience to applaud him 'by whose cares and directions this Stage is govern'd, who had for many yeares both in his fathers dayes, and since directed Poets to write and Players to speak till he traind up these youths here to what they are now' (p. 272), he wrote with a consciousness of his theatre as an institution with a separate and continuous professional history, a sense which could only be reinforced by the various occasional prologues and inductions employed to mark special events, such as an exchange of theatres between companies, or a re-opening after a plague closure, and by the inter-company rivalries which he, and Davenant, Massinger, Shirley and Nabbes all at one time or another fought out from the stage or in print.[1] Certainly the King's Men do seem deliberately to have capitalized on court favour: Henrietta Maria visited the Blackfriars four times and received private drama-coaching from their leading actor, and they incorporated courtier plays into their repertory and appeared at court, in our period, nearly three times more often than all the other companies put together.[2] Nevertheless, out of the sixty-one plays the King's Men were protecting from piracy in 1641, only ten were courtier plays (or less, depending how Davenant is counted),[3] while their earnings at court never amounted to so much as a tenth of their annual income;[4] the proportion for the other companies was considerably less, if not almost non-existent. The vast bulk of the players' incomes came commercially, in their day-to-day playing in town; their services to the court, on the other hand, were principally seasonal, and centred on the Christmas months of November to February (and then usually on Tuesdays and Thursdays), and were only sporadic thereafter. Nor were the king and queen even notable patrons of individual dramatists; they often accepted the dedications of religious and scientific literature, but only one published play was ever addressed to Charles (Cartwright's *The Siege*), and that appeared after his execution. Charles's main interest was painting, and his known encouragement of playwrights does not, with the single exception of Shirley's *The Gamester* (1633), extend to non-courtiers. It is naive and frankly starry-eyed to suppose that the professional dramatists were tumbling over each other in a pell-mell race for court favours; they only had to look at Jonson – paralysed, penniless and forgotten – to see where that road led.

Wit's market

London's rapid growth in the seventy years 1570 to 1640, a source of discomfort to both economists and moralists, had as one dimension the creation of an industry purely devoted to leisure and entertainments. In the 1630s the law student John Greene recorded visits to Hyde Park and Greenwich gardens; he saw 'the shew of the artillery', the arrival of the Palatine Prince and the Lincoln's Inn Christmas revels. Marmaduke Rawdon (a merchant's nephew) visited court to kiss the king's hands; he played bowls, saw the king's horses and the Royal Sovereign; he spent many evenings at feasts. The Essex gentleman Sir Humphrey Mildmay witnessed executions, wrestling matches, state installations, trials, the arrivals of ambassadors and the queen mother, and the city pageants. He visited a glass furnace, Tradescant's gardens, Covent Garden, the musters and the Exchanges. He went maying in Hyde Park, boating on the Thames, heard sermons at St James's and saw the royal family 'in Hyde Park all the day in all state'. And so the list goes on.[5]

The 1630s saw the appearance of the precursors of the Restoration *beau monde*, a class coming to London principally as a place of leisure. The correspondence of the period is full of allusions to families coming up to town to visit their acquaintance. Sir John North reported in 1635 'heare is now good company in towne'. Lady Cornwallis could not deliver a letter to a friend in 1629 for 'there was soe much company I could not speak with her as I desired'. The chief delight of Hyde Park, said Sir Kenelm Digby, 'is the meeting of the company and the going together to encrease the entertainment by conuersation and mirth'. Edward Hyde too always kept aside dinner for those 'who used to meet together at that hour', 'where they enjoyed themselves with great delight and public reputation, for the innocence, and sharpness, and learning of their conversation'. London was becoming a place for news, duels, and matchmaking. The many contemporary newsletters invite country-dwellers to town and apologize for retailing gossip but these things 'we that live in London cannot help, and they are as great news to men that sit in Boxes at Black-Fryars, as the affairs of love to Flannel-Weavers'.[6]

The theatres, as my last quotation shows, were involved in this gay round. The Lord Keeper complained in 1632 that the gentry commonly 'goe from ordinaries to dicing houses, and from thence to play houses', and their wives go to Hyde Park. Margaret Cavendish described how her sisters used 'in winter time to go sometimes to plays, or to ride in their coaches about the streets to see the concourse and recourse of people; and in the spring time to visit the Spring-garden, Hide-park, and the like places; and sometimes they would have music, and sup in barges upon the water'. Mary Rich spent her time 'in seeing and reading plays and romances, and in exquisite and curious dressing' and being courted by gallants.[7] London society grouped around itself a parasitic body of luxury traders, porters, coachmen, water-men, fencing- and dancing-masters,[8] a development of which the theatres were a part. They too provided a professional service, and this is marked by a semantic shift. 'Playing' is a holiday skill, potentially in all, but 'acting' is a professional qualification and this the theatres had to sell. In 1631, Jonson protested his *New Inn* was 'never *acted*, but most negligently *play'd*, by some, the Kings Seruants'. Two years before, John Earle said a player's life was 'not idle, for it is all Action', and in 1634 Marmion praised John Taylor's 'action' as a quality distinct from the play he was performing in;[9] there are many similar uses of the word. Players have changed from entertainers *of* the audience to entertainers *to* the audience, and Shirley acknowledged this by describing the theatres as 'wit's market', another place of trade:[10]

And as at a great Mart, or Faire, we see
Some things of price, which all men do not buy;
But guided by their eye, or strength of purse,
Lay out their pence upon a Hobby-horse
Sometime, or a Childs Rattle; so we are
In this wits Market, furnish'd with all ware,
But please your selves, and buy what you like best,
Some deep commodities mingle with the rest.

Records left in contemporary diaries suggest how central the theatres were to high society. When Sir Humphrey Mildmay was in London, play-going was an intensive activity for him. He saw five plays in the three months November 1632 to January 1633, five in November to December 1635, and in February 1639 he saw plays on the 12th, 13th, 14th and 18th. The Kent gentleman Sir Edward Dering, in London in the 1620s, might see four plays a month (in December 1623 he visited the theatres on the 3rd, 4th, 5th, 6th, 8th and 9th; the 7th was a Sunday!). Edward Heath, a law student, saw thirty-six plays in a single year (1629).[11] The diaries also show how sociable play-going was. Dering and Mildmay often went with friends; 'dinner and a play' was habitual for Mildmay, the Countess of Arundel and Shirley's Aretina.[12] Margaret Cavendish would go with her sisters 'in a flock agreeing so well, there seemed but one mind amongst them'; Sir John Digby was 'accompanied with two friends then casuallie present' when Suckling attacked him at the Blackfriars; John Greene recorded in 1635 that 'all the batchelors, we were at a play, some at cockpit, some at blackfriars'; Mildmay squandered a whole day at 'the Newe play att Bl: fryers wth my Company' in 1640.[13] Anne Halkett, who 'loved well to see plays and to walke in the Spring Garden sometimes', remembered how, careful for her maidenly honour, she

was the first that proposed and practised itt, for 3 or 4 of us going together withoutt any man, and everyone paying for themselves by giving the mony to the footman who waited on us, and he gave itt in the playhouse. And this I did first on hearing some gentlemen telling what ladys they had waited on to plays, and how much itt had cost them; upon which I resolved none should say the same of mee.

This demonstrated the rise of the coach as a form of group transport, but also the development of the playhouses as distinct environments with their own conventions and traditions of behaviour.[14]

At the end of the century James Wright lamented that 'the more Civilized part of the Town' now shunned the theatres 'as they would a House of Scandal', whereas the theatres of the last age could support themselves even without scenery but 'meerly from their own Merit'.[15] By contrast, the Caroline theatres were respectable places of entertainment, and had some prestige (the Blackfriars, for example, reputedly possessed London's best orchestra), and it is clear that a flourishing literary world was gradually being established around them. Much literary activity still took place on an intimate, personal level, prior to print. Earle's *Microcosmography* and Suckling's *Discourse of Religion by Reason*, for example, first circulated in manuscript, and Waller's poems 'pass'd up and downe through many hands amongst persons of the best quallity'; Sir Kenelm Digby recounted how Sir Thomas Hawkins read him 'some ingenious compositions of a friend of his', while correspondents of Viscount Conway and the Earl of Newcastle sent them verses, prose characters, 'our new ballets' and an 'excellent song, which privately passes about, of all the Lords and Ladies in town' in the 1630s.[16] Such literary interchange was characteristic too of the theatres. Courtly plays often circulated in manuscript copies, but so too did more popular plays such as Brome's *The English Moor*, Shirley and Newcastle's *Country Captain* and Middleton's scurrilous *Game at Chess*; five of Fletcher's plays survive in private transcript, and such transcripts underlie the printed texts of four more plays in the 1647 Beaumont and Fletcher folio. The publisher Humphrey Moseley explained that the actors would provide transcripts for 'private friends [who] desir'd a Copy', and Sir Aston Cockayne recorded being sent such a transcript by his friend Charles Cotton. When the actors lent the prompt-copy of *The Wild Goose Chase* to 'a *Person of Quality*' they were unable to get it back.[17] Viscount Falkland, writing to borrow a playbook from his 'Cosin', desired leave to 'reade it to a ffreind or two, [that] are

Judges, (if it be possible) fitt for it', and, returning it later, asked for a copy of it, explaining, 'if I valued it so at the single hearing, when myne eares could not catch half the wordes, what must I do now, in the reading when I may pause uppon it'. Another person, 'one of ye fayrest, wittiest & newest widdows of o[ur] tyme, my lady Dorothy Sherly longs extremely to read it, and hath sent to beg a sight of it'.[18] Another society lady wished in 1639 to see 'the newe playe a friend of mine sent to Sr John Sucklyn and Tom Carew (the best witts of the time) to correct'.[19] Descriptions of masques were commonly sent into the country, Viscount Conway paying 1s. 6d. in 1634 to have one written out.[20] Francis Lenton published a series of epigrams on the ladies who danced *Luminalia* (1638) and the lawyers who appeared in the *Triumph of Peace* (1634), books obviously intended for perusal among theatre-going circles. Jonson's valediction to the professional stage, the *Ode to Himself* (1629), provoked several answers in verse from the audience, and Sir Richard Baker's polemical reply to *Histriomastix*, *Theatrum Redivivum* (*c.* 1634), circulated in manuscript until 1661 and was cast in the form of a review of another book, a device common among written tracts passing around the Kent gentry from whom Baker hailed.[21] Prynne complained that six playbooks were sold for every sermon, and this was indeed an outstanding decade for the publication and purchase of drama;[22] theatre-going and the collection of playbooks were becoming new areas of connoisseurship for the gentlemanly amateur.

When the Venetian ambassador visited a playhouse in 1617 he saw 'so much nobility in such excellent array listening as silently and soberly as possible',[23] a description which is probably representative of later decades also. He was correct to emphasize the audience's concentration for there is plenty of evidence to suggest that these playgoers did not have 'jaded palates' which Clifford Leech attributes to them but were closely and seriously attentive to the plays they witnessed. Many Caroline plays allude to earlier plays, their meaning depending on the audience recognizing the sub-text below the surface (*Othello* underlies the situations of many; *The Tempest* looms behind Suckling's *The*

Goblins; Glapthorne's plays rework situations from *Julius Caesar*, *Richard III*, *The Changeling*, and so forth). Brome's city plays adopt a deliberately Jonsonian style to bring forward certain assumptions about human society and behaviour; his *City Wit* (1629?) has a revival prologue which asks the audience to recollect the first performance. Ford makes numerous dramatic and non-dramatic allusions, even quoting from himself (the line 'Brother unkind, unkind' appears in three plays).[24] The prologue to Massinger's *A Very Woman* (1634), a reworking of an earlier play, began by admitting

> *such (and some there are, no question here,)*
> *Who happy in their memories do bear*
> *This subject long since acted, and can say*
> *Truly, we have seen something like this play.*   (1.1)

These playwrights are assuming an audience already conversant with the stage repertoire, and they also had pretensions to being critics of the acting. Cast-lists start to accompany published play-texts in the late 1620s, and Sir Richard Baker in 1634 wrote that a play acted was superior to a play read, and accounted '*Gracefulness* of *action*' as 'the greatest pleasure of a *Play*'.[25] The revival prologue for *The Jew of Malta* (Phoenix, 1633) asked the audience to compare Perkins's performance as Barabas with Alleyn's; three performances are compared in the revival prologue to *Bussy D'Ambois* (Blackfriars, 1634, 1638). In a prologue of 1633, John Lowin reminded the Blackfriars audience he had served them for a lifetime; Ezekiel Fenn (Phoenix) spoke a special prologue when he first took a man's part; Stephen Hammerton (Blackfriars) is named in three epilogues of about 1640; another actor reminded the audience of Glapthorne's *Revenge for Honour* (1641) that they had 'grac'd me sometimes in another sphere'.[26] After the theatres closed, gazettes continued to report the actors' fortunes, and Tatham's *Knavery in all Trades* (1664) depicts the wits reminiscing about the Caroline actors and their roles.[27]

Much more telling is the fact that this is the first audience to leave traces of widespread critical discussion of plays. The epilogue to Suckling's *Goblins* protests at this:

into how many peeces a poore Play
Is taken still before the second day . . .
One will like all the ill things in a Play,
Another, some o'th'good, but the wrong way;
So from one poore Play there comes t'arise
At severall Tables, severall Comedies.   (l.13)

Richard Brathwaite wrote in 1635 that the spectators talked the plays over while going home from them in their coaches; according to Edmund Gayton, they would invite the players to repeat scenes afterwards in taverns, and 'came home, as able Actors as themselves'.[28] James Wright's father made a series of short notes on individual plays, even comparing the technique of Shirley's *Young Admiral* (1633) with Barclay's prose romance *Argenis*; Robert Baron praised a friend's tragicomedy by comparing it with *Catiline*; Aston Cockayne, expressing his love for a friend, invoked the arguments of Jonson's *New Inn*.[29] One society lady of 1639 wished she was in town 'to see the Alchymist, which I heare this tearme is reviv'd'; Thomas Fuller recommended that Jonson's plays be seen several times to be properly appreciated.[30] Lord Falkland was said to have defended Henry Killigrew's *The Conspiracy* (1635) from criticism at the Blackfriars by saying that the intelligence displayed by the seventeen-year-old hero was not improbable for he '*that made him speak in that manner, and writ the whole Play, was Himself no Older*';[31] it is a rare insight into the continual commentary and assessment of the plays that must have been commonplace among these cultivated audiences. Similarly, the many prologues and epilogues of the decade repeatedly defer to the spectator's judgment; they imply an audience of active taste, critical, discriminating and alert.

There are several contemporary testimonies to the character of Whitehall as restrained to the point of strangulation: Edward Hyde said that the king 'kept state to the full, which made his Court very orderly; no man presuming to be seen in a place where he had no pretence to be'.[32] It seems clear that the convivial life which undoubtedly was upheld in Caroline London was less an aspect of membership of Charles's rather costive court than of participation in the activities of the 'Town', that fashionable society which, though partly overlapping with the court, was also definitely distinct from it and had a separateness and identity of its own. I am suggesting that we should regard the Caroline 'private' theatres as belonging much more firmly in this environment, a world with which they had far more regular and intimate connections than they ever did with the court and which provided them with an audience of some enthusiasm and sensitivity. Or, to put it the other way round, the development of this semi-independent *beau monde*, which was in large measure a creation of the late 1620s and 1630s, was itself facilitated by the special conditions which the fashionable theatres fostered, a point I now wish to pursue with more detail.

The theatres and the gentry presence in London

It must be emphasized that the Caroline world of fashion was only newly in the process of formation. The permanent London social round was only made possible after 1660 when large numbers of gentry chose, or were able, to forgo close supervision of their land, but such regular absenteeism was practised in the 1630s only by a minority of men of rank and fortune. Much the major part of England's wealth was still tied up in the country and the Caroline gentry remained stubbornly provincial in outlook, the pull of their local allegiances tending to draw them away from the centre. Kent, for example, had 800 gentry in 1640, many of parochial status, intermarrying and closely committed to their properties (some even writing on estate management); twenty were MPs, thirty or so were courtiers, only twenty had houses in town. Similarly, Somerset gentry at this time rarely spent more than a month a year in London. London was principally a business centre; permanent London living was expensive, and someone like Aurelian Townshend, dancing attendance on the court but inadequately financed, might live in embarrassing poverty. The seventeenth century saw a vast and revolutionary development of London's fashionable western suburbs which would transform the face of the city, but this was a new and still embryonic growth in the 1620s. The 1632 census demonstrated that only a quarter of the peerage, a sixth of the baronetage and knightage and less than a hundredth of the squirarchy and gentry were residing in London.[33] Sir Humphrey Mildmay, the diarist, had two large country estates, yet when in London he only rented a house from his brother-in-law, and that was in unfashionable Clerkenwell; Covent Garden, an area of stylish housing, was just being built in 1632. As a class, the gentry were still very dispersed; the letters of Sir Thomas Knyvett and Lady Cornwallis show that they, in London in the 1630s, tended to rely on circles of relatives or of friends whom they knew from the country. They would have approved of Henry Peacham's warning (of 1642) against coming to town unless one knew people there already.[34] In Peacham's *Thalia's Banquet*, a collection of witty pieces of the 1620s, society poems to Drayton, Jonson and Selden rub shoulders with large quantities of epigrams to members of the Norfolk gentry; his gallant society is only just beginning to emerge from its county roots.

So Caroline high society was unlike the later Restoration *beau monde* in being less exclusive and developed, and bringing together men of a broader social and geographical differentiation. It lacked the narrow courtly homogeneity of the Restoration town, but in the development of its own tone the position of the theatres was crucial. Unlike France, England had no salons, and it still wanted the regular round of concerts and balls of later years (Shirley's *The Ball* (1632) registers the very first appearance of this institution, possibly even coining the name). The gentry's need for an environment in which to meet and establish its own unity was fulfilled precisely by the theatres. The theatres were neutral zones, independent of the court, where the gentry gathered casually, but also on a regular basis and with interests that were widely shared, and where ideas and attitudes were actively exchanged. They were both public settings and areas of unrivalled personal interchange, environments where manners and *mores* could be determined and established on a communal level.

We can see, for example, that the drama was providing this society with models for its behaviour. Plays by Brome, Shirley and Davenant offered the audience images of themselves in parks, squares, taverns and gaming houses, supplying standards against which forms and codes of behaviour could be established, scrutinized and adjusted, and that these comedies of manners are among the best plays of the period is a measure of the importance of this function for the theatres. The process can be watched explicitly in *The Academy of Compliments* (London, 1640), an anonymous compilation of 'Complementall, Amorous, High expressions, and formes of speaking' (t.p.), the centre of this guide to proper deportment being eighty pages of dialogues to cover all likely social situations. Each dialogue is essentially a little playlet, often recalling the stock situations and characters of the drama, as when a gallant is depicted planning to help a friend 'beare away the Vsurers daughter' (p. 96). Here society's forms are developing in a manner directly parasitic on theatrical prototypes.

Secondly, the atmosphere of the theatres seems to have been affable and familiar. The sheer quantity of prologues and epilogues increased in the decade,[35] creating a dialogue between players and audience which linked the theatrical conversation with the world of play. Bulstrode Whitelocke was so well known as a *habitué* that his coranto was played every time he visited the Blackfriars (p. 92 above). Published plays appeared with large quantities of commendatory verses, expressing the goodwill of friends who had seen them on stage; Massinger used the dedication of *The Picture* (London, 1630) to his lawyer friends to say he 'had rather inioy (as I haue donne) the reall proofes of their friendship, then mountebancke like boast their numbers in a Catalogue' (sigs.A3^{r-v}). This feeling for shared experience was turned devastatingly against Prynne by Sir Richard Baker in his *Theatrum Redivivum* (London, 1661) which attacked him as an undesirable outsider. Baker pointed to Prynne's hysteria ('what is all his *Book*, but a bundle of *scoulding Invectives*, and *railing* instead of *reasoning*?' (p. 17)), contrasting it with the cultivated dignity of the '*Courteous* reader' to whom he addressed himself (sig.A2^{r}). The theatres also witnessed several quarrels,[36] and these have the air of a society defining its own internal boundaries. The auditorium was becoming a forum for social assertion and display.

Thirdly, the interchange of manuscripts and discussion would be a principal means by which this society could establish its common tone. Viscount Conway, for example, enlisted the aid of friends to obtain books from abroad for his library, and in 1634 is found giving 5s. to 'my Lord Goring's footman that brought books'. At sea in 1636–37, he arranged for George Garrard to send him playbooks and news, and complained he had not yet received a copy of *Aglaura*:[37]

if you would have gone any farther then wishes the play booke would have endured cariadge, and although it be none of yours, you might have stollen it; both your conscience and ours would have endured it; a seaman, an usurer, and a thiefe put into a bagge when they come out, a theife comes first; but if it be not a [second?] play we need it not.

Conway's literary interests developed into witty, complimental correspondences which must have been a bantering extension of the Blackfriars and Phoenix milieu with which he was already familiar (p. 93 above), and the creation of a fully realized social manner out of the exchange of books, poems and views is even more marked in the dozens of letters collected by James Howell. The conversation of Thomas Killigrew in Geneva in 1640 was also said to have been 'very sweet and delectable'.[38]

It seems likely, then, that the theatres were important as a focus around which this society could constitute itself and develop its own self-consciousness. It is possible to begin to distinguish the various internal circles of intimates who participated in the Caroline social round, and it is notable how recurrent the theatres were as centres linking members of these groups together. Jonson, of course, had his 'sons'. One of these, James Howell, described his convivial dinners with Jonson in his letters, and alluded to a wide circle of acquaintance, legal and literary: Kenelm Digby, Philip Warwick, Selden, Herbert of Cherbury, Sir Richard Baker and so forth. One friend Howell invited to the Blackfriars to see 'a Play spick and span new, and the *Cockpit* with another'.[39] Selden and Digby were also among the circle described by Edward Hyde which included the poet-dramatists May and Carew, and Edmund Waller, Sidney Godolphin and Charles Cotton; Cotton himself had poems addressed to him by the dramatists Cockayne and Glapthorne ('May there be/In your carouses, Wit and Companie/Fit for your dear enjoying').[40] Hyde also moved, with Davenant and Ford, among a group of lawyers providing dedicatory verses for one another in the years 1629–34; he himself had verses (along with Habington) in Davenant's *Albovine* (pub. 1629).[41] Ford's plays, published with verses, marginal comments and, in one instance, an anagram instead of a name on the title page, suggest a context of intimates with literary–dramatic interests. One of his friends, William Singleton, joined Aston Cockayne in writing verses for Massinger's *Emperor of the East* (pub. 1632). Massinger saw himself as poetic 'father' to James Smith who, in his verse letters of 1640 to the minor poet John Mennis, described his clubbing life at 'Viscount *Conwaies* house' with, among others, Kenelm Digby.[42] Smith, a clergyman and protégé of Holland, was censured in 1633 'for keeping excessive company with players, and that he and the others styled themselves of "The Order of the Fancy, whose practice was to drink excessively and speak nonsense" '.[43] Selden explained how men of different counties would come up to London and form separate clubs, each with their own rules;[44] such clubbing is mocked in Brome's *Weeding of Covent Garden* (1632) and Glapthorne's *The Hollander* (1636). Even the humble Thomas Dekker had verses in Brome's *Northern Lass* (London, 1632) 'To my sonne Brome' (sig.A4ʳ). Clearly, the theatres were an important meeting-ground for a wide spectrum of people.

We may exemplify the process by which the theatres could unify a large collection of people of disparate backgrounds into a more homogeneous social group by examining the different links that one theatre-goer, Sir Humphrey Mildmay, could make between himself and other figures in the theatre auditorium. For Mildmay, and probably many like him, the audiences were criss-crossed by a network of friendship and kinship the extraordinary complexity of which must have made the environment at once public and intimate (the density of my description may be

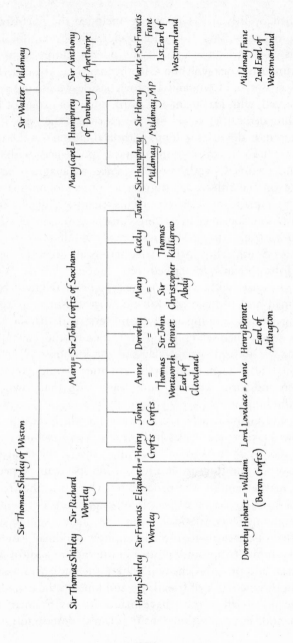

Table 1. Family tree of Mildmay and Crofts (simplified).

alleviated by reference to table 1). Mildmay's family were recent, Tudor gentry, who had profited from the dissolution of the monasteries, and his fortune was part of the fruits of office of his grandfather, Elizabeth's chancellor; but he was not of the eldest line, and although his brother held office and he himself accompanied the wife of the Secretary of State, Sir John Coke, to 'a pretty Masque of Ladyes',[45] he was essentially of the country and town rather than of the court. His London connections in the theatres would have been all the more significant for him, enabling him to find a sense of belonging in the metropolis outside the charmed circle of the court.

Mildmay accompanied to the theatres, or could have met in an audience or in theatrical circles, many people with whom he would have been familiar simply through family connections. His own family was linked to the Fanes, a family of small gentry originally from Kent who, through dint of judicious marriages, had newly (1624) risen to the peerage, and he was cousin to Mildmay Fane, poet and friend of Herrick who wrote and produced plays on his Northamptonshire estate in the 1640s. The two cousins dined together in 1639; another Fane, Sir Francis (Mildmay Fane's nephew) would also write plays after the Restoration.[46] His wife's stock, on her mother's side, were Shirleys, a Sussex family of some antiquity (though her line had recently suffered some pecuniary distress) and even notoriety: Jane Mildmay's uncles were the adventuring Shirleys who inspired Day's play *The Travels of Three English Brothers* (1607). Moreover, her cousin was another minor dramatist, Henry Shirley, author of *The Martyred Soldier* (1619?) and other lost plays of the 1620s.[47]

On her father's side, his wife belonged to the Crofts of Suffolk, a 'county' clan of similar status to the Mildmays and Shirleys, but one pursuing their advancement with considerable determination, and consolidating their favour at court. They also had a number of interesting literary connections. The wife of Mildmay's eldest brother-in-law, Henry Crofts, was sister to a 'son of Ben', the minor poet Sir Francis Wortley, whose verses on Jonson appeared in *Jonsonus Virbius* (1638). Mildmay was intimate with his son, with whom he saw *Volpone* in 1638, and Henry's son William created scandal in 1634 by quarrelling with Lord Digby at the Blackfriars theatre. William Crofts later followed the court into exile and was ennobled by Charles II; his sister married into the Cornwallis family, whose society letters I have already quoted.[48] A sister of Mildmay's wife married Thomas Wentworth, Earl of Cleveland, and became the mother of Lovelace's 'Lucasta'; her death produced a funeral elegy from Francis Quarles. Mildmay went to a play after dining with a Wentworth in November 1634.[49] Another brother-in-law, John Crofts, was a gentleman in the employ of Herbert of Cherbury, and a friend of Carew, who wrote verses for him to speak to the king in Suffolk in the 1620s. Mildmay owned copies of the poems of both Herbert and Carew; if, as seems likely, he knew Carew, he was in contact with a very wide circle of wits indeed.[50]

Two more sisters of Jane Mildmay married into powerful and wealthy city dynasties, the Abdys and the Bennets. These important commercial families held aldermanic power in the Clothworkers' and Mercers' companies respectively, and were involved in civic administration and trade to America and the east; the Bennets had produced a lord mayor (1603), and both families were rising towards baronetcies.[51] Sir Humphrey went to the theatre with his brother-in-law Sir Christopher Abdy, and his nephew, Henry Bennet (later Earl of Arlington and member of Charles II's Cabal) wrote verses for Killigrew's *The Prisoners* (1641) alongside two sons of Ben. The Bennets also connected Mildmay with another playgoer, for in 1630 Bulstrode Whitelocke married Rebecca Bennet, a first cousin of Mildmay's brother-in-law John Bennet and herself the daughter of an alderman and sheriff of London (1619). Another Bennet widow was stepmother to Henry Shirley the dramatist.[52]

Further theatrical connections were provided by the marriage of Mildmay's sister-in-law Cecilia Crofts to the dramatist Thomas Killigrew, for the Killigrews, an old Cornish family, were well-known courtiers with strong links to the queen's circle who produced three amateur dramatists (Thomas, Henry and, after 1660, William) and were cousins to a fourth (William Berkeley, author of *The Lost Lady* (1638)). Mildmay feasted 'Dame Sisly Croftes' and her theatrical 'sweete harte Mr Tho: Killigraue' in 1634, and he was a guest of Berkeley's brother in Somerset in 1642.[53] Thomas Killigrew's sister Anne married the courtier George Kirke, a friend of Kenelm Digby and patron of the masque writer Aurelian Townshend; another sister, Elizabeth, married Francis Boyle, brother to Roger, Earl of Orrery, who may already have been writing plays in the 1630s.[54] The Boyles lived ostentatiously in the Savoy and 'drew a very great resort thither'. Mary Boyle described how her Killigrew sister-in-law led her into 'reading and seeing plays, and in going to court and Hide Park and Spring Garden'; the husband she was courting at this time was Charles Rich, whose father, the Earl of Warwick, was a patron of the amateur dramatist Arthur Wilson.[55] Through Sir Peter Killigrew, second cousin of Thomas, who married Mary Lucas, the Killigrews also had a tie with the Suffolk gentry family of Lucas whose visits to the theatre in the 1630s Mary's sister Margaret Cavendish (*née* Lucas) described (p. 103 above).[56]

Mildmay also mentions supper after a play with his 'cousin' Thomas Chicheley, a member of a leading Cambridgeshire county family who had more distant links by marriage with Mildmay Fane and, later, the son of the playgoer Sir Edward Dering.[57] Finally, Mildmay was a friend of Giovanni Biondi, an Italian historian and author of romantic novellas which had some vogue at the Inns of Court. Among Biondi's friends who contributed verses to an English version of his *Eromena* (1632) were Jonson's 'son' James Howell, and the amateur dramatist Thomas Salusbury of Denbighshire who was himself closely connected to Sir Thomas Myddleton (patron of Middleton the dramatist) and the Stanley and Egerton families, sponsors of provincial drama in the 1630s.[58]

These are Mildmay's most direct connections among people we know to have gone to plays, and similar networks could probably have been constructed for other theatre-goers had their diaries too survived. Mildmay was no courtier, but with a theatrical milieu so rich and intimate he had no need of the court in order to cultivate his social life in London. The playhouses were environments which stimulated acquaintance and in which friendship and kinship could thrive, sufficiently private to develop their own tone but sufficiently open to avoid the narrow exclusiveness of the *beau monde* of the 1660s and 1670s; they provided conditions ideally suited to enable such a society to constitute and establish itself.

These developments had significant political consequences, for the court profoundly distrusted the prospect of the creation of a semi-permanent, independent gentry presence in London. The early Stuarts were, of course, opposed to the growth of London in general and issued proclamations designed to forestall it. London was an economic canker, wealthy out of all proportion to the rest of England, and a social and moral canker, for it was in the widest sense a place of disorder where 'all sorts reside, noble and simple, rich and poor, young and old'.[59] The lavish spending and promiscuous social interaction that occurred in London threatened morality and the stability of rank. James had tried without success to prevent the resort of the gentry to London, but in 1632 Charles issued his own proclamation against this behaviour, followed it up with a series of vigorous show trials of offenders and instituted a regular census of gentry numbers in London. Mildmay was among those in 1633 forced to request permission to remain.[60] On one level, this was an extension of the strategies of prerogative government. To rule personally and effectively, Charles needed to reinforce his authority in all parts of the realm, and he would establish peace and conformity in the countryside by sending back the magistrates and natural rulers to serve 'the King according to their Degrees and Ranks, in aid of the Government' (as his proclamation said); he also sent to all magistrates a book of directives concerning the maintenance of local order and discipline.[61] But on another level, Charles's anxiety expressed his fear of the political pressure such a gentry presence at the centre could exert. Historians have suggested that in the absence of parliament political discussion may have been given some continuity in the country in the regular meetings of gentry at quarter sessions.[62] London society was also becoming a new and dangerously permanent area in which political views could be canvassed and interchanged, and the proclamation to the gentry may be seen in part as an attempt to disperse a potentially critical opposition.[63]

London society and politics

As early as 1623, London society was being described as a place of 'a great deale of vncertaine newes . . . every man expecting what wilbe the conclusion of our princes match'. In 1626, the summoning of parliament caused all 'other kind of nuse . . . exsept itt have some relacion to the Parlement' to lie dead. The next year a country gentleman, incensed by demands for coat-and-conduct money, threatened to make 'ordinary [i.e. tavern] tables at London . . . ring of our letters'. John Earle wrote in 1629 that a tavern was 'a broacher of more newes than Hogsheads'. After the collapse of the 1629 parliament, the arrested MPs were asked what houses and taverns they resorted to in London, and Selden confessed 'he was at dinner at the three Cranes in London' with 'Sr John Eliott & divers other parliament men'.[64]

In 1633, Gervase Clifton was told that 'The most wonder' in town was about the gentlemen prosecuted 'for their stay here contrary to proclamacion'; the next year a letter on foreign affairs said the 'towne heardly did more abound with newes then now it doeth'. In 1635 Clifton again was told that 'Here is nothing but crying out and pittifully complayning for this great tax for shipping'. The Venetian ambassador reported London gossip to be commenting on the proportion of ecclesiastics in high office 'to the prejudice of the nobility and governing houses', and also that while Charles was in the country the nobility 'try to divert themselves by discussing what are considered the most essential affairs . . . The one thing they all join in maintaining with vigour is the report that Parliament will meet soon'. In 1637, a wanted puritan was said to be hiding in Drury Lane. A Norfolk gentleman wrote home that 'The busines nowe talkt on in towne is all about the Question of the shipp moneye' and complained he could not get to hear Hampden's trial, 'the crowd was so great'.

Bastwick said that the report of the romanism of a Laudian priest was 'talked over towne and country'.[65]

With the approach of parliament, the town's excitement increased; many of the future parliamentarian leaders had houses in town. In 1639, Suckling said 'one part of the town is in a whisper'. Strafford suggested using militia against the Scots in 1640 but was warned the 'Towne [was] full of nobility, who will talke of it'. The rumour of the Short Parliament's dissolution caused 'a murmure about the Towne'. In 1641 Laud was complaining that libels against him were circulating in taverns, and a pamphlet on Strafford recounted 'the opinion of all and the best judgements here about town'. A country gentleman dined with Sir John Hobart, 'his discourse nothing but state affaiers'. Essex was on a bowling green when he told Hyde of his antagonism to Strafford, and Fiennes declared his readiness to go to war when out riding with him. In mid-1641 a chief reason for coming to London was that there was 'soe much talke of the parliament busines'; six months later, one would readily meet 'a Cluster of Gentlemen equally divided in opinion and resolution'. When new appointments were made, the Verneys recorded, 'all ye Towne full of it'. Waller said that 'ladies of great honour . . . had spoke to him in their chambers of the proceedings of the Houses'. Jermyn first mentioned the Army Plot to Goring in Covent Garden, and Suckling arranged meetings for the conspirators 'at the Sparagus Garden at Supper', at 'the Dog Taverne in Westminster' and 'at the Dolphin in Grayes Inn lane'. Petitions and news sheets were read aloud and circulated 'by daily Tavern clubs in each ward' of the city.[66]

Hollar's engraving of the Royal Exchange (plate 1), with its tight knots of gentlemen engaged in discussion, gives a good impression of this highly-politicized society. In effect, political discussion was another of the forms of entertainment London could offer. One country gentleman said it was 'worth riding a hundred mile to see the court and stately presence' at Strafford's trial; another that it produced 'the most glorious assemblie the Isle could afford' and that there was 'much public eating not only of confections but of flesh and bread, bottles of beer and wine

Plate 1. Wenceslaus Hollar, *The Royal Exchange*.

going thick from mouth to mouth without cups'.[67] The newsletters that in the 1630s recounted town gossip turned readily in
the 1640s to discuss the relations of king and parliament. There
is every reason to suppose that the theatres, a key element in this
society and a highly articulate environment, could be settings for
such discussion, and a further scrutiny of the backgrounds of
some known theatre-goers will show that such discussion would
not have been limited to merely 'Cavalier' opinion.

The family of Sir Humphrey Mildmay, for example, had a
distinctly puritan tradition. His grandfather, Sir Walter, had
sympathized with Elizabethan puritanism against its episcopal
persecutors, and had founded that renowned centre of godliness
and learning, Cambridge's Emmanuel College. Sir Humphrey
was educated at Emmanuel and knew Bastwick there, and he
maintained the connection with him for he visited him in prison

and accepted a copy of one of his books. He himself was unsympathetic to the religious radicalism of the 1640s, but his sister Mary would serve meat on Fridays ('a dinner of flesh, like a Puritan'), and his cousin, Henry Mildmay of Graces, Essex, was a Presbyterian and parliamentarian colonel, who besieged Colchester under Fairfax and sat in Cromwell's parliaments and on the Cambridge committee of the Eastern Association. On his mother's side, Sir Humphrey was also related to the New England families of Gurdon and Winthrop.[68]

Sir Humphrey's brother, Sir Henry Mildmay, achieved considerable notoriety as a regicide (although he did not sign the death warrant, he sat among Charles's judges). He has come in for some stick as a turncoat and a scoundrel, but already in the 1620s he had spoken against Arminianism and helped the puritan divine Thomas Preston; in the 1640s he became a parliamentary commissioner for the revenue and a member of various councils of state. Imprisoned and exiled after the Restoration, he had a death-bed portrait painted to show that a regicide *could* die in bed. Another brother, Anthony Mildmay, described himself as 'a great opposer of tyranny and Popery' and fought against the king under the Earl of Bedford in 1642. Parliament employed him as an attendant on Charles at Carisbrooke in 1648, 'a charge great and dangerous . . . did not God enable us', and he accounted the king simply 'the most perfidious man that ever lived'. Sir Humphrey was not very close to his brother Henry, but several times he and Anthony saw plays together.[69]

The Mildmays also had a distinguished parliamentary record. Sir Henry and old Sir Walter had both sat in parliament, and the family was linked with the Northamptonshire parliamentary dynasty of the Fitzwilliams and the Chicheleys of Cambridgeshire. Several other MPs sitting in the Long Parliament were related to the Mildmays; we may note, for example, Sir Henry's second cousin, Arthur Capel of Raines Hall. Capel later contributed richly to the royalist effort, but he also had refused to contribute to Charles's 1639 expedition against the Scots and carried a petition of grievances to the king at York in 1640; in 1640–41 he was urging prosecution of Strafford, and the debate on grievances began with his presentation of the Hertfordshire petition. He was also a friend of the play-going puritan Sir Thomas Barrington.[70]

Sir Humphrey's cousin Mildmay Fane had also sat in parliament for his county, and he is a good example of the kind of moderate opinion which Charles and his followers so rashly alienated. Fane suffered to the tune of £19,000 in fines for alleged forest encroachments (a device of Charles's to raise finance by unparliamentary means), and in 1640 he was complaining of Charles's indifference to his services. Nevertheless, he was an early supporter of the king and was imprisoned for his activities, but in 1644, with the king's party increasingly under the sway of Cavalier extremists, he repudiated his old allegiances and petitioned to be allowed to take the Covenant, avowing horror at the 'Malignity of those who practised [the] Destruction' of church and state.[71] In his play *Candia Restaurata*, privately performed in Northamptonshire in 1641, countrymen lamented that their temples were defiled with new worship, and complained of judges who had introduced new laws, and of Ship Money, fen drainage schemes, depopulation of the countryside, monopolists and forest fines. Dr Psunodark, who restored this suffering realm to health, quite clearly stood for parliament; he had been banished the land these thirteen years. The play concluded hopefully, expecting men would now be 'monopolye, and proiect free'.[72] It is a remarkable demonstration of the freedoms the stage might take when totally beyond the reach of Charles's censorship.

Mildmay had other interesting connections. Sir John Bramston, son of the judge who decided against the king in Hampden's case, married an Abdy girl and had a Mildmay and a Crofts to his godparents. We do not know whether he went to the theatres, but he did dance in the Middle Temple *Triumphs of the Prince d'Amour*.[73] The wife of Secretary Coke whom Mildmay took to a masque was the widow of an alderman and daughter of a mayor and merchant tailor of London. Her husband was of course a royal servant, but Laud suspected him of sympathies with puritanism, and his eldest son supported parliament.[74] Mildmay also saw several plays in the company of Dr Isaac Dorislaus. Dorislaus was a Dutch historian brought to Cambridge in 1628 by the puritan Lord Brooke to lecture on Tacitus, which he did do, briefly, to the scandal of the University. He used the opportunity to comment on contemporary politics, inveighing against Spanish oppression in Holland, and he 'was conceived of by some to speak too much for the defence of the liberties of the people, though he spoke with great moderation and with exception of such monarchies as ours'. His radical views on authority placed 'the right of monarchy in the people's voluntary submission'; Laud had him silenced quickly. His other friends in the 1630s included Digby and Selden, and he reappears in 1649 as a manager of the charge of high treason against Charles at his trial. The same year he was assassinated while on the continent by royalist militants in exile. Parliament interred his body in Westminster Abbey; Charles II dug him up again in 1661.[75]

Mildmay, then, brought many significant and non-Cavalier strands to the theatres. Another striking figure was Sir Edward Dering who, as MP for Kent 1640–42, had a turbulent parliamentary career. He was a prominent figure in these years, having been elected on the radical platform, especially as a spokesman for ecclesiastical reform and the furtherance of a godly reformation. He chaired the Commons committee on religion and introduced the Root and Branch bill into the House, which proposed the total abolition of episcopacy; he was lobbied by Brownists and others complaining of Romish corruption in the English church, and was fêted in the streets by the London mob; his speeches were avidly read in Kent. However, disturbed by the breakdown of public order, he gradually swung back to the right, arguing in favour of a moderated episcopacy, and opposing the Grand Remonstrance in November 1641; his self-justifying pamphlet of 1642 earned him imprisonment for contempt. He went over to the king as a reluctant supporter, active in arms, yet wishing for 'a composing third way'; in 1644, he abandoned the king again and took the Covenant.[76] This radical MP was also the author of the first Shakespearean adaptation, a version of *Henry IV* which he produced (with other plays besides) with amateur actors on his estate in Kent. He amassed a large collection of playbooks, and a surviving diary for 1619–27 shows him attending the theatres frequently when in London.[77] Probably he continued to do so in the 1630s; an account book for 1637–39 records more payments for playbooks and their binding, and he began to sketch out the plot of another amateur play sometime early in the decade.[78] His son certainly visited the playhouses, for he had verses in the 1651 collection of Cartwright's plays; he was later a member of the 'Orinda' circle around Katherine Phillips the poetess.

Dering was a respected county figure (he was Lieutenant of Dover Castle) and like Mildmay had extensive links with other local parliamentary gentry, some of whom he would have been likely to find himself beside in the London theatres (see table 2). On his mother's side, he was grandson to a Speaker of the Commons, Sir Robert Bell; on his father's, he was cousin to the statesman Sir Henry Vane (whose son was the Independent leader Henry Vane). The Fanes were a branch of the Vanes, and Dering had a distant connection with Mildmay Fane; at one time they were rivals for the Kent county seat in parliament.[79] His mother's brother was MP for Aldborough, and his daughter married another Speaker, Sir Heneage Finch, and bore him a son who later became Earl of Nottingham and a prominent Restoration statesman; Finch's brother received the dedication of Webster's *The Devil's Law Case* (1623). Finch's second marriage was into the Bennet family to which Sir Humphrey Mildmay was related, and his daughter by this match, a child in the 1630s, would later marry the son of the theatre-going Viscount Conway; she was the Viscountess Conway who corresponded with the philosopher Henry More.[80]

Dering's diary mentions theatre-going with his cousin, Sir John Hobart, also the grandson of another Speaker of the Commons. The Hobarts were a Norfolk dynasty of relatively new gentry, but one possessing great wealth and prestige, consolidating a fortune made at law which destined the family to national prominence in succeeding generations. After the breakdown they tended to side firmly behind parliament; a Hobart regiment was active in the Eastern Association in the 1640s. Dering's companion in the playhouse was himself an MP in 1621,

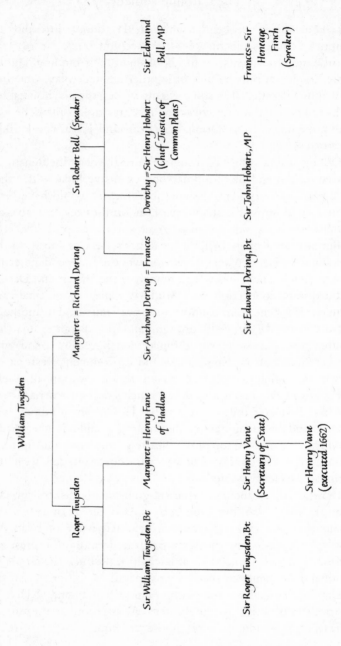

Table 2. Family tree of Dering and Hobart (simplified).

1624 and 1626; he was distantly related to the Sir Miles Hobart who participated in the scandalous attempt to prevent the dissolution of the 1629 parliament. Sir John Hobart sat in the Long Parliament beside his brother-in-law Sir Robert Crane, and his nephew sat in Cromwell's parliaments. Another brother-in-law, John Lisle, was a regicide; a third was William Crofts, Humphrey Mildmay's nephew. Sir John had another Kent connection through his marriage to Philippa Sidney, a niece of Sir Philip Sidney; his second wife, Frances Egerton, made him brother-in-law to the Egerton children who acted in 1634 in Milton's *Comus*.[81]

So Dering brought distinctly parliamentary touches to the London theatres. He also shows how the theatres could act as a bridge between political discussion at a county level and in London. Recent historians have demonstrated how politics in the provinces took its shape from pre-existing local alignments, a feature particularly marked in Kent where the peculiar twists and turns of Interregnum politics in part reflected the nature of the social constitution of the county. Kent was a county of many, relatively small gentry very closely interrelated. No one figure nor group dominated the county, and though Dering was elected on the basis of intense personal canvassing in 1640, he could never lead opinion; after his defection, another radical candidate quickly replaced him. Within this open environment ideas and opinions could circulate freely, and the Kent gentry maintained a flourishing intellectual life. There were several important literary families – the Lovelaces, Sidneys, Wallers, Filmers, Evelyns, Wottons and Diggeses, for example – and in these circles manuscripts were exchanged and ideas debated. Politics and literature cannot be fully separated in this interchange; the groups included such noted political theorists as Dering's cousin, Roger Twysden, and Sir Robert Filmer, a friend also of George Herbert and William Camden. Filmer's political treatise *Patriarcha* continued in manuscript in his lifetime.[82]

Dering would probably have found the atmosphere of these London theatres as I have described it a congenial metropolitan extension of these provincial circles, and his diary shows him several times in the theatres with members of leading Kentish families. The Tuftons who accompanied him were members of his wife's family. The 'Lady Wotton' whom he mentions was probably related to Thomas Baron Wotton who acted in Dering's amateur production of *The Spanish Curate*. Thomas Wotton was a nephew of the poet Henry Wotton, and married a cousin of the Lucas sisters; one of his daughters married a Tufton, another a member of the Stanhope family that performed Aston Cockayne's *Masque at Bretby* (1640).[83] The 'Lady Sedley' whom Dering also mentions seems to have been a relative of his close friend Sir John Sedley, who helped him in his 1640 election campaign and had a reputation as a fierce court opponent; he was also second cousin to the future Restoration dramatist, Sir Charles Sedley.[84] Dering might also have met in the theatres Sir Richard Baker, author of the *Theatrum Redivivum*, friend of Edward Wotton, and a poor scion of a wealthy Kent family related to the Tuftons.[85] Like Mildmay, Dering could have found in the theatres an extension of both his family and his county backgrounds.

Finally, Dering was well-known as an antiquary. Caroline antiquarianism was mostly in the hands of gentlemanly amateurs interested in their genealogy, for whom it reinforced an awareness of their 'county' roots, but it was also a politically sensitive hobby that touched on matters of state and dealt with precedents from which constitutional principles could be argued. Dering used his family history to speculate on the origins of government, and himself unearthed and sent to his friend Sir Robert Cotton a copy of Magna Carta; Charles's parliamentary critics found Cotton's famous library increasingly useful in the 1620s, and Cotton's career collapsed disastrously when his library was closed by royal command in 1629 after the circulation of a scandalous pamphlet originating from his collection.[86] Like the theatres, antiquarianism focused a wide range of discussion and friendship, for its practitioners relied on personal contacts to obtain access to material or its loan; Dering had a semi-formal arrangement with other antiquaries of the 1630s to exchange records and information.[87] At several points, theatrical and antiquarian circles overlapped. Simonds D'Ewes's autobiography records how his researches brought him into contact with a varied collection of gentry, including Sir Thomas Barrington, Sir Robert Crane, Sir John Hobart's father and Sir John Lucas (father of Mary Killigrew). Ben Jonson helped Selden compile his *Titles of Honour* (1614), and he was intimate with Cotton and was called into question about seditious verses he had seen at Cotton's house in 1628; Jonson's copy of Spenser came to Dering's hands.[88] Another antiquarian friend of Dering's (and cousin of Cotton's), Sir Thomas Shirley, belonged to a branch of the Shirleys with whom Mildmay was linked; his sister-in-law Dorothy was the dedicatee of James Shirley's *The Changes* (1632).[89] Antiquaries were familiar figures on the Caroline stage. The courtly Cartwright ridiculed one unmercifully in *The Ordinary* (1634), while Nabbes was gentler to Horten in *The Bride* (1638) whom he allowed a few words of defence. Shakerley Marmion's *The Antiquary* (*c.* 1631?) deals with the gulling of an old antiquary and the confiscation of his collection by a duke as part of his witty intrigues. It has been proposed that Marmion intended this to be read as a comment on Cotton's disgrace and ruthless treatment at the hands of Charles.[90]

The audience and the closing of the theatres

After this detailed investigation into the Caroline audience, a number of important conclusions suggest themselves. Firstly, it should be clear how inadequate is the description of the private theatre audience simply as an aristocratic and courtly coterie. Both in terms of social differentiation and political leanings, the theatres embraced a collection of spectators much broader and more varied than this view allows. Of course, my description has touched on a number of people who were as familiar with Whitehall as they were with Drury Lane, but I have also tried to suggest that the theatres had, nevertheless, a far less exclusive and closed climate than the hothouse atmosphere of the court. As a milieu, they were more open and outward-looking, distinct from Whitehall and self-sustaining; I have been arguing that they provided the conditions needed by a fashionable world to establish itself in London without everlasting dependence on the court. The audiences were societies still only in the process of developing towards a condition of greater exclusiveness, and the most striking demonstrations of this are the strong provincial ties which still bound many theatre-goers, and the surprising presence of spectators who had close connections with commercial or mercantile families; there is a tension existing in the 1630s between the progressive centralization of this milieu and its stubbornly decentralized roots. What seems to me to be characteristic of this period is that we have a distinctively *gentry* audience that is unlike both the wider early-Jacobean and narrower Restoration audiences. In attempting to delineate the Caroline audience, I have had to return over and again to the major county families and their scions; the bafflingly complex internal interrelationships of this audience are themselves reflections of one peculiar feature of the gentry world.

Admittedly, the commercial families I have discussed were no ordinary citizens and numbered among London's leading merchant dynasties, but there is evidence to suggest that the smaller citizen and comparable ranks still continued to be represented in the indoor theatres in our period. In *The Magnetic Lady*, Jonson mentions the 'sinful sixpenny mechanics' who sat in 'the oblique caves and wedges' of the Blackfriars in 1632, and the epilogue to Lovelace's *The Scholars* (Salisbury Court, c. 1637?) distinguishes between the 'gentlemen o'th'pit', and the less witty audience sitting in the galleries.[91] The prostitute in Thomas Cranley's moral poem *Amanda, or the Reformed Whore* (1635) goes to the theatre disguised alternately as a great lady, a chambermaid, a country wench and a neat citizen, while a vacation prologue by Henry Glapthorne, having described how the courtiers, ladies and gentlemen are out of town for the vacation, addresses itself to the ordinary citizens who still are visiting the theatre:[92]

> You are our daily and most constant Guests,
> Whom neither Countrey bus'nesse nor the Gests
> Can ravish from the Citie; 'tis your care
> To keep your Shops, 'lesse when to take the Ayr
> You walke abroad, as you have done to day,
> To bring your Wives and Daughters to a Play.

And there are more references besides.[93] Unlike the gentlemen, these classes did not leave diaries and account books and so tend to figure less prominently in accounts of the theatre audiences, but it may well have been they who were partly responsible for example for the hissing, hooting and 'pippin-pelting' of French actresses from the Blackfriars stage in 1629.[94]

Perhaps the assumption that the dominant audience of the 1630s was a wholly courtly grouping has been induced by too emphatic a distinction between the 'private' and 'public' theatres, a rift usually seen as getting only progressively wider with time. In fact, although a courtly writer like Cartwright might denigrate Shakespeare as 'Old fashion'd wit',[95] low and plebeian, the taste of the private theatre audience was still very mixed. We know from theatre records and from Greene's and Mildmay's diaries that *Hamlet*, *Henry IV*, *Othello*, *Richard III*, *Midsummer Night's Dream* and other Shakespearean plays were still current in the private theatre repertoire. So too were Jonson's *Volpone* and *The Alchemist*, Marston's *The Malcontent*, and other Elizabethan and Jacobean plays besides; I shall be exploring some implications of these continuing revivals in chapter 8 below. There were indeed two types of theatre and repertoire, catering for an elegant audience and for 'citizens, and the meaner sort of People' respectively,[96] but the two 'traditions' they inspired, none the less, cannot be absolutely distinguished even at this date. For example, the King's Men alternated between their indoor and outdoor playhouses according to season, and their private theatre audience seems to have followed them to the Globe quite readily. Sir Humphrey Mildmay went there several times; Buckingham and Holland were at the Globe in 1628 and in 1632 the Earl of Salisbury paid for his son, Viscount Cranborne, to see plays there.[97] In 1629, a satirist lampooned an Inns of Court man in his 'silken garments, and his sattin robe/That hath so often visited the Globe', and a Globe prologue of 1635 affects to perceive 'Besides rich gaudy sirs, some that rely/More on their judgement than their clothes'.[98] In 1632, the Globe was described as 'a World of *Beauties*, and brave *Spirits*', while at the Hope there was a 'mixt Society, yet there were many Noble Worthies amongst them'.[99] The reference to 'the splendour of the curved theatre' in Milton's 1626 elegy would fit a public theatre better than a private house, and in 1654 Edmund Gayton, an ex-Oxford man, described a festive riot at the Fortune or the Bull, apparently from personal observation. During the Interregnum, reports of raids on illegal play performances show that an audience of quality was still prepared to attend the public theatres when no other playhouse was open.[100] It appears that although the 'two traditions' are broadly and unmistakably distinct a considerable degree of interaction and cross-fertilization still took place between them, and the critical terminology that divides 'private' from 'public' implies misleadingly that the Blackfriars, Phoenix and Salisbury Court catered for a more withdrawn and restricted clientele than in fact they did. The *court* stage constituted such a 'private' theatre; the town stages (which, after all, were open indiscriminately to anyone who could afford the admission prices) did not. A modification of the critical language used in discussing the two types of theatre is called for here. I propose that we should replace the terms 'private' and 'public' with 'popular' and 'elite' which, though they go against contemporary usage, provide a more appropriate and precise means of describing the *de facto* relationship of the two traditions, identifying the greater sophistication of the indoor theatres while avoiding the suggestion that their audiences were less a public than a band of specially invited and (somehow) privileged spectators.

It is also striking that we can link with these audiences many county families who were rising towards positions of considerable prestige. Several of them were among James's first baronetage creations – the Hobarts, Barringtons, Cottons, Wortleys, Tuftons, Bakers, Sedleys, Mildmays of Mulsham and Shirleys of Staunton Harold were all ennobled in 1611; Dering's baronetage came in 1627. The city dynasties too held positions of great trust. Three Abdy brothers of this generation each received baronetcies; Mildmay's nephew Henry Bennet became Earl of Arlington, three of his Bennet cousins became baronets and another Bennet line later produced the Dukes of Grafton and Marquises of Salisbury. Some of these were very wealthy families; of the malignants who compounded between 1643 and 1660, Mildmay Fane was the second richest peer, and Sir John Baker the second richest baronet.[101] By no means are we dealing with the 'decadent' end of the Caroline social structure.

This was, of course, a class that contributed a substantial proportion of MPs to the Long Parliament, and to the gentry who went there the atmosphere of the theatres must have been in some limited senses comparable with that which they met with in parliament. Historians have highlighted just such complicated interrelating circles of friendship and kinship as I have been describing as a distinctive and significant element among the membership of the House of Commons, where the solvent of politics was the 'connection' or 'association' rather than the 'party'.[102] Parliamentary politics in the 1640s involved a shifting complex of alliances or groupings founded on local correspondences of interest, outlook or friendship which had to be manipulated into larger coalitions by parliamentary leaders in a manner only analogous to party manoeuvring. Regional or kinship ties were exploited to build up a majority or a lobby; they must also have contributed greatly to the parliament's sense of political identity, its unity as a body. Peter Laslett has argued that in the 1630s the circles of Kent gentry acted in a similar manner as channels enabling political feeling to crystallize and coalesce. They were 'a medium of political consciousness: they were units through which political attitudes were formulated and spread about'.[103] In the absence of parliament, the theatres also were a meeting-ground where the gentry who would normally have been at Westminster might associate and cultivate their connections, and I suggest that it is quite likely that they too may have served a similar purpose. It is especially notable that the theatres brought together a range of opinion much wider *geographically* than any that could be met with in county circles. In particular, they brought into contact leading gentry of the adjacent counties of the south-east (the area that supported parliament most consistently in the 1640s): the Crofts were from

Suffolk, Mildmay and the Lucases from Essex, the Barringtons from Hertfordshire, Dering from Kent. In such rudimentary ways a purely local political consciousness might gain a more than local dissemination, and a purely social phenomenon, the creation of a gentry presence in London, would have wider political resonances. The development of the gentry's political unity is bound up with its development as a discrete social group and the theatres were a prime medium through which its group consciousness was established. They offered a sort of continuity between the meetings of gentlemen at Westminster in 1629 and 1640, and it is not fanciful to suppose that some of the matters which were under discussion in the parliaments of the 1620s would have come up again in personal interchange in the following decade in the theatres.

Obviously, such political dialogue as the theatres could sustain could at best be only sporadic, and many of the theatre-goers I have mentioned would later trend towards firm support for the king. But the theatres were places where free association and interaction might take place, and which were much more open to radically opposed points of view than is usually allowed. Theatrical circles overlapped revealingly with the personnel of the Long Parliament. Dering sat at Westminster in 1640–42 among representatives from Kentish families, Sir Henry Mildmay amongst his connections; Barrington, Whitelocke and Henry Killigrew were related to many MPs.[104] Other MPs who were theatre-goers or who were closely connected with theatre-goers could be mentioned (such as the Earl of Falkland, Viscount Cranborne, Edward Hyde and Mildmay Fane's brother); the dramatist Tom May later became associated with the republican Henry Marten; Thomas Heywood already was a friend of the Presbyterian Harbottle Grimston.[105] Simonds D'Ewes complained in May 1641 that the afternoon sessions of parliament were being disrupted because 'the greater parte' of its members disappeared to 'Hide Park & playes & bowling grounds'; we know by chance that Peter Legh, the member for the Cheshire borough of Newton, was at a playhouse in January 1642 for he died after a duel sparked off by a quarrel there.[106] Seven years later, a number of MPs were among the audience surprised by a raid on an illegal play performance at the Salisbury Court.[107] The persistent presence in the playhouses of such people, as well as of Cromwell's privy councillor (Whitelocke), Charles's gaoler (Anthony Mildmay) and of the lawyer who framed the charge against the king at his trial (Dorislaus), is perhaps the most decisive refutation of the notion of the 'Cavalier audience'. One might also mention that John Bradshaw, the president of the king's judges and the man who sentenced Charles to death, paid for plays to be performed in Cheshire in 1632.[108]

It is evident that in these last years the theatres were staging politically dangerous material with increasing frequency and freedom. Remarkably, within six years each company without exception ran into trouble with the royal authorities for touching on sensitive issues.[109] In 1634, Sir Henry Herbert intervened to prevent the King's Revels from using a church robe in a play about 'a Flamen, a priest of the heathens'. It seems highly likely that some reflection on the church under Laud was suspected here, and five years later it was Laud himself who prosecuted the Fortune players for performing inflammatory scenes in an old play *The Cardinal's Conspiracy*, 'revived on purpose in contempt of the ceremonies of the Church' (as Viscount Conway's correspondent readily recognized). After a brief imprisonment, the players had their revenge by reviving *The Valiant Scot* which, because of its ironic appropriateness to Charles's contemporaneous attempt to impose ecclesiastical conformity on the Scots by military force, 'vext the Bishops worse then the other, insomuch, as they were forbidden Playing it any more; and some of them prohibited ever Playing again'.[110] Later that year the Prince's Men were called into question by the privy council for satirizing monopolies and ecclesiastical officials in *The Whore New Vamped*; the year before the king intervened in person to prohibit the King's Men from staging parts of Massinger's *The King and the Subject* which dealt with unparliamentary taxation (see p. 72 above). Finally, there seems to have been a tremendous row in May 1640 when Beeston's Boys risked staging Brome's *The Court Beggar*, a wholesale attack on the Scottish war and on the court itself, without a licence. In defiance of a royal command to forbear, the players continued to act 'the sayd Play & others' (what these last were can only be speculated), and were thrown into prison and their theatre closed down, not to reopen until a safe courtier, Sir William Davenant, had been imposed on the recalcitrant company in place of its old manager, William Beeston.[111] Significantly, only two of these six or more plays ever reached print; had the others come down to us, the history of this last decade might have looked very different from how it appears now.

It seems to me that the parliamentary order closing the theatres in September 1642 makes much more sense in relation to these recent and repeated collisions between the authorities and the playhouses over the drama's political freedom, as part of already existing anxieties about the subversiveness of the theatres and about the politically alert and involved audiences they played to, than it does as the climax of a sustained puritan anti-theatrical campaign (the existence of which is doubtful) or as a petty parliamentary revenge on a courtly amusement. The theatres were dangerously volatile and articulate institutions with a recent history of inflammatory performances, and, as areas where gentry of parliamentary status were accustomed to meet and discuss affairs, rather like the conventicles of dissenters which were later presumed to be hotbeds of secret radicalism, they were places where debate was suspiciously free and association uncontrolled. Moreover, in the perspective of several generations of theatre regulation, parliament's repressive acts in the 1640s and 1650s appear less as aggressive moves than as typically precautionary measures such as had often been taken before at times of crisis or instability when governments wished to disperse the people and maintain a tight rein on law and order. The playhouses had been shut down at the deaths of Queen Elizabeth (1603) and of Prince Henry (1612), and in the 1620s and 1630s they were subject to repeated closures, sometimes for months at a stretch, when the plague was prevalent. These latter instances were commanded to prevent danger of infection, but also to guard against popular disorder when many people in authority had fled to the country and left the city lawless (as happened in the great plague visitation of 1636–37).[112]

September 1642 was, after all, a moment of unprecedented crisis in English history, of major social division, political breakdown and near disaster. The first blood of the Civil War had already been shed; Charles raised his standard at Nottingham on 22 August and the parliamentary ordinance of 2 September justified closing the theatres by reference to the sudden and terrible calamities threatening the peace and safety of the realm from within and without, 'the distressed Estate of Ireland, steeped in her own Blood, and the distracted Estate of England, threatned with a Cloud of Blood, by a Civill Warre'[113] – there seems no reason to suppose that this apprehensive order meant any more or any less than it said. Precisely the same reasons had been advanced in January 1642 when the closure of the theatres had been suggested in a debate on the recent, shocking rebellion in Ireland, that playhouses were needlessly disruptive 'in these times of calamity in Ireland and the distractions in this kingdom', and they were repeated again at the Middle Temple in November when the lawyers decided to put down their Christmas revels for fear of drawing unwanted company into their society, 'and this in respect of the danger and troublesomeness of the times'.[114] On the day that parliament issued its closing order its members also heard debates on how to secure the Tower armoury and the munitions at Bristol and Droitwich, on the nomination of deputy lieutenants, on the levying of money to suppress the Irish revolt and on the need to ensure the safety of the seas.[115] The minds of MPs at this critical juncture were not set on a programme of moral and social reform but on the fundamental political necessity of establishing the security of London and the kingdom, a security the theatres' freedom was only likely to disrupt. Rarely is it mentioned that the ordinance came before the public as the second in a pair issued together, the first of which was a declaration 'for the appeasing and quietting of all unlawfull Tumults and Insurrections in the severall Counties of England' and for the suppression of riots newly disturbing the peace of Essex.[116] In other words, the 1642 order contains nothing that is doctrinally 'puritan' or which is unusual in the steps taken to secure public calm in a turbulent time, and although the idea that plays are anti-christian amusements which have provoked God's vengeance was indeed advanced in the 1648 parliamentary ordinance against the theatres, it was significantly absent from the 1642 order. Rather, the statement of 1642 that 'publike Sports doe not well agree with publike Calamities, nor publike Stageplayes with the Seasons of Humiliation' reiterates closely the form of words which the privy council had used when putting down plays during the mourning for Prince Henry, 'that these tymes doe not suite with such playes and idle shewes, as are daily to be seene in and neere the citie of London, to the scandall of Order and good governement at all occasions when they are most tollerable'.[117]

Furthermore, if we take the closure of the theatres to have been an act of public safety rather than of puritan reform, some inconsistencies in the subsequent history of the parliamentary ban begin to make sense. It is clear, for example, that parliament did not go about to restrain the theatres with an unchanging resolution; in January 1642 the proposal was to close the theatres only 'for a season', in September it was to be 'while these sad Causes and set times of Humiliation doe continue', in 1646 the King's Men were awarded arrears of pay by parliament, and the order of July 1647 closed the stages only for a temporary period of six months.[118] It would appear that a permanent closure of the theatres was only one of a number of options which parliament was willing to consider (no doubt those gentlemanly MPs who in their leisure hours gravitated naturally towards the theatres would have wished, once security was restored, to have returned to the enjoyment of those pastimes which could not be tolerated in a society embroiled in civil war).

Secondly, parliament's hostility to plays was of an uneven intensity, and was most active at times of increased political instability. Not only was the 1642 order issued at a moment of unprecedented crisis, but the second wave of repression (the three orders of July 1647 to February 1648) coincided with renewed agricultural depression and economic distress, with the growing militancy of the Levellers, with parliament made desperately weak by its chaotic internal struggles between Presbyterians and Independents, with riots at Westminster and the army occupying London, and with the outbreak of the second Civil War. It is surely appropriate to see parliament's renewal of its earlier measures as a response to this situation of crisis upon crisis and to its own embattled position of being under attack from both royalists and radicals, rather than as the implementation of a theological and moral programme. Indeed, a royalist newsbook of 1648 did interpret the suppression of plays as part of parliament's strategy against the Levellers, putting them down 'for fear all in time should be published on the house-tops'. Similarly, the famous concerted raids by the army on the Phoenix, Salisbury Court, Red Bull and Fortune theatres, all on 1 January 1649, were probably planned with a view to removing potential points of public meeting and disorder before the trial of the king, the speedy preparations for which were already under way; marching the Salisbury Court players off, 'they oftentimes tooke the Crown from his head who acted the King, and in sport would oftentimes put it on again'.[119] The same cautions were implemented by Cromwell's shaky and unpopular regime in 1656, when the council of state instructed officers in the provinces to take securities for good obedience from known malignants, to close unlicensed taverns and 'to observe the behaviour of all the disaffected, and what meetings they hold, and to suppress such as are dangerous; also to suppress all horse-races, cock-fighting, bear-baiting, stage-playes, or other unlawful assemblies'. The Venetian ambassador commented that because 'the government dreads gathering of people, all conventicles and meetings are forbidden, and plays and parties in particular, from fear that under the guise of recreation they may be plotting something against the present rulers', while another observer described the closure of bear-baiting and cock-fighting houses, explaining 'all this [is] done for preventing any great meeting of the people'.[120] I suggest that considerations such as these, rather than an overriding and specifically puritan doctrinal and moral disapproval of play-acting (which, as we have seen, many MPs would not have gone along with anyway), must have been the really decisive factor in getting the playhouses closed in September 1642.

There are, then, other and much more likely interpretations of the suppression of the theatres than as an act of puritan aggression against an institution irretrievably riddled with 'royalism'. It is by no means clear that the court looked to the playhouses as to little islands of sympathetic elegance in the city, nor that the players were ever content to be the docile puppets of a wayward and intolerant royal master. Parliament was evidently correct to suppose that the theatres, performing in the disturbed conditions after 1642 and before the highly politicized audiences which they attracted, could quite easily have had extremely disruptive and divisive effects. If we turn to the drama they were staging in the previous decade we shall find that plays on sensitive topics were not exceptions in the repertoire, occasionally provoking the wrath of the censor, but that the theatres were used to discussing the affairs and issues of their day with a frequency and freedom far from acceptably subservient to either the wishes or the dignity of the powers set over them, and very unlikely to induce an unquestioning acceptance in their spectators of the authority and actions of their rulers, divinely ordained or otherwise.

7

City comedies: courtiers and gentlemen

POLITICS BELONG to cities. The word derives from *polis*, a city or state, and properly signifies the science of human relations in the public sphere, as opposed to *ethics*, the science of human relations in the private sphere. Politics govern the relationships between the various elements of society, the means by which they compose themselves into a unity, and from Babel downwards the city has been the ancient and archetypal symbol of man in his complete society. Man, as a social animal, tends to live in cities, and this decision to form a community has produced *politics*.

Comedies too belong to cities. They are 'an imitation of the common errors of our life' represented in 'the most ridiculous and scornful sort that may be'. While tragedy takes place among high characters and the extraordinary, comedy deals with low figures and the ordinary. Its characters are ones 'which we plaie naturally' and which 'if we saw walke in Stage names' would produce 'delightful laughter, and teaching delightfulnesse'.[1] Politics are a natural subject for comedy because they concern the adjustments man has to make to live in society. That man should be forced to accommodate his behaviour, to undergo deformity for the sake of conformity, is inherently comic.

I have been arguing that the 1630s were witnessing a long-term alteration in the shape of society. The traditional configuration of court, city and country now had a fourth term, the town, and the adjustments Caroline city comedy is specially concerned with are adjustments society was making to accommodate this new element. A distinctive feature of this comedy is the large social perspective in which the audience are invited to contemplate the rise of the town: the town is in the foreground but behind it is implied the presence of society's other constituents, court, city and country. Thus Caroline comedy is not simply a comedy of social life, interested only in the finer niceties of manners in a prescribed environment, but a comedy of political life too, interested as much in the relationships between society's various parts as those within only one of those parts. Manners are important, but their significance is as an index to the more complex adjustments taking place beneath.

In the perfectly balanced society, the individual would be perfectly behaved, so by bringing forward the interaction between manners and social change the dramatists also raise the issue of changes in patterns of moral behaviour. Morals reflect on politics too, for in a society ruled by personal will, the moral qualities of society's governors are as important as their political capabilities. Caroline city comedy, presenting manners, morals and politics as interrelated aspects of a complex whole, seems to me to have this comprehensiveness and this seriousness about it.

So when the city comedies of the 1630s took the rise of the town for their subject they were addressing themselves to political issues and ones which, I have suggested in my previous chapter, were newly becoming controversial. The gentry's acquirement of selfconsciousness as an autonomous group with its own values, distinct from the court and potentially in tension with it, implies a corresponding growth in political consciousness and confidence, and these developments Charles's proroguing of parliament and proclamation to the gentry were intended to frustrate. The plays which specifically consider the problems raised by the growth of the town, a series beginning with *Hyde Park* in 1632 and ending with *The Constant Maid* of *c.* 1637 (Shirley gave none of his comedies after 1637 a London setting), all belong to the five years following Charles's initiation of his campaign against the town; it would appear that the issues they are concerned with had suddenly become pressing. They are often regarded as among the best plays of the period; their quality is not merely a reflection of their 'realism', but a measure of their serious engagement with what were the most significant and problematic developments of their day. They are helping the town create itself by providing it with a model of the norm of good manners; but they are also constituting a political inquiry into the significance of those manners, and into the permanent place now claimed by the gentry class in the structure of the complete society, the *polis* that is England.

Attack and defence

There are three plays which explicitly take up the question of the establishment of the permanent presence of a large group of gentry in London, and one of these adopts a position on the issue diametrically opposed to that of the other two. Davenant's *The Wits* (January 1634; pub. London, 1636) is about the antics of two country gentlemen, Pallatine the elder and Sir Morglay Thwack, who have come to town with the resolution of living by their wits. Leaving their estates in trust, they 'disdaine/ Suppliment from [their] Lands' (sig.F1ʳ) and rely instead on their personal abilities to bring them a living. They are

> Two that have tasted *Natures* kindnesse[,] Arts,
> And men, have shin'd in moving Camps, have seene
> Courts in their solemne businesse, and vaine pride;
> Convers'd so long i'th towne here that [they] know
> Each Signe, and Pibble in the streets . . .   (sig.C2ʳ)

However, their intention is frustrated by Pallatine's younger brother in association with a lady of the town, Lady Ample, who put the supposed 'wits' through a series of humiliations. Pallatine the elder discovers that his 'lazie method, and slow rules of Thrift' are no match for the arts of his brother who is 'Votary to chance' (sig.E3ʳ), and he marvels that while he loses face his brother appears ever more and more flourishing, a prosperity, he admits, which is the result of neither office, law, nor trade, but simply the natural propensity a younger brother has to thrive by his wits. By Act IV he has been hilariously taken prisoner in a chest, and is forced to endure a lecture on his behaviour from his brother, criticizing him for attempting a course of action to which he is not suited:

> Brother, you have prayd well [for patience], heaven send her you!
> You must forsake your faire fertile soyle
> To live here by your Wits!
>   ... I meane to take
> Possession sir, and patiently converse
> With all those Hindes, those Heards, and Flocks
> That you disdain'd in fulnesse of your Wit!   (sigs.H2^v–3^r)

Thwack's experiences force him too to acknowledge that his abilities fit him better for his place in the country than for witty living in the town, and says he will

> write down to'th Country, to dehort
> The Gentry from comming hither, Letters
> Of strange dire Newes; You shall disperse them Sir! ...
> That there are Lents, six yeares long proclam'd by th'State! ...
> That our Theaters are raz'd downe; and where
> They stood, hoarse Midnight Lectures preach'd by Wives
> Of *Comb-makers*, and Mid-wives of *Tower-Wharfe*!   (sig.H3^v)

The associates of the younger Pallatine approve his reform:

> This cannot chuse but fright the Gentry hence;
> And more impoverish the Towne, than a
> Subversion of the Faire of *Bartholomew*,
> The absence of the Termes, and Court!   (sig.H4^r)

In the last act, Pallatine the elder repents and admits to the 'crimes' his brother accuses him of, 'misleading/Morglay, your old friend; then, neglect of mee,/And haughty over-vallewing your selfe' (sig.K1^v). He and Thwack return to the country, but first confer rewards for superior wittiness on the younger brother.

Clearly, Thwack's letter into the country is a comic equivalent of Charles's proclamation to the gentry, and the intrigues 'prove' that slightly old-fashioned gentry like Thwack are unsuited to London life and should stay at home in the provinces. Charles's proclamation, I have suggested, was intended to prod the gentry back to their role of local justicers and to reinforce his national paternalism with a strong local paternalism, and Davenant similarly urges onto his country gentlemen their proper place and function. Ironically, the country, traditionally a place of purity, must be taught chastity in *The Wits*. Pallatine the elder is mortified by his confinement in the chest (and in a graveyard) and admits his intentions of living off town ladies were sinful, and Thwack is taught to kiss Ample in a pure manner ("'Tis the first leading Kisse that I intend/For after chastitie' (sig.K1ʳ)). The gentlemen are also reminded of their roles as society's governors. The play opens with Pallatine the younger taking two discharged soldiers, under no authority, into his witty company, and there is much talk of following the 'Colours of Queene *Ample*' or 'King *Pall*' (sigs.I3ʳ, B4ʳ). The play's low characters, a constable and his watch, are farcically controlled by Pallatine the younger through offers of drink or through his influence with the constable's wife; Pallatine claims, "th Constable obayes no Law, but mine' (sig.K2ʳ). Finally, in the last act the wits dress Thwack up as a justice to pass mock-sentence on Lady Ample's avaricious guardian. Through such ironic versions of authority's forms, the gentry are prompted to give over a witty life and return to their true function in the country as arbiters of government.

Although Davenant discourages country gentry like Thwack and Pallatine from coming to London, the town, which looks 'as it would invite the Countrey/To a Feast' (sig.B4ʳ), remains attractive as a place. Davenant does stage a wit combat in Act II, in which the gentlemen rail against the vanity and frivolity of the town and the town ladies reply with the country's dullness, yet the two terms remain balanced equally against each other. In earlier and later London comedies one term tends to eclipse the other: in Jacobean city comedies country wealth is a prey for the rapacity of the city, while in Restoration versions the gaiety of town life destroys any sympathy for the values of the country, backward as it is. This mutually destructive aspect is absent from the antagonism between the two in *The Wits*. Davenant's town respects the wealth of the country: there are allusions to Elder Pallatine's 'young Heifers', 'faire fertile soyle' and his 'Hindes, those Heards, and Flockes' (sigs. C1ʳ, H2ᵛ-3ʳ). On the other side, the country gentry have left their estates behind in trust, so the usual criticism of town life, that its excesses destroy the achievements of country frugality, does not operate. At the end of the play, the Elder Pallatine is rewarded with Lady Ample, the younger with a manor in the country. Town and country are not mutually exclusive terms here; indeed, the continuities between the two are conspicuous, for the two Pallatines are brothers and therefore of near-equal status. Rather, town and country represent two contrasting environments to which different personal characteristics are suited, but which may and should coexist harmoniously. What Davenant is doing, in the interests of the political moral he wishes to draw, is to introduce a distinction within the gentry class between those whose capacities fit them for the town (younger brothers and female wards of undisclosed background) and those whose responsibilities tie them to the country (old-fashioned knights and heirs of land). This distinction anticipates the terms of many Restoration comedies, and Davenant produces a play very much like Etherege's *She Would if She Could* (1668), for example. In Etherege, though, the country/town antithesis is marked more definitely by an age/youth opposition, whereas Davenant's brothers are of the same generation and obviously much more alike, and this opens up the possibility that Davenant's distinction might well have been received by his audience as a sophistication. As we have seen, in the 1630s town and country were only just beginning to separate and it seems to me unlikely that such neatly drawn lines of demarcation as Davenant makes would have been readily acceptable to the Caroline audience (many of whom would have been men more of the stamp of the elder Pallatine than of his brother). This may account for some of the difficulties the play faced. The dedication speaks of trouble 'from a cruel Faction' (sig.A3ʳ), and Carew's commendatory verses try to forestall criticism; the prologue is amazed to meet '*A Session, and a Faction at his Play*' and worries about '*cruell Spies*' in the audience (sig.A4ʳ). The play was reported to have 'had a various fate on the stage, and at court',[2] and this may well reflect the slanting of Davenant's social commentary towards the point of view of the king. *The Wits* is not a 'town' play at all, but embodies a courtier's attitude to the town, as a place where younger brothers (rather like Davenant himself, though of a higher rank) might gather, but from which the men of real substance, the leading country gentry, are best excluded.[3]

The Wits, then, may be elucidated with reference to the proclamation of 1632, but it is possible also that it was responding to two other plays of *c.* 1632–34 by Richard Brome and Thomas Nabbes, both professional playwrights, which approach the question of royal hostility to the town but from the opposite side. Both plays are set, with great attention to detail, in Covent Garden, which was the newest and most prominent example of the gentry's foothold in London. The square was designed deliberately as an area of fashionable housing, and its early inhabitants included Sir Edmund Verney, the Earl of Essex, Sir Henry Vane and Denzil Holles. It offended against another royal proclamation also, one which prohibited new building in London, and its construction was made possible only through the good offices of its architect, Inigo Jones, who as a commissioner for new buildings could authorize rebuilding on old foundations if done with 'Uniformitie and Decency'.[4] The owner and developer of the land was the Earl of Bedford, a peer not in favour at court. Bedford had been a critic of the court in the parliaments of the 1620s, notably in the debates on the Petition of Right (1628), and he spent six months in prison for his part in the events which led to the closing of Cotton's library. During Charles's personal rule he shunned participation in public life and was mainly engaged in fen drainage; in 1640 he was one of the twelve noblemen who petitioned the king at York to recall parliament. Widely respected both as a popular peer and a moderate, it was hoped he might be able to bring Charles to a compromise with his critics, but he died before it could be effected. His son subsequently had a tortuous political career, fighting against Charles at Edgehill, for him at Newbury, then throwing himself on parliament's mercy again.[5] Like Salisbury's Royal Exchange, Covent Garden was a prestigious assertion of dynastic wealth and power right at the heart of London. It was also a challenge to Laud's conforming ministry. Covent Garden church was the first church to be built in London since the Reformation and the puritan earl reserved its patronage to himself, resisting the attempts of the vicar of St Martin-in-the-Fields to control the living. Architecturally, it reflected the earl's principles, being built in the deliberately plain

Tuscan style, the lowest of the five orders and usually treated by architects as a purely theoretical style (see plate 2); it implied a return to the primitive and vernacular. The square too, an Italianate piazza, was unlike anything in London; perhaps it would have reminded contemporaries of the wealth and republican values of Venice.[6]

Such associations and more are behind Brome's and Nabbes's Covent Garden plays. R. J. Kaufmann has shown that Brome's *Weeding of Covent Garden* is larded with allusions to the intensified royal paternalism of 1632–34, as Charles tried to bring the country's economic and social life under his direct regulation: there are references to the royal proclamation on prices, the Book of Sports, the licensing of taverns, the creation of the soap monopoly, and so forth.[7] As these authors present Covent Garden, it is full of implications for the way Charles rules, as a place where the newly developing independent gentry class and the forces of court authority and interference collide. It focuses the friction between the gentry in town and the court.

In Nabbes's *Covent Garden* (1633; pub. London, 1638), the defence of the gentry's moral behaviour in town leads naturally

Plate 2. Wenceslaus Hollar, *Covent Garden church and piazza.*

to reflections on their political character. The piazza is ambiguously a place of high fashion or of vice masquerading as gentility, and in the central romantic plot, the courtship of Dorothy by Artlove, the gentry in Covent Garden are exonerated from any suspicion of misbehaviour. Artlove's courtship is the golden mean between the excessively boisterous and lascivious jeerers and the absurdly nervous Littleword (who speaks only one word in the play). This discrimination between types of behaviour at the same horizontal (social) level is complemented by a vertical distinction between Artlove and the comic passions of the servants who quarrel over a lady's maid and fight a cowardly mock-duel. The servants ape gentle manners but are betrayed by their own lowness, the lady's maid getting drunk and insisting at length that she is a 'gentleuman' (p. 59), and Artlove's social correctness is further established in contrast with the excesses of a 'complementing Vintener' (sig.A4^v) whose language is too high for his social station. Nabbes has isolated Artlove as an example of a gentleman with manners ideal for his situation and a model to his class.

Artlove's moral integrity is tested by Dorothy who questions the sincerity of the intentions underlying his manners and parodies his mannered speech, but she is conquered by his goodness, the play affirming that his manners are not affected but an index to his true worth. He is, however, also tested by Dorothy's brother who suspects his intentions because he is of a slightly lower rank of gentry than their family (Artlove, we learn, has £1,000 a year (p. 8)). The brother confronts Dorothy and Artlove in turn with his suspicions and fears for his sister's honour, and the reaction of each is identical. Both angrily retort the brother's doubts back against himself, Dorothy asserting that she can distinguish 'true desert' from 'outward glosse' without his interference (p. 29) and accusing him of being the baser one himself for harbouring such mean suspicions ('Guilt is aptest still/To be suspitious' (p. 28)). For Artlove too, Dorothy's brother's jealousies only prove his own lack of gentility:

> What base suspition
> Poysons his jealous thoughts! (p. 40)

> What a prophane breath from his blacke mouth flies . . .
> He is not sure her brother, but some impostor,
> That onely counterfeit's his worthier person. (p. 42)

Their immediate response is outrage that anyone could be so base as to doubt their integrity, and this aggressive feeling for the identity of good manners and worthy behaviour is a characteristically 'gentry' attitude which we will find explored more fully in Shirley's plays. The other element in this shock is resentment at her brother for attempting to control their freedom of choice (especially as his doubts of them cast suspicion on his own gentility). The brother, Dorothy sees, has taken it as his 'prerogative' to make such an inquiry (p. 29) but she claims the right of relying on her own judgment to rule her actions. When the situation is repeated in the last act, Dorothy openly demands to have the 'freedom of my will before your counsell' (p. 64). She and Artlove are resisting an interfering paternalist authority that attempts to limit what is theirs by right; and their sense of their right is founded precisely on their feeling for their innate gentility.

So Nabbes demonstrates that because the basis of the gentry's actions is virtue they are capable of acting responsibly in private without being controlled, and the rest of the play draws the political consequences of this. Artlove is shown drinking with the jeerers. He behaves temperately in an intemperate place ('Thou know'st my temperance doth not oft frequent/These publique places' (p. 46)); when he does drink, it is to Dorothy's health:

> Whose active climbings carry her desires
> To th'utmost height of nobleness and honour. (p. 48)

Similarly, Dorothy will assure her brother that 'without mature consideration/I dare not doe an act; on which depends/Such dangerous events'; and in a subplot her step-mother, tempted to lewdness, replies 'Such [desires] are in me; but not to satisfaction' (pp. 62, 60). This insistence that the gentry can regulate themselves and that the abuse of pleasures, but not their use, needs

suppressing is turned in the tavern scene by one of the jeerers
against a representative of public authority. A magistrate intrudes
to suppress their drinking session but is told

> Sir, we are Gentlemen; and by that *priviledge*[,]
> Though we submit to politique Government
> In publique things[,] may be our owne law-makers
> In morall life. If we offend the law
> The law may punish us; which onely strives
> To take away excesse, not the necessity
> Or use of what's indifferent, and is made
> Or good or bad by'ts use . . .
> Then good Sir, (though you find enormities
> Amongst the rabble) be not so suspitious
> Of our more carefull carriage, that are gentlemen.
>
> (pp. 50–51, my italics)

Such interruptions were actually occurring in Covent Garden,
for Charles was attempting to restrict the number of alehouses
there,[8] and in the following scene the ungentlemanly complimenting vintner mistakes Littleword for a government informer
who supposes that his affected talk of 'kingdoms' and 'commands'
is seditious. But in their retort, the gallants base their defence
both on the responsibility of their behaviour and on the innate
dignity that gentility can claim, its 'privilege'. Such interference
is offensive to their credit as gentlemen, and they warn the
magistrate 'Some busie ones have arrogated much [power];/But
being told their owne have ever since/Given Gentlemen a due
respect' (p. 51). The whole play concludes with a satire on
authority, the local constable and his clerk being 'tried' by two
country clowns whom the gallants raise to be mock-justices. It is
made plain that justices are bribeable, and the heavily ironic
moral is drawn 'that Clownes and fooles be not made Justices in
earnest' (p. 70) – it being implied that of course they are. In
Nabbes's Covent Garden, an independently minded gentry indignantly criticize the rigours of a repressive authority.[9]

Brome's *The Weeding of Covent Garden* (c. 1632–34?),[10] which
argues that 'Wine in it self is good . . . though the excesse be
nought' (p. 61), takes a similar stance to Nabbes's play on the use

and abuse of pleasures. But Covent Garden, a symbol of present disorder and potential good order, raises wider doubts for Brome about the theoretical basis of Charles's personal government. Simonds D'Ewes complained that the proclamation to the gentry was symbolic of the assault that Charles was making on the basic rights of his subjects since it 'took away men's liberties at one blow, constraining them to reside at their own houses, and not permitting them freedom to live where they pleased within the King's dominions'.[11] Brome too perceives what is at stake if the fiat of Charles's single will is capable of restricting so radically the freedoms of many, and his treatment of the issue probes insistently into the justification (and the implications) of the authority by which Charles does these acts.

The play's action is founded on three sets of parallel relationships between fathers and children and a parody version of the same in Captain Driblow and his 'sons', the roistering 'Philoblathici' ('Lovers of the Blade') who, though farcical, have definite roots in the realities of the clubbing circles of Caroline London. This structure focuses attention on the play's main conflicts, which are between parental authority and the children's freedom.

The embodiment of parental authority is Crosswill who, modelled on the Jonsonian humour, is more a mode of behaviour than a character. His humour of *crossness* arises with a paradoxical but serenely inexorable logic from his position of wilful power: he commands his children, on their obedience, not to obey him. As his daughter says, 'he will like nothing, no not those actions which he himself cannot deny they are vertuous; he will crosse us in all we do, as if there were no other way to shew his power over our obedience' (p. 50). Crosswill sees authority simply as power, the dominion of one will over another, and his crossing of his children is a way of establishing the dominance of his authority over them; the most 'arbitrary' thing an arbitrary authority can command is that it should not be obeyed. Conversely, he takes obedience to his will to be a device to limit his own freedom of action: when his daughter offers to accept any husband he will nominate, he exclaims, 'Make me her matchmaker! Must I obey her, or she me, ha? . . . How subtly she seeks dominion over me' (p. 6). Any agreement with Crosswill is thus a challenge to his freedom to have his own independent and wholly singular will. There are two notions encapsulated here: rule by personal will, and the necessary and contradictory arbitrariness of the absolutely supreme authority. Crosswill's wilfulness over his children is a government by conflict rather than love, and this crossness he extends to a principle of action in ordinary life. He enjoys being contradicted and contradicting everyone, even including himself; when alone on stage, his soliloquy concludes, naturally, with him beating himself (p. 77).

Crosswill's humour is at the heart of the play and a key to its meaning and to the significance of all the other forms of rule which are also competing for precedence in Brome's Covent Garden. Legal authority is figured in Cockbrain (one of the parents) who, a latter-day Overdo, disguises himself in order to 'weed' the garden of its enormities. Devoted to an abstract ideal of law, his authority is, like Overdo's, continually undercut by human error. He regards the law almost as personal property, and is motivated as much by pride as by genuine care for the public good, being 'ambitious to be call'd into authority by notice taken of some special service he is able to do the state aforehand' (p. 76). Cockbrain confuses the authority of law with his own private capacities, and he works by interference, provoking crimes as much as discovering them. His methods are so devious he is suspected to be 'some disguiz'd villain' who should be hanged 'presently without examination' (p. 59). Cockbrain's use of law stimulates crime as something it may profit from, just as Crosswill's authority prides itself on the resistance it generates but also rather as Charles's fiscal devices created new categories of offence in order to benefit from the revenue they would automatically yield in fines, in effect profiting from 'the sale of pretended nuisances', as the Grand Remonstrance later complained.[12]

Authority and will are also confused in Crosswill's son, Gabriel, a puritan who judges the lawfulness of things by his inner light. He too subjects what is ideally right to what is pragmatically right for his own purposes, describing how his personal sense of virtue would have authorized him to have taken a sinner and 'smote him, smote him with great force, yea, smote him unto the earth, until he had prayed that the evil might be taken from him' (p. 62). The punishing of sin has become the inflicting of one will onto another; his brother, Mihil, comments, 'This is their way of loving enemies, to beat 'em into goodnesse' (p. 62). Gabriel's idea of law is balanced against that of the anarchic Philoblathici who swear obedience to their own roistering set of rules, laws which command them deliberately to defy legal authorities and commit them to lawlessness. Their motivation too is wilful opposition to other people, and, like the vapourers of *Bartholomew Fair*, they purposely quarrel amongst themselves.

Mihil actually is a law student. However, he uses law to confuse and defraud his creditors, and his father complains he is 'learning a language that I understand not a word of' (p. 23). There is also present the idea of the law of whores who complain of 'the bondage of Authority' and wish for 'that freedome/The famous Curtezans have in *Italy*' (p. 9). Then there are tradesmen who have 'made a Law within your selves to put no trust in Gentlemen' (pp. 20–1), and innkeepers who reckon bills wrongly to demonstrate that 'All's law, I tell you, all's law in Tavernes' (p. 46). Finally, all are ruled by money: 'O thou powerful metal! what authority is in thee! Thou art the Key to all mens mouthes. With thee a man may lock up the jawes of an informer, and without thee he cannot [open] the lips of a lawyer' (p. 28).

The play is episodic and almost plotless, Brome simply setting these various sorts of authority at war with one another, the point being that no one figure can claim any more 'authority' than the next, since the actions of each arise from a narrow personal (and often contradictory) idea of what constitutes law. Brome demonstrates that while each 'law' excludes the claims of the others, each is really alike. For example, the Philoblathici and their polar opposite, Gabriel, meet in Act IV. The origins of each aberration are the same, for Gabriel took to puritanism after his cousin fell to prostitution ('His purity and your disgrace fell on you both about a time, I faith' (p. 66)). And the two sides get on famously. Gabriel mistakes the bawd for 'a Sister or a Matron' and confers 'devoutly' with her (pp. 66–7). The Philoblathici tell him they too are brothers and sisters, and an extended parallel is drawn; they are

as factious as you, though we differ in the Grounds; for you, sir, defie Orders, so do we; you of the Church, we of the Civil Magistrate; many of us speak i'th'nose, as you do; you out of humility of spirit, we by the wantonnesse of the flesh [i.e. because of the ravages of the pox]; now in devotion we go beyond you, for you will not kneel to a ghostly father, and we do to a carnal Mystresse.

(p. 71)

Gabriel joins them readily, declaring 'I'le drink, I'le dance, I'le kisse, or do any thing, any living thing with any of you, that is Brother or Sister' and the roarers respond, 'I vow, thou art a brother after my own heart' (p. 71). By Act V, Gabriel is become a roarer and Mihil, an erstwhile roarer, is a puritan. For all their ostensible differences, all these forms of exclusive authority are alike, each trying to impose their will on the world around them.

Kaufmann reads the play as a Jonsonian attack on extremism of behaviour centring on the antithesis between puritan and libertine.[13] But this instance of extremism is only one in a society ruled by a more pervasive *wilfulness*, and Brome is careful to locate its sources. On several occasions, for example, Crosswill's children get what they want out of him only by pretending that they do not want it, crossing him to make him cross them in return and give what they really want from him. Mihil refuses money from Crosswill who then forces twice the original amount on him, the servant commenting, 'He swears he will try whether you or he shall have his will' (p. 27). Moreover, Crosswill and Cockbrain both date their problems with their children from the time when they opposed a match between them, another instance of arbitrary interference for, as Crosswill says, 'on a sudden he and I both consented to a dislike of the match and broke it, and have both repented it an hundred times since' (p. 77). Rooksbill, the third father, also tries to force his will on his children, by selecting Gabriel (of whom, as a puritan, he approves) for his daughter. When asked if she agrees he replies, 'The same affection governes her [i.e. as does me], she is not mine else' (p. 32). Just as Crosswill's wilfulness causes answering crossness from Mihil, so the other children are reacting to a parental tyranny of will.

Not only has wilfulness among the parents generated the children's wilfulness but, as we have seen in Cockbrain, Crosswill, Gabriel and the Philoblathici, authority and the capricious will have become inextricably mingled. In Covent Garden, authority thrives only where there is wilfulness and disorder. This is clearest with Crosswill who admits his addiction to the confusion of London. Brome introduces a series of noisy tavern cries which Crosswill praises as 'all excellent ill sounds' (p. 33), and although he breaks up a meeting of the Philoblathici he secretly avows he enjoys it, and disrupts it so crossly that the roisterers are 'struck with admiration at the old Blades humour' (p. 75). The contribution to disorder of the wilfulness of authority is pointed up by Captain Driblow, the leader of the Philoblathici, whose authority actively *encourages* his 'sons' to disorder; he is 'that old Ruffian, the Incendiarie, that sets the youthfull bloods on fire here with his Infernal discipline' (p. 92).

It should be becoming clear that the play's topicality (its frequent reference to Charles's social and financial schemes) and Crosswill's humour are intimately interrelated: they are complementary aspects of Brome's analysis of the manner and consequences of Charles's personal government. Cockbrain goes about his weeding of society *In Heavens name and the Kings* (p. 2), while Crosswill's behaviour is the obverse of this interfering paternalism, for he was never 'fully bent' on living in town 'until the Proclamation of restraint spurr'd him up' (p. 19) – his crossness directly answers the crossness of those who govern him. At his trial, Charles was accused of having upheld 'a personal interest of Will, power and pretended prerogative to himself and his family against the public interest, common right, liberty, justice and peace of the people of this nation';[14] *The Weeding of Covent Garden* shows a society in which exactly this is happening, where government has become a simple tyranny of will, imposed without regard to the interest or consent of those governed. In Brome's account of Crosswill's despotism over his children is a protest to Charles about the contradictions inherent in arbitrary rule. Crosswill's wilful government *creates* the resistance of his children, for he needs opposition against which to exert his own will and measure his strength. Moreover, an entirely arbitrary government has already devalued and subverted any authority by which it operates, for where government is at will, authority is reduced to mere naked power: the most authoritative men in Brome's play are those who can shout the loudest, coerce, bully or contradict the greatest number of their fellows. Brome's Covent Garden is full of law of all varieties, but order and authority there is none; and this is the lamentable state of England under Charles's personal rule.

Parental wilfulness is circumvented in the marriages and reconciliations which conclude the play; Crosswill gives over 'wrangling' (p. 95) and a new order seems set to emerge, based on understanding and consent. But Brome has also contrived to suggest that there may be a positive value to Crosswill's humour, which he criticizes less severely than Gabriel's puritanism and Cockbrain's authoritarianism. A further aspect of Crosswill's encouragement of crossness in his children is the independence he wishes them to develop. He would have his daughter responsible for her own marriage, scorning that she should 'be under correction at these yeares' (p. 6); he wishes Mihil to 'learn fashions and manners, that thou mightst carry thy self like a Gentleman' (p. 23); he is offended when Gabriel swings from puritanism into roistering, but comments 'to say truth, this is the better madnesse' (p. 90). There are suggestions here that a certain crossness – a pride and spirited freedom – are essential elements of gentility, to be cultivated and asserted when occasion demands. Crosswill is a symptom of a disordered rule but also implies how the gentry may well respond to it: a repressive and wilful authority is likely to provoke an answering crossness or impatience from those ranks who value most jealously the fundamental liberties which arbitrary government threatens to invade and destroy.

Town and country

In his intelligent and complex play, Brome finds in Covent Garden, the symbol of the new permanent gentry presence (and crossness) in London, an occasion for defending the gentry's developing political character and for making a general critique of the personal rule. In turning to Shirley's town plays we find a society more confident in its own autonomy, and one of Shirley's main aims, consequently, is simply the elucidation of the new codes of manners as they act as internal standards to regulate and censure behaviour. But for Shirley as for Brome, these manners are resonant with political meanings; the problem is that these have been obscured by an obliquity of interpretation, a treatment of Caroline city comedy as largely either post-Jacobean or pre-Restoration. In fact, Shirley's preoccupations and anxieties rest on notions about the shape of society and the whereabouts of its points of tension different from those obtaining in both periods; we will not understand the significance of his comedies until we treat them as characteristically Caroline, and not merely adjunct to but fully distinct from both their predecessors and successors.

To conduct the kind of inquiry he wished for in *The Weeding of Covent Garden*, Brome adopted a deliberately old-fashioned style, playing the severe moralist in the Jonsonian mould, more concerned with humours than manners; his model is obviously *Bartholomew Fair*. Broadly speaking, Jacobean city comedy is moral rather than social, and takes greed and folly for its principal preoccupations; it also evinces little direct interest in the court. The main social antagonism with which it deals is between citizen and gentleman, Money and Land; London means the city, a place of legalism and sharp practice. This polarization did not greatly obsess the dramatists of our period. London in the 1630s implies the Strand, not Cheapside, and the motives to action are less commercial than amorous, so although London comedy is still a serious form, the vices it castigates are promiscuity and pride rather than greed, and its yardstick is civilized behaviour rather than human kindness. Moreover, as we have seen, many playgoers were making connections with the rich merchant classes, and the plays they saw rarely suggested that the city was out to destroy the gentry. I have argued elsewhere[15] that the great apparent exception, Massinger's *The City Madam* (1632) actually proves the rule; Massinger attacks civic avarice and social-climbing but from the standpoint of Sir John Frugal, a dignified citizen of alder-manic rank who associates with and counsels the nobleman, Lord Lacy, yet who is also a thrifty and highly successful businessman. Frugal cures the ladies of his family of pride above their station; nevertheless he still marries one daughter to a gentleman, the other to Lord Lacy's son.

Fletcher's city comedies begin to deal more obviously with London's leisured classes and develop an interest in 'wit' as a social value ('accomplishment' or 'breeding') as opposed to the 'wit' of Middleton's heroes which represents their capacity to swindle. However, his gallants are still footloose and their 'wit' is a nervous reaction, 'a flourish of indifference towards money'[16] and the obligations it brings with it; 'wit' rationalizes their rootlessness in terms of London's competitiveness, providing a weapon against insecurity. In *Wit Without Money* (*c.* 1614) Valentine, even though an elder brother, decides to live in London by his wits and attractively but outrageously parades his contempt of responsibility. His 'wit' converts his sense of displacement into aggression; Fletcher's plays are still largely without much sense of a communal social round such as becomes commonplace for the 1630s. Valentine walks the streets or visits taverns; in *Wit at Several Weapons* (*c.* 1609?) the clown kills time by wandering around 'the new River by Islington, there they shall have me looking upon the Pipes, and whistling'.[17] In Caroline plays people never simply lack anything to do but participate in an established and socially sanctioned Town. So although Shirley depicts 'wits', their *otium* is never, like Valen-tine's, radically at variance with their *negotium*. Caroline London plays continually demand that 'wit' be reconciled with more traditional notions of 'worth', and that it should cease to be the badge only of the *déclassé*.

It is more essential to distinguish Caroline comedy from its counterpart in the 1660s and 1670s because here critics have found the similarities most compelling (even though Shirley was felt to be out of date by 1667).[18] Restoration comedy spoke principally to a metropolitan audience accustoming itself to absenteeism and establishing permanent roots in London, itself rapidly becoming the only centre of political power. The centre of the stage has been taken over by the Town, and the criteria of behaviour have become urbanity and a cultivated and detached civility. 'Wit' has developed into an electric, sophisticated and sardonic mode of discourse entirely unlike anything in the 1630s (the nearest equivalent is the compliment, always regarded suspiciously by Caroline dramatists),[19] and marriage and romantic love are treated realistically and sceptically, perhaps fully for the first time. Clearly much has changed – including the attitudes to society and politics.

The precedence of the town in the 1660s and 1670s is established by a continual comparison with country dullness. This issue is examined most searchingly in Wycherley's *The Country Wife* (1675) in which, although the value of Margery Pinchwife's rural 'naturalness' is plain, her husband's error is to take it for something which is antithetical to the habits of the town. Her innocence exerts no positive pressure at all; it is simply lack of experience, and she quickly discovers it is as 'natural' for herself to prefer the town to the country as it is for any more sophisticated person ('how shou'd I help it, Sister').[20] 'Nature' is everywhere outraged in *The Country Wife*, but as a prescriptive system of value it hardly exists. Rather, in Wycherley's Hobbesian human zoo men are 'naturally' predatory and pleasure-seeking, just as it is 'natural' for jealous husbands, like Pinchwife, to be cuckolded. Ironically, it is the town which best fulfils these conditions, and is witty man's 'state of nature'. In Etherege's plays, the country is similarly a place of dullness or sterility, the 'Wildness' of the heroine of *The Man of Mode* (1676)[21] is exactly that quality which allies her with the town against the country. Any suggestion that the town fulfils man's 'nature' or represents the sum of experience in this way is wholly alien to the 1630s.

Alongside this devaluation of the country is a shift in the political position of the town. The Cavalier–puritan polarity absent from the 1630s is much in evidence in the 1660s and 1670s. A main butt of Etherege's seminal comedy *The Comical Revenge* (1664) is '*Sir Nich'las Culley*, one whom *Oliver*, for the transcendent knavery and disloyalty of his Father, has dishonour'd with Knight-hood' and who therefore is allowed no serious qualities; the hero, Bruce, is a loyal Cavalier who has to vindicate himself from puritan slanders ('Look on your Friend; your drooping Country view;/And think how much they both expect from you').[22] The tendency of these comedies, even within a single play, to over- and under-seriousness reflects the self-images towards which the exiled courtiers were forced in the Interregnum, either heroic Prince Ruperts or debauched devil-may-cares. In Dryden's *Marriage-à-la-Mode* (1672), and many like it, the play world simply splits into two contrasting halves, one prose, one verse, which coexist yet barely interact except as versions of these extreme, alternating mentalities. The place of the town in this is quite evident. Sedley's *The Mulberry Garden* (1668) opens with an apparently objective debate on the freedom of town pleasures, recalling similar discussions in Caroline comedies, but its seriousness is suddenly undermined when the critic of the town is revealed as a puritan and hence a killjoy who in the overplot prevents his daughter from wedding a heroic Cavalier loyal to the exiled king. Throughout the play the puritan is satirized and humiliated, and the success of true love is signalled by the return of Charles II and the vindication of loyalty and the gaiety of the town. A comparable re-alignment is observable in more serious drama too.[23]

Evidently the experiences of 1642–60 have undermined the Town's independence and forced it into a close association with the court and into opposition to city, country and puritanism of any brand. Dryden formulated his criticisms of the drama of the previous age precisely in terms of its lack of courtliness. Accusing Jonson of 'meanness of thought', he complained that the wit of his contemporaries

was not that of gentlemen; there was ever somewhat that was ill-bred and clownish in it, and which confessed the conversation of the authors . . . In the age wherein these poets lived, there was less of gallantry than in ours; neither did they keep the best company of theirs . . . I cannot find that any of them were conversant in courts, except Ben Jonson: and his genius lay not so much that way as to make an improvement by it . . .

The present (1672) refinement he ascribed to the influence of 'the Court: and, in it, particularly to the King, whose example gives a law to it'; later (1679) he attacked Fletcher for allowing kings who were not usurpers to appear bad, and for failing to provide 'those royal marks which ought to appear in a lawful successor of the throne'.[24] There is a unity of artistic and political outlook here in which a dislike of 'lowness' in art reinforces a rejection of ungentlemanly behaviour in politics, and specifically of 'country' distrust of and opposition to the king. The dramatic equivalents of Dryden's precepts are Lady Woodvill in *The Man of Mode* (she being an absurd 'admirer of the Forms and Civility of the last Age') and Old Bellair whose ridiculous rustic obstinacy ('go, bid her dance no more, it don't become her, it don't become her, tell her I say so; a Dod I love her') is a deft parody of the deliberate stubbornness associated with the political idea of the 'country';[25] sixty years later, Chesterfield was quite certain about what the involvement of the Restoration dramatists with the court had meant for the political attitudes they had expressed.[26] It is this narrow courtliness in politics which it is tempting, but most misleading, to read back into the Town plays of the 1630s. These are the attitudes of a society purposefully retreating from serious political engagement, not of one moving towards it.

In several Caroline plays, the country is indeed ridiculed in a figure who has come to London and failed to reproduce society's good manners. However, the social pretender is always satirized not for his *rusticity* but for his *lowness* and his attempt to clamber into a higher rank than he deserves. In Shirley's *The Changes* (1632; pub. London, 1632) a country knight, Simple, finally returns to the provinces to sell his servant his 'Knighthood for halfe the mony it cost me, and turne Yeoman in the country agen' (p. 69). In *The Constant Maid* (c. 1637; pub. London, 1640), Startup, claiming gentility, admits 'my father was/A Yeoman . . . my Grandfather was a Nobleman['s] Foot-man, and indeed he [ran] his countrey; my father did outrun the Constable' (sig.C2ᵛ);

he is contrasted with the dignified figure of a countryman whose daughter he has wronged. Other figures abused for their lack of gentility rather than urbanity are Brome's Tim Hoyden (in *The Sparagus Garden*, 1635) and Cavendish's Simpleton (in *The Variety*, c. 1641–42), the latter's attempted rape of the play's heroine making him a most undesirable character. The attitudes are social and moral, not anti-rural; rather, this feeling that rank ought to be answerable to a standard of worth seems to me to be a characteristically 'country' conviction.

I have been suggesting that the roots of Caroline high society were still firmly linked to the provinces, and the instinctive sympathy of Caroline city comedies (and Shirley's in particular) for the outlook and attitudes of the country is a feature which significantly distinguishes them from their Restoration successors. This sympathy is made explicit in Shirley's *The Witty Fair One* (London, 1633), written shortly before our main period (1628). The heroine's social placing is very carefully detailed:

> Her Father is a man who though he write
> Himselfe but Knight, keepes a warme house i'the Countrey
> 'Mongst his Tenants, takes no Lordly pride
> To trauell with a Footman and a Page
> To *London*, humbly rides th old fashion
> With halfe a douzen wholesome Liueries,
> To whom he gives Christian wages and not countenance
> Alone to liue on, can spend by th'yeare
> Eight hundred pounds, and put vp fine sleepes quietly
> Without dreaming on Morgages or Statutes
> Or such like curses on his Land, can number
> May be ten thousand pound in ready coyne
> Of's own, yet neuer bought an office for't
> Ha's plate no question, and Iewels too
> In's old Ladies cabinet, beside
> Other things worth an Inuentory, and all this
> His daughter is an heyre to . . .   (sig.B3^r)

Sir George Richley, described here, typifies the traditional country values – conservative, hospitable, plain yet wealthy, knowing his place yet independent of the court ('never bought an office'), and he is contrasted with the foolish Sir Nicholas Treedle who lacks love for his servants, pursues foreign fashions and is 'a Knight & no Gentleman' (sig.K1ᵛ). Although Richley opposes his daughter's match, the play exhibits considerable respect for the attitudes represented in this speech. The best characters are shown acting in a magnanimous, dignified manner, and their generous language matches their deeds. Typical are the scenes in which Richley's daughter's suitor is counselled by her uncle, or in which the subsidiary heroine is aided by two anonymous gentlemen to reform her rakish suitor:

> 2 GENTLEMAN.   Gentle Lady
>   And if it prove fortunate, the designe
>   Will be your honour, and the deed it selfe
>   Reward us in his benefit, he was ever wilde
> 1 GENTLEMAN. Assured your ends are noble, we are happy in'[t].
> (sigs.I2ʳ⁻ᵛ)

The play is permeated with the values and speech of a gentry class moving to London yet conscious of its traditional duties of courtesy and responsibility, and this feeling for 'country' values continually recurs in London plays of the 1630s. For example, Shirley's *Constant Maid* opens with the hero bidding a sad farewell to the family retainers he can no longer support, one of whom refuses to leave him; and in Thomas May's *The Old Couple* (1636), the Jacobean city comedy motifs of usury and avarice have been imposed, with little sense of incongruity, on a story set amongst country gentry and emphasizing values of charity and neighbourliness.

Another feature distinguishing Caroline from Restoration comedy is that in the former the Town is not the only centre of attention, but the other localities of the realm are invoked besides and the behaviour of the metropolis is measured against them. The completest example is, again, Shirley's *Constant Maid* whose hero, we have seen, has a country background and who, at the nadir of his fortunes, leaves the town for the fields. The city is present in a usurer, Hornet, who opposes his daughter's marriage, and the court is represented in burlesque by a group of servants who dress up as courtiers to help fool Hornet out of his daughter. So although the town gallants triumph, the town is placed against

a broad context of all the estates of the realm in a manner quite
unlike Restoration comedy. In the ease with which the tyrannous
Hornet is deceived by the fake courtiers' talk of monopolies and
projects (and in his readiness to threaten the gallants with a
prosecution in Star Chamber), Shirley seems to be associating
city and court together as both unattractive and avaricious,
whereas the gallants, with their dignity and resistance to parental
attempts to force their affections, adopt a 'country' outspokenness
and respect for free judgment and action. For example, one of
the girls resists her mother's oppression indignantly:

> Though in imagination [i.e. in thought] I allow you
> The greatest woman in the earth, whose frowne
> Could kill . . . I durst tell you
> Though all your terrours were prepared to punish
> My bold defence; you were a tyrant . . .
> My soul's above your tyranny, and would
> From torturing flame, receive new fire of love.   (sigs.G1^{r-v})

Although in comedy parents traditionally oppose lovers' freedoms, the violence of this retort and its language of 'tyranny'
(and the girl's insistence on her essential obedience and willing-
ness to submit despite her speaking her mind) seem to me wholly
characteristic of the tone of this drama with its instinctive feeling
for the gentry's inviolable dignity and for the freedom due to
their 'place'. This 'country' sense of *place* derives from the
gentry's identity as the principal propertied class; it both defines
their social position, and protects their independence from the
encroachments of other ranks.

Country gentry in town, such as Sir Humphrey Mildmay and
Sir Edward Dering, would have felt much sympathy with these
characters on the Caroline stage, and much continuity exists
between the respect for gentility, responsibility and worth in
these plays and the sentiments which are commonplace in the
memoirs, letters and notebooks preserved by such people as Sir
George Sondes, Sir John Oglander, the Verneys of Buckingham-
shire and Oxindens of Kent, men deeply conscious of the
traditions and responsibilities the ownership of land confers.
Although this serious aspect of Caroline comedy has been

dismissed by critics as an anticipation of Augustan sentimentality, or as 'dubious grace',[27] it is something that runs very deep in this period. It also carries a considerable political charge. There is, for instance, much common ground between the distaste for parental tyranny in *The Constant Maid* and the reflections on 'political nobilitie' made by the Kent gentleman Henry Oxinden. Oxinden felt that the aristocracy should be esteemed according to their behaviour, not their titles:[28]

The knowledge and consideration whereof hath caused mee not to value anie man by having anie inward respect or conceite of him beefore another, beecause he excells in degrees of honour, but according to the concomitant ornaments, as vertue, riches, wisdom, power etc. etc.

If I see a man of what low degree or quality soever that is vertuous, rich, wise or powerful, him will I preferre beefore the greatest Lord in the kingdome that comes short of him in these . . .

The implications for the political attitudes of the Caroline gentry of this respect for traditional dignities and valuation of virtue above title are worked out most fully in Shirley's two major comedies.

Town and court

Shirley's *The Lady of Pleasure* (1635; pub. London, 1637) opens with an attack by Sir Thomas Bornwell (and his steward) on the extravagance of his wife, Aretina, which is destroying their wealth in the country, and the play is often read as if it were a moralistic rejection of the behaviour of the town from the point of view of a rural society outraged and threatened by it. Shirley's opening, though, must be balanced against the scene in the second act in which Bornwell visits the other 'lady of pleasure', Celestina, apparently also to 'test' her behaviour in town. After acting towards her in the bawdy manner of the gallants with whom his own wife consorts, he finds that her manners are not a blind for lascivious or over-liberal behaviour but a reflection of her true, virtuous nature, and he apologizes to her and praises her innocence. The scene acts as a norm of social behaviour which Shirley admires, and thereafter Bornwell associates with the 'good' lady of pleasure rather than with Aretina, in order to cure the latter's misbehaviour. Bornwell and Celestina are two prongs in one argument – country attack of the town's excess, and an example of what it should be. The play parallels the careers of Celestina and Aretina, demonstrating in the former that the achievement of a social code enshrines positive values and enables free social intercourse by defining its limits, and attacking in the latter those who misuse the social codes for ambition and lasciviousness.[29]

The main force of the Aretina plot is moral. Shirley attacks fashionable ladies for whom manners contradict morality ('Praying's forgot./'Tis out of fashion' (sig.C1ᵛ)), and the plot culminates with Aretina's reawakening to virtue as she realizes the degeneracy of her lover and her nephew (whose attempted rape of her is the fruit of the fashionable dissipation to which she has encouraged him). But this moral failure is related in the first scene to a political failure. Aretina's extravagance is an attempt to make her household like the court, and she encourages her husband to use his wealth to procure offices:

> A narrow minded husband is a theefe
> To his owne fame, and his preferment too,
> He shuts his parts and fortunes from the world
> While from the popular vote and knowledge men
> Rise to imployment in the state.
>   BORNWELL. I have
> No great ambition to buy preferment
> At so deare rate.   (sig.B3ʳ)

'Deare' here implies expense to the pocket and to honour. Aretina is (quite literally) prostituting herself to the court, and Bornwell responds to this as to a subversion of his 'gentry' integrity. Her court-centred attitudes are realized in her language, for she justifies her actions, as Charles his prerogative rule, on the grounds of 'privilege':

> I finde you would intrench and wound the liberty
> I was borne with, were my desires unpriviledged
> By example . . .
> You ought not to oppose.   (sig.B3ʳ)

With this 'privilege' she subordinates Bornwell's freedom, keeping him in awe of her 'kinsmen great and powerfull,/It'h State', and he admits that if she does not have her will 'the house [will] be shooke with names/Of all her kindred, tis a servitude,/I may in time shake off' (sigs.B2^r, B3^v). Her extravagance is related to court tyranny; Bornwell complains she makes gaming 'Not a Pastime but a tyrannie, and vexe/Your selfe and my estate by't' (sig.B2^v). This distinction between court and town has been obscured by critics who have persistently referred to Sir Thomas Bornwell as 'Lord Bornwell'. There is, though, a clear correlation between Aretina's behaviour and her desertion to the court; she offends against the values of the town gentry morally, economically and politically.

Whereas Aretina's steward criticizes her expenditure, Celestina's questions her morals:

> tis not for
> My profit, that I manage your estate,
> And save expence, but for your honour Madam.
> CELESTINA. How sir, my honour? STEWARD. Though you heare it not
> Mens toungues are liberall in your character,
> Since you began to live thus high, I know
> Your fame is precious to you. (sigs.C2$^{r–v}$)

The steward's suspicions reflect on his baseness, not Celestina's, and she strikes him for them. Such criticisms the play's action shows to be false, for Celestina is a town lady whose expense is the true image of her 'generosity' – both her financial openness and her dignified gentility (the word derives from *generosus*, meaning 'of high birth'). It does not compromise her modesty but marks the freedom proper to her 'place'; she and her women are resolved to possess

> Our pleasure with security of our honour,
> And that preservd, I welcome all the joyes
> My fancy can let in. (sig.D3^r)

So although Celestina resists Bornwell's temptations, she rebukes one of her women for not freely returning a courteous kiss that she is given. Liberality is thus the outward sign of inner gentility, and suited to her social position. She is not, then, overbearing like Aretina, but her freedom is precisely that natural behaviour proper to a gentlewoman. She reverses Aretina's position, establishing herself in opposition to, not emulation of, the court; she will

> Be hospitable then, and spare no cost
> That may engage all *generous* report
> To trumpet forth my bounty and my braverie,
> Till the Court envie, and remove . . .   (sig.C2ᵛ, my italics)

Whereas the ridiculousness of the courtiers with whom Aretina consorts exposes them, Celestina herself satirizes the worthlessness of those who visit her. One she slyly guesses is a courtier 'by your confidence' (sig.C2ᵛ); another she characterizes as

> a wanton emissarie
> Or scout for *Venus* wild [fowl], which made tame
> He thinkes no shame to stand court centinell,
> In hope of the reversion.   (sigs.D3ʳ⁻ᵛ)

This implicit friction between court and town becomes explicit in the fourth act in which Celestina undergoes a test of courtesy with an unnamed lord.

The great court lord who is thrown Celestina's way is a platonic in love after the manner fashionable at Henrietta Maria's Whitehall in mid decade. When he first appears, he is professing an elaborate and rather pompous fidelity to a dead mistress, Bella Maria: he boasts of having 'a heart, 'bove all licentious flame' and of having loved Bella Maria for her beauty rather than her person, so that he claims now not merely to be mourning her loss but still to be in love with her 'Idea' as his 'Saint' (sigs.E4ʳ⁻ᵛ, I4ʳ). Celestina 'tests' the lord rather as Bornwell tested her and is pleased to find at first that his professions are matched by a real purity, and are not a merely fashionable courtly pose:

> Nor will I thinke these noble thoughts grew first
> From melancholy, for some femall losse,
> As the phantasticke world beleeves, but from
> Truth, and your love of Innocence . . .   (sig.H4ʳ)

However, in the final act he reverses his position and succumbs to Celestina's charms. As base as her steward, he now supposes that her personal openness indicates she has lascivious intentions like Aretina's:

> These widowes are so full of circumstance,
> Ile undertake in this time I ha courted
> Your Ladiship for the toy, to ha broken ten,
> Nay twenty colts, Virgins I meane, and taught em
> The amble, or what pace I most affected.   (sig.K1ʳ)

He now disowns his earlier constancy as 'A noble folly' and offers her instead a platonic love that really is, like Aretina's manners, only the superficies of respectability, a mask for looser practices ('Your sexe doth hold it no dishonour/To become Mistris to a noble servant/In the now court, Platonicke way' (sig.I4ᵛ)). He goes on to woo her with an elaborate flowery speech, perhaps intended to recall the language of Davenant's platonic plays. Celestina only regains him for virtue by narrating an exemplary fable about a social upstart who tried to purchase honour equivalent to his, implying his honour is worth no more than bought honour if not matched with personal integrity. Thus the town corrects the court, its virtue being shown to have a more solid foundation than the artificialities of courtly platonism, and Celestina's moral point is underlined (in a manner typical of Shirley) in the action immediately following in which a minor courtier defends his gentility honourably and exposes the lack of gentility of another, merely fashionable, courtier (sigs.K1ᵛ–2ʳ).

The lord's tactics are also tyrannous, like Aretina's. He appeals to his status, expecting that his position at court can validate his behaviour:

> consider
> Who tis that pleades to you, my birth, and present
> Value can be no stain to your embrace . . .   (sig.I4ᵛ)

Celestina admits that 'gay men have a priviledge', but warns the lord that by presuming on this privilege 'you doe forget/Your selfe and me' (sigs.K1ʳ⁻ᵛ). That is to say, in respecting the lord's privilege, she expects an answering respect for *her* privilege: the system of 'privilege' defines the freedom of behaviour appropriate to every rank within that system but its operation demands that the 'privilege' of each rank is as inviolable as that of the next. By assuming that because his privilege is courtly it is in some way superior to Celestina's, the lord invades and destroys her privilege – in the language of opposition to Charles, it is an *encroachment* on her rights. This too is the burden of the fable Celestina instructs the lord in, that the attempt of the parvenu to purchase honour like the lord's renders the system within which it operates meaningless and destroys the very basis of that honour. Privilege and honour are forces which determine social boundaries, but cannot be used to override them for that would turn them against themselves; the sanction of society's values, they are not strategies to exceed them. By disrespecting Celestina's privilege and resorting to *tyranny* the lord has destroyed the guarantee of his own freedom, the privilege which protects his rights as well as hers.

Clearly, this incident, and the fable with which Celestina corrects the lord, have far-reaching social and political implications. It is not merely that the lord is using the authority of his 'honour' dishonourably, but Celestina's rebuke reaches out impressively to imply a wide social system of checks and balances in which each man respects the freedom and integrity of those around him and in which the respect he can command is a guarantee of his own freedom. It is a mature, comprehensive picture of the workings of society, depending for its dynamic on the gentry sense of one's 'place', a position in which one can act and speak freely without encroaching on the freedoms of others. This has obvious continuities with the attitudes of Charles's critics in parliament whose anxiety for their liberty of life and person was bound up with a concern for their property rights, the security of the possession of their goods from court encroachment. Denzil Holles complained in 1641 that Charles's judges 'have removed our land marks, have taken away the bound stones of the Propriety of the subject, have left no *meum* and *tuum*; but he that had most might had most right and the law was sure to be of his side'.[30] Celestina, arguing that the privilege which gives the lord his freedom does not sanction his attempt to override her freedom, is anticipating Holles's argument.

Celestina's free speaking here is also a form of resistance to the court's centralizing tendencies. Her answer of course attacks the lord's notion that his status enables him to arbitrate all moral value according to his uncontrolled will. But on a different level, she is replying to the extremely flowery platonizing speech with which he tries to tempt her. It is a long, over-poetic description of the delights she can expect in his paradise of love, and she parodies it as 'linsey woolsie, to no purpose' (sig.K1ʳ). But it does have a purpose – to overwhelm her resistance with a catalogue of sensual delights, subjugating her with a stream of all varieties of pleasure. Just as the court laid claim to a monopoly of authority, this speech shows the lord claiming a monopoly of experience, destroying value (and Celestina's freedom to act morally) by invoking all value. This is a common *topos* with Shirley. In *The Example* (1634; pub. London, 1637), Lord Fitzavarice (whose name suggests the economic encroachments which parallel his moral encroachments) tries to overwhelm the wife of an absent gentleman with extravagant poetry:

> consent, deere Ladie, to
> Be mine, and thou shat tast more happinesse,
> Then womans fierce ambition can persue;
> Shift more delights, then the warme-spring can boast
> Varietie of leaves, or wealthie harvest
> Graine from the teeming earth. Joy shall dry all
> Thy teares, and take his throne up, in thy eies,
> Where it shall sit, and blesse what e're they shine on.
> The night shall Sowe her pleasures in thy bosome,
> And morning shall rise only to salute thee.   (sig.D1ʳ)

Fitzavarice's expressions suggest he can control all experience and hence all value, a monopoly of authority which destroys discrimination (his creature, Confident – Shirley's typical name for a courtier – claims that to inquire 'The meaning of a Jewell, sent by a Lord,/ ...'tis a thing/At Court, is not in fashion' (sig.A4ᵛ)). The tempted gentlewoman heroically resists this sensual assault:

> not your estate,
> Though multiplied to Kingdomes, and those wasted

With your invention, to serue my pleasures,
Have power to bribe my life away from him,
To whose use I am bid to weare it . . .
Ile rather choose to die
Poore wife to *Peregrine*, then live a Kings
Inglorious strumpet

(sigs.D1^{r-v})

Shirley presents us again with another gentlewoman preserving her moral independence against a courtier who claims to control all value.[31] The blasphemous echoes in his speech ('Joy shall dry all/Thy teares . . .') recall the assertions that were being made about Charles's divinity in court masques, and in *Love's Cruelty* (1631) an explicit link is made by the courtier Hippolito who, instructed by the duke to seduce a gentlewoman for him, once more embarks on such another speech of the rapturous delights of the court which culminates in a description of the scenic wonders of Jonson's masque *Neptune's Triumph* (1624). Here Shirley penetrates to the heart of the court's ethos. The masque, a symbol of the king's power, shows all nature subjected to him and obedient to his magical will as the scenes range over all times and places. The masque is thus the highest expression of the court's imperialism,[32] making the king the lord of all possible experience and value, and it is this imperialism with which Shirley's courtiers try to tyrannize Celestina and her counterparts.

This pattern, in which the town criticizes and restrains the court's monopolizing tendencies, underlies all Shirley's major city plays with the exception of *The Gamester* (1633) which, significantly, he wrote specifically for court performance. It can be found in *Hyde Park*, *The Example*, the collaborative play *The Country Captain* (c. 1641) and, in modified form, *The Constant Maid*.[33] *The Ball* (1632) seems to follow the pattern, but it is ambiguous because of the alterations Shirley was forced, by court interference, to make in the play. One would dearly like to know more about those people 'personated so naturally, both of lords and others of the court' that Sir Henry Herbert insisted Shirley cut out.[34] Evidently the pattern represents for Shirley something very basic and challenging about the town's position in the social structure; nevertheless, he does not offer to present the town as replacing the court but balancing it, and modifying its excesses. The pattern shows the court being restrained from usurping the centre of value but equally prevents the town from doing the same (and in this Shirley's plays are typical of the broad perspective characteristic of Caroline city comedy in general). While Celestina's cautionary fable criticizes the court's misuse of its status, she has no quarrel with the system that grants it its privilege. She is not so much attacking the court as defending the *status quo* (the system of honour) which is unbalanced by the lord's exceeding of his place. The lord's failure to match his 'worth' to his 'status' (the two ideas suggested by 'honour') disrupts and nullifies the system; Celestina's riposte suggests that the system is prescriptive and that, to deserve his status, the lord must recognize the responsibilities, as well as the privileges, that it confers (this is the same argument that seemed so ineffective when advanced in Shirley's *The Duke's Mistress* (chapter 3 above). An admonition to the court to fulfil its proper social/political role carries a different pressure depending on the context in which it is made; the court's and town's conceptions of this role would not have been identical.)

It was exactly such a notion of a balanced system, the members of which sustain and restrain each other, to which the parliamentary leaders frequently appealed in defence of the rights which Charles's government seemed increasingly to be eroding. Pym argued in 1628 that the constitution was one of finely balanced 'mutual relation and intercourse'; the 'form of government is that which doth actuate and dispose every part and member of the state to the common good; and as those parts give strength and ornament to the whole, so they receive from it again strength and protection in their several stations and degrees'. If these degrees are exceeded, 'there should remain no more industry, no more justice, no more courage; for who will contend, who will endanger himself for that which is not his own?' Clarendon similarly urged in 1641 that if either king or parliament tried to increase its dominance, it hurt the very basis of its power: 'if the least branch of the prerogative was torn off, or parted with, the subject suffered by it, and . . . his right was impaired: and he [Clarendon] was as much troubled when the crown exceeded its just limits, and thought its prerogative hurt by it'. In 1647 his solution was that 'the frame and constitution of the Kingdom [should] be observed, and the known laws and bounds between the King's power and the Subjects' right'.[35] These are the constitutionalist sentiments of a gentry class concerned for the survival of their interests and wishing for reform but reluctant to provoke social revolution in the process. Similarly, Shirley reforms his stage-courtiers, but then puts his trust in their future good faith. In *The Example*, Fitzavarice is rebuked in the third act, and thereafter acts in a wholly noble way, even being allowed to defend his honour in a duel. He ends taking to wife the heroine's sister (though 'not for any titles' but 'for [his] noble nature' (sig.I2ᵛ)). Once he acknowledges the responsibilities lying on him, he resumes his place in a properly reformed world, in which the checks and balances inherent in the system will ensure its just operation. Both court and gentry have their *place* in this order; but the gentry maintain their freedom and dignity by reminding the courtiers that they will only receive their dignity – their *place* – by respecting the dignity – the *place* – of others. 'Respect' and 'restraint' are the forces that bind together, and simultaneously distinguish, the various components of this society.

Shirley's completest account of this harmoniously balanced society is drawn in that beautifully achieved play *Hyde Park* (1632; pub. London, 1637).[36] The action follows three parallel courtships of three ladies, the spirited Carol, her suitor Fairfield's sister Julietta, and Mrs Bonavent, a merchant's wife and, supposedly, his widow. The Julietta plot presents another gentry–courtier contrast. Julietta is tested by her gallant, the aptly named Trier, who exposes her to the dubious attentions of Lord Bonvile, having secretly assured Bonvile she is a courtesan. Her innocent openness to Bonvile is based on her understanding that her integrity will be protected by the social forms, giving Bonvile all respect since

> It is my duty, where the king has seal'd
> His favours, I should shew humility
> My best obedience to his act. (sig.H4ᵛ)

The credit she allows Bonvile is that which answers his social position ('There's nothing in the verge of my command/That should not serve your Lordship' (sig.E2ʳ)), and she refuses to probe the sincerity of his behaviour for he is 'one it becomes not me to censure' (sig.E3ʳ). Such respectful, dignified language matches her ideal of civil, generous behaviour and clearly she expects Bonvile will treat her respectfully in return. But he is full of ambiguous compliments. Where her language has been that of 'plaine humilitie', his is dark, leading her to protest 'Ile not beleeve my Lord you meane so wantonly/As you professe' (sigs.E2ʳ ᵛ). In fact, he wishes simply to violate the proper boundaries of social place which her careful language acknowledges. Quite literally, he would approach her too closely:

> LORD. Come, that [word] humble was
> But complement in you too.
> JULIETTA. I wood not
> Be guilty of dissembling with your Lordship,
> I know [no] words have more proportion
> With my distance to your birth and fortune,
> Then humble servant.
> LORD. I doe not love these distances. (sig.C2ʳ[=D2ʳ])

Julietta's faith in the protecting system of decorum is thus rendered useless by the lord who does not recognize the constraints of that system. He is another tyrannizing courtier, expecting absolute deference from all ranks beneath him (when Julietta offers her 'best obedience', he says, 'So should/All hansome women that will be good subjects' (sig.H4ᵛ)). In a short episode after this initial seduction scene, Bonvile's page tries to rape Julietta's woman, spurred on by his master's example, Shirley implying that Bonvile's contempt for decorum causes similar disruption at all levels, and threatens the whole basis of society's order.

The plot culminates with another rebuking scene. Julietta tells Bonvile his disrespect for her dignity destroys his own dignity, and that true status is dependent on the hierarchy of virtue to which he, as much as any man, must submit:

> this addition
> Of vertue is above all shine of State,
> And will draw more admirers . . .
> Were every petty Mannor you possesse
> A Kingdome, and the bloud of many Princes
> Vnited in your veynes, with these had you
> A person that had more attraction
> Then Poesie can furnish, love withall,
> Yet I, I in such infinite distance am
> As much above you in my innocence.   (sig.I1ʳ)

Julietta's defiant assertion echoes Henry Oxinden's regard for virtue above degree (p. 166 above). In her, the town criticizes the court from a standpoint of independent, disinterested judgment, while still reserving its essential duty ('Tis the first libertie/I ever tooke to speake my selfe' (sig.I1ʳ)), and desiring to see the order reformed, rather than overturned (Julietta admonishes Bonvile, 'Live my Lord to be/Your Countries honour and support' (sig.I1ʳ)). On the last page, Bonvile has his place and Julietta's respect, but it is based on his answering respect for her virtue, and, one feels, for the town's.

By contrast, Trier has been rejected as a suitable husband for her. His behaviour has travestied gentility. He has degraded her before Bonvile, and by thinking her virtue needed testing, he has shown his own baseness and lost her respect (Lord Bonvile rebukes him, 'Oh fie *Franke*, practice jealousie so soone,/Distrust the truth of her thou lov'st[?] suspect/Thy owne heart sooner' (sig.I3ᵛ)). He assents to the moral and social view of the unreformed Bonvile, allowing that 'his honour/May priviledge more sinnes' (sig.B2ᵛ). Having degraded Julietta he degrades himself before Bonvile, using the very basest compliments:

> TRIER. If [you] knew Lady, what
> Perfection of honour dwels in him,
> You would be studious with all ceremony
> To entertaine him! beside, to me
> His Lordship's goodnes hath so flow'd, you cannot
> Study, what will oblige more then in his welcome!
> LORD. Come, you Complement!   (sig.C1ᵛ)

Of course he compliments! Not only is he being insincere and putting place above worth, he is compromising the integrity of the town as Aretina had done, making it a place of courtship rather than of true judgment.

This association of insincerity with ungentility is related to the play's main antithesis between nature and chance. Trier belongs with the other characters who are only game-players, uncommitted to anything but fortune, and seeing courtship only as an amusement to be dabbled in. In the first scene, Carol's suitors approach courtship as a game in which one will defeat the others; the widow's suitor sees her as a business venture, a 'voyage' he makes, or a 'bond' to be cashed (sig.B1^r). The supreme gamester, Carol, uses games to avoid commitment. Her freeness allies her with court rather than town, for it involves a tyranny of personal will:

> Keepe him [a lover] still to be your servant,
> Imitate me . . . I
> Dispose my frownes, and favours like a Princesse
> Deject, advance, undo, create againe
> It keepes the subjects in obedience,
> And teaches em to looke at me with distance. (sig.C3^v)

The play shows her learning to put aside wilfulness, relinquishing games for a serious personal relationship. The mere gamesters and complimenters are rejected and 'nature' is allowed to triumph. Carol describes flattery of a mistress or a lord as offensive to man's 'natural' dignity:

> You neglect
> Your selves, the Nobleness of your birth and nature
> By servile flattery of this jigging,
> And that coy Mistresse[.] Keepe your priviledge
> Your Masculine property.
> FAIRFIELD. Is there
> So great a happinesse in nature! (sig.C2^r)

This speech recommends an idea of *natural* 'privilege', man's freedom to be his dignified self, and the term 'property' here is close to Denzil Holles's notion of 'propriety' (p. 171 above), meaning that which is *proper* to each man, his by right of possession (with all its attendant political suggestions). Similarly, in the horse-racing and betting scenes of Act IV, Bonvile attributes his success to his belief in nature, not chance ('Won, won, I knew by instinct,/The mare would put some trick upon him' (sig.G4^v)). In the third plot, the return of the widow's husband comes as the restoration of a deeper, natural order:

> Welcome to life agen, I see a providence
> In this, and I obey it. (sig.K1^r)

This sense of nature taking over is clearest in the bird calls of the central scenes. Nature greets the winners with the nightingale, the losers with the cuckoo, endorsing those who have chosen a respectful, responsible mode of loving, and in whom outward status is matched by nobility of mind.

It is thus in the park itself that man's natural condition – 'the Nobleness...of birth and nature' to which Carol refers – can be most fully realized. Hyde Park, a green world in urban London, is both country and town, nature and art. It is a cultivated nature, expressing the dual character (of town and country) of the gentry who frequent it and who are 'cultivating' themselves. The agents of this cultivation are 'good manners', also simultaneously artificial yet natural to those for whom courteous deportment reflects inner respectfulness. The park is both the natural environment of this gentry and a symbol of their values, for enshrined in the manners of this high society are the ideals of decorum and balance, social and moral distance, which Julietta brings to bear against Bonvile. In Hyde Park and high society, England's political character is harmonized, for here the court and the country are brought into a mutually respectful, mutually beneficial relationship. [37]

So in exploring the manners of London's developing fashionable world, Shirley's city comedies are also concerned with the moral attitudes they protect and the political adjustments they make possible; the three are inextricably mixed, and the purely social ideal of respect acts as a key to the relationships which Shirley, and the genteel audience he addresses, would see obtaining between the political entities of court and country, nobleman and gentleman. Although this reinforces the structure of the system as Shirley finds it, it leaves the gentry in the key position in that structure, for it is precisely they, with their 'country' sense of responsibility and place, who are most aware when 'place' is being exceeded and may best act as the arbiters of this hierarchy of deference. Court and country do not exist in isolation, for each term implies the other; but it is the gentry, and their developing town midway between the two, who see themselves as reconciling and balancing the various constituents of the political nation.

There is a suggestively proto-Whiggish admixture in these plays of fashionable London life which makes them ideal vehicles for expressing the outlook of a landed but discontented class. The gentry (broadly speaking) may increasingly have felt politically excluded, yet nevertheless they were well and firmly entrenched socially and in so far as they can be said to have desired revolution, it was only revolution in their favour – change taking place within careful limits, and governed by a respect for traditional and constitutional forms and principles. I have tried to show that the admiration which distinctively marks these plays for balance and 'propriety' in manners and politics arises from a feeling for the sacredness of 'property' – a concern for secure enjoyment of one's liberties, protected by customary restraints from the depradations of arbitrary and irresponsible powers.[38] But not only the landed interest was spoken for from the Caroline stage. The popular stages were still active and, apparently, successful, and on the more fashionable theatres they exerted an important and much underestimated influence. Alongside the comedies of manners another and more plebeian, varied and eclectic tradition of drama coexisted. Inevitably, the political sentiments to which it gave voice were far more disturbing and subversive of established values and hierarchies than the comedies of elegant society could possibly be.

8

The survival of the popular tradition

The pattern of revivals

ALTHOUGH such open-air playhouses as the Curtain, Hope, Swan and Rose had ceased mounting plays long before Caroline times, plays continued to be seen at the Fortune and the Red Bull (and, of course, the Globe) throughout the 1630s. This is perhaps the single most underrated fact in the history of the English theatre. It passes unacknowledged because, although there was a general decline in the numbers of new plays written annually from about 1615,[1] at the popular theatres in particular the quota diminished almost to nothing, and since we measure a theatre's importance by its creativity, these stages tend to disappear from our notice. Yet they continued to perform, with self-evident success: G. E. Bentley was amazed that the Prince's Men held together during the long plague closure of 1636–37 when better companies went down, and that the 'Red Bull-King's' company survived the £1,000 fine they incurred in 1639.[2] We have little enough idea of what was happening at the popular theatres in these years, but what evidence there is all points in one direction – backwards. They were known mainly for spectacular plays of chivalry and romance, or farce and devilry such as *Dr Faustus* ('red bull phrase', said John Cleveland, was 'enter three devills *solus*'), and for vigorous and old-fashioned pseudo-histories of love and conquest (Richard Fowler 'drew much Company' to the Fortune to see him in the 'Conquering parts', while the Red Bull was remembered for its 'Drums, Trumpets, Battels, and Hero's'). Marlowe's *Tamburlaine* (1587), and *Jugurtha King of Numidia* (1600) were instanced as characteristic pieces; the Prince's Men may still have been playing John Day's rollicking chronicle of life under

Henry VI, *The Blind Beggar of Bethnal Green* (1600).[3] In 1638, Jasper Mayne contrasted Jonson favourably with those popular writers who were still bringing '*Monsters*' onto the stage:[4]

> no hard *Plot*
> Call'd down a *God* t'untie th'unlikely *knot*.
> The *Stage* was still a *Stage*, two entrances
> Were not two parts oth'*World*, disjoyn'd by *Seas*.
> Thine were *land-Tragedies*, no Prince was found
> To swim a whole *Scoene* out, then oth' *Stage* drown'd;
> Pitch't fields, as *Red-Bull* wars, still felt thy doome,
> Thou laidst no sieges to the *Musique-Roome* . . .

A third genre was the apprentice's adventuring play, the fantasy of fame and heroism for the ordinary artisan. Thomas Heywood's *Four Prentices of London* (*c.* 1600), set in the crusades, seems still to have been performed, and William Rowley's *A Shoemaker a Gentleman* (1608), in which the apprentice, a disguised prince, earns glory fighting abroad as a common soldier, was published in 1638 as an old play 'which is often Acted' at the Red Bull and 'well approved' by its shoemakerly spectators 'with your loud alarums, (I meane your clapping of hands)'.[5] Perhaps repeatedly reissued plays such as Dekker's *Shoemaker's Holiday* (5th edn, 1631) and the old pastoral *Mucedorus* (14th(!) edn, 1639) still had theatre audiences too. These indications are borne out by the few new popular-theatre plays that appeared, which conform to old and tried patterns. *The Knave in Grain* (> 1639) and Thomas Jordan's *The Walks of Islington* (1641) are jolly plays of low life and roguery among brothels and prisons; the *Valiant Scot* (> 1637) is a ranting chronicle of war and clowning about the border ballad-hero Wallace; and John Kirke's *Seven Champions of Christendom* (> 1638)[6] is a full-blown adventure packed with spectacle, devilry and magic, starring St George and based on a popular Elizabethan prose romance. The (lost) Fortune play of 1641, 'the Doge & the Dragon',[7] looks very like a transcriber's error for 'St George and the Dragon'.

In retrospect it is hard to restore the continual impact that the activity of these stages would have had on the theatrical map; but it must have been immense. There was, in effect, a third, alternative tradition of theatre in Caroline London, running concurrently with the private court stage and the elite professional theatres, one capable of sustaining two large, old-style popular playhouses (three in summer, when the Globe operated) and which, judging from surviving descriptions, was received with riotous enthusiasm. Obviously, such a repertoire presupposes a largely plebeian audience of apprentices, 'Citizens, and the meaner sort',[8] but it cannot be entirely accounted for by social considerations alone (for example, social factors do not explain why there were so few *new* popular plays). Rather, though popular drama was low, its more crucial feature was that it was old-fashioned. Its social indecorum – the mingling of clowns and kings – was only one aspect of a more complex set of preferences for the manner of Alleyn, Marlowe and their contemporaries, a style festive, ranting, traditional, nostalgic and Elizabethan – the old 'national' taste, in fact. The popular stages, with all their vigour and tenacity, were not in decline but simply conservative – they continued to give expression to those traditions from which Whitehall and Blackfriars had largely turned away but for which, plainly, a sizeable audience still existed.

It is helpful to see the open-air stages as catering for older tastes rather than merely as backward, because these were not isolated preferences; frequently the more popular end of the fashionable spectrum participated in the Elizabethan tradition too. The Phoenix demonstrably kept a high proportion of old plays current in its repertoire in the 1630s,[9] not only Jacobean melodramas such as Rowley's *All's Lost by Lust* (1619) and *The Witch of Edmonton* (1621), but also plays like Marlowe's *Jew of Malta* (1590), and the anonymous *George a Greene* (1599) in which, astonishingly, the mythical folk-heroes Robin Hood and the valiant Yorkshire yeoman of the title would still have been treading the boards. There is no way of telling whether the violent, spectacular and ranting tyrant play *The Bloody Banquet* was new or (as it appears to be) very old when the Phoenix company protected it in 1639, but that in itself is significant. Here Thomas Heywood's middle-class chronicles were revived: his spirited Elizabethan adventure fantasy *The Fair Maid of the West* (*c.* 1600?), his pious biography of Elizabeth as a sainted Protestant queen, *If You Know Not Me You Know Nobody* (1605), and *The Rape of Lucrece* (1608), the latter, an extraordinary political tragedy-cum-gallimaufrey with its songs, garboils and clown, having originally been a Red Bull play. Possibly his boisterous pseudo-history *The Royal King and Loyal Subject* (1602?), published in 1637 as acted by the Queen's Men, was still being performed. So too in 1631 Henry Chettle's huffing revenge play *The Tragedy of Hoffman* (*c.* 1602) was published as acted at the Phoenix, and Dekker's *Match Me in London* (1611?) claimed to have been 'often Presented; First, at the Bull in St. IOHNS-street; And lately, at the Priuate-House in DRVRY-Lane' (t.p.). Similarly, seven years later, the title page of Kirke's *Seven Champions of Christendom* claimed performances at the Phoenix and the Red Bull, while Henry Shirley's *The Martyred Soldier* (*c.* 1619) had been acted 'at the Private house in Drury lane, and at other publicke Theaters' (t.p.).

As for the Salisbury Court, though an indoor theatre there are surprisingly few new titles associated with it, and it may well have been dependent on a much more 'popular' or antiquated repertoire than we usually take it to have been. There certainly were revivals here (*Sir Giles Goosecap* (1602), *A Mad World My Masters* (1606) and *Dr Lambe and the Witches*, an 'ould play'),[10] and two of its occupying companies, the Prince's Men (1632–*c.* 1634) and the King's Revels (*c.* 1634–36), transferred to or from open-air theatres. The actors' names in the manuscript of that vigorous popular chronicle of British resistance to Danish tyranny, *Edmond Ironside* (*c.* 1598), show it to have been revived by one of these two troupes *c.* 1631–34; it is just possible that the Salisbury Court also staged the tyrant play *Woodstock* (1594), which is closely linked with *Edmond Ironside* in the same manuscript collection.[11]

By concentrating on those elements in a period which to hindsight appear progressive we subtly but inevitably misrepresent the way things looked to contemporaries. We tend to describe audience demand in terms of what changes or is new, but clearly a substantial part of Caroline taste was backward-looking, and this is of enormous significance, both theatrically and politically. Caroline refinement was continually modified by more Elizabethan styles, and their survival suggests that the attitudes on which they were founded – their traditional and highly-charged popular sympathies and values – were still felt to be strongly relevant to England in the 1630s. The taste for revivals and for the Elizabethan manner made available a drama that was sceptical, critical and levelling, in which common men rubbed shoulders with kings; the Master of the Revels who required all revived plays to be re-submitted to him for censorship of the 'offensive matter' they might contain,[12] clearly perceived how suspect they could be. I shall be exploring some implications of these revivals and of the survival of theatrical and political 'Elizabethanism', and particularly in relation to the work of a group of dramatists who, though writing for the elite theatres, remained closely in touch with these older forms and voiced social and political sentiments much more traditional, popular and radical than obtain in the work of other elite-theatre writers, such as Shirley. I believe they deserve much greater attention than they have had hitherto for they demonstrate how the popular drama continued to be capable of further valuable and exciting development. To Caroline eyes these playwrights, drawing off both the elite and popular traditions, would have looked far more like principal heirs to the Elizabethan mainstream than they do today.

Conveniently, these dramatists declare themselves as a distinct self-conscious group because they are forward among a number of writers who enthusiastically exchanged commendatory verses one with another in a series of publications beginning in 1637. The relevant cross-commendations I have summarized in table 3; from the Phoenix we have Thomas Heywood, Robert Davenport, the jest-book author Robert Chamberlain, and Shakerley Marmion; from the Salisbury Court Brome, Nabbes, Thomas Rawlins and Nathanael Richards; Thomas Jordan and John Tatham wrote for the Red Bull. Of their non-theatrical friends, C.G., R.W., and E.B. signed their verses with their initials. Heywood, in Jonsonian fashion, calls the minor versifier Humphrey Mill 'my adopted sonne', and Stephen Bradwell is elsewhere known as a friend of his.[13] Significantly, none of these was a very fashionable writer. At least three (Brome, Heywood, Jordan) had experience of both the elite and popular theatres, and their distinctness as a group is reinforced by their reiterated and parallel complaints about the 'stormes of Critticks' who have vilified their writings, 'censuring Criticks', '*squint*-ey'd *critickes*', '*a stocke of brothers,/Thought wise by praysing and dispraysing others*', 'Zoylists', '*a certaine Sect of selfe-affecters*' who express the '*envious condition of these carping times*' and discharge on them the 'rage/Of Criticisme', the 'disease of dislike, censuring what ere is writ/with ignorance'. It would seem to be the more courtly, fashionable playwrights from whom this scorn has come, since they describe them as '*Patentees of censure*' who 'have no mercy on the Paper rheames,/But produce plaies as scole-boyes do write theams'. A reference to '*those that surfet with their bayes*' is perhaps a side-swipe at Davenant and his friends.[14]

Throughout these occasional verses may be traced, sporadically but coherently, an alternative account of the function of literature which consciously opposes it, morally and socially, to the elegant triflings of society poets. This view is most fully set out in Humphrey Mill's *A Night's Search* (London, 1640), a voluminous but undistinguished collection of satires on the Caroline under-world of rogues and prostitutes for which six members of our circle contributed commendatory verses. Mill was nervous about the reception of a volume on such a subject, and he justifies his poetic procedures at some length, explaining that although his subject is wanton his style is chaste, and describing how he has avoided 'knotty words' and 'rocky expressions' [sig.):(7ʳ], prefer-ring to use what he elsewhere calls '*tearmes nearest at hand*' and 'plaine dressing':[15]

> this ingenious Poet doth rehearse
> Things as they are, or should be, and his verse
> Not stuft with clouded words, or conjuring straines,
> Nor thunder-claps, which might distract the braines
> Of honest readers: but in tearmes most fit
> T'expresse his matter, and to teach them wit.
> He doth refine conceits, and raise them higher,
> His musique's next unto the angels quire.   (p. 10)

TITLE	Nabbes	Brome	'C.G.'	Chamberlain	'E.B.'	'R.W.'	Heywood	Rawlins	Richards	Jordan	Davenport	Tatham	Bradwell	Dedicatee
1637														
Cupid and Psyche (Marmion)	V	V					V							
Microcosmus (Nabbes)	Λ	V												William Balle
Poetical Varieties (Jordan)	V	V					V			Λ				
1638														
The Spring's Glory (Nabbes)	Λ		V	V										
Nocturnal Lucubrations (Chamberlain)	V			Λ										Peter Balle (father of above)
1639														
The Rebellion (Rawlins)		V	V	V	V	V		Λ	V	V	V	V		
Messallina (Richards)								V	Λ	V	V		V	Viscount Rochford
Conceits, Clinches, Flashes and Whimzies (Chamberlain)				Λ				V						
1640														
The Sparagus Garden (Brome)		Λ	V			V								Earl of Newcastle
The Unfortunate Mother (Nabbes)	Λ		V		V	V								
A Night's Search (Mill)	V	V	V	V			V						V	Earl of Essex
The Swaggering Damsel (Chamberlain)			V	Λ				V						
The Antipodes (Brome)		Λ	V	V										Earl of Hertford
The Fancies Theatre (Tatham)	V	V	V	V				V				Λ		
Jocabella (Chamberlain)			V	Λ				V						
1652														
A Jovial Crew (Brome)		Λ										V		
1657														
The Walks of Islington and Hogsdon (Jordan)				V						Λ				

Key V = Includes commendatory verses by   Λ = Author

Table 3. Dedications and commendatory verses in published popular literature 1637–41.

There is here a unity of style and ethical intention. Mill stresses that, because his aim is moral seriousness, he has chosen a style that is perspicuous and direct, and shows things as they are, or ought to be:

> A Poets pen should ever strike at vice,
> And raise true vertue to a noble price:
> And honour truth, dash falshood out of favour,
> Shame foolish Imps, and praise a sweet behaviour;
> Or else the Devill may a Poet prove,
> To honour lust, and give it termes of love. (p. 15)

But this stylistic and moral chastity has a social dimension too, for his is a 'plain' Muse who addresses those who value plainness in word and action ('Muse, thou are honest, I must take thy part,/ Though thou art plain, let none thy truth despise'),[16] and she is firmly contrasted with bad poets who write ornately on bawdy or heathen subjects, 'fictions vaine', as degenerate in morality as in style (p. 13). In their contributions to his volume, Mill's friends attacked the *'loose-lin'd Rimers'* who now *'Infect the Aire'* with their *'Meere flashy Poems'* designed for a readership of *'men to Novels of the times inclin'd'* (sigs.B1ᵛ, B6ʳ).

Mill also suggests that a plain stage, properly reformed, could become a powerful ethical weapon:

> He that's Dramatick, and doth purge the stage
> From scurrill drosse, and shewes this simple age
> Their moulded trophies; and doth always strive
> To keep both persons names, and things alive,
> His end is good . . . (p. 12)

He was perhaps echoing the views of his poetic 'father', Heywood, who had already complained in a prologue of *c.* 1635 that modern playwrights[17]

> strive to flie
> In their low pitch, who never could soare hie:
> For now the common argument intreats,
> Of puling Lovers, craftie Bawdes or cheates . . .
> I only wish that they would sometimes bend
> To memorise the valours of such men,

> Whose verie names might dignifie the Pen,
> And that our (once applauded) Roscian straine,
> In acting such might be reviv'd againe . . .

Comparable opinions concerning the seriousness and usefulness of the stage and damning recent theatrical fashions circulated freely among this group. Chamberlain's *Swaggering Damsel* (London, 1640) was praised because 'No debaucht Scenes, nor such base mirth as we/Place in the Scenes, of obscene Ribaldry,/ Pollutes thy Pen' (sig.A3ᵛ), while in Richards's *Messallina* 'things immodest, modestly were writ'.[18] Davenport avowed he wrote '*rather with a native familiarity than an impertinent Elegancy*', and Nabbes's *Microcosmus* was described as '*instruction mingled with delight*'.[19] In Brome's hands, Mill's rejection of 'Love-subjects' as 'too thredbare now adayes' (*Night's Search*, p. 1) became a forthright assault on those who have neglected '*the old way of* Playes' for a '*new strayne of wit*' which he personally repudiates, defying his audience to hope that any '*gaudy Scaene*' or '*handsome Love-toy shall your time beguile*'. The adoption of plain style and subjects instead of more elegant language and themes has both a serious and a social purpose: '*low and home-bred* Subjects *have their use*'.[20]

Of course, Brome was especially attacking the scenic innovations associated with the courtier-dramatists, their faddish extravagances of language and sumptuous staging, '*Scene magnificent and language high:|And Cloathes worth all the rest*'; his verse satire on Suckling's *Aglaura* was widely circulated.[21] There is indeed much spectacle in the plays of his friends, but it is different in kind from the ostentatious and often redundant splendour of royal theatricals. Usually it carries particular moral significance, as may be instanced from the little masque in Davenport's *A New Trick to Cheat the Devil* (Phoenix, > 1639) in which a scrivener is brought on dancing with a knave, a prodigal with a beggar, a puritan with a whore and a usurer with a devil, the whole antic presided over by the devil himself. Davenport's device is deliberately emblematic, employing popular theatrical stereotypes to make moral points visually and memorably. There are similar dumb-shows in Heywood's *Love's Mistress* (Phoenix, 1634), including a prodigal, drunkard, usurer, king and beggar, and in Richards's *Messallina* (Salisbury Court, *c.* 1635) in which three furies incite the evil Roman empress on to further crimes. Similar effects are achieved in the curious hybrid plays which are found solely among the work of this group. Nabbes's *Microcosmus* (Salisbury Court, 1637), which calls itself a 'morall maske', is a morality play with songs and dances on man's creation and fall, a throwback to an otherwise extinct form, and Jordan's *Money is an Ass* (King's Revels?, *c.* 1635) is a city intrigue on one level but is also overlaid with features from the interludes; its personae include Money, Credit, Gold, Silver, Felixina and Feminia, it has a usurer who is referred to as 'Faustus' (p. 16)[22] or 'the Devil' (p. 5) and who lives in 'hell' (p. 16) with his 'black and horrid' servant, Calumny (p. 29).

Such interweaving of social and moral types is a common characteristic of these dramatists. It suggests they are drawing on very old, even outmoded dramatic styles and forms such as moralities, jigs and antics, but it also points to the relationship between the plays and the non-dramatic verse connected with the group, among which their satires often include elaborate and theatrical parades of social types. In a satire of Tatham's we find[23]

> dunghill Doublets, muskt and sented forth:
> The Gallants Feather, and his tatling Spurre,
> The Citie Miser wrapt in's Neighbours Furre,
> The Countrey-dolthead Mungrell brought to land . . .
> (Reserv'd for laughter till his wealth is done)
> Gulls were ordain'd wits pastime . . .

Tatham writes as one familiar with the character-types that had been developed for the stage, and his friends continually return to such emblematic, visual effects. Nathanael Richards provides a gallery of courtiers, strumpets, Jesuits and even the devil himself in his verse satires, and Mill's *Poems Occasioned by a Melancholy Vision* (1639) mix social types – the Magistrate, Heir, Clerk, Sexton – with moral abstractions – Ignorance, Covetousness, Lust, Pride, Sin and Death. In his *Night's Search* the world has been virtually anatomized into generic types such as Whores, Pimps, Thieves, Prodigals, Gallants and Beggars, and their ruler, the Devil, is a strongly realized controlling presence. Mill depicts a world that sin is simultaneously turning into a hell, as men are made devilish by their sins, or led on by devils in the guise of pimps and whores; here a real and a moralized landscape constantly interpenetrate. In the plays too characterization is frequently nothing more than the animation of conventional social types – the usurer, scrivener and prodigal in Davenport's *New Trick*, the usurer, shark and informer who disguise themselves, morality-fashion, as upright aldermanic figures to poke fun at respectable hypocrisy in the anonymous play *The Wasp* (Salisbury Court, *c.* 1635). Though simple, these devices are not crude, but carry considerable analytic potential, as a schema by which society may be satirically dissected, piece by piece, into its constituent estates.

Occasionally, too, this connection works in the opposite direction, for in the case of the moral eclogues and dialogues written by Jordan and Tatham, and of Davenport's *A Crown for a Conqueror* (1639), a series of discourses between Christ, the soul and various personifications, the poems seem to be on the edge of becoming quasi-dramatic pieces. With these might also be linked that odd volume of 1641 by the erstwhile popular playwright John Day, *The Parliament of Bees*. This collection of semi-dramatic monologues by various character-types including a rich man, a soldier, a poet, a prodigal and a usurer demonstrates clearly how the social attitudes of the popular theatre survived in other forms right down to the Civil War, for it makes hearty complaints against usurers, lawyers, rack-renters, hoarders and rich men who grind the poor, and demands for justice and reforms. Day also attacks flattering poets, but the blame for the nation's crimes and corruptions is laid firmly on its ruler, the 'Master Bee', Prorex himself, when his lord, Oberon, finally comes to judge him. Significantly for 1641, the title page shows the Master Bee dispensing justice in his parliament.

If we knew this group merely by their non-dramatic writings we would have a very singular impression of them, for much of their published verse has a sternly pious character. Mill's *Poems Occasioned by a Melancholy Vision* and Chamberlain's *Nocturnal*

Lucubrations (1638) are largely religious meditations in the plain style. Heywood's work in the 1630s included his anthology of angel-lore *The Hierarchy of the Blessed Angels* (1635) and a city pageant, *Londini Status Pacatus* (London, 1639), praising the 'free and frequent Preaching of the Word and Gospell' (sig.C2ʳ). Nathanael Richards's two volumes of sacred poems were intended 'to direct soules from the dangerous Passage indirect', while Nabbes's and Jordan's poetry was 'Morall *some, and some* Divine'.²⁴ The jewels of a Christian's crown enumerated in Davenport's *Crown for a Conqueror* are²⁵

> *Election, Creation,*
> *Redemption,* and that middle lemme *Vocation;*
> *Sanctification, Iustification,* and
> *Glorification.*

Davenport is speaking here in the persona of the dying Calvinist saint, anticipating the rewards due to God's Elect, and it would not be inappropriate to think of these men as dramatists with strongly 'puritan' inclinations, in their serious moral and religious concern but also in their deliberate cultivation of the plain style and their commitment to the social and political attitudes which go with it. In fact, the dramatist Thomas Rawlins went so far as to call Richards's melodrama on the wicked life and death of the Roman empress *Messallina* (pub. London, 1640) a play '*whose veines can stirre/* Religious thoughts, *though in a Theator*' (sig.A8ᵛ). Rawlins no doubt had in mind the series of virtuous characters who stand aside from the corrupt imperial court and improve their time with 'superstitious lecturing' (sig.C7ʳ) or heavenly contemplation:

> [Sit,] my deare friend, and I will reade to thee
> Of that high Majestic puissant *Ens,*
> From whom we have our being, life, and soule,
> Which should dull flintie inconsiderate man,
> When with black deeds 'ith myrie bog of sinne,
> Beast like he wallows; consider right . . .
> . . . he then no more
> Would dare t'offend his Maker, but with teares,

Lament his soules pollution, which doth give,
Matter, by which mens soules immortall live ... (sigs.D5^{r-v})

Equally 'puritan' is Richards's withering depiction of the vices of
the rich and powerful, and the debauched pleasures of the court;
for some spectators, Messallina, a 'Circe' (sigs.C3^r, F4^r) who
intoxicates men and drags them to damnation, may have carried
theological overtones associating her with that other great Whore
of Rome, the Catholic church. In the last act the heavens
intervene spectacularly, and the libidinous courtiers are swallowed up by the earth or struck down by an avenging angel,
while Messallina's courtly masques are overtaken by a greater
'Tragedy' (sig.F2^r) in which she plays an unexpected part. The
play is shot through with allusions to the stage and acting:
Richards is presenting events as a great theatre of vengeance in
which divine justice on sinners and great men is displayed for the
astonishment and warning of all. He realizes, in actual theatrical
terms, the inherently dramatic tendencies of those popular puritan
manuals, such as Thomas Beard's *Theatre of God's Judgments* (3rd
edn, London, 1631), which describe how God's wrath is 'thrown
effectually vpon the heads of the mightie ones of the world' in 'a
strange and admirable order' (sigs.A4^v, A5^r). Rawlins praised
Richards for using the stage 'For to convert not to corrupt this
Age' (*Messallina*, sig.A8^v).[26]

These impressions are strengthened if we inspect some of the
patrons to whom these men addressed themselves. *Messallina* was
dedicated to Viscount Rochford, a man who in 1629 had shown
his sympathies with Charles's critic Sir John Eliot by visiting
him in the Tower; Rochford's father received the dedication of
Heywood's *Pleasant Dialogues and Dramas* (1637). Richards's *Poems
Sacred and Satirical* (1641) were addressed to Alderman Thomas
Soames who had achieved some popularity as a critic of Ship
Money, and was elected in 1640 with other radicals as MP for the
city.[27]

Both Brome and Mill were courting the attention of the Rich–
Devereux–Seymour group, immensely prestigious and powerful
noble dynasties closely tied by blood but also by common

contempt for Charles's government. Brome dedicated *The Antipodes* to William Seymour, Earl of Hertford, and provided him with a manuscript copy of *The English Moor*; Mill's *Night's Search* was addressed to Hertford's brother-in-law, Robert Devereux, Earl of Essex, while the second edition (1652) went to Essex's cousin, Robert Rich, Earl of Warwick. The Earl of Winchilsea, dedicatee of Mill's *Poems* (1639), had a son who, though a zealous royalist in the 1640s, later married Hertford's daughter Mary Seymour. Essex, Warwick and Hertford were perhaps the most determined of Charles's aristocratic critics, who in the 1630s had entirely ceased frequenting the court; all three were among the popular noblemen who in 1640 petitioned Charles to recall parliament. Hertford and Essex had already been notoriously disobliged by King James, Hertford over his stolen marriage with Arabella Stuart (1610) and Essex by his divorce which James engineered to gratify his corrupt favourite, Carr (1613). Essex distinguished himself by his active support for the continental protestant cause and by his bitter hatred of Strafford; by 1640 this 'man beloved of the people' had become 'the most popular man of the kingdom'. Hertford was his close political associate (they shared a house in London), a man with 'many eyes... upon him' in 1639; his appointment in 1641 as governor of the Prince of Wales was 'to the satisfaction and joy of the whole kingdom'.[28] They broke up in 1642 when Hertford declared for the king, but Essex became Lord General of the army for parliament, and his ally Warwick was parliament's admiral. The fiercely puritan dramatist Arthur Wilson was employed in the Essex and Warwick households, and the Essex family's interest in the theatre is well-attested.[29] Essex himself would pass his leisure times 'in the perusall of some labourd Poeme' and applauded 'the professors of that Art, as high as their desert, and... [rewarded] them above it', not accepting the 'sullen opinion' of those who censured poetry as 'unlavvfull and unprofitable';[30] his contemporary biographer may well have been thinking of Brome and his friends here. Perhaps too the 'C.G.' who in 1646 published *An Elegy upon... Robert Earl of Essex* was the C.G. who wrote verses among our group.

Finally, the dedicatee of some of Davenport's religious verse and of Brome's *The Sparagus Garden* (1640) was William Cavendish, then Earl of Newcastle. Brome must have established a fairly close connection with him for he wrote verses in praise of Newcastle's own comedy, *The Variety* (*c.* 1641). Newcastle was no puritan, but neither was he a simple courtier for, by birth (as a scion of a great Tudor family) and temperament an Elizabethan, he was out of his depth in Charles's progressive court, isolated, distrustful and saddened by the decline of the English nobility. In 1632 he declared himself a lord of misrule, for 'I take that for an honor in these dayes rather then the other more common title'; in 1636 he found 'a great deal of venom against me' at court, and in 1639 he was said not 'to grow much in thear Maties esteemation'.[31] Later he complained reproachfully that Charles had neglected the old, established nobility and surrounded himself with 'meane People' that 'woulde Jeer the greateste Noble man in Englande iff hee did nott make the laste monthes Reverence A La Mode thatt Came with the laste Danser frome Paris'.[32] There had been 'no manner off Regarde off the Nobiletye'; parasites who 'lived off the kinge' were in favour and those who 'did nott make le Bon Reverance & could nott dance a Sereban' were despised. Newcastle told Charles II that his father's fatal error had been his failure to maintain Ceremony and degrees of honour, which brought the nobility and ultimately his own person into weakness and contempt:

Seremoneye though Itt Is nothing In Itt selfe yett Itt doth Everye thinge – For what Is a Kinge more then a Subiecte butt for seremoneye & order when that fayles him hees Ruinde...Whatt Is a Lorde more then a foot-man withoute seremoneye & order, – a dispisde Title...

Despising Whitehall's modishness, Newcastle cast back to the days of Elizabeth who had valued her nobility (including his own uncle, Shrewsbury, 'a wise man & had a Gentle Sole & a Loyall') and built her success on them, men 'no fooles butt verye wise Counselors'. Princes should choose ministers who 'are borne to Leade, & nott to followe, To teach, & nott to Learne, butt ther are butt fewe off them, – Sr Walter Rawleye was one off them'.

Those times had been 'the best Presedente for Englandes Govermente absolutlye'.[33]

Newcastle tried personally to imitate 'the examp[l]es of our heroic ancestors';[34] he (twice) feasted Charles prodigally, challenged Holland to a duel for a supposed slight on the royal honour, and even invited Fairfax to fight a pitched battle in 1643. He also wrote two plays (c. 1639–41) which, as a courtier's plays, were staged at the Blackfriars. However, their plain and satirical style associates them with the manner of the more popular playwrights (the prologue to *The Country Captain*[35] scorns '*new strong lines*' and those who present '*a glorious painted Scene . . . in stead of wit*' or '*lines well writ*' (sig.A1 + 1ʳ), and the heroine of *The Variety* demands to be courted (p. 11) 'in a phrase is fit to own and understand'), and they advance political ideas similar to the advice to Charles II. Monsieur Device, the butt of the satire in *The Country Captain*, is a frivolous gallant 'governd by the mode, as waters by the moone' (p. 11) who explains elaborately the science of wearing different coloured ribbons. He is merely absurd, but Sir Francis Courtwell, 'a powerfull friend at court, whose favor is worth preservinge' (p. 13) and whose attempts to cuckold a country knight the play charts, is more severely condemned. He is contrasted with his nephew, who woos lawfully, adopting the seriousness and modesty of a puritan (specifically, an Anabaptist), and who argues for frankness of speech and intention. One scene of this courtship is set in a field – it contrasts court with 'country' wooing.

These themes are pursued more explicitly in *The Variety*. Here the man of mode is Galliard, a specimen of those new courtiers who are undermining Charles's authority. He represents the Frenchifying tendencies of the court: he is unpatriotic, a pursuer of foreign fashions, and he values men according to their elegance, laughing at statesmen who make 'de estrange a Sir reverence' and wondering 'dat dey will suffer a des men to be neere a de King . . . dey vil marra de understanding very mush' (p. 17). Dancing he interprets as a form of good government, for making 'reverences' instils obedience, and gay music dispels melancholy and rebellion (pp. 17, 36) – Charles is to dance his subjects into obedience.

Newcastle was Ben Jonson's last patron, and Galliard is, of course, travestying Jonson's noble concept of the dance as the image of harmony and wisdom; he parodies what Charles was doing with his court masques, in which symbols for good government and national harmony were increasingly becoming substitutes for what they symbolized. In Galliard's view, dancing has replaced statesmanship, 'for de Courtier Alamode, dere de vit lie in de foot . . . dere is nobodie can be viseman, dat does no make a de most excellent reverence' (p. 17); ironically, the courtiers who dance with Charles are indeed only wise in their feet. *The Variety* has its own masque, a drunken affair staged by the humorous gentleman Newman. The room of the tavern becomes 'the field of *Tempe*', and a hypocritical usher and a whore are hoisted aloft in a throne, accompanied by the 'Musick of the Spheres'; their glasses are their sceptres, their wine their 'blood royall', and the whore is 'Queene of grapes'. Newman explains he has 'built this Elisium; and when bright Sack hath crown'd my brow, how soon I am made immortall, you may guesse' (pp. 69–70). It is an unidealized, disillusioned version of the Whitehall masques; for Newcastle, masquing carries the same ironic meanings it does in the masque of whores dressed as queens in *Messallina*, or in the masque of beggars in Brome's *A Jovial Crew* (1641).

Against this degenerate society is set Manly, a gentleman whose humour is to dress as the Elizabethan Earl of Leicester. Galliard derides his old-fashioned costume, but Manly frightens him away and has a *five-page* speech in praise of

> those honest dayes, when Knights were Gentlemen, and proper men tooke the
> walls of dwarfes . . . these things were worne when men of honor flourish'd,
> that tam'd the wealth of Spaine, set up the States, help'd the French King, and
> brought Rebellion to reason Gentlemen. (p. 39)

He extols English clothes and dances, sings patriotic songs, and recalls the greatness of St George's day feasts when 'Every Knight had his hundreds', not merely 'a page and a barber' as they do now (p. 41). The heroine falls in love with him and endorses his beliefs, declaring 'there wants but such a noble leader to reduce, and make this habit fashionable; it shews a proper man' (p. 44). The opinions of Manly – patriotic, nostalgic for England's Elizabethan greatness – express Newcastle's own discontent with a Frenchified, unheroic court and its king.

Elizabethanism in theatre and politics

Newcastle was essentially a good king's man whose disappointment with Charles was pushing him into uncomfortable company (Sir John Eliot had also complained that places of honour were filled with 'men of mean and poor parts for singing and dancing'); the England to which he wished to return was an idealized and ultra-conservative never-never land where everyone had contentedly known their places under a Wise and Just Monarch.[36] But it cannot be emphasized enough that for others Caroline nostalgia for better days was not at all 'nostalgic'. Everywhere the government of James and Charles provoked, unintentionally, a quite extraordinary cult of the memory of Elizabeth – the pictures and biographies of her endlessly reprinted, the sermons, and bonfires and bell-ringing year after year on her Accession Day[37] – which, for all its veneration of monarchy and attachment to the past, was sweeping the country relentlessly towards the challenge to the king, not away from it. Elizabeth was not merely remembered fondly; rather, she was enthusiastically reverenced, and not just for her personal stature which threw Charles the man into an uncomplimentary shadow, but because of the aims and policies which men remembered (or thought they remembered) her as pursuing but which under the Stuarts had been either abandoned or reversed. At the heart of the Elizabethan cult was an emotional concern for *values* – opposition to Spain and the Pope, support for international Protestantism, aggression abroad, unity at home in a church properly reformed under a godly prince – the values of the old national myth of England's greatness which Elizabeth was supposed to have been furthering and which Charles certainly was not, and which cast suspicion on

Plate 3. Queen Elizabeth, from the title page of T. Heywood, *If You Know Not Me, You Know Nobody* (6th edition, 1623).

the whole tendency of Stuart government. It was this myth that the 1620s parliaments constantly threw in Charles's face, that 'that never to be forgotten excellence, queen Elizabeth' had maintained a loving accord with her parliaments, kept religion up, helped her allies, prosecuted Catholics and made England great, because under her 'God and [England] were friends', whereas the present is distinguished only by 'grievances and

199

Plate 4. Henry VIII, from the title page of S. Rowley, *When You See Me You Know Me* (2nd edition, 1613).

oppressions, wholly inferred and raised since the connivance with the papists'.[38] Far from being a valedictory yearning for a lost Golden Age, the myth fuelled popular and puritan fervour for a *recovery* of that neglected national destiny, now identified with the Elizabethan past: 'all goes backwards since this connivance in religion came in ... whereas in Queen Elizabeth's time, who stood firm in God's cause all things did flourish'.[39] It rebounded with enormous force against Charles when the godly ministers preaching to parliament in 1640 urged MPs to take up the reformation where Elizabeth had left off.

Nowhere are these significances better seen than in the survival of Foxean history plays onto the stage of the 1630s. Heywood's

If You Know Not Me, revived at the Phoenix, dramatized the idea of Elizabeth, descending from Foxe's *Book of Martyrs*, as a noble saint, a godly queen steadfast – like Prynne, Burton and Bastwick – under the persecution of cruel papists, corrupt petty officials and pompous prelates, and finally entering triumphantly into her rule, English Bible in hand. Moreover, she is a popular queen; she loves and cares for the poor, the common soldiers pity her mistreatment. This play, in its eighth edition in 1639, was plainly one of the most popular of its age, and perhaps Rowley's companion piece on Henry VIII's merry japes, Wolsey's dismissal and the godly education of Edward VI, *When You See Me You Know Me* (1604), which reached its fourth edition in 1632, was still being performed alongside it. If so, it must have been an astonishing spectacle in Charles's London to see Elizabeth and Henry striding the indoor stages[40] as they appeared on the title-pages (plates 3 and 4), icons of good princes piously furthering the gospel whose presence implicitly damned a king who had failed to further the continuing process of reform and preaching of the gospel which Foxe demanded. Contemporaries would not have missed the effect; when Buckingham in 1628, two weeks before his assassination, saw a revival of Shakespeare's Foxean play, *Henry VIII*, at the Globe, they quickly pointed out his resemblance to Wolsey, a 'lively type of himself, having governed this kingdome eighteene yeares, as he hath done fourteen'.[41] And Foxean plays were still being written: Davenport, in *King John and Matilda* (c. 1634), dramatizing an English king on his knees offering his own crown to the Pope's legate seated in the chair of state, while his barons stood by astonished at the loss of their liberties, was putting onto the Phoenix stage an icon of papal tyranny which, in the pages of Foxe, could be seen in every church in the land (see plate 5), and the relevance of which was immediately plain to anyone anxious about Charles's romanized church and innovations in the state.

The old-style adventuring drama acted as a vehicle for identical sentiments. To go only a little way out of our period, the revival in the winter of 1630–31 of Heywood's *Fair Maid of the West*, with its pell-mell enthusiasm for war with Spain, its depiction of

Plate 5. King John submitting to the Pope's legate; from J. Foxe, *Acts
and Monuments* (6th edition, London, 1610), I, p. 722.

the Englishman's honest plain valour and its heroine named Bess,
was a calculated appeal to traditional patriotic anti-Spanish
feelings precisely at the moment that Charles was signing the
Treaty of Madrid with Philip IV (November 1630) and while the
rest of England was newly applauding the entry of the Swedish
King Gustavus into the European war on the Protestant side.
The play actually brought on stage in a dumb show the second
Earl of Essex, the great Elizabethan champion against Spain who
had been resurrected in the crisis of 1624 by the puritan
pamphleteer Thomas Scott, as *Robert Earl of Essex his Ghost*, to
protest anxiously against the proposals to marry Charles to the
Infanta, and Heywood wrote a new second part which, though
not anti-Spanish, was barely less patriotic in its praise of English

valour and beauty. Five years later he returned to the lists with
A Challenge for Beauty (pub. London, 1636), another chauvinistic
adventure in which a Spanish queen, boasting her beauty, finds
herself put down by the superior perfections of an English lady,
while the English gentleman Ferrers similarly proves himself to
be 'The wonder,/And abstract of all vertues' (sig.H1ʳ). Heywood's popular plot of slandered beauty enabled him to make
other political points too; the tyrannical Spanish rulers who
demand unthinking obedience from their subjects are shamed
into self-knowledge and juster government, and the honest
truth-telling good counsellor Bonavida is allowed to defeat the
two time-serving courtiers who have been flattering their royal
mistress up to the hilt. The title-page claims performance at both
the Blackfriars and the open-air Globe.

The case of the apprentice drama is very similar. At the
popular theatres, plays like *The Four Prentices* and *A Shoemaker a
Gentleman* epitomized all that was most festive, Elizabethan and
plebeian about the popular tradition, with their fantastic displays
of apprentice heroism in foreign wars, and their levelling plots in
which unprivileged men challenge rank by becoming princes and
marrying noble ladies. Yet, amazingly, these revivals had a
Caroline progeny too. We can only speculate about Heywood
and Brome's lost play *The Apprentice's Prize*,[42] but Thomas
Rawlins's *The Rebellion* (> 1636)[43] rants splendidly, and has some
extravagantly Marlovian villains, especially the evil Spanish
courtier Machvile who despises the people and tries to seize
power for himself and his ambitious wife. His opponent is
Antonio, a plain aristocrat and popular general in the mould of
Essex, who, though his loyalty is slandered by Machvile, is
eagerly rescued from arrest by the citizens who love him. Rawlins
celebrates citizen honour in love and war. The merry tailors
resolve to prove themselves in the festive style of the 1590s:

> Come my bold fellowes, let us eternize,
> For our Countries good, some noble act
> That may by time be Regestred at full;
> And as the yeare renewes, so shall our fame
> Be fresh to after times: the Taylers name,

> So much trod under, and the scorne of all
> Shall by this act be high whilst others fall.   (sigs.C2ᵛ–3ʳ)

The hero Giovanni later turns out to be of noble birth, but he woos Antonio's sister and fights valiantly disguised as a tailor, much to the envy of the courtiers (''Tis not to be borne: a Tayler!' (sig.E3ʳ)) who reward his honest pains with banishment; he retorts by taunting them as 'pamperd flesh' and 'Pomander boxes' not 'worth my breath' (sigs.E2ᵛ, E3ᵛ). The despised tailors lament this world's neglect of virtue, and attack the rich as devils in fine clothing:

> If our Hell afford a Divell, but I see none
> Unlesse he appeare in a delicious remnant of
> Nim'd Sattin, and by my faith that's a courteous
> Divill, that suffers the Brokers to hang him
> In their ragged Wardrobe; and us'd to sell his
> Divelship for mony . . .   (sig.E3ᵛ)

But it is the tailors who save the king from Machvile's plots, hiding him (and Antonio) in their shop. The king is reinstated, but he is overwhelmed with a consciousness of his obligations to those ordinary men whose 'loyall love, makes thy King poore'; he 'can't enough pay thy alone deserts,/Kings may be poore, when Subjects are like thee' (sigs.H4ᵛ, K2ᵛ). He even admires their ladies above court beauties, and the tailors sing of how *they* intend to cuckold gentlemen (sig.H1ᵛ).

Some vestiges of apprentice drama survive in the anonymous play *The Costly Whore* (pub. London, 1633),[44] in which the Prince of Saxony, who has revolted from his father the Duke for his dotage on a courtesan, does battle energetically and with some hilarity: '*They fight, Fredericke beats them off, and courses the Dutchesse over the stage*' (sig.E3ᵛ). The plot closely parallels Brome's *Queen and Concubine* (also a Salisbury Court play), with its whore and evil counsellors inciting the arbitrary and doting Duke against the 'busie-headed rabble' who 'plead reformation to depose you' (sig.F4ᵛ). Physically opposed by his people for his bad rule, the Duke eventually repents and abdicates in favour of the good and popular prince. Much space is devoted to depicting the Duke's brothers Hatto and Alfrid, 'catterpillars of the state' and 'realmesucking slaues' (sig.H3ʳ) who improve their already swollen profits by deliberately seeking to aggravate the lot of the poor, whom they hate as 'paltry wormes' (sig.D4ʳ):

> ... what course can you take to plague these dogges?
> Hatto. Why, buy up all the corne, and make a dearth,
> So thousands of them will die under stalles.
> Alfrid. And send it unto forraine nations,
> To bring in toies, to make the wealthy poore.
> Hatto. Or make our land beare wood instead of wheate.
> Alfrid. Inclose the commons, and make white meates deare.
> Hatto. Turne pasture into Parke grounds, and starve cattle,
> Or twentie other honest thriving courses;
> The meanest of these, will beggar halfe a Kingdome.   (sig.B4ʳ)

Hatto and Alfrid are archetypal rack-renting landlords, living luxuriously off wealth got by grinding those unable to resist, and they do it with royal connivance, for their devices are those hated preferential economic controls, the patent and the monopoly:

> Alfrid. I have a commission drawne for making glasse,
> Now if the Duke come, as I thinke he will;
> Twill be an excellent meanes to lavish wood,
> And then the cold will kill them, had they bread.
> Hatto. The yron Mills are excellent for that,
> I have a pattent drawne to that effect,
> If they goe up, downe goes the goodly trees,
> Ile make them search the earth to find new fire.   (sig.B4ʳ)

Such speeches are distinguished by the vividness with which they image the plight of the poor, but they sound notes that are heard throughout the drama of the 1630s in which the manner of the 1590s is still current – sympathy for the feelings of the under- or unprivileged, a sceptical understanding of society's hierarchies and the injustices of the rich and powerful, and intense, radical hopes for political changes under which society's inequalities and corruptions will be resolved or dealt with, even if these hopes can still only be conceptualized in terms of reformed or popular monarchs who have taken the interests of society's critics or underdogs to heart. It is a powerful combination of a plebeian point of view with one we otherwise would think of as 'puritan'.

Levelling sentiments were voiced at the Phoenix and Salisbury

Court even in plays which have no explicitly political dimension, such as Nabbes's 1638 Phoenix play, *The Bride* (pub. London, 1640), in which the citizen hero beats the gallants who are pursuing his girl and rebukes them for being 'Declin'd from men', telling them to 'Go to th'warres, and save the Citty/The chargeable reparing of their prisons' (sigs.E2ʳ⁻ᵛ), or in Davenport's *New Trick to Cheat the Devil*, a play full of bitter reflections on birth and rank in which the heroine, having dropped her true lover, a reduced gentleman, for the sake of marrying a lord and being a lady, finds that the courtier is not, in all that really matters, a patch on the man she has abandoned:[45]

> his Lordship? good, now,
> Tell me, in what place of his body lyes it?
> If in the face or foot, the Crowne or Toe,
> The Body, arme, or legge, the backe, or bosome,
> Without him, or within? I see no more
> In him than in another Gentleman.

Significantly, the play's totally digressive central episode dramatizes an old popular fabliau that has numerous analogues throughout Europe. It seems quite likely too that it was either the Phoenix or Salisbury Court that would have hosted Sir Aston Cockayne's rewriting of an Italian *commedia dell' arte* scenario, *Trappolin Supposed a Prince* (1633),[46] in which the Harlequin figure, the common pimp Trappolin, changes places (by a magical contrivance) with the Duke of Florence and rules far better than he, throwing the pompous nobles into prison, marrying off lovers that are true but of unequal birth, improving Florence vastly by madly turning hierarchy and authority upside-down. Cockayne's pimp is finally rewarded with a real earldom; the plebeian sympathies and style of his play would have attuned it well to performance at either of these theatres.

Perhaps the most telling survival into the 1630s is that of the popular history or pseudo-history of the 1590s. Political plays like *The Rebellion* or Davenport's *John and Matilda*, which contrast dishonest, parasitic evil counsellors, who are subverting or perverting their prince's government for their own ends, with idealized popular noblemen who are friends to their country and its people and are prepared boldly to tell their prince of his wrongs to his face ('perform with us,/You shall walk over us; if not, we stand/Our injur'd Countries Justicers', Davenport's barons tell John),[47] are consciously imitating the manner of those Elizabethan chronicles whose later stage-history links them with these theatres – *Edmond Ironside*, *Woodstock*, Heywood's *Royal King and Loyal Subject*, Day's *Blind Beggar* – and which display the same vigorous combination of patriotic fervour for the national good, entrenched (and justified) suspicion of the men who actually have the royal ear, and frequent concessions to the opinions of honest yeomen or downright servants who can perceive without fear or favour the wrongs done in high places. This political analysis has remained virtually unchanged for forty years, but clearly it was felt to have enormous truth in pre-Civil-War England. The figure that continually returns in these plays is the plain lord who dresses like a subject, criticizes the pride of courtiers, and gives honest counsel, no matter how unwelcome, and for whom the archetype is Thomas of Woodstock: there is Fitzwater who 'must tell truth still' in Davenport's *King John*,[48] Antonio in Rawlins's *Rebellion*, the eccentric Lord Letoy in Brome's *Antipodes* who makes his servants play rustic games such as football and despises the court's 'publique shewes, and braveries' (p. 245), and 'old Tom: plaine home spon Archibald' in the anonymous *Wasp*,[49] a true nobleman whom the court favourite derides as 'the kersy Lord, the lynsy wollsy gentleman the yeomanly Barron, The bottome of Browne thred' (ll.261, 266). Such characters are popular idealizations of what the nobility ought to be, but behind them we readily sense the presence of real popular aristocrats like Essex, Warwick and Hertford, men politically more 'country' than court and who, it was hoped, were more champions of their country's good than the courtiers seemed to be. In *The Wasp*, Archibald avows himself a 'country' lord, belonging to a rural England where nobles and people live in harmony but whose traditional peace the court's new ways are ·disturbing: 'my contry Bred me, myne owne shepe clothe me & myne owne beefe feeds me' (l.268). When he disguises himself as the blunt and discontented northerner Percy, there seems to be a direct reference to the reputation of the Percy family, Earls of Northumberland; and the mistreatment of the 'Earle of clare' (l.294) earlier in the play would surely have directed attention to the contemporary dis-courted earl of the same name.[50]

The Wasp, with its vigorous action, violent clashes of character and racy language, is an extraordinary demonstration of the tenacity of older forms, and of the pointedness of their perspec-tives on recent politics. The play is – nominally – set in the Roman occupation of Britain, and the Prorex governs arbitrarily over an enslaved nation:

> DEVON. . . . the poore he makes
> slaves, & like horses yoakes 'em vp in Teames
> to till our owne Land for the Romaines vse,
> ARCHIBALD. our wifes & daughters they make prostitutes
> eat vp the rich, make bondslaves of the poore
> & oppresse all
> CONON. nay we that Are the peeres
> & barrones of the Land, are howrly fleicd,
> off Titles & additionns   (l.14)

His favourite, Varletti, is a courtier of Buckingham's stamp, promoted for his dancing skills and who schemes alternately to overthrow the Prorex or to marry into his family. He is fiercely opposed by Archibald and the old nobility who demand to have their 'Antient priviledges & customes' restored, and refuse to stand bare-headed to him (ll.308, 367); the scene in which they are made to give up their staves of ministerial office, which are then conferred on a prodigal and a reveller (ll.1680–1707), brings strongly to mind the comparable incident in *Woodstock* (II.ii). Tyranny produces its own punishment: the Prorex is overthrown by the villains he has himself promoted ('I deservt/For plucking downe the trew Nobillity/& raiseing Boyes & vpstarts' (l.2171)) and is saved only by the intervention of the faithful counsellors who, as the manuscript breaks off, are explaining the true use and dignity of kingship. This is the framework for a fierce philippic on an astonishing range of grievances in court and state: the sale of honours, the begging of forfeit estates, the system of wardship, the legal profession, the decline of hospitality, 'Exaction, op^{r}ssion monopoly, symonye, transportacion, extortion, Rack rent vsery Brokery Bribery knavery knavery, all manner of knaverye, not an honest British name amongst em' (l.2036) – a comprehensive indictment of the unpatriotic rule of an alien tyrant under whom public interest has been supplanted by private, against which Charles, with all *his* supposed leanings towards modern Rome, stands condemned.

Worst of all is the Prorex's treatment of Archibald. Even though he perceives Archibald's taintless loyalty and admires his worth, because he will not reconcile with his bad courtiers he throws him into prison, sets him to the mill with a miserable diet, and beggars his wife and son, while Archibald himself suffers with unequalled patience, accuses his own son of plotting to help him escape and is full of apparently sincere praise for the Prorex's goodness as a monarch; there is an *intentional* dishonouring by the Prorex of those who are most faithful to him (Archibald's son retorts to the threats of torments, 'whip thy doggs: whip thy pesants & fawneing Parasites, my father is a better gentleman & nobler borne, then the proudest [Roman] of y^w all' (l.1515)). This motif of vicious oppression of one's own best subjects, who remain utterly loyal to the limits of their endurance, with its violent and paradoxical expression of complete devotion to the crown even (especially) in the midst of the very worst sufferings at the monarch's hands, looks peculiar but is reiterated elsewhere, in Brome's *Queen and Concubine*, for example, and Heywood's *Royal King and Loyal Subject*. It corresponds to a central element in the experience of the period, one I have already suggested is indicated by the hiatus in the language of politics in the 1630s and of the puritan tracts, which extravagantly appealed to the king for their vindication even while perceiving his complete hostility to them (pp. 20, 89 above) – a powerful sentiment that men of real worth and fidelity are being deliberately, calculatedly excluded and abused, while the basest parasites are graced as though they only were faithful and true. In the scrupulous loyalty of the suffering Archibald, drinking on his knees 'a harty health to my kings wellfare' in the puddle water which the Prorex allows him (l.1727), spectators may have heard echoes of another voice:[51]

It is not unknown what calmness I have used, how little patience I have lost, in the length of all this sufferance, wherein, I here profess and my God knoweth, no thoughts havē possessed me of the personal injury to myself, nor hath my circumstance been able to move me but as it might impart a prejudice to the public, a prejudice to this house, a prejudice to the kingdom.

These are the accents of Sir John Eliot, dying in the Tower: they were repeated again in the letters of the imprisoned John Bastwick professing his unstained loyalty in his sufferings to the best, but most misguided of kings (p. 90 above).

Brome's estates satires

It is clear, even from this brief survey, how challenging the drama was that was being performed at these fashionable theatres. Their playwrights were expressing plenty of reasons for being dissatisfied with England under Charles, and in an aggressive popular manner that made no concessions to the tender feelings of courtiers and wealthy politicians but presented them with their counterparts in self-interested evil counsellors and principal villains in distrusted and discredited regimes. It is with this milieu that Brome's major comedies of 1637–41 emphatically belong, and I wish to look at them in greater detail not only because they are particularly accomplished plays but because of their very considerable originality, that they achieve something which, for all their indebtedness to the Elizabethan tradition, looks genuinely new on the English stage. Though plainly popular in style, it is hard to find exact models for them in the earlier drama; it seems to me that Brome is searching for new forms to his conceit, starting to effect a transformation in dramatic form to order and articulate his changing perception of his society. These plays are adumbrating a kind of mature comedy of political life – complex, ironic, shrewd, subversive – which is continued in *A Jovial Crew* (1641) but the further development of which was cut off by the closure of the theatres in 1642.

Brome's maturer manner begins to crystallize in *The Damoiselle* (Salisbury Court, 1637), a sweeping broadside against the systems of usury and law in which his sympathies are unequivocally with the victims of these two professions, the beggar-maids and ruined gentlemen cast off from society. The play proclaims its popular roots: like a morality or folk-play, 'the World's turn'd prodigall' or 'turn'd/Quite upside downe' (pp. 428–9). There are suggestions of a beast-fable too. The villain, a larger-than-life usurer, is 'a ravenous Beast, a Wolfe' (p. 457), a sly fox ('The Fox here learns to sing' (p. 429)), his son is 'a Wolfe' (p. 383), and he is trying to wed his daughter to a 'Dunghill Scarab,/A water-Dog Knight' (p. 386) who cares more for his dog than for a woman. The usurer is significantly called Vermine, a name Thomas Rawlins gave to one of his characters, apparently for the sake of a single joke: 'there's a great many Courtiers Virmine indeed:/ Those are they that beg poore mens livings'.[52] Brome's Vermine is 'the Monster of our time' (p. 381), inhumanely and cruelly devoted to getting wealth, and who ends the play merely as 'vermin' assailed as a common pest by his enemies (p. 441). He is conflated with another traditional type associated with usury, the devil. He loves 'The Devill 'bove all' (p. 389), his countenance is 'hellish' (p. 439), his breath 'stinkes of brimstone' (p. 399), and his son is a 'Devilish Rascall' ('Had I rak'd *Limbo*, as I did the *Compter*,/I were not better fitted with a Copesmate' (pp. 416–17)). He even has his hypocritical 'Usurers Scripture', by which he gives 'good admonition with [his] Money' (p. 380). Hell and London, Limbo and the Compter interpenetrate visually as they do in Mill's *Night's Search*, social and moral types (usury and devilry) overlapping. This is the emblematic style of Brome's friends; it is also the caricature of the avaricious usurer that was popularized by the godly preachers in their moral treatises. Frequently Brome's good characters break out into attacks on Vermine and usury that are almost little sermons:

> how slight a thing
> It is, for such base Worldlings to be rich?
> That study nothing but to scrape and save.
> That have no Faith, but in their ready money,
> Nor love to Worldly pleasures above those
> Poor Coblers use.   (p. 386)

These orations expand into general denunciations of an oppressing society:

> What corrupt Lawyer, or usurious Citizen,
> Oppressing Landlord, or unrighteous Judge,
> But leaves the World with horror? (p. 440)

The heirs of such will 'Turne Idiots, Lunaticks, Prodigals, or Strumpets' (p. 440) and, finally, beggars.

This parading of social types in the language is realized vividly on stage by their visual embodiment in the dramatis personae. Brome depicts a known and named environment (rather like the realism of Shirley's London plays), but he peoples it emblematically. Vermine is brought to 'the Temple Walks' (p. 398), and there '*Lawyers and others passe over the Stage as conferring by two and two*' (p. 407); they are watched by Brookeall, a man 'Undone by Suits' and wearing 'a ragged one' (p. 437), and Phillis, a beggar, emblems of the victims of usury and law. In this, and a similar scene later, Brookeall and Phillis become choric commentators or presenters of a picture. Brookeall instructs the audience to observe 'The Giants, that over-threw him: Though they strut/ And are swolne bigger by his emptiness', and he cries out 'See the *Vermine,*/That hath devoured me living' (p. 437), his language effecting a transition from Vermine the individual to *vermin* in the collective, the rats he imagines gnawing at his body. Brookeall protests against the 'false and mercilesse' system and declares Law has become

> Supportresse of oppression;
> Ruine of Families, past the bloody rage
> Of Rape or Murder: All the crying sins
> Negotiating for Hell in her wild practise. (p. 408)

To confirm this indictment, an attorney enters to invite Brookeall to sell his conscience by becoming a hired witness, a Knight of the Post, an invitation he angrily refuses. Phillis too explains that in the Temple Walks are found

> Brokers, Projectors, Common Bail, or Bankrupts,
> Pandars, and Cheaters of all sorts, that mix here
> Mongst men of honor, worship, lands and money. (pp. 406–7)

The Walks are a realistic setting which the presenters lead us to understand symbolically. It is a displaying of the professions; we see less people than a gallery of social types that the pervasive imagery of hell and devils invite us to reinterpret as a moral gallery too, an anatomy of the world. As Brookeall moralizes it, the symbolic aspect of the scene takes in all men, for we are all, like these people, living on credit:

> Nature sent us
> All naked hither; and all the Goods we had
> We onely took on Credit with the World.
> And that the best of men are but meer borrowers:
> Though some take longer day.   (p. 409)

The visual parade of emblematic types has become a *theatrum mundi*, an exposure of a society bound together by law not love. Usury and Law here share the stage with their unacknowledged allies, Beggary and Ruin.

These satirical types are added to in the language of subsequent scenes. Phillis supposes that her father must have been a courtier, since beggary, which she has inherited from him, is characteristic of courtiers everywhere. In the subplot, which concerns a pretended project to raffle off a girl's maidenhead, we are told that Lords, justices, usurers and merchants are contributing (p. 424), and the raffle itself adds the Whore who is raffled, the Projector her bawd and the 'Devill' her pandar (p. 425). Brome's picture of society anatomized into all its ranks or 'estates' looks back to Elizabethan plays like Wilson's *Three Ladies of London* (1588) and to the Tudor social morality, as well as to the world of popular ballad and complaint, but without ever becoming merely stiff and schematic. The strategy enables his indictment of a corrupt England to be comprehensive and memorable while remaining fully dramatic.

To be brief, around these estates-types and symbolic scenes Brome weaves a complex plot in which the inhuman system of bonds and warrants associated with the usurer and lawyers is broadly contrasted with the values of conscience, charity and brotherliness upheld by the hero, Dryground, who intrigues to thwart and ultimately reform Vermine. There is a general political moral here: the law was a traditional satiric target, but it was also a particularly sensitive area at a time when Charles was using the law courts as a means of enforcing policy, developing legal devices as fiscal expedients, and appealing to judicial opinions as a substitute for a sanction he could not rely on parliament to provide. The Londoners who saw *The Damoiselle* had listened to Hampden's case the same year, and Dryground's benevolent familial care and paternalism acts as an implicit rebuff to the lovelessness of public paternalism. More specifically, the supposed raffle which he organizes is repeatedly described as a 'project' (pp. 380, 415, 416, 425, 457, 464, 466) and Brome may well have had in mind here the legal monopolies and 'projects' to which Charles turned as a means of indirect taxation. Dryground's project turns out to be a sham designed to reunite his family, and the rafflers 'all recanted/The barbarous purpose' (p. 461); it shows that projects have a right and a wrong use, and that when used to exploit, as Dryground's apparently is, they are both illegal and inhumane.

There is a strikingly Shakespearean side to *The Damoiselle*; its characters all learn from their experience. The final reconciliation is a finding of one's true nature after a temporary period of madness, obstruction or disguise, and these echoes are stronger still in *The Antipodes* (Phoenix/Salisbury Court, 1638) which revolves around a series of cures and imitates the Shakespearean motifs of beneficial madness and the inverted world. In the London house of Lord Letoy, the madman Peregrine is cured of his delusions by being taken, in a play-within-the-play, to London's antipodes, where everything directly inverts the normalities of home; in the process, the members of his family are drawn unwittingly into the illusion and find their own melancholy or anxieties dissolving too. At the centre of *The Antipodes*, in the play-in-the-play, is a parade of estates even more explicitly emblematic than that in *The Damoiselle*, but it is not distanced by intervening moralizing commentators or by extravagant language of devils and vermin. Rather, the very process of inverting normality is integrated with the major concerns of the play, and the emblematic manner, once enabled to issue into the level of action, becomes disturbing in itself, the ambiguities of inversion challenging the normality or healthiness of real London and functioning as a brilliant structural and analytic tool.

For example, in Letoy's Anti-London we have inversions which are simply amusing, confirming our confidence in our certainties. Here coachmen beat captains, women fight, men are ducked, old men go to school and merchants ask gentlemen to cuckold them. But these are mixed with more problematic inversions – women ruling their husbands, wives seducing their servants, aldermen who lack wit, ladies being taught by their parrots. These are already established as satiric *topoi* in real London, so that Anti-London is not always an inversion of normality but a revelation of what normality ordinarily hides; inversion – sickness – is a part of 'normal' life. Brome underlines this ambiguity by having a running commentary on the play from Peregrine's step-mother Diana, which goes 'How finely contrary th'are still to ours' (p. 284). For example, he presents a beggar who uses courtly language, and a courtier who begs. Diana comments:

> how feelingly
> He begges; then as the beggers are the best
> Courtiers, it seemes the Courtiers are best beggers
> In the *Antipodes*; how contrary in all
> Are they to us? (p. 282)

Then we see a lawyer forcing money from a beggar ('True Antipodeans still') and a usurer giving him charity. The usurers, we are told, are

> Souldiers, and Courtiers chiefly;
> And some that passe for grave and pious Church-men.
> DIANA. How finely contrary th'are still to ours. (p. 284)

Diana's fatuousness suggests that the direct opposite is true, that the Antipodes is what *is*, not what is not. Her ironic obviousness provokes the conclusions that courtiers *are* beggars, that lawyers make beggars, that courtiers and churchmen really are usurers. And the memorable visual, emblematic presentation makes the ambiguity pervasive. Not only do we see satirical types, but these types – beggars, courtiers, soldiers and usurers – come to stand for their whole estate. The point is not that some courtiers are like beggars, but that London and Anti-London are indistinguishable: courtiers and beggars are simply interchangeable.

Of course it is courtiers and high-churchmen such as these against whom inversion rebounds most forcefully; Brome's sharpest barbs are reserved for absurdities in Anti-London which have counterparts in real abuses existing in the true London. The Antipodean statesmen patronize projects and monopolies, all of which are useless or just foolish (such as a design to cover horses with sheepskins to increase wool); the project for the charitable recovery of decayed gamesters and criminals makes the sly point that monopolies are being used to 'finde reliefe for Cheaters, Bawdes, and Thieves' (p. 311). Another inversion is the 'odde/ Jeering Judge' who refuses to be ruled by the law:

> you shall know
> I can give judgement, be it right or wrong,
> Without their needlesse proving and defending ... (p.288)

The self-opinionated judge belongs in a traditional line descending from Jonson's Justice Clement and including the corrupt or eccentric justices of Brome's own *Jovial Crew* and Cavendish's *Variety*, and the double-dealing lawyer in Robert Chamberlain's *The Swaggering Damsel* (> 1640), but by 'needlesse proving and defending' Brome may also have been thinking of the drawn-out arguments and delayed judgment of the Ship Money case. The sword of justice by which Charles rules has come to look very like the sword with which Peregrine tries to knight his Antipodean judge, only a property dagger of lath.[53] Similarly, the play's doctor is said to have had court officers come to him for cure

> and men of place,
> Whose sences were so numm'd, they understood not
> Bribes from dew fees, and fell on premunires,
> He has cur'd diverse, that can now distinguish,
> And know both when, and how to take, of both;
> And grow most safely rich by't ... (p. 235)

This seems to be alluding to the inquiry of 1635 into the behaviour of Sir James Bagg ('Bottomless Bagg') to whom another courtier had fruitlessly given £2,500 for his services as an intermediary in an attempt to get repayment of a debt of £6,000 from the Lord Treasurer. The episode was highly embarrassing for the government for it highlighted its insolvency and the large part played by bribes and gifts in the normal course of the court's business. Charles, who expected his courtiers to take the fruits of their place as remuneration for attendance, gave judgment for Bagg.[54]

So the illusion which Brome's characters watch disturbs and criticizes the reality of *their* audience; it demonstrates how upside-down is the real England under Charles. But like other topsy-turvy worlds, the Antipodes also has a positive, normative side, and is partly a land of Cockayne in which the inversion improves on the reality. Here lawyers are honest, sergeants merciful, aldermen enjoy poetry and poets are paid by the verse. High fantasy it may be, but Brome makes it more than wishful thinking because the play of the Antipodes is set within a realistic frame (the play, *The Antipodes*) in which the stage Londoners are *cured* of their melancholy by their co-operation with Anti-London. On a simple level, the framing characters gain from a correcting sense of the balance of normal life, but, more deeply, they are drawn into their Antipodes, first by responding sympathetically as spectators, but then actually by entering the play-in-the-play as actors or participants, and their readiness to take part with their opposite restores them to wholeness. This is a time-honoured apology for the dignity of the imagination, the ability of illusion to better reality,[55] but it is also an argument for the desirability of inversion in real life. The fictional Londoners who enter the play of Antipodes within the play are implicitly parallel with the real Londoners who themselves watch Brome's play of *The Antipodes* and respond sympathetically to it, and at the outset he notes that they too are sick, for he alludes to the severe plague of 1636–37 which closed the theatres, and during which his play may well have been planned. The play-within-the-play extends the diagnosis by demonstrating other sorts of sickness outside the play in 'real' London, but it is simultaneously the device by which it is to be cured. Just as the stage Londoners are cured by going to the Antipodes, so real London needs curing by being turned upside-down.

In effect, *The Antipodes* is a play about the other England, 'New England', a locale to which the mad Peregrine, who has adopted the role of player 'King' of the Antipodes, specifically alludes as he begins to return to sanity:

> PEREGRINE. What if I crav'd? a Counsell from New *England*?
> The old will spare me none.
> DOCTOR. Is this man mad?
> My cure goes fairely on. (p. 307)

Peregrine's concern for his lack of counsel in 'old' England refers directly to the absence of parliament from real London, and the proposal to co-operate with 'New' England is a solution which is more than merely imaginary. New England really was the inverse of the old, for it was the refuge of those subjects who were opposite to Charles's rule, the puritans who had fled from the persecutions of Laud's drive for conformity. On several occasions the truth of the Antipodean subjects is stressed:

> DIANA. What subjects there are
> In the *Antipodes*.
> LETOY. None in the world so loving. (p. 293)

On Peregrine's entry to his Anti-London, a satiric commonplace has more than laughter value:

> PEREGRINE. All I have seene since my arrivall, are
> Wonders. But your humanity excells.
> BYPLAY. Vertue in the *Antipodes* onely dwells. (p. 273)

To some of Charles's subjects, even to such a moderate as George Herbert, virtue *did* only dwell in the Antipodes ('Religion stands on tiptoe in our land,/Ready to pass to the *American* strand').[56] By having his mad king restored to his wits and to good rule by seeking counsel from his subjects, and specifically from New England, Brome hints at a political moral, that Charles will rule better by turning his government upside-down, attending to more puritanical opinion and returning to rule with the sanction of a parliament.

An important figure in the play is Letoy, the lord who organizes the cure. He has a special relationship with illusion. He steps in and out of the play, and like Hamlet is familiar with the actors. He incorporates the play's inversion into his normal life, for he is a plain lord who though of noble birth dresses like a pedlar and consorts with common men in the idealized Elizabethan manner of harmony between ruler and ruled. He is thus a member of (fictional) real London and topsy-turvydom simultaneously, and though himself a creature of illusion the audience may have recognized the similarity between Letoy and the play's dedicatee, Hertford, another noble with Antipodean views, 'A loyall Lord' but 'a wondrous plaine one' (p. 293). It is through participating in the dance of harmony with such other-England figures that health will be restored; the only alternative is to remain locked, like Peregrine, in melancholy and madness.

Hence only by reading *The Antipodes* as essentially a comedy of political life does the full coherence of its splendid design become apparent. It is this idea of co-operating with one's apparent opposite which provides the fundamental link between the subject of the outer play, the cure of individuals, and the pervasive concerns of the inner play with the problem of the sick state, and it also indicates the relevance of the presence of Letoy and of having Peregrine's recovery come about in the role of a king reforming his upside-down country. Here satire and solution are identical. Inverting society shows what is wrong with it and how it may be cured, and the whole is unified into a particularly fine statement about the potential political usefulness of the stage: just as the stage Londoners are cured through their antipodes, so real Londoners will find the play *The Antipodes* beneficial if they accept its diagnosis. *The Antipodes* is brilliantly successful in its combination of popular satiric devices and sophisticated dramatic technique in the interests of a comprehensive political statement; it is difficult and multi-layered, yet Brome is wholly in control at every point. Moreover, the complex ironies of his antipodal inversions produced a play which is much more double-edged and sharply critical than *The Damoiselle*. Underlying *The Antipodes* is a nexus of popular motifs linked with the Saturnalia – passage through release or madness, overturning of degree, flouting of authority – which are normally thought of as acting as safety-valves for society's repressed energies but which in Brome's hands turn into a far more specifically political, potentially radical critique of Charles's government.

These subversive possibilities of the popular style were finally, and fully realized in *The Court Beggar* which, performed at the Phoenix in May 1640 while the new but ill-fated Short Parliament was still sitting, brought the wrath of the king crashing down onto the company and virtually wrecked the career of its manager, William Beeston. It has already been demonstrated that the play mocks Suckling in the courtier Sir Ferdinand and – perhaps – Davenant in the poetic Court-wit;⁵⁷ but we can go much further than this, for the royal objection to the play was not simply irritation at ill-advised personal satire. Rather, the court's furious reaction shows that it recognized how dangerous the play was; *The Court Beggar* is a full-blooded and uncompromising demonstration of the bankruptcy of the personal rule and an attack on all that the court, by 1640, had come to represent.

Sir Henry Herbert recorded that the play 'had relation to the passages of the [King's] journey into the Northe',⁵⁸ by which he must mean the delusions of the mad Ferdinand/Suckling that he is still at Berwick fighting the Scots in Charles's disastrous and unpopular northern war (pp. 218–19), in which Suckling had earned himself enormous derision as a coward and a bungler. But there is much in the play besides this that would have highly offended Whitehall. Ferdinand may have some specific traits of Suckling, but he also functions as a portrait of the courtier in general, 'a Man rising in the favour Royall' (p. 186), a favourite typical for being a liar, blackguard and a vicious libertine. Ferdinand has designs on Charissa, the daughter of his client Mendicant with whom he has ingratiated himself merely to get access to her; but he also intends to rape the attractive widow Lady Strangelove, and to facilitate this he pretends to be mad. His condition the others interpret as natural to a courtier, to be

> Mad with conceit of being a favorite
> Before your time, that is, before you had merit . . .
> When you were counted wise, great, valiant, and what not
> That cryes a Courtier up, and gives him power
> To trample on his betters.   (pp. 246–7)

Ferdinand is contrasted with the worthy but unmoneyed Frederick, who loves Charissa truly, and Brome establishes the antithesis
between them as an opposition between honest Merit and courtly
Favour:

> Merit only
> It is that smoothes the brow of Majesty,
> And takes the comfort of those precious beauties
> Which shine from grace Divine: and hee's a Traytor
> (No way to stand a courtier) that to feed
> His Lusts, and Riots, works out of his Subjects
> The meanes, by forging grants of the Kings favour.   (p. 235)

The 'lusts and riots' of courtiers we actually see, for Lady
Strangelove has to be rescued forcibly from Ferdinand's violent
sexual assault on her. He is paired with his client and associate,
Mendicant, the court beggar of the play's title. Mendicant, 'an
old Knight, turnd a projector' (p. 183), stands on the fringes of
the court begging for the grants of favour alluded to above
which Ferdinand may obtain for him from the king and which he
can then put to his own use. He searches out

> Where such a forfeiture is to be begg'd;
> Where one would purchase a Reprieve, another
> A Pardon or a lease of Life Rope-free
> For ready money: Then where Goods or Lands
> Are found of men that make away themselfes,
> And so of fooles and madmen; All to set
> Your trade of Begging up, and still you beg . . .   (p. 188)

There are three types of clientage under attack here. Firstly,
Mendicant is another Sir James Bagg, acting as an intermediary
between great courtiers and non-courtiers who need to pursue
business at court but have no direct access to it; hence he can
turn the workings of justice or of court affairs into a source of
profit to himself. Secondly, he competes to be allowed to

administer estates which, through the incapacity of their owners, have fallen into the gift of the crown; this system, closely related to the unpopular but hugely profitable arrangement for the wardship of minors, exploits those without full rights, yet whose exploitation it was expressly designed to prevent. Thirdly, he is an aspiring patentee, who works with a trio of 'projectors', 'project Beagles' (p. 188) who hunt out suitable schemes for him to beg from the king to be granted as a monopoly, another device, and one of the most hated grievances of early Stuart England, by which he may make his own private profit out of what is, supposedly, public business. Brome's attack is two-pronged: in Ferdinand is figured the worthlessness of courtiers, in Mendicant the corrupt and immoral practices by which they capitalize on their favoured place.

Brome is trespassing onto extremely sensitive areas. Without parliamentary levies to fall back on, wardship, monopolies and forfeitures were crucial sources of revenue for the crown. Charles made great play with schemes such as fines for default of knighthood or for (imaginary) encroachments on the royal forests, and with monopolies over a vast range of products, which his courtiers devised for him and then implemented on his behalf; nationally, these aroused enormous suspicion and resentment. Moreover, the making of grants to favoured courtiers was a means of getting business done in the absence of a regular paid bureaucracy, while patents and monopolies were developed, haphazardly and inefficiently, as a form of economic regulation or simply interference. Of course, the impecunious Mendicant is not a *successful* speculator; the leitmotif of court beggary cuts deeper than complaints about the wealth of courtiers. Rather, Brome's point appears to be a condemnation of the whole system of preference of which Mendicant is a part, that, operating through the channels of a hierarchy of parasitic courtiers – court beggars – Charles implements a justice which is unjust, an economic policy which is in itself uneconomic, for they involved the perpetual gratification of an army of useless middlemen who merely burden, unproductively, the labours of others. For example, the schemes devised by the projectors in Act I are not merely foolish, but redundant (such as a tax on fashions, or on child-getting, to be operated by them). They promise good returns to the king, but they also envisage gigantic profits to Mendicant and themselves, and all 'Without all grievance unto the subject'; Mendicant's servant comments sarcastically, 'That's no little marvaile' (p. 192). In the 1630s the puritan Simonds D'Ewes complained that England laboured under numerous monopolies which were 'to the enriching of some few projectors, and the impoverishing of all the kingdom beside'.[59] Brome's point is the same, but is more sharply imaged: he mentions the monopoly of sedans, under which 'The subject groanes, when for the ease of one/Two abler men must suffer' (p. 194). Not only Mendicant, but the entire court superstructure is sponging off the rest of the country, and this is what lies behind Charissa's rebuke to her father, which opens the play, for having come up to London as a court hanger-on, to the total neglect of the good estate he had in the country:

> Large fruitfull Fields, rich Medowes and sweet pastures
> Well cropt with corne and stockd as well with Cattell,
> A parke well stor'd with Deere too, and Fishponds in't,
> And all this [left] for a lodging in the Strand now . . .
> Your own fed Beefes and Muttons, Fowle and Poultry
> Loaded your long boords then; and you had then
> Neighbours could boast your hospitality,
> And poore, that for the remnants prayd for you,
> Now all concludes upon a two-dishd table.   (pp. 187–8)

Mendicant's 'numerous Family/Of Servants and Attendants' has degenerated into 'a Varlet Coachman, and Footboy', a life of spurious fashion and gentility replacing the old worthy ways which he once upheld. Charissa's rebuke – the complaint of country against court, provinces against the centre – announces impoverishment as the play's central concern, that the tremendous dominance of the court and its clients is dragging all wealth and power from the rest of the country to London, there to be frittered away. Beggary is more than the condition of the court, it is a prospect which the court is forcing onto the whole realm.

The history of Mendicant demonstrates how beggarly the

clientage system is, characterized as it is by continual rapacity and a correspondingly accelerating impoverishment. Mendicant at first intends to marry Charissa off to Ferdinand, but hearing of his madness he sets about to beg his estate. No sooner has he achieved his ends, but he is himself accused on a trumped-up murder charge, and his own estate is snatched from his hands; another courtier has 'beg'd the Begger' (p. 264). There is a strong moral charge in this attack. Mendicant is quite happy to live by begging, for 'The Beggers best is that he feeles no shame' (p. 197), and this is something which also reflects very badly on the king. The suggestion is present that not only are Charles's finances mendacious, but that his rule is penurious too: the justice which is sold, and the economic devices which are uneconomic are already discredited, and the court which employs them must be morally beggared. Charles presides at the top of a hierarchy of scroungers, each courtier begging off the one above and exploiting those below. With courtiers like Mendicant, he can be only 'Lord of Beggers' (p. 196).

So in the Mendicant plot, the comparison of courtiers with beggars is developed with considerable analytic and emblematic force until beggary becomes a telling symbol for the economic state of the country, and the moral state of the court. On the other side, the Ferdinand plot is dominated by the idea of the madness which he has assumed to rape the widow. Again, madness is elaborated as a condition common to courtiers. Ferdinand is 'as mad,/As you can thinke a Courtier must be/That is more mad then all the rest' (p. 189), and he confesses he was expecting that a court lady would prefer a madman and allow him to be free with her, since

> Monkeyes, Fooles, and Madmen,
> That cannot blab, or must not be believ'd
> Receave strange favours. (p. 250)

In a striking stage emblem, the lunatic courtier is brought on bound and hooded like a hawk, and put through his mad tricks. Madness infects the others too: Lady Strangelove pretends madness to further her counter-plots, and in the last act everyone is so preoccupied with preparing a masque that a visitor imagines they 'are bewitch'd . . . All Lunatick . . . Never was I in such a Wildernesse' (pp. 262–3). Only the news that Mendicant has begged him causes Ferdinand to drop the pretence, and betrayed and disgraced, he is forced to make reparations (though Lady Strangelove finally weds him regardless). For his part, Mendicant's dreams of great, unrealizable wealth are an additional form of madness ('When shall you take possession, thinke you,' he is asked, 'of your/Lordship of Lunacy in the *Cynthian* Orbe?' (p. 237)), and when his designs fall to the ground he runs mad indeed; however, his recovery to sanity, the climax of the play, is effected in a most singular and pointed manner.

The concluding action is a masque which, though arranged to celebrate the stolen marriage of Frederick and Charissa, functions satirically rather as the masque in Newcastle's *The Variety*. Performed by seven minor characters, there are ironic relation-ships between some of the masquers and the parts they play. Mercury is represented by Dainty, a fashionable picture-drawer, yet who has just been exposed as a real thief; Venus is Strange-love's maid, whose whoredom has been established, and her bastard son stands in as Cupid. Having undercut the courtly pretensions of his mock-masque, Brome allows Mendicant to blunder into it, in 'wild distraction and phantastick fury' (p. 267), and heralded by his projectors, themselves announced as messen-gers from the underworld:

> FERDINAND. What black Tragedian's this?
> RAPHAEL. Some *Nuntius* sent from Hell.   (p. 266)

'News newly arriving from hell' was a motif which Brome picked up from the common stock of popular satirical literature, and one which had already been used by some of his friends. The hero of Rawlins's *Rebellion* runs temporarily mad and thinks himself in hell where the great sinners of the world are getting their just deserts:

> Here on a Wheele, turn'd by a Furies hand,
> Hangs a distracted States-man, that had spent
> The little wit Heaven to strange purpose lent him,

To suppresse right, make beggers, and get meanes
To be a Traytor. Ha, ha, ha, and here
A Vsurer fat with the curses of so many heires
His Extortion had undone, sate to the Chin
In a warme bath, made of new melted gold . . .   (sig.G1ʳ)

He sees beside a whore-master, a punk, a prodigal, a glutton and a foolish gallant. In Richards's *Messallina*, Messallina's mother madly describes politic statesmen and painted ladies in hell, urging the devils to 'Note with your grim aspects the courts of Kings' (sig.C7ᵛ), and there are comparable effects in Davenport's *New Trick to Cheat the Devil*. In the *Court Beggar*, Ferdinand, feigning a mad fit, pretended he was transported to hell which he described as 'a trobled world in want of Statesmen' and great ladies to promote pride and new fashions, and he invited the court to follow him there and 'raise a new Plantation' (p. 221). Mendicant's arrival from hell comes as the animating of one of these established satiric types, especially since he is decked out with the emblems of his trade: '*Enter Mendicant attir'd all in Patents; A Windmill on his head*' (p. 267). Thus, attended by his projectors, he is established as a caricature of the generic type, the Monopolist; his windmill is the commonplace satirical badge of mad or fanciful enterprises. Mendicant enumerates his crazy monopolies and, in an excited, festive conclusion, he dances while the others pull off his patents, and the projectors' cloaks, '*who appeare all ragged*' underneath and are finally '*thrust forth*' (p. 268). The 'excellent Morrall' is drawn: 'The Projects are all cancel'd, and the Projectors turnd out o' dores' (p. 268).

What Brome is doing in this extraordinary sequence is quite clear. The masque, set apart by its extreme stylization, encapsulates memorably and graphically the themes of the play. More than in any earlier piece, Brome provides a dance of emblems, an animated picture of wholly symbolic characters in fantastic but significant costume, accompanied by a moralizing commentary. Its effect is to universalize the various estates-types we see dancing so that, just as beggary was expanded into a symbol for all courtiers, the masque dissects its society into a panorama composed almost entirely of projectors, monopolists, beggars, madmen, whores and thieves. It is a full-scale Displaying, or Anatomy of the Times: the visual contradictions implicit in the casting of the Thief and Whore in the courtly masque become an explicit *exposure* in the case of the projectors who are revealed for what they are with a theatrical flourish. Furthermore, as the masque uncovers the times' errors, it also enacts Brome's proposed solution for reforming them. Mendicant addresses himself to his astonished audience as if to parliament:

> Roome here: a Hall for a Monopolist,
> You, Common-wealths informers lead me on.
> Bring me before the great Assembly. See,
> Fathers Conscript, I present all I have
> For you to cancell . . .
>   . . . I submit
> Myselfe to your most honorable censure.
>   CIT-WIT. What dos he take us for?
>   SWAYNE-WIT. Powers, Powers; A lower house at least. (pp. 267–8)

Mendicant's language involves his stage-spectators, and through them the real audience, in the game he is playing, in which they take part as members of the 'lower house'; his dance is an emblem of the greater cancelling of patents in which Brome invites them to participate. The Monopolist – in the abstract, as it were – is brought to parliament from his home in hell and divested of his projects, and in the extended epilogue which follows the whole cast turns openly to the audience and warns them directly against patronizing courtly plays. More fully and imaginatively than in any other play of the period, Brome is exploiting the spectacular resources of the popular style in the service of a distinct, and highly radical, political moral. The concluding masque turns the play into a great festive, Saturnalian overthrowing of monopolies and grievances, in which players and audience, on a wave of anti-court feeling, vigorously celebrate their political expectations and anticipate their success. It would have taken little effort to have connected Brome's concluding masque with the hopes vested in the new parliament, sitting at that moment for the first time in eleven years.

From popular style to political polemic

The Court Beggar presents us definitively with that fully achieved political drama which was always a latent possibility in the popular theatrical tradition. In his mature comedies, with their satiric inversions, plays-in-the-play, Shakespearean echoes, generic characters taken from chapbook and ballad, inclusive social perspective, feeling for the unprivileged and distrust of the present, Brome writes as a dramatist engaged passionately with the most pressing and significant concerns of his day and who, simultaneously, is bidding not for the attention of a small courtly elite but for a truly national audience, all those who in the spring of 1640 were looking to the new parliament to represent their interests and right their grievances. His carnivalesque plays may have filled a gap (London was unusual in seventeenth-century Europe for its lack of a period of carnival and organized public merry-making),[60] but in the process of transference from ephemeral outdoor game to written play, the licensed freedoms of carnival sports have been turned into something more disturbing than a single day's carnival could be: Brome converts the festival notion of turning the world upside-down from a gay but transient fantasy into a radical and enduring criticism of his society. Like Middleton's *Game at Chess* which in 1624 had rallied public abhorrence for James's pro-Spanish policies, *The Court Beggar* articulated sentiments that were widely held but utterly unpalatable to the king (indeed, it *accelerates* resentment against the court; though no one man dabbled in all varieties of monopolies, Mendicant appears as the Monopolist, a kind of composite villain who focuses the repugnance felt for them all). The Phoenix was closed down and the actors thrown into prison on 4 May 1640; the following day, Charles dissolved the parliament which had sat for only three weeks.

The Court Beggar belongs to a specific, significant moment in English politics; nevertheless it must not be represented as an exceptional case. Mendicant, attired in his patents, stands in a long and particular stage line: he is plainly a grotesque, an *antic*, closely related to the puppet-like figures – prodigal, beggar, usurer, devil, and so forth – who dance in satirically-paired groups in Davenport's *New Trick to Cheat the Devil* and who are identified by their emblematic costumes: '*Enter an* ANTICKE *habited in Parchment Indentures. Bills, Bonds, Waxes, Seales, and Pen, and Inkhornes: on his breast writ,* I am a Scrivener'.[61] Hybrid characters of this type, part man, part beast, part emblem, stretch back into the sixteenth century and beyond, especially in the literature of political and religious controversy. Cruel, scurrilous and sometimes obscene, they were a plebeian substitute for learned argument, vividly compressed polemical statements immediately comprehensible even to an unlettered audience. Mendicant has many prototypes in popularly-circulating wood-cuts and broadsides, but also in theatrical performances, such as the anti-Catholic mummings of the 1560s in which asses and wolves appeared dressed as cardinals and friars, and the Martin Marprelate scandal of 1588 to 1590, when Martin was brought onto the stage 'with a cocks combe, an apes face, a wolfs bellie, cats claws &c'.[62] Brome's lampoon on the Monopolist continues a popular tradition of racy stage caricature, but it was by no means unique in the 1630s. Apart from Davenport's grotesques, six projectors rode as antics in the procession preceding Shirley's masque *The Triumph of Peace* (1634), bearing emblems of their absurd patents (one wearing a bunch of carrots on his head, another a furnace, a third encased in a device for breathing under water); the city spectators were highly gratified by this protest about 'the unfitness and ridiculousness of these Projects against the Law'.[63] A few months later, on the death of the Attorney-General, William Noy, who had devised some of Charles's most notorious monopolies and fiscal schemes, the players were said to have caricatured him publicly in a lost play, *A Projector Lately Dead*:[64]

wherein they bring him in his Lawyers robes upon the Stage, and openly dissecting him, find 100. Proclamations in his head, a bundle of motheaten records in his maw, halfe a barrell of new white sope in his belly, which made him to scoure [i.e. purge] so much, and yet, say they, he is still very black & foule within.

This slapstick revenge on a hated politician is a direct predecessor

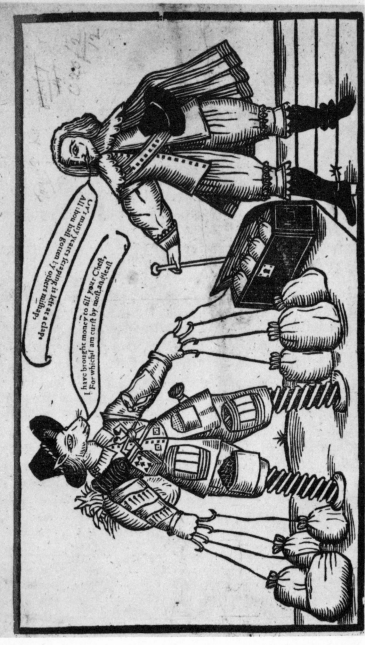

Plate 6. Tenterhook the projector and Dodger the patentee, from J. Taylor, *The Complaint of Mr Tenterhook* (1641).

of Brome's de-patenting of Mendicant, and what such figures must have looked like in the theatres is graphically shown by the woodcut which heads John Taylor's 1641 satirical broadside *The Complaint of Mr Tenterhook the Projector and Sir Thomas Dodger the Patentee* (plate 6). Here the patentee – the man of Mendicant's interests – is obviously a courtier, fashionably dressed with lace collar, spurs and cane, but the projector corresponds closely to what Brome demands for Mendicant, being hung about with the symbols of his patents for wine, soap, coals, tobacco, pins, playing-cards, dice and so on. Tenterhook's other features are explained in the verses which Taylor puts into his mouth, like a stage monologue:

> My legs were Screwes, to raise thee high or low,
> According as your power did *Ebbe* or *Flow* . . .
> For you, I made my *Fingers fish-hookes* still
> To catch at all *Trades*, either good or ill . . .
> I put a *Swines face* on, an *Asses eares*,
> The one to listen unto all I heard
> Wherein your worships profit was prefer'd.
> The other to tast all things, good or bad
> (As Hogs will doe) where profit may be had.

He also has, like Brome's projectors, a 'cloak of honesty' with which to hide his foulness. Dodger[65] replies that they had almost monopolized the whole land, '*Silke, Tallow, Hobby-horses, Wood, red-herring,/Law, Conscience, Iustice, swearing,* and *For-swearing*', but now parliament has returned they are ruined. Taylor describes them as '*Vermine*' that '*or'e this Land did crawle,/And grew so rich, they gaind the Devill and all*', and his squib demonstrates clearly how, with the collapse of the censorship in 1641, the satirical devices and political concerns of the popular stages were quickly and readily assimilated into the work of purely political pamphleteers. It may be that Taylor's picture derives from actual theatrical portrayals of such pairs of antics, or even that he designed his grotesques with some possibility of stage performance in mind (a character called Tenterhook appears in the short pamphlet-play of 1641 *The Counter's Discourse*, an estates satire on the inhumanity of law- and prison-officers which recalls Brome's *Damoiselle* and would not have been unstageable). Certainly the antic figure of the projector was widely disseminated, for it crops up again in later political satires,[66] and achieved the dignity of being engraved by Wenceslaus Hollar.

Similarly, the arrival of Mendicant as a rogue out of hell owes much to the popular ballad or pamphlet of burlesque news, the kind of political satire which re-emerges energetically after 1640 in such ribald lampoons as *News from Avernus* (1642), *An Epistle from Lucifer* (1642) and John Taylor's *The Hellish Parliament* and *The Devil Turned Roundhead* (1641). The common features are well displayed in the anonymous satire *Machiavel as He Lately Appeared to His Dear Sons, the Modern Projectors* (London, 1641). Here Machiavel comes to England from hell and, in a heavily ironic speech, praises the industry and inventiveness of the projectors, and rebukes those who dare 'disturbe my Darlings, or compell/ Them 'fore their time to take their Thrones in hell' (sig.A3ᵛ). A character of that *'pestilent Vermine'* the Projector follows, and an account of his practices, recent sickness, death and epitaph. But Mendicant's devilishness is also indebted to archaic yet still current theatrical models too. When Middleton threw the condemned black pieces into the 'bag' at the end of his *Game at Chess* he was relying for his full effect on its association with the medieval hell-mouth, or perhaps even still using that old stage prop.[67] The hell-mouth *did* survive in a lost provincial play of 1621 in order that 'Landlords and puritanes and Sheriffs bailiffs' that 'puke and poole, & peele' poor men and tenants could be consigned into it, and in 1628 the Star Chamber was anxiously investigating a play performed by Yorkshire recusants in which King James had been carried off to hell on the devil's back, like the vice in Ulpian Fulwell's morality *Like Will to Like* (> 1568).[68] Devils, we recall, were staple fare at the Fortune and Red Bull.

What I am suggesting is that *The Court Beggar* represents the tip of an iceberg of popular political drama, the exact size of which can only be inadequately guessed at and which is now almost totally beyond reconstruction. Some idea of what passes unseen in the decade can be gathered from the massive explosion of political commentary and satire which occurred in the 1640s when the collapse of the censorship took the lid off a seething lower-class world of heresy, scepticism and dissent; obviously this rich flood of radical ideas could not have been created out of nothing. There is a real problem of interpretation here, that such evidence as I have collected in the paragraphs above is not of the sort to have got into print or to have survived at all except under the most unusual circumstances (for example, we only know of *A Projector Lately Dead* from an impeccably puritan pamphlet of 1636 and from a letter to the godly New Englander John Winthrop). Nevertheless, this need not limit us completely. The evidence brought together above is sporadic but at least does indicate the existence of a tradition; it may be discontinuous, but it contains clear and significant continuities.

Once again, the great unknown is the question of the open-air theatres, and in this context the lack of information about their repertoire is a crippling gap, not least because of the serious imbalance it poses in respect of the increasingly vociferous demands made by the lower sort of people for a political voice. The establishment of a permanent popular political consciousness, although not new in the 1630s was in large measure a creation of these years. One thinks of the great crowds that applauded Prynne, Burton and Bastwick on the scaffold in 1637 and lined the streets in 1640 when they returned triumphantly from exile, strewing flowers and laurel in their path; the organized attack on Lambeth palace in 1640; the tumultuous demonstrations against Laud, Strafford and the Catholics day after day at Westminster in 1641–42, calling for justice and jostling the bishops as they tried to get into parliament; the petitions with thousands of signatures presented to the Commons by citizen delegations; the sheer tenseness of London in these months with its fears of plots, violence and riots.[69] Amongst these plebeian crowds enthusiastically urging parliament on faster than it wished to go must have been many of the '*Rables, Apple-wives* and Chimney-boyes'[70] who had stood in the playhouse yards in the previous decade and for whom the popular drama, with its celebration of the dignity of artisan life and responsiveness to the feelings of the ordinary citizen, would have fostered their consciousness of belonging to a distinct social group with political interests and opinions that were not contemptible (several of the later Leveller leaders were younger sons of gentry in apprenticeships in the 1630s;[71] perhaps they would have aspired to visit the more fashionable theatres too). The drama's ability to crystallize and shape political expectations would have had an incalculable effect on their thinking; the apprentices who invaded parliament in July 1647 and expelled the Independent MPs would not have understood plays like *The Rebellion* and *A Shoemaker a Gentleman* merely as extravagant fantasies.

We can, however, begin cautiously to fill in some of these lacunae by considering, firstly, the few indications of openly political activity at the popular theatres that have come down to us and, secondly, the evidence of those satirical tracts of 1641–42 which seem to have been strongly influenced by memories of theatrical performance. In the first instance, such traces as we have tend to suggest that it was the popular rather than the elite theatres which staged plays directly commenting on or dealing with recent affairs. The one complete surviving example is Henry Glapthorne's *Albertus Wallenstein* (c. 1634–39), a lurid melodrama depicting the ill-led life and violent death of the Catholic-Imperial general, a monstrous bogeyman well calculated to incense the indignation of an audience avid for Protestant success in the continental war. Acted by the King's Men, this was performed at the Globe, but apparently not at the Blackfriars.[72] A comparable case is *The Valiant Scot* which though set in a long-distant and heroic past had, in the context of Charles's catastrophic attempt to impose Laud's prayer-book on the Scottish Kirk by force of arms, suddenly acquired a new relevance. According to a puritan newsbook, this chronicle on the heroism of the Scots rebel Wallace and the villainy of the English tyrants he is fighting got the Fortune company into great trouble when they played it for 'five dayes with great applause' while Charles's army was still heading north to disaster.[73] Other plays on public events have been lost and we can say little about them, but their titles look more like those of outdoor than indoor plays. *The Irish Rebellion* of 1642 certainly was a Red Bull play, and the following year Mildmay saw an illegal performance somewhere of 'a Playe of Warre'.[74] Dekker's lost *Gustavus King of Sweden* (1632) was presumably a play on Gustavus's recent continental victories against the Catholics, and Heywood and Brome's lost play 'The Life & Death of S[r]. Martyn Skink. wth y[e] warres of y[e] Low Countries' would seem to be designed to exploit interest in the siege of the Spanish garrison at Schenck's Sconce in 1635–36.[75] Possibly too the otherwise unknown *Play of the Netherlands*[76] belongs with this group on the European conflict with the Emperor.

Obviously, this list is tentative and incomplete, but such written records as have survived do preserve vestiges of a performance tradition of clownery and political burlesque at the popular theatres which in the absence of literary *texts* has vanished from view. The best-reported instance is the 'scandalous and libellous' lost play *The Whore New Vamped* which was acted at the Red Bull in 1639 'for many days together' until the Privy Council hurriedly banned it. This seems to have been a play of the 'estates satire' type, for it 'personated not only some of the aldermen of the city of London and some other persons of quality, but also scandalized and libelled the whole profession of proctors belonging to the Court of Probate, and reflected upon the present Government'. The council specifically objected to comic dialogue in which the company's clown, Andrew Cane, mentioned the unpopular monopoly on wine and called its patentee, the city alderman William Abell, 'a base, drunken, sottish knave'. In another exchange on monopolies and projects, a character listed the patents he was supposed to have been granted including one 'for 12*d.* a piece upon every proctor and proctor's man who was not a knave. Said another, Was there ever known any proctor but he was an arrant knave?'[77] Proctors probably came under fire since that was the profession of Abell's co-monopolist Richard Kilvert, but the incident demonstrates how quickly satire on a single individual escalated into a general attack on fundamental grievances, in this case Laud's hated ecclesiastical courts and officials. Earlier in 1639, the wrath of the same church courts had descended on the Fortune company for their revival of an ecclesiastically-sensitive play, *The Cardinal's Conspiracy*, 'in as great state as they could, with *Altars, Images, Crosses, Crucifixes*, and the like, to set forth his pomp and pride' – a spectacular visual statement of the offensiveness of the Laudian church to puritan sensibilities. The King's Revels had been prevented from attempting something similar five years before when they tried to bring on stage 'a Flamen, a priest of the heathens' in a real church vestment, and in 1639 the Fortune players excused themselves as presenting only 'an altar to the heathen gods, yet' (said an observer of the event) 'it was apparent that this play was revived in purpose in contempt of the ceremonies of the Church'.[78] In 1641 Milton, while inveighing against the 'se[n]suall Idolatry' into which the church had fallen, pursued the same comparison and complained of the 'fantastick dresses in Palls, and Miters, golds, and guegaw's fetcht from *Arons* old wardrope, or the *Flamins vestry*' which the Laudian clergy wore;[79] perhaps he had seen or heard of these performances.

By this date, even the Blackfriars theatre was joining in the popular-puritan tide of denunciation of the bishops: Shirley's *The Cardinal* (1641) portrays the downfall of a scheming, Machiavellian prelate whose dying confession to his king is[80]

> My life hath been prodigiously wicked,
> My blood is now the Kingdoms balm; oh Sir,
> I have abus'd your ear, your trust, your people,
> And my own sacred Office, my conscience
> Feels now the sting . . .

Laud, imprisoned in the Tower and awaiting a state trial, would scarcely have been pleased to learn of this speech, but he may already have known that still more explicit and hostile dramatizations of him had begun to circulate around London in quantity. With the abolition of the Star Chamber in 1641, the way was cleared for the extraordinary inundation of printed literature of controversy, polemic and satire that so distinguished these years, and it is especially remarkable that among the scores of pamphlets that appeared before the playhouses closed in 1642 were many that were cast in dramatic or semi-dramatic form. Astonishingly, these have excited almost no attention from theatre historians,[81] yet I have found over sixty for 1641–42 and, for completeness, I list them below in Appendix I. Most of these are dialogues of one sort or another, and 'dramatic' here is often a misnomer; dialogue form was simply a suitable means of exposition or argument. Nevertheless, the sheer volume of controversy that was conducted in this way is in itself interesting and suggests how familiar the public was with having its politics dramatized, as well as how naturally the inversions and freedoms of festive play were transmuted into a language of real political subversion: the *Dialogue Betwixt Roundhead and Rattlehead* (E134/19)[82] advertised itself as 'Full of mirth, and repleat with witty Inventions' (t.p.), while Archbishop Laud is depicted in *A New Disputation Between the Two Lordly Bishops York and Canterbury* (E1113/2) as comically exasperated by the 'rayling manner' in which Bishop Williams is laughing at his distress (p. 6).

Moreover, a significant proportion of these tracts are, as little playlets, fully and coherently achieved. For many, dramatic garb was more than merely a convenience, but a lively device designed to speak familiarly and entertainingly to as wide an audience as possible. Broadly speaking, they divide into three groups. Firstly, there are playlets which dramatize the great politicians of their day: Laud is most frequently depicted, but Strafford, Noy, Lord Keeper Finch and the papist secretary of state, Sir Francis Windebank, also appear. A second group animates estates figures, courtiers, bishops and monopolists but also Henrietta Maria's friars and Jesuits and even the Pope. Such figures are usually imagined as discussing recent events nervously with each other, or abjectly confessing their crimes, or lamenting their recent downfalls.[83] Thirdly, there are pamphlet-plays in which ordinary citizens, or rogues such as pimps and whores who have most felt the power of the church courts, meet to discuss the times and rejoice at their oppressors' ruin, and retail scandalous gossip about the corruptions of ecclesiastical officials.[84] Frequently these are violently anti-Catholic in tone, and at the very least they mark a transition between stage performance and popular printed prose, suggesting how the energy of the theatrical traditions ran into other channels after the closing of the playhouses. But, given their undeniable signs of contact with and understanding of the forms and conventions of the popular drama, it may also be that some are indeed survivals of terse and scurrilous performances that could actually have taken place, surreptitiously and irregularly, at the outdoor theatres in these last months. It is notable, for example, that the monopolists and proctors whom we know to have been ridiculed on stage in the lost *Whore New Vamped* repeatedly re-appear as satiric targets in the printed playlets. There are two playlets on the wine monopolists Abell and Kilvert, *A Dialogue or Accidental Discourse* (E156/16) and *The Last Discourse* (E156/18), in which the two friends admit their deceptions and curse one another; and the officials of the church courts are the subjects of yet more vigorous and frequent abuse, such as in *The Spiritual Courts Epitomized in a Dialogue Betwixt two Proctors, Busie Body and Scrape All* (E157/15) and *The Proctor and the Parator their Mourning . . . Being a True Dialogue Relating the Fearful Abuses and Exorbitancies of Those Spiritual Courts, under the Names of Sponge the Proctor and Hunter the Parator* (E156/13), the titles of which sufficiently indicate their contents. In Richard Newrobe's nondramatic satire *Farewell Mitre* (E134/33), the odious Laudian bishop Matthew Wren is represented as saying in despair 'Is all turn'd to this?/A pris'ner now, poore WREN is in a *Cage*;/Alas poore Bird, sing, act on every Stage' (p. 4) and this seems to be more than just a turn of phrase. In fact, Newrobe may well be referring to a specific playlet, for in *Canterbury his Change of Diet* (E177/8), probably written by the future Leveller pamphleteer Richard Overton, Laud actually was put into a cage with his confessor and mocked by a fool (see plate 7). No doubt the Bull or Fortune would have had Bajazet's cage handy after their revivals of *Tamburlaine*.

It seems quite possible that these playlets represent a further development of the jig or afterpiece, that satirical dialogue or song-and-dance by the clowns so popular in the Elizabethan theatre. No jigs have reached us from the 1630s, but several

Plate 7. Laud and his confessor caged, from R. Overton, *A New Play Called Canterbury his Change of Diet* (London, 1641), t.p.

independent testimonies that they were still being performed exist, including a comic induction at the Salisbury Court in 1638 in which a citizen in the audience asks for his money back and goes off to the Bull or Fortune to see 'A Play for two pense, with a Jig to boot'.[85] In at least six pamphlet-plays of 1641–42 there are embedded jigs: two each in Thomas Herbert's *News out of Islington* and *Keep Within Compass, Dick and Robin* (1641) and in Overton's *Vox Borealis* (E177/5), and single instances in *Roundhead and Rattlehead*, *A New Disputation* and *Canterbury his Change of Diet*. Except for *Vox Borealis*, all these playlets are conceivably performable. Their jigs are political, and retail news and satire about Laud, the bishops, monopolies, the Scots War, the guilty flight of the Lord Keeper and so forth. In the jig that concludes *Canterbury his Change of Diet* the play's fool makes fun of one of Laud's proctors (blue and red caps refer to the Scots and English armies respectively):

> PARITOR. What newes sir, what newes, I pray you know you,
> FOOLE. Correction doth waite sir, to catch up his due.
> PARITOR. His due sir, whats that, I pray you tell me,

239

FOOLE. not blew cap, nor red cap, but cap of the See,
PARITOR. What caps are these pray you, shall I never know,
FOOLE. The caps that would us, and our Church overthrow,
They both sing, O wellady, wellady, what shall wee doe then,
    Weel weare tippet foole caps, and never undoe men.   (sig.A4ᵛ)

In two more equally lively verses, the parator admits his projects, and says he is now *'turnd out of doore'*. In the case of Herbert's *News out of Islington* (London, 1641), the jig is a song complaining of monopolists and wishing that they were hanged (*'Some did England molest,/And the poor much opprest,/And I dare to protest,/They did it not in iest'* (p. 12)), and it is preceded by a dialogue 'very merry and pleasant betwixt a knavish *Projector*, and honest *Clod* the Plough-man' (t.p.), in which Clod rejoices for the return of parliament and punctures the projector's pretensions. The projector seems to have been conceived as an antic like Tenter-hook, for he boasts, 'Those which I thought would not easily be brought to my purpose, I allured them by my golden hook, and so drawed them unto mee' (p. 4). It is difficult to see how a play such as *A Projector Lately Dead* could have got onto the stage except in this way, as a topical afterpiece, and perhaps other occasional forms were elaborated in a political direction also. In *Read and Wonder* (n.p., 1641) the devil visits the Pope attended by a pageant of the Seven Deadly Sins, and *A Dialogue or Accidental Discourse* promises a description of 'how Projectors and Patentees have [rode] a Tilting in a Parlamant time' (t.p.), behind which may lie the kind of burlesque procession or 'riding' such as concludes the Fortune play *The Knave in Grain*.

The one playlet which for its verve and theatricality looks almost certain to have achieved stage realization is *Canterbury his Change of Diet*. The title is a visual pun; the 'diet' this archbishop convenes is a meal of the ears of his puritan critics. Laud here is a giant ogre, his dinner a grim spoof of his real cruelty to Prynne, Burton and Bastwick:

BISHOP. What would you have my Lord?
CANTERBURY. Them fellowes, bring them to me.
DOCTOR. What will your Lordship doe with me.
CANTERBURY. Onely cut off your eares.

DOCTOR. That would be an unchristian action, a practice without

[a precedent,

O cruelty, tyranny! Hold me, hold me, or else I dye:

Heavens support me under this tyrant.

    CANTERBURY. Come Lawyer, your two eares will make 4.

That is almost a little dish for rarity.   (sig.A2ᵛ)

Laud's victims have become estates-types, Lawyer, Doctor and Divine,[86] but as plate 8 shows they could have been individually recognized at once, and the effect of the play must have been similar to that of an animated newspaper cartoon, a bold and brutal caricature of political events and motives. The following scenes turn the tables. Laud goes to a carpenter's to sharpen his knife, but is himself picked up by the common carpenter and held to the grindstone (perhaps the same prop that honest Archibald turned in prison in *The Wasp?*). Having got a bloody nose, he is caged, and mocked by the fool, then the fool and the parator dance the jig. His attendants seem to have been stage antics, bishops *'with muskets in their necks, bandeleeres, and swords by their sides'* (sig.A2ᵛ; see plate 8), whose attributes are designed to

Plate 8. Laud dining on the ears of his puritan critics, from R. Overton,
A New Play Called Canterbury his Change of Diet, sig.A2ʳ.

label them as instigators of the unpopular Scottish war. This particular hybrid may have been seen more frequently on the stage, for it reappeared several times in later satirical drawings (two instances are shown in plates 9 and 10), and the jig on the bellicose bishops in *A Dialogue Betwixt Roundhead and Rattlehead* comments on them as antics wearing symbolic costume:

> Take your Miter to the field,
> Let it serve you for a shield,
> 'Twill pay your Ransome if you yeeld:
>   We have resolv'd it so
>   To lay you low.

> Let Lawn-sleeves serve instead of Buffe,
> And for your Armes your partled ruffe,
> You may be fierce 'tis pistoll proofe:
>   It is your dismall fate
>   Come downe Prelate.   (sig.A4ᵛ)

Another playlet with a good claim to performance is *The Bishop's Potion* (E165/1). This has only two characters, Laud, who complains of feeling unwell, and his doctor, who administers an emetic to him which induces a violent purge. Laud vomits up a series of objects he has swallowed, symbols of his crimes – the tobacco patent, the Book of Sports, the Star Chamber order against Prynne, a bundle of church livings and, finally, his mitre. It is easy to see how farcically effective this could be made on stage, and it has famous satirical-dramatic predecessors: Crispinus vomiting hard words in Jonson's *Poetaster* (1601), Divinity casting up dignities and promotions, and Martin Marprelate let blood by 'launcing and worming him ... vpon the common Stage' in 1589,[87] Avarice being squeezed in the morality *Respublica* (1553), but it had been done recently too. Noy was dissected and revealed as full of soap[88] and proclamations in *A Projector Lately Dead*; in Newcastle's *Country Captain* a minor character is a projector who falls sick and throws up his monopolies off-stage – pins, dice, hides, wine, soap and tobacco; and in Francis Quarles's privately performed tragicomedy *The Virgin Widow* (c. 1642), a doctor casts the water of Lady Albion and Lady Temple, and diagnoses the latter is troubled with 'a Liturgie', 'Let her

Plate 9. Bishop Williams ready for war, by Wenceslaus Hollar.

Fasting be frequent, and her Prayers, Common'.[89] There are two
strong external testimonies that *The Bishop's Potion* actually was
performed: in the *New Disputation Between the Two Lordly Bishops*,
Bishop Williams twits Laud by asking, 'I pray you tell me one
thing if you can remember it, how hath your body fared since

your Doctor gave you the purge, which made you vomit up the Crosse-keyes and the Miter? me thinkes you looke very costive upon the matters' (p. 3), and a fine satirical engraving exists of Laud bringing up just those items he vomited in the playlet, and this could well have been taken from a production (plate 11). The engraving suggests that on stage the doctor was personified as Laud's erstwhile victim, Henry Burton, now having his revenge on his persecutor. Moreover, the playlet seems to have

Plate 10. Bishops carrying muskets and pikes, a detail from *Magna Britannia Divisa* (1642).

And so yow will till Head from body part.

O Mr Burton, I am sick at Heart.

TOBACO

Standar No Sabath

An Order of Star Chamber

CANONS AND CONSTITV TIONS

aw-meats, o Bishop bredd sharp Cruditis
Eares from the Pillory? other Cruelties
As Prisonments, by your high Inquisition
That makes your Vomits have no intermision.

My disease bredd by to much Plenitude
Of Power, Riches : The rude multitude
Did aye invy, and curbing of the zeale
Of lamps, now shyning in the Common weale.

Plate 11. Laud being purged by Henry Burton, contemporary satirical print.

245

inspired an obvious sequel in *Canterbury's Will* (E156/5), a closely similar dialogue in which Laud, fearing his imminent demise, calls his scrivener to him to witness his last will. He bequeathes away his mitre, books, rosary and so on, and leaves solemn advice to the bishops not to be proud nor dumb dogs but to preach 'painfully and purely, that it may prove to the edification and salvation of the people' (p. 7). His scrivener has a clown's bawdy patter: 'LAUD. . . . preethee come to the purpose./ SCRIVENER. As the priest said, when he did you wot what' (pp. 4–5). Several other unpopular characters also made mock-wills in playlets, including the Pope (*Read and Wonder*), Cheapside Cross (*Articles of High Treason*, E134/23) and the defunct church court Doctor's Commons (*The Pimp's Prerogative*, 669f4/27). Doctor's Commons has a burlesque recital of his dozens of now-redundant officers, and his bequests included a popular-theatre joke: 'All my great Books of Acts to be divided between the Fortune and the Bull; for they spoyle many a good Play for want of Action.' He could quite conceivably have been brought onto the stage as a grotesque.

There seems to be, then, a number of likely reasons to suppose that these playlets, and perhaps others like them, were to be seen on the London stages in their last months, and if this was the case then the shaky parliament of September 1642, declining in popularity and in its members' attendance and newly embarking on a war for which it was ill-prepared, had indeed good incentives to be determined to prevent the playhouses from continuing. Parliament was crucially dependent on maintaining its credibility with that solid middle-ground of opinion which was prepared to go to the length of fighting the king to get the limited change that it desired, but which was direfully apprehensive about the social consequences of its own actions and deeply suspicious of the pressure parliament was under from lobbies who desired to see more radical achievements.[90] The satirical devices of popular theatre, the purging and caging of hated statesmen, the anatomizing of the times, encapsulated the new political expectations with vividness and immediacy, but received the applause of a tumultuous multitude who were normally excluded from political life. The great festive overturning of an insufferable regime, celebrated in this riotous way by these pamphlets, was something which threatened to go yet further – it brought into question all obedience, order, rank, government and discipline. Parliament closed the playhouses before the volatile, radical theatre of a Leveller such as Overton had time fully to develop.

Essentially, the devices employed by these playlets *are* performance devices. Their appeal is visual and theatrical rather than literary, and they work not merely by describing but by *presenting* a slapstick version of events. But even if only a proportion of them are stageable, they are still significant for their demonstration of the real continuity between the concerns of the Caroline drama and of the political pamphleteering which took over the mass market from it in the following decades, that 1642 did not mark a dead-end but that the developments of the revolutionary years took place on ground which the theatres had helped, energetically, to prepare. In the Long Parliament Sir John Culpepper appropriated the theatrical language of vermin when, complaining of the throngs of monopolists, he described them as[91]

a Nest of *Wasps*, or *Swarm of Vermin*, which have overcrept the Land, I mean the *Monopolers* and *Polers* of the People; These, like the *Frogs of* Egypt, have gotten the possession of our Dwellings ... They sup in our *Cup*, they dip in our *Dish* ...they have *marked and sealed* us from head to foot.

There are many similar examples besides; this is a broad and angry linguistic consensus in which both the politicians and Brome and his friends are participating.[92] Similarly, there is a multiplicity of points of contact between the regular theatre and irregular playlets, and the non-dramatic political satires which appeared in profusion after 1640 – the characters, anatomies, complaints, news reports, mock-wills and sermons which register pervasively the influence of the spoken, dramatic word. One example must suffice for many. *Pig's Coranto* (London, 1642) is a jesting commentary on recent events posing as yet another newsbook, whose anonymous author ridicules projectors (as 'vermine' and 'Crabb-lice' (p. 4)), bishops and the prerogative courts, but also finds the citizen trained-bands irresistibly funny, and contrives to deflate the courtier-playwrights and Charles's northern expedition in the same breath by scoffing at those 'babes and sucklings' who went to war in Scotland but found 'the play were spoyled, and . . . no time to alter it again from a Tragedy to a Comedy, nor to repent themselves they were Actors where they might have been but spectators only' (p. 5) – references to Suckling's revised version of *Aglaura* and unheroic flight from Berwick. The world, it seems, has gone mad, and each estate is trying to pass the blame onto the next:

the usurer layes the fault on the prodigall, the prodigall on the Scrivener, the Scribe on the broker, the broker on the Gallant, the gallant on the Cittizen, the cittizen on the courtier, the courtier on the projector . . .   (p. 6)

It looks to the author as though everything has been turned upside-down, that fantasy has definitively superseded reality:

all are acting the Antipodes young boyes command old Souldiers, wise men stand cap in hand to fine fooles, maidens woe widowes, married women rule their husbands, Clergymen turne Lawyers, and Lawyers honest men, Masters obey their servants and favorites lay their faults on their Prince; It was not so in *Temporibus Noah*, ah no.   (p. 7)

The complex, detached, disillusioned tone of this pamphlet, with its feeling that the whole world has gone wrong and no easy solution is possible, is essentially dramatic; the jest of Brome's *Antipodes* has become part of the experience of the 1640s.

Finally, in tracing the survival of the energies of the popular theatre into the political world of the Civil War, it remains to note that the *Actor's Remonstrance* (London, 1643) claimed that 'some of our ablest ordinarie Poets', now that the closing of the theatres had destroyed their usual source of earnings, were 'compelled to get a living by writing contemptible penny-pamphlets' (p. 7). Possibly some of the dialogues I have been discussing were the work of professional playwrights; the few dramatists whose pamphleteering we know about were all connected with the Phoenix–Salisbury Court circle. Thomas Jordan wrote five short tracts in 1641–42, including a burlesque news-book; broadly, these tend towards defence of the king's position, and exhortations to obedience. More interesting is Heywood's verse satire of 1641, *Reader, Here You'll Plainly See Judgment Perverted by These Three* (E171/2); the three in question are bishops, judges and monopolists. Heywood is no Presbyterian (he would not do away with good bishops), but he writes with a patriotic concern for the purity of the Protestant church and faith; had not the bishops

> . . . inclining to the *Arminian* Sect,
> And preaching in the Romish Dialect,
> . . . labor'd 'mongst us Protestants to intrude
> What our Reformed Church did quite exclude?
> New Cannons, Oathes and Altars, bending low,
> To where in time the Images must grow? (p. 2)

Laud he compares with those 'proud priests' who before the Reformation tried to subordinate state power to their own authority, '*Wolstan, Becket, Wolsey,* who durst write,/*I and my King,* even in his Soveraigns sight' (p. 1); the offenders must be 'punisht and remov'd' (p. 3). So too must the judges who have perverted England's laws, taken bribes and given false judgment (Heywood was thinking of the Ship Money case); on them will fall 'the *Magna Charta's* curse' (p. 4). Heywood's feelings are with the ordinary man most vulnerable to misused authority:

> Nor wonder is't; when some as grave and great,
> Have in the same or like Judiciall Seat,
> (Only to give his wit some vaine applause)
> Jested and jeer'd a poore man from his Cause. (p. 3)

Jeering judges were already familiar from *The Antipodes, The Wasp* and *The Variety.* As for monopolists, they are a 'swarme of Locusts', a 'crew of moaths and cankers that bereaves/Our flourishing Orchard both of fruit and leaves' (p. 5). Heywood enumerates their projects with disgust, but has special venom for 'your brave skarlet Patentees' who promoted the soap and wine monopolies: 'The subject suffers in each draught he swallows,/ For which may they be doomb'd unto the gallows' (pp. 5–6). Another contribution to the list of pamphlet-plays, *Mercurius Britannicus* (1641), was written by a friend of Heywood's, the

popular miscellanist and courtesy-book author Richard Brathwaite (who also received the dedication of Nabbes's play *The
Unfortunate Mother* (1640)). Brathwaite's play is a dramatized
anticipation of the trial and condemnation of the judges involved
in the Ship Money case, elaborately worked in four acts with a
large cast including onlooking commentators and even a ghost
(of Strafford). It is set in no less a place than the House of
Commons itself, thinly disguised as a Roman senate, and the MPs
appear as '*Consuls of true piety*',[93] pursuing their reformation of the
state cautiously but with whole-hearted zeal. I have argued
elsewhere that the title-page claim to performance at Paris may
refer to the amateur theatricals which were sponsored there by
the English ambassador, the Earl of Leicester, in the ambassa-
dorial household;[94] possibly it saw the boards in England too, for
it was several times reprinted. And last of all, a late, colourful
addition to the circle of Humphrey Mill was Sir Edward Peyton,
a Fifth Monarchist who fought against Charles at Edgehill,
Newbury and Naseby and wrote pamphlet attacks on the Laudian
church and on Charles's violations of parliamentary privilege 'for
which he was condemned to die', though he survived until
1657.[95] In 1652, the same year that he contributed verses to the
second edition of Mill's *Night's Search*, he published a scandalous
and vitriolic attack on the whole royal line, *The Divine Catastrophe
of the Kingly Family of the House of Stuarts*, which sweepingly
damned them as an irredeemably corrupt and degenerate dynasty,
known only for their tyrannies, murders, blasphemies, fornica-
tions, sodomies, obstinacies, hostility to parliaments and general
debauchery, and he gleefully greeted their ruin as God's just
vengeance on a perfidious family. Bizarre *The Divine Catastrophe*
may have been, but it was not entirely unprecedented; it was the
ultimate extension of that scepticism about kings and their courts
that was in part at least a legacy left by the Caroline theatres.

9

Concepts of the country in the drama

Court and country

THE TWO LEADING MODES of the official Caroline court culture
– that sponsored directly by the king or queen – were the pastoral
and the masque. The courtier-play which created the vogue for
Whitehall's amateur theatricals, Walter Montagu's *The Shepherd's
Paradise*, was a pastoral; portraits in rustic manner subsequently
became fashionable among Caroline courtiers and their ladies.
Henrietta Maria, who on her arrival in England was reported to
have been 'delighted with the River of Thames and doth love to
walk on the meadows and look upon the haymakers, and will
sometimes take a rake and sportingly make hay with them',
particularly enjoyed playing at being a shepherdess; her private
amusements with her maids were 'pastorals and comedies and
other pleasant diversions'.[1] She acted in *The Shepherd's Paradise*
and in an earlier court pastoral;[2] only a pregnancy prevented her
from performing in *Florimène* (1635). These three were all
elaborately and expensively mounted with scenes, and so too was
Fletcher's *Faithful Shepherdess*, revived for the queen at Somerset
House in 1635, and on which occasion Davenant wrote a special
prologue inviting Charles to share his wife's country world of
refreshment and repose:[3]

> Welcome as Peace to wealthy Cities, when
> Famine and Sword have left more Graves then Men;
> As Spring to Birds, or *Phebus* to the old
> Poor Mountain *Muscovite* congeal'd with cold;
> As Shore to Pilots in a safe-known Coast,
> Their Cards being broken and their Rudders lost.

The masque, on the other hand, was the expression and vindication of Charles's princely power, especially in relation to *his* 'country'. Charles danced his masques as an individual, but their form realized and celebrated his public, kingly character which was normally invisible but which could be suggested through the mechanics of Inigo Jones's stagecraft. The movement of Jones's machines, with their wild and sudden transitions, historically and geographically, imitated the kinetic forces of nature, now apparently harmonized and ordered to the disposal of England's god-like ruler, and responsive to his imperial will. Meaningless except in the illuminating presence of the King, the masque projected Charles's sovereign capacity, dramatizing him as the soul of his kingdom which without him would be but a disunified aggregate of miscellaneous individuals. In Carew's *Coelum Britannicum* (1634), Charles was accorded the homage of all who ever had been, or were to be, British subjects, as well Britain's 'antient Worthies' and 'moderne Heroes' as 'the naturall Inhabitants of this Isle': 'what-ever elder times can boast,/ Noble, or Great . . . they in Prophesie/Were all but what you are'.[4]

Masque and pastoral were both making assertions about the nature of princely government, the relationship between ruler and ruled, the king and the sort of 'country' over which he reigned. In her pastorals, Henrietta Maria was marked out for superiority by her inherent loveliness, a rustic queen who ruled 'naturally' over a country of elegant shepherds and shepherdesses, the most elegant of all. The masques (like the figure on the title-page of Hobbes's *Leviathan*, a giant king composed of the bodies of his people) premised that all the king's subjects were mystically *in* him, that he *was* the country in a way no one else could be. Idealized though they undoubtedly were, these were not illusory dream-worlds destined to be swept inexorably away, but political statements which were entirely valid in the circumstances prevailing down to 1641 and whose validity might easily have endured afterwards had the court not failed to retain the confidence of the nation as a whole. Had Charles taken a slightly more conciliatory (and trustworthy) line in 1642 and sought to reach a compromise with his critics instead of forcing them to resort to war as the only effective means of securing their objectives, it can be quite readily imagined how, with political life continuing to be centred on the court at Whitehall, masque and pastoral would have been sustained into the succeeding decades. Indeed, some elements of these forms were picked up again by the restored court after 1660.

On the other hand, some of Charles's subjects who in the 1630s were dissatisfied with the direction of his rule were developing radically different understandings of what was meant by the 'country' which would contribute importantly to undermining faith in the court. Two alternative senses of 'the country' I have already noted in passing. In Shirley's comedies, the country impinges as an actual presence, the countryside, a system of economic and social relationships affected by political change. More schematically, elaborated as it had been for example in Nicholas Breton's *The Court and the Country* (1618), the country could signify a set of attitudes, values, or interests opposed in a general way to those typified by 'the court', a contrast we have found in *The Queen and Concubine*, *The Bashful Lover* and other plays, where characters are placed symbolically in rustic settings to establish their alienation from the court even though they have no real economic connection with the country at all. To conclude this study, I wish to examine some of these dissenting versions in the drama of what is meant by the country, first in three plays which deal with outlawry (the very oddity of their subject inviting us to consider them as a group), and secondly in a series of plays by Richard Brome. I shall be arguing that the ideas of the country – what it is, and what it represents – propounded in these plays were seriously at variance with the version that descends in masque and pastoral, and correspond to political sentiments and opinions critical of the court and with which the court would have to come to terms if it were to establish (as in fact it failed to do) a successful accommodation on which to found its rule after 1642. Furthermore, in Brome's hands, the country comes to represent something which, for its complexity and sensitivity, strains politics to its very limits, and perhaps goes beyond politics altogether.

Massinger's *The Guardian* (1633) is an attractive comedy set in Naples which frequently, though unobtrusively and without any obvious design, brings to mind the political overtones of romantic material such as were exploited in courtier drama or in Shirley's comedies of tyrannizing parents and waywardness in love. The guardian of the title, Durazzo, is a humorous and indulgent figure who encourages his ward, Caldoro, to such free and open exercise of his pleasures as suits his place as an heir and a gentleman:

> Riots! what riots?
> He wears rich clothes, I do so; keeps horses; games, and wenches;
> 'Tis not amiss, so it be done with decorum:
> In an Heir 'tis ten times more excusable
> Then to be over-thrifty. (I.i.49)

The play's principal action follows Caldoro in his pursuit of the affections of the young gentlewoman Caliste, the achievement of which is to them as the accomplishment of a private kingdom, submission to a perfect monarchy in love:

> these favors
> (How ere my passions rag'd) could not provoke me
> To one act of rebellion against
> My loyalty to you; the soveraign
> To whom I ow obedience. (IV.i.103)

Caliste, though, is subject to a despotic parent, her mother Iolante, who will not allow her the modest freedom she deserves, but is afraid her daughter's amours will sully her own pure reputation. She even threatens to imprison her:

> I'll chain thee like a slave in some dark corner,
> Prescribe thy daily labor: Which omitted,
> Expect the usage of a Fury from me,
> Not an indulgent Mothers. (I.ii.75)

Caliste's maid calls this 'Flat tyranny, insupportable tyranny/To a Lady of your Blood' (I.ii.93). However, Iolante is hypocritical, for while denying Caliste her freedom, she herself secretly runs

after attractive men, an internal tyranny of appetite to which she
is no less a slave:

> I am full of perplexed thoughts: Imperious Blood,
> Thou only art a tyrant; Judgment, Reason,
> To whatsoever thy Edicts proclaim,
> With vassal fear subscribe against themselves.   (III.vi.1)

The subsidiary action deals with Iolante's exposure by her
husband, Severino, and their subsequent reconciliation. The same
kind of internal tyranny of blood also affects Caldoro's rival for
Caliste's hand, Adorio, for he is a noted libertine, enslaved to his
desires. When he is converted to a wholesome love for Caliste he
moralizes:

> What Sacrifice of Thanks can I return
> Her pious Charity, that not alone
> Redeems me from the worst of slavery,
> The tyranny of my beastly appetites,
> To which, I long obsequiously have bow'd . . .   (II.iii.86)

Against such violent and unbalanced behaviour, the dignified and
gentle language of Caliste and Caldoro provides an admirable
corrective and balance.

These two plots, which Massinger combines so deftly, are
lifted directly from a single source,[5] and if this was all the play
was it would have little interest for us. What does make it
significant is Massinger's modification of his source and expansion
of these political hints into an encompassing overplot, that he
makes Caliste's family into one 'Not gracious with the times'
(I.i.58), the king having banished her father Severino from Naples
for (supposedly) having killed her mother's brother in a duel (by
marrying Caliste, Durazzo says, Caldoro will 'scape Court-
visitants,/And not be eaten out of house and home/In a
Summer-progress' (I.i.59)). Severino passes his exile in the forest
with a band of outlaws which Massinger characterizes as an
alternative woodland monarchy defying the king's rule. Severino
'lives like a King/Among the *Banditi*' (IV.iii.11), he is as royal as
Alexander, who was only a greater thief (V.iv.34). His men
address him as their monarch:

1.   What's your will?
2. Hail Soveraign of these Woods.
3.   We lay our lives
At your Highness feet.
4.   And will confess no King,
Nor Laws, but what come from your mouth; and those
We gladly will subscribe to.   (II.iv.62)

They shout before him, 'Long live *Severino.*/And perish all such cullions as repine/At his new Monarchy' (II.iv.115). In the fifth act Severino brings Iolante back to the forest, and her induction as a May Queen strongly recalls *The Queen and Concubine*. The foresters hymn her:

> *From you our Swords take edge, our Hearts grow bold.*
> *From you in Fee, their lives your Liegemen hold.*
> *These Groves your Kingdom, and our Law your will;*
> *Smile, and we spare; but if you frown, we kill.*   (V.i.11)

Thus Severino's woodland outlawry is made into a country kingdom specifically in antithesis to the Neapolitan norm.

The foresters are clearly not a realistic band, and Massinger uses them almost symbolically as righters of society's wrongs. They have articled to rob only certain types of men:

> The Cormorant that lives in expectation
> Of a long wish'd for dearth, and smiling grindes
> The faces of the poor, you may make spoil of;
> Even theft to such is Justice...
> The grand Incloser of the Commons, for
> His private profit...
>   ... If a Usurer,
> Greedy at his own price, to make a purchase,
> Taking advantage upon Bond, or Morgage,
> From a Prodigal, pass through our Territories,
> I' the way of custom, or of tribute to us,
> You may ease him of his burthen...
> Builders of Iron Mills, that grub up Forests,
> With Timber Trees for shipping...   (II.iv.79)

The list of social and economic grievances is not Neapolitan but English; it recalls the grievances complained against in the *The*

Costly Whore, its manner is reminiscent of Brome's emblematic satires. The thieves specifically exempt the poor and oppressed from their attention. They will not rob women, scholars, nor

> Soldiers that have bled in their Countries service,
> The Rent-rack'd Farmer, needy Market folks,
> The sweaty Laborer, Carriers that transport
> The goods of other men, are priviledg'd ...   (II.iv.108)

Massinger's thieves are not robbers but reformers, amending the wrongs perpetrated in the normal life of Naples. As outlaws they are free of the normal corruptions of law, their country justice is a fantasy version of the justice that really ought to operate in everyday affairs.

· This scene (II.iv) is carefully isolated to provide a stylized contrast to the rest of the first three acts, but the play as a whole forms a diptych in which the characters progress, in a series of steps invented by Massinger, from city to country where together they are made whole. In the country Caliste accepts Caldoro into the monarchy of her love, and Iolante becomes 'Cinthia' (V.i.2), the chaste forest queen, Severino achieving more royalty with his wife in the woods than can be found in the real court at home:

> as a Queen be honor'd
> By such as stile me Soveraign; already
> My banishment is repeal'd, thou being present:
> The Neapolitan Court a place of exile
> When thou art absent ...   (III.vi.271)

The whole story is resolved in a final testing scene in which the king has the outlaws secretly surrounded, then allows himself to be captured disguised as an old man carrying money as a ransom for his sons enslaved by the Turk. Severino responds to his appeal and makes his men contribute to free Christians from 'Turkish servitude' (V.iv.145). When the king reveals himself, Severino is pardoned ostensibly because his dead brother-in-law still lives, but the inclusion of the elaborate false tale makes his pardon appear to be more specifically a consequence of his deep and generous commitment to justice and liberty. The country is vindicated through a plot contrivance, but also one feels because of the particular values which it has espoused and is upholding.

The same overlaying of stereotyped romantic material with a structural contrast between an everyday kingdom and a country kingdom was repeated about seven years later by Suckling in *The Goblins*. In Suckling's imaginary realm of Francelia the outlaw band is even more plainly an alternative to the ruling political group for they are the family of the Tamorens, rivals to the present prince who are now in outlawry after a blood-feud between these two principal Francelian noble houses. Like Massinger's outlaws, Suckling's thieves correct social abuses, but they also dress themselves as goblins:

> The common people thinke them a race
> Of honest and familiar Devills,
> For they do hurt to none, unlesse resisted;
> They seldome take away, but with exchange;
> And to the poore they often give,
> Returne the hurt and sicke recover'd,
> Reward or punish, as they do find cause.   (I.i.124)

They are, then, another country band that reforms the corruptions of orthodox society, but most of the satire is directed exclusively against courtiers. In one scene, a courtier whom they have captured confesses hilariously to the seduction of vast numbers of women of all ranks (III.vii). Another captured courtier is accused of flattery, worthlessness and sheer witlessness: 'you fill a place about his Grace, and keep out men of parts, d'you not? ... A foolish Utensill of State, which like old Plate upon a Gaudy day, 'sbrought forth to make a show, and that is all ... You thinke there is no wisedom but in forme; nor any knowledge like to that of whispers' (III.i.19). This individual has prevented his prince from hearing the truth and caused him to be blamed for errors which he himself has committed, the same complaint against evil counsellors, that they 'have unmannerly and slubber-ingly cast all their Projects, all their Machinations upon the King',[6] which was advanced in the new parliament in 1640, around which time Suckling may well have been writing. Two stage courtiers consider turning beggars or thieves but reflect

'That's the same thing at Court: begging is but a kind of robbing th'Exchequer' (IV.i.15), and elsewhere they suppose that one of them is suited to steering 'the Helme of State' because he is 'so full of nimble Stratagems, that I should have ordered affaires, and carried it against the streame of a Faction' (IV.i.101). Suckling was of course a courtier looking for office to fit his talents; but though his play was romantic, there is no evidence of court performance, and its satire of courtiers links it more closely with the public stages than with the court.

The play follows the fortunes of Orsabrin, the lost brother to the reigning prince, and his faithful friend Samorat, noble heroes whose selfless gentility is in dazzling contrast to the base duplicity of the courtiers with whom they come into conflict. Although their generosity is a measure of their princeliness, it is also at first ambiguously the common decency of ordinary men (something which is a Shakespearean legacy in Suckling, whose play is studded with echoes of Shakespeare). Orsabrin may be a prince, but his identity initially is only hinted at, and his early adventures are bawdy, comical and vulgar (he is mistakenly arrested for debt, he stumbles into a brothel); when in the opening scene, he comes across Samorat, as yet unknown to him, duelling alone against two opponents, he rises almost instinctively to his rescue. The gentility of these heroes is an innate, 'natural' quality in them, which associates them with the country rather than with a court where the rustic ideals of candour and manliness are continually outraged by the mean and treacherous courtiers.[7]

This same set of preferences, country over court, is the burden of their interwoven amorous adventures. Orsabrin, captured by the Tamorens, falls in love with the young heiress, Reginella, of that rebel family. Samorat loves the lady Sabrina, but his rival is the prince himself, and he is the object of the bitter hatred of Sabrina's brothers, courtiers who are determined their sister should not be thrown away when she could have the prince for a husband. Samorat is pursued violently and treacherously by them; one brother advises the prince to earn Sabrina's affections by offering Samorat a false pardon for his part in the opening duel:

The censure past,
His death shall follow without noise:
'Tis but not owning of the fact,
Disgracing for a time a Secretarie,
Or so – the thing's not new –
Put on forgiving looks Sir . . .   (V.ii.13)

The brother is exactly a type of the evil counsellor already exposed by the outlaws. Only after criticism from Sabrina does the prince realize the injustice of his actions and thereafter emulates the behaviour of his rival. The play concludes with him pleading with Sabrina to take her time over deciding between his affections and Samorat's, but the worthiness and superior claim of the ordinary man has already been conclusively established. For this last scene, Suckling engineers a grand resolution, in which the Tamorens reveal themselves, restore Orsabrin to the state and make their peace with the ruling family by the match between Orsabrin and Reginella, thus bringing about a beneficial reunion in both private and public spheres. There is here a deliberate, careful orchestration of conventional yet pointed romantic motifs – Sabrina urging the prince 'for your owne sake Sir be mercifull' (V.ii.41), the Tamorens deciding to come forward once 'some new troubles in the State should happen,/Or faire occasion to make knowne our selves/Offer it selfe' (V.iii.25), the reconciliation of court and country, the miraculous finding of a new, more popular prince – which suggests very strongly that the play belongs to 1640 and is capitalizing on the particular set of expectations engendered by the recall of parliament. Writing in the shadow of exciting and charged events, Suckling anticipates, in fictional terms, the rapprochement which it was widely hoped was about to be effected between Charles and *his* 'country' critics.

An idealized, generous woodland existence had long been enshrined in the popular ballads of Robin Hood, but the particular social and political reflections raised by these plays on outlawry gesture towards a more specific, and less literary background.[8] Broadly speaking, contemporaries perceived the English countryside as dual in character, divided between pasture and cultivated land on one hand, and wilder woods, heaths, fens and commons (the environment of the imaginary outlaw bands) on the other. The remote wilds were only partly under the control of law or the parochial system; they were the areas where peasant revolt occurred, over enclosure, disafforestation and fen drainage, and where men lived like 'the very savages amongst the infidels'.[9] They also sustained heresy and religious free-thinking. Brownists and radical dissenters could meet 'in woods, in fields, in stables,/In hollow trees' and preach in 'thickets, and under hedges, to a great many of poore people'; nonconformity went to ground in the wilds of the north, west and Weald of Kent.[10] The radical associations of the uncultivated areas give added significance to the organization of these stage bands as alternative political bodies, woodland monarchies, yet the outlaws themselves hail essentially from a different social context. In *The Guardian*, for example, the outlaw king Severino is 'an unfortunate Gentleman,/Not born to these low courses' (V.iv.66) and his men are 'courteous English Theeves' (V.iii.11) admired by Durazzo as 'A fair fraternity' (V.iv.87); here the move to the country is one both to the woods and to Durazzo's 'Country-villa' where all 'variety of delights' is promised (I.i.293, 310) – rising early, hunting, hawking, flirting with Durazzo's tenants' daughters. These are the activities of the *cultivated* countryside.

What seems to be happening is that gentlemanly figures from the pasturelands are being 'naturalized' against the more radical background of the forests, and the embodying of this distinctive blend of courtesy and criticism in terms of reforming country commonwealths has suggestive correspondences with the contemporary understanding of the term *country* to characterize a set of interests (usually of Charles's gentlemanly or middle-ranking critics) other than, and occasionally opposed to, the court. To the MPs of the 1620s and 1640s their 'country' was (to each) the group of local gentry who had chosen them to represent their grievances at Westminster; much later, in the 1670s and 1680s, the Country came to signify a distinct political grouping in parliament. Recently historians have emphasized that the term 'country' is ambivalent in the 1630s. In the absence of parliament the 'country' as a discrete political unit did not exist, and country opinion needed to have a foot inside the court in order to obtain a hearing. However, the appearance in these plays of alternative and idealized monarchies suggests that the dramatists were endeavouring to conceptualize the country forcefully and formally as a separate and independent corporate body even while the actual conditions of politics remained court-centred; they could embody an idea of the country imaginatively, in a fiction, which answered to some of the attitudes of the court's critics even though such a bloc could not be realized in practice. The woodland plays do not indicate the existence of an organized country faction but are responding to, and helping to shape, expectations in their audience which would eventually create the conditions for such an autonomous, nationally-based consensus.[11]

There is a third band of thieves in a late play of Shirley's, *The Sisters*, which belongs to April 1642.[12] They are not reformers though, and are only adjuncts to the main plot, but the action is one which makes great play with notions of court and country. In characteristic fashion, Shirley contrasts two sisters, Paulina, a proud heiress, and Angellina, who is humble and plain. Paulina has delusions of grandeur, for she turns her house into a country court of which she thinks herself queen, giving her servants white staves to complete the parody of Whitehall's protocol. Her uncle Antonio sarcastically rebukes her as if she were a monarch:

> are not you
> Some Queen conceald?
> PAULINA. I am Independent, and sole regent here.
> ANTONIO. So, so,
> Where's your Nobility? they are to blame
> Not to attend . . .
> Your grace should be a little more reserv'd,
> And entertain none that did treat of Mariage
> To your private conference, untill they had
> In publick receiv'd audience like Ambassadors.   (pp. 8–9)

Paulina actually does believe the prince intends to woo her, and gives regal audience to a courtier, Contarini, who fuels her pride by making out that he is ambassador from 'The most immortall

Prince of Love', that is, Cupid himself (p. 15). Paulina's sister
Angellina subscribes to a different view of the country:

> my Lord, you talk too fine a language
> For me to understand; we are far from Court,
> Where though you may speak Truth, you cloath it with
> Such trim and gay apparell, we that only
> Know her in plainness, and simplicity,
> Cannot tell how to trust our ears, or know,
> When men dissemble.   (p. 17)

As in Shirley's city comedies, Angellina's behaviour is governed
by a feeling for *place*, which controls the values of the play. The
uncle Antonio tries to build Angellina into a competing country
queen, but she rules her 'court' with humility, eschewing fashionable gentlewomen and pride beyond her station. This awareness
of place makes Paulina (= 'the little one') appear patently absurd,
though equally the courtier Contarini is put down when he too
fails to fulfil his social obligations (he has jilted his beloved). Last
act revelations turn the tables: Paulina is shown to have been a
changeling and is disgraced, and Angellina, now the true heir,
finds herself wooed and wedded by the prince indeed.

The part played by the thieves is in boosting the delusions of
Paulina. They disguise their captain as the prince and visit her in
state, and Paulina is about to marry the mock-prince when the
real one arrives and deflates both them and her. But the effect of
this contrast of true and false princes is not simple. In some
senses, the bandit Frapolo *is* a prince. As in Massinger's and
Suckling's plays, the thieves have their own little kingdom which
imitates and defies the normal political forms:

> We are safe within our Woods, and Territories,
> And are above [the prince's] Edicts; Have not wee
> A Common-wealth among our selves, ye *Tripolites*?
> A Common-wealth? a Kingdom; and I am
> The Prince of *Qui-Vala's*, your Sovereign theef,
> And you are all my Subjects.   (p. 1)

The thieves' articles draw attention, right at the beginning of the
play, to the political and religious uncertainties of spring 1642.
They impudently repudiate the laws ('Hang Laws,/And those

263

that make 'em' (p. 2)); they have their own religious debates which run parallel to the controversies in which the Long Parliament was beginning to embroil itself. There is 'a kind of Religion/We Outlaws must observe', their king insisting he is defender of the faith ('Yee shall be of what Religion I please') but then determining ironically 'every man shall be of all Religions... Why should I clog your Conscience, or confine it' (pp. 2–3). In the last scene, the mock-prince, however comical he may be, does retain some sympathy as he attempts to preserve his regal pose while being outfaced by the real prince:

> Have all my cares and watchings to preserve
> Your lives, and dearest liberties, deserv'd
> This strange return, and at a time when most
> Your happiness is concern'd [i.e. his marriage with Paulina] ...
> 'Tis time your Prince were dead, and when I am
> Companion to my Fathers dust, these tumults
> Fomented by seditious men, that are
> Weary of Plenty, and delights of Peace,
> Shall not approach to interrupt the calm
> Good Princes after Death enjoy.   (pp. 55–6)

His accents are uncannily similar to those to which Charles himself had danced in that plaintive and conciliatory last masque, Davenant's *Salmacida Spolia* (1640), in which the murmuring people were urged not to forget his love for them, and the blessings of his reign:[13]

> I know it is the People's vice
> To lay too mean, too cheap a price
> On ev'ry blessing they possess.
> Th'enjoying makes them think it less...
> O who but he could thus endure
> To live and govern in a sullen age,
> When it is harder far to cure
> The People's folly than resist their rage?

In the prologue to *The Sisters* Shirley reminded his audience that at that moment Charles's court was in fact a country court, for he had left London in March and gone to York in an attempt to rally his northern support which culminated with the shocking scene before Hull in which Sir John Hotham refused to admit him into the town.[14] It is not far-fetched to suppose that in the parallel that Shirley suggests between Charles and Frapolo he is hinting that Charles's failure validly to maintain his regality has already reduced his credibility to little more than that of a mock king.

Beyond politics: country as county

The dramatist who gave the deepest and most prolonged thought to the concept of the country was Richard Brome, and it is fitting to end the whole study with a consideration of some of his plays for he is the playwright whose career was most obviously still at its height and full of promise when it was cut unnaturally short by the parliamentary ban of 1642. His final play shows that even as the theatres closed the drama was continuing to develop and to respond to the changes around it with intelligence and energy, and that he, with his finger firmly on the nerve of events, was already identifying those areas of anxiety which would be of most concern to men in the immediate future.

Brome was the Caroline dramatist most sensitive throughout the 1630s to country hostility towards the court. We have already seen with what aggressiveness and determination he advanced the country versus court analysis in *The Queen and Concubine*, and in two more plays we find him repeating himself very closely. The first is *The Queen's Exchange*, set in the Saxon England to which the antiquaries looked for evidence of England's ancient liberties, but which in this instance is ruled by a wilful queen who cannot stomach the objections to the marriage she wishes to make raised by the free-spoken but well-intentioned counsellor Segebert, who is anxious for the 'wholsome Laws,/Customes, and all the nerves of Government' which have 'enricht this Land' in the past but which her actions are now overturning (p. 458). For his faithfulness and honest care, Segebert is disgraced and exiled, and he finds sanctuary in the wilds with a hermit, an emblem of the piety, patience and goodness of the country; the queen, though, irresponsibly yields herself, and *her* country, to the embraces of the mad king of Northumbria. His madness poses similar problems for his subjects, who in desperation have taken rule into their own hands, in the name of the national good, though reserving their duty, like Decastro in *The Queen of Aragon*: 'and if your Majesty/Will tread our due allegiance into dust,/We are prepar'd to suffer' (p. 527). As in *The Queen and Concubine*, the main point at issue is how far the monarch is free to act unrestrained, and the subject justified in resisting. Brome works out his plots comically with a tissue of trickery, identically-twinned characters and dream-like awakenings from lunacy, but points to a serious moral. The Northumbrian king applauds his subjects for having opposed him for his own good:

> Thy trespasse is thine honour...
> And I must thank your care my Lords, as it deserves,
> Your over-reaching care to give my Dignity
> As much as in you lay unto another. (p. 546)

The queen too is happy to wed a son of Segebert's who looks just like the king, thus rewarding Segebert's suffering and acknowledging the claims of the 'country' he represents. The effect of the arch, overtly theatrical ending is to diminish those whose fortunes it manipulates; king and queen are content to defer to the playwright's capricious providence.

Once again, Brome's main contrast is drawn between selfless but frankly-spoken loyalty and self-seeking flattery, plain rustic and plush courtier, honest fool and knavish favourite (pp. 529–30). It is the same opposition as that between Edgar and Oswald in *King Lear*, and the play borrows a great deal from Shakespeare's tragedy. There is a truth-telling fool; Segebert is a Kent figure, a good counsellor whose honesty has caused him to be cast out; the subplot contrasts the sons of Segebert, like the daughters of Lear, one who flatters his father yet attempts his life, the other who professes only due respect yet is faithful to him in all adversity; and Brome evinces a Shakespearean respect for the voices and opinions of ordinary, common men – the Segebert plot is wound up by a group of lively and attractive rustics who punish Segebert's vicious son in the disguise of devils, like the outlaws in *The Goblins*. Both Brome and Suckling employ Shakespearean motifs as a means of overcoming (and criticizing) the limitations of romantic drama; not only do they respond to Shakespeare's feeling for nature and the natural in life, they are using these echoes to reinforce a more national sense of the 'country' and opening the drama's frame of reference to encompass a greater spectrum of attitudes and variety of social types. In Brome's case, it produces a play that looks courtly but in fact is much more popular and spirited.

The second instance is *The Lovesick Court* which goes even further by being a full-scale parody of the absurdities of courtier drama.[15] Court life, as seen through the drama the court prefers, is a ludicrous farrago of extravagant, conflicting intrigues, remote sensibilities and impossible fastidiousness. In this court, making love has become more important than matters of state. The love of two equally-deserving courtiers for the same princess recalls the situation of Matilda in *The Bashful Lover*:

> Were it a Kingdom onely, we could part it
> Without the quarrel of the *Thebean* brothers;
> Or, were it heaven it self, *Castor* and *Pollux*
> Should have our imitation. But *Eudina*
> Is onely indivisible.   (p. 152)

The alternative to this is the good intentions and assistance of the countrymen who intervene to rescue the lovers from assassination by an ambitious courtier. These rustics are

> the heads of *Tempe*; and the chief
> Swain heads of *Thessaly* (the King has known us)
> And here we came to lay our heads together
> For good of commonwealth.   (p. 145)

They meet in Tempe as a sort of country council, and though they are deferential to the princes they handle the politic nobleman roughly; they intend to 'discharge/Our Countrey loyalty with discretion' (p. 147). The play concludes with them entertaining the court with 'a Rustick round' (p. 168) to demonstrate that there are witty heads in the country, even 'though hear at Court, like courtiers/We'll shew it in our heels' (p. 159).

Brome was principally a writer of realistic and satiric comedy.

As a romantic play, *The Queen and Concubine* stands some way aside from the general tendency of his writings, and these two plays, the only other items in his canon which are remotely similar, self-evidently form with it a distinct Bromean group. *The Queen's Exchange* belonged to the King's Men and so cannot be later than about 1634; *The Lovesick Court* parodies that strain of courtly tragicomedy being newly exploited in mid-decade by Davenant, Montagu and Carlell. It would appear to be quite a plausible supposition, then, that all three belong roughly to the same stage in his career – those months in the mid-1630s when the queen was intriguing dangerously with dissident lords at court, some of whom had connections with openly discourted peers, and in which period freer speech became possible at court than could be used under more stable conditions. Had these plays been performed at court as *The Queen and Concubine* had been, the effect would have been the creation of a kind of theatrical country-at-court: the introduction of country settings and rustic characters, the fierce Prynne-like combination of extravagant declarations of deference to the king with severe criticism of royal favourites, the familiarization of good counsellors from the country who are vindicated by their loyalty and wisdom. If this was the case, it would have been the only time in Brome's career when he was writing for a court audience as much as for a public-theatre audience; though we must say at once that it is not at all representative of the tastes, only superficially similar, that normally prevailed at Whitehall.

With the demise of the queen's country alliance these conditions disappeared, and Brome returned to writing in a style more suited to the ambience of the Phoenix and Salisbury Court. He continued, however, to incorporate 'country' criticism and voices into his plays; we have already noticed, for example, the concern for the destruction of traditional patterns of economic life in the provinces prominently displayed in *The Court Beggar*. This play includes a character who is manifestly a spokesman for the attitudes of the country, Swayn-wit, a downright countryman who contrasts favourably with Court-wit and Cit-wit, representatives of the other 'estates' of the realm. Though Swayn-Wit visits Lady Strangelove, he is no courtier to dance attendance on her and efface his sense of his own dignity ('I come not as one o' your fooles to make you any [mirth] though' (p. 209)), and he upholds plain open honesty, manly valour, and unaffected directness in word and deed. His harshest rebukes are for Cit-wit who is infuriatingly double-faced ('thou wilt speake outragiously of all men behinde their backs, and darst not answer Ba— to the face of a sheep, o I could pommell thee' (p. 202)) and who is too cowardly to acknowledge a commitment to any political values at all:

COURT-WIT. You may safely say for Religion, King or Countrey.

SWAYN-WIT. Darst thou fight for Religion? say.

CIT-WIT. Who that has any Religion will fight I say? . . .

SWAYN-WIT. La you. Hee'l say he has no King neither, rather then fight.

COURT-WIT. Why if he will not fight for him he is no Subject, and no Subject no King.

CIT-WIT. I thank you sir, I would ha' said so . . .

SWAYN-WIT. And for thy Countrey, I dare sweare thou wouldst rather run it then fight for't.

CIT-WIT. Run my Countrey I cannot, for I was borne i'the City, I am no clown to run my Countrey. (p. 230)

Swayn-wit is the typical country voice, a true Englishman but also a fearless and stubborn, though just, critic of others. He is clearly the type who has opinions, and Brome identifies almost personally with him, bringing him forward at the end to speak the long epilogue for him. A few years later Brome adopted a similar persona in the verses he contributed to the Beaumont and Fletcher 1647 folio, when he posed as the common porter opening the door to the rest of the volume.

In his last play of all, Brome produced the period's fullest account of what is implied by the country. This is *A Jovial Crew, or the Merry Beggars* (1641), one of the best and most attractive achievements of the decade. Brome's later assertion, in the dedicatory epistle, that the play '*had the luck to tumble last of all in the* Epidemicall *ruine of the* Scene' (p. 344) – by which, presumably, he meant that it was being performed as the theatres closed, rather than that it was the last play to be written, which it plainly wasn't – has given it a certain poignancy which it would not originally have possessed and caused it to have become famed as a Cavalier escapist fantasy written in the face of a disastrous political reality. But the Cavalier interpretation is impossible to maintain consistently, for the play's dominant estates-type of the beggar acts as it did in *The Court Beggar*, as a sharp rebuke to the court for its economic and political bankruptcy. Brome's prologue announces the whole play as a travesty of the romantic dramas favoured at court, with their *'afflicted Wanderers'* and *'stout Chevalry'* (p. 351), and he makes several gibes about the beggary of court life and includes a verse satire attacking courtiers who beg 'by Covetise, not Need' (p. 367) which is recited by a beggar-poet to the acclaim of his audience. In the play's main plot, the four lovers, Rachel, Meriel, Vincent and Hilliard, who steal away from the girls' father's home in the country to find out what life is like among the merry beggars, are said to constitute a mock 'Camp Royal' (p. 377) and to be making a royal summer 'progress' (pp. 372, 375, 377, 381), but it is one

> That the most happy Courts could never boast
> In all their Tramplings on the Countries cost;
> Whose envy we shall draw, when they shall reade
> We out-beg them, and for as little Need. (p. 381)

Such well-spoken beggars prompt the amazed reflection 'The Court goes a begging, I think' from a passer-by (p. 400). The court's delight in playing at being rustic is deliciously parodied in Act IV when the beggar-band take courtly airs on themselves. They organize a mock-masque under their 'Master of their Revels', the beggars' *'Poet Laureat'*, whose inspiration shines 'as warm under a Hedge bottom, as on the tops of *Palaces'*, in celebration of the ludicrous marriage of an old beggar couple, one blind, the other lame, who are accorded the honour of being 'King *and* Queen' for the occasion, 'the old Couple in State' (pp. 427–9). Even the play's final joke is another swipe at courtiers for being beggars and 'Fool-Royals' (p. 451).

As Brome's epistle clearly states, the play's valedictory aspect was due to *luck*, not *intention*; the outcome of the current political confusion, and the closure of the theatres, were hardly foreseeable eventualities in 1641. Escapism is indeed Brome's theme, but the play is about escapism rather than itself escapist. Brome was himself no fugitive from reality; his prologue specifically demanded that the audience should relate the play's action to the political uncertainties through which they were living and which were the major concern of all:[16]

> THe Title of our *Play*, A Joviall Crew,
> May seem to promise Mirth: Which were a new,
> And forc'd thing, in these sad and tragick daies,
> For you to finde, or we expresse in *Playes*.
> We wish you, then, would change that expectation,
> Since Joviall Mirth is now grown out of fashion.   (p. 351)

Brome's multiple plots are deliberately designed to confront the question of escapism from cares and obligations, or from troubling events. The four lovers leave the house of Oldrents because of the oppressiveness of Oldrents's inexplicable melancholy, but also to escape the 'continual steam of hot Hospitality' that he dutifully keeps there (p. 370). The life they seek with the beggars (epitomized in the beggars' song) is one free from just such responsibilities and from the perplexities of politics:

> Come away; why do we stay?
> We have no debt or rent to pay.
> No bargains or accounts to make;
> Nor Land or Lease to let or take:
> Or if we had, should that remore us,
> When all the world's our own before us,
> And where we pass, or make resort,
> It is our Kingdom and our Court.   (p. 370)

Once established with the beggars, they meet Amie who is also running away from an unwanted marriage being organized for her by her guardian, Justice Clack. Meanwhile Oldrents, left behind, decides to abjure all his worries and forces himself into a life of jovial merry-making, refusing to concern himself about the mysterious disappearance of his daughters, and extravagantly dispensing with affairs: 'can you be so discourteous, as to tell me, or my Friend, any thing like businesse. If you come to be merry

271

with Me, you are welcome, If you have any businesse, forget it: You forget where you are else, and so to Dinner' (p. 421). He dismisses the burdens of 'Wealth and Power' as only 'a meer load of outward complement' (p. 388).

But as the plots unfold, the attractions of escapism are undermined by the continuing, troubling claims of wealth, power and, simply, convenience. Oldrents's joviality is highly enjoyable, but not wholly admirable; having once been a good and careful landlord, he now turns his household upside-down, singing a catch which encapsulates a visual criticism of his behaviour, for Brome directs '*The Singers are all Graybeards*' (p. 419). His joviality is merely another humour, the opposite extreme to his earlier unreasonable melancholy (and Brome points this up by introducing another humorous character, Talboy, who weeps all the time). Oldrents's friend Hearty, by contrast, indulges himself while retaining a detached awareness of the consequences of his indulgence:

> I ha' not so much Wealth to weigh me down,
> Nor so little (I thank *Chance*) as to daunce naked.   (p. 389)

As for the lovers, Brome mercilessly demonstrates the hardships of the life they have romantically sought out with the beggars, and their idealism and easy nostalgia quickly disintegrate. In Acts II and III, beggar life is explored merrily but realistically, as one remarkable for its indignities, squalor, deceit and predatory nature. The women are open to prostitution (p. 392), or to rape by the unsavoury gentleman Oliver (a cruel exposure of the artificialities of court pastoral, the chaste shepherdesses of which would, in real life, have been unprotected from such violations). The men are beaten; the threat of the whip is perpetually present (pp. 391, 398, 432, 442, 444). The beggars' merriment is maintained in the teeth of their experience, and the lovers find that the life that lacks cares also lacks comforts. At the end of Act II, while Oldrents admires the merry noise of the beggars in the barn, Brome brings together his criticism of both him and his children: Hearty tells him that the beggars are laughing loudly only to disguise the cries of a beggar-woman in labour, who must be on the road again the next day. Brome's point appears to be that however strong the desire to escape from one's troubles may be in 1641 it is none the less reprehensible and potentially disastrous. His play reasserts the importance of a mature and balanced recognition of the commitments one owes to everyday life; it is, implicitly, a morality of social and political responsibility.

It is true that Brome also presents his beggar-band in a more positive mode, but he isolates these scenes from the central realistic episodes, and in them he uses the beggars differently. In Acts I and IV the beggars appear unrealistically, no longer speaking in cant language and rather themselves social commentators than the object of social comment, and Brome imitates the device used in the earlier woodland–commonwealth plays of ordering them into an alternative kingdom which mirrors real England, a little realm within the greater country. Their world repeats Caroline society at every point, with its own estates of lawyers, soldiers, poets, courtiers and clergy, and it has a beggar-king too, Springlove, 'the great Commander of the *Maunders*, and King of *Canters*' (p. 377) who wields all 'Power . . . [and] Command/I'th' *Beggars* Commonwealth' (pp. 379–80). This mirror device enables Brome to raise a different set of issues; he emphasizes that the distinctive feature of the beggars' government, and what makes it so merry, is its perfect, natural freedom. The lovers, smarting under 'our Father's Rule and Government' yearn for 'absolute freedom; such as the very Beggars have . . . Liberty! the birds of the aire can take no more' (p. 371). They describe the beggars as 'the only people, can boast the benefit of a free state, in the full enioyment of Liberty, Mirth and Ease' (p. 370), and envy them for being

> The onely Freemen of a Common-wealth;
> Free above *Scot-free*; that observe no Law,
> Obey no Governour, use no Religion,
> But what they draw from their own ancient custom,
> Or constitute themselves, yet are no Rebels. (p. 376)

Couched in these terms, the freedom which the lovers seek in the beggars' state is pregnant with political significance; *A Jovial Crew* was staged at a time when parliament was professedly intent on vindicating the liberties of the subject and when, indeed, the very basis of the understanding of political liberty was being brought into question.[17] The lack of restraint of the beggars is also an oblique mirroring of the political freedom newly current in 1641. Their numbers include musicians 'that being within the reach of the Lash for singing libellous Songs at London, were fain to fly into our Covie, and here they sing all our Poet's Ditties' (p. 368) – such as his satire on court beggary – and their beggar-clergyman, Patrico, is a 'Hedge Priest', '*Parson Under-Hedge*', that is, a dissenting unlearned preacher such as might be found in the heretical woodlands (pp. 425, 436). Patrico tells Oldrents that ministers of his calling 'As well as those oth'Presbyterie,/Take wives and defie Dignitie' (p. 390); he and his flock take their cue from the political and religious turbulence to which the prologue refers. Moreover, the realistic scenes add different senses of the term 'liberty', for in these episodes the beggars' freedom is that of the politically unfree, the disfranchised, who are subject to whatever 'liberties' the enfranchised – such as the wayward Justice Clack or the obnoxious Oliver – may freely take with them and against which they have no redress. Besides availing himself through the beggars of the freedom of speech of the times, Brome is also using them to suggest, extraordinarily precisely, what it means to be without political rights altogether. In the world of Acts II and III, the beggars' liberty is the freedom of choice between equal miseries.

In these scenes, Brome confronts an ideal value, liberty, with the reality of its embodiment in practice, and this same process, of testing an abstraction, political or otherwise, against its practical realization, is a fundamental dynamic in *A Jovial Crew*. In a real world, monarchy may be realized only in a Springlove, a king of beggars. Justice may be reduced to *a* justice, Justice Clack – vain, talkative and inclined to punish first and examine after (p. 434). In the history of Amie, the young girl discovers that romantic flight with a lover is far from pleasurable, and bitterly complains 'that's a most lying Proverb, that saies, Where

Love is, there's no Lack' (p. 408). Most important of all, while in political life the question of the good of the country was being bandied back and forth, Brome asks insistently what the 'country' *is*. It is notable that his play about escapism is one of the most determinedly realistic of the entire period. Brome's country is not the literary pastoral of the court, nor the fantasy Sherwood of Massinger and Suckling in which what is hinted at by the 'country' matters more than the stage country itself. Rather, Brome created a wholly localized environment, not pastoral but manorial, the antecedents of which are in plays like *King Lear*, *A Woman Killed with Kindness* and *The Witch of Edmonton*. It has barns, hedges, ditches, roads and houses; its inhabitants are landlords, stewards, tenants and almsmen; ordinary moral activities – business, amusement, charity – take place here. It is a nexus of social and economic relationships, concrete at just those points where Massinger and Suckling were vague. The pressure of this contentious realism is to assert that for any political settlement to have meaning beyond the world of Westminster and its constitutional arguments, for any political group to 'represent' England, it must be in touch with the England 'represented' here dramatically in all its human detail.

The most striking thing about *A Jovial Crew*, then, is that it should be there, that at a major moment of crisis in English history a dramatist should evoke so completely the continuity, the particularity and the presence of English life, and Brome reinforces the effect theatrically by his fifth-act introduction of a band of strolling players, themselves legally rogues and vagabonds and consorting with the beggars, which makes the play read as if casting back to the very earliest days of the English stage (with its specially close relationship with the country) and taking stock of the whole great achievement of the English theatre too. *A Jovial Crew* is a truly national play written at a turning-point in the history of the English stage and the English nation, and Brome is wholly conscious of that fact and of all that is at stake; at a moment when England was embroiled in a political crisis more grave and uncertain than anything within living memory, the play stood as an eloquent plea for everything that was valuable, permanent and sanctioned by time in the English way of life. It seems to me that Brome is here making a brilliant and astonishing anticipation of the provincialism in politics of the mid- and late-1640s; that he is already sensitive to that 'neutralist' or 'localist' sentiment which was to emerge spontaneously and nationally as an expression of the country's horror and amazement at the failure of the London politicians to reach a settlement and at the stark choice between king or parliament with which the nation was presented, and which generated regional determinations to preserve the integrity of the locality by obstructing fighting and preventing the political conflict from threatening the fabric of provincial life (see p. 18 above). In few other plays is the feeling for the tight-knit, interdependent local community, the country as county, so carefully and richly created; it is entirely characteristic that Oldrents's servant Randall should confess he has never gone twelve miles distant from his home in his life (p. 438). Events open with Oldrents looking over his household accounts, and with Hearty praising him as a wise, conscientious country gentleman, prayed for by his neighbours and tenants 'as duly as/ For King and Realme':

> Whose Rent did ever you exact? whose have
> You not remitted, when by casualties
> Of fire, of floods, of common dearth, or sickness,
> Poor men were brought behind hand? Nay, whose losses
> Have you not piously repair'd? . . .
> What Hariots have you tane from forlorne Widows?
> What Acre of your thousands have you rack'd?   (p. 356)

We hear further of his 'Cattel, Wool, Corn', 'House-keeping, Buildings and Repairs', liveries and charities (p. 358), of the surveying of his lands (p. 383), of the good wages he gives his servants (pp. 414–15), of the charitable maintaining of poor men's children, aged labourers and young married couples (p. 362). Oldrents – as his name suggests – is the perfect local squire, and his escapism is in part a repudiation of this profoundly fulfilling relationship with his country, a flight into a deliberate neglect of his obligations which is increasingly mad and monstrous ('Lack we Motives to laugh? Are not all things, any thing, every thing to be laugh'd at? And if nothing were to be seen, felt, heard, or understood, we would laugh at It too' (p. 441)). Oldrents finally returns to an acknowledgment of his duty to his dependants, but the play's general movement, from Oldrents's hospitable household to the 'Miser's Feast' at the house of Justice Clack (p. 442), pessimistically confirms Brome's fears of deterioration in the texture of provincial England at large. And the inhabitants of this other household – the self-opinionated Clack, the opportunist Oliver, the mean-minded Martin and the ludicrously weak-spirited Talboy – have qualities which not only mark them out as unworthy leaders of their local society but augur ill for the achievement of a wise political settlement at the centre.

So Brome's dramatic testament is set in a lovingly drawn English landscape as a measure of all that is worth preserving in the present crisis, and of the commitment to the country and to its survival which he is urging onto his audience. These implicit meanings are made explicit in the beggars' masque of Act IV, which is set apart in the play almost as a direct, embedded authorial comment on the dangers that face the nation at the present moment. It is introduced by the speech of Vincent and Hilliard on the delightfulness of the beggars' kingdom, that it is free precisely from the political strife all around them in 1641:

> With them there is no Grievance or Perplexity;
> No fear of war, or State Disturbances.
> No Alteration in a Common-wealth,
> Or Innovation, shakes a Thought of theirs . . .
> We have no fear of lessening our Estates;
> Nor any grudge with us (without Taxation)
> To lend or give, upon command, the whole
> Strength of our Wealth for publick Benefit:
> While some, that are held rich in their Abundance,
> (Which is their Misery, indeed) will see
> Rather a generall ruine upon all,
> Then give a Scruple to prevent the Fall. (p. 426)

This speech registers the attractiveness of escapism into a world where politics does not happen, from which the grievances and fears of innovation at that moment being voiced at Westminster are absent. But its ironies are slippery and seem to invite several interpretations simultaneously (one problem is that Vincent and Hilliard are only pretending to like being beggars, in order not to lose face before the girls). From another angle, the speech is arguing that the responsibilities of political life must be accepted because the beggars' peacefulness is due to their poverty, that they have no fears and grudges about unparliamentary taxation only because they have no estates to lose in the first place. And again, the speech operates also as a direct admonition to those involved in politics to compound their differences and find a resolution of the political dilemma, and to avoid destroying the nation for the sake of 'a Scruple'. The plans for the beggars' masque follow. This is intended to display 'a Common-wealth; *Utopia*, With all her Branches and Consistencies' (p. 429), represented by the beggar-courtier, merchant, gentleman, clergyman and lawyer:

POET. I would have the *Country*, the *City*, and the *Court*, be at great variance for *Superiority*. Then would I have *Divinity* and *Law* stretch their wide throats to appease and reconcile them: Then would I have the *Souldier* cudgell them all together, and overtop them all. Stay, yet I want another person.

HILLIARD. What must he be?

POET. A *Beggar*.

VINCENT. Here's enough of us, I think. What must the *Beggar* do?

POET. He must, at last, overcome the *Souldier*; and bring them all to *Beggars-Hall*. (p. 430)

This is a firm, uncompromising conviction that the only victor in the battle of estates can be the beggar, and it formulates into a single statement tendencies that are at work throughout the play. Here the gentry go begging in courtly language, as in *The Antipodes* except that this is real England, not Anti-England. We see Oliver seducing beggar girls (beggar-niggling) and the last-act revelations disclose that Oldrents has fathered a beggar's bastard, and that his estate is partly founded on a cheat practised by his grandfather. The wandering players turn out to be the lost gentry; and there is a general reminder that all people on stage are players, and so potentially vagabonds. The closing mood is reconciliation, but really nothing is concluded. The play remains open-ended, fearful for the future and acutely aware of this society's proximity to disintegration into its lowest parts – thieves, beggars and beggar-nigglers.

A Jovial Crew, then, is not in the least escapist, and is only nostalgic in the false perspective created by later events, that the inability of the politicians to resolve the crisis did in fact have the disastrous consequences that Brome foresees and pleads may be averted. In fact Brome was perhaps the first person of his day, both within the theatres and without, to voice openly the possibility of a full-scale social division that was real and not merely fictional; if this is so, *A Jovial Crew* is an extraordinary achievement. It is a profoundly historical play, giving vigorous expression to the most central preoccupations of its time, and painfully sensitive to the uniqueness of the moment at which it was being performed, that English history was standing upon a point of decisive transformation; its vigorousness demonstrates the quality of Brome's understanding of the pressures of the moment, his sense of the tension between the values that had to be preserved and the impending loss. The effect of his provincial perspective on events at the centre is to suggest that politics alone is not enough – that politics must be the servant and not the master of those continuities, traditions and balances which are the products of long and difficult development but which once destroyed cannot be restored; that the language of politics must have relation to life as it is lived; and that it is no use fighting for England if England is destroyed in the process. Above all, the play comes close to saying that we are all responsible for the good of the country and for the probity of actions done in its name – Brome seems to be moving towards a significantly modern ethic of political obligation, for this is a sentiment which belongs in the post-revolutionary world and for which there was little place in the society of Charles and Laud. For his part, Brome is concerned for both puritan and cavalier, for the integrity, continuity and survival of the English way of life. Deeply reflecting on the destiny of the nation, he writes the most committed play of the decade.

10

Some conclusions

I HAVE BEEN ARGUING that the drama of 1632–42 has been undeservedly neglected and astonishingly undervalued. While no one is going to maintain that these plays exert the same claims on our attention as do their predecessors of the 1590s and 1600s, there is still much here that is valuable and genuinely exciting; moreover, it seems to me that in the 1630s the one literary medium which more than any other is focusing and responding sensitively and articulately to the major needs and anxieties of its society is the drama. It is beyond doubt that the theatrical tradition that was cut short in September 1642 was neither exhausted nor in retreat. Indeed, with the collapse of the censorship and with the leading gentry once again returning to London to attend parliament, the conditions of 1641–42 were ripe for a theatrical boom rather than a termination. The popular stages had been enjoying for the first time a series of successful 'runs' of consecutive performances of plays;[1] the period's leading playwright, Richard Brome, was at the height of his powers when his career was so tantalizingly disrupted; and some of the decade's best achievements and most suggestive new departures – such as *The Queen of Aragon*, *A Jovial Crew*, *The Sophy* and *Canterbury his Change of Diet* – belong to these last months. The superannuated notion of the 'decadence' has little place here. It took the most catastrophic social and political crisis of early modern England to destroy the tradition of the Elizabethan theatre; we might have expected no less.

The root causes of this neglect are political. The Caroline drama has been dismissed for its escapist tendencies; yet as a body it is perhaps most remarkable for its consistent, insistent political interests. It has been derided for its servility to an unpopular and intolerant regime; yet it is full of suspicion and hostility towards the court and courtiers. Richard Brome now goes almost totally unread; yet there is some reason to consider him as a political playwright of major significance. Brome's artistic importance for the Caroline theatre, that he is simply the best Caroline playwright, is indistinguishable from his centrality within the period, that as the author of plays which articulate the points of view of courtly or aristocratic dissidence, of nascent gentlemanly 'localism' and of popular and puritan radicalism, he seems to be in touch with an amazingly diverse range of feeling, with the most lively and challenging currents of opinion in the decade. As a political playwright, Massinger comes close behind him, and even Shirley, whose fashionable manner has been mistaken for mere courtliness, deserves fuller recognition as an independent and intelligent critic of his society. In play after play of this decade, politics is not just an occasional or ephemeral issue but is the basic, fundamental concern and the principal determinant of dramatic form; far from being innately conservative and traditional, this is a drama which cautiously yet firmly is seeking to change its world. The playwrights were dramatizing the conflicts and tensions at work in their society, embodying men's dilemmas and voicing their grievances, anxieties and frustrations. In fictional settings they were able to suggest and explore hypothetical modes of action, formulate political expectations, instil changed attitudes and shape and educate new kinds of political consciousness. Their drama was not merely the product of its society but was itself part of the historical process, an agent of change as much as the mirror of change, a participant engaged *with* its society's compromises and not merely an observer *of* them: the collision of irreconcilable attitudes, desires and misgivings which it reveals and advances fictionally was one which, as the theatres closed, was already issuing into real social and political upheaval. In its uneasily integrated society the drama registered the impact of politics but in important and lasting ways it also had its own impact upon politics; formed by its society, it was itself helping to transform it.[2]

Clearly, the recognition of the intense political concerns of the Caroline theatre goes against the grain of much that has been asserted about the political conformism and orthodoxy of the earlier, greater drama, and in other ways too the evidence of this crucial final decade contradicts many tendencies which are commonly assumed to have been latent or inherent in the drama's previous history – its dependence on the court, its hostility to puritanism, the eclipsing of the popular theatre tradition by the success of the more fashionable playhouses, the gradual but inexorable metamorphosis of the socially inclusive Elizabethan theatre into the socially exclusive Restoration stage. Too many of these assumptions rest on an easy, questionable correlation of the state of the theatre as it closed down in 1642 with the state of the theatre as it was restored in 1660, but on examination the theatre of the 1630s does not fit readily into an inevitable, step-by-step progression from Elizabethan to Restoration. Rather, there was much going on in the drama before 1642 which would find no place on the stage after 1660, and 1642, instead of marking a moment of continuity, represents one of real, decisive discontinuity, for the stage that was restored after 1660 had been reorganized on a radically altered basis. To put it another way, would we now have seen the same straightforward progression between 1642 and 1660 had Charles reached an understanding with parliament, averted a national political breakdown and so allowed the theatres to continue playing? It seems highly unlikely that had the professional theatres been operating after 1642 their repertoires would have been simply and comfortably 'Cavalier'.

What needs the strongest emphasis is the variety of the drama that was closed down in 1642. The Elizabethan theatrical inheritance was not single and unique; seven stages were playing throughout the 1630s, not just one, and these divide broadly into three traditions – what I have termed the courtly, the elite and the popular theatres. The difference between 1642 and 1660 is partly explained by the narrowing of this rich interplay of competing traditions (James Wright complained in 1699 that 'the

Town[,] much less than at present, could then maintain Five Companies, and yet now Two can hardly Subsist'),[3] but more particularly by the fact that the restored theatre took over much (such as heroic drama, scenery and actresses) that before 1642 belonged principally to the court stage and had little or no currency in the professional theatres. Most interested in explaining the antecedents of the Restoration drama, the history of the immediately pre-1642 theatre has been written almost exclusively from the point of view of the court stage, yet this, I have suggested, was the weakest and least important tradition in its own time, significant only where (as in the plays I discuss in chapters 3 and 4 above) it shows most signs of contact with the more vigorous and questioning non-courtly drama. The court stage can be made to appear to be the theatrical mainstream only in the most teleological account of the period. In spite of all that Harbage offers in *Cavalier Drama*, it is surely clear that the influence of courtiers like Walter Montagu and Lodowick Carlell on the contemporary professional stage was virtually negligible. A few courtly plays written principally for private performance (or even just for reading) could modify only minutely the brilliant, established, historic dramatic tradition to which the working playwrights belonged far more inextricably than they ever could to the world of court theatricals. This tradition was still in performance or in print; the vast bulk, and most important part, of the Caroline drama participated in or built on it; some of its giants were still alive. The courtier drama, except where it emulated the greater inclusiveness and openness of the public stages, is frankly of little lasting interest or importance, and I have not discussed it; the real future in 1642 still seems to be in the hands of the professionals.

For, after all, the crucial theatrical division in the period falls not between the elite and popular theatres at all, but between the courtly and the professional stages (the genuineness of this division is underlined by the notorious antagonisms which subsisted between the courtier and the professional playwrights), and in 1642 the Caroline mainstream lay emphatically on the professional side of this great divide, and much closer to the popular end of the spectrum than is usually supposed. Early Stuart culture has been habitually equated with the culture of the early Stuart court, but this is profoundly misleading, falsifying the nature of the crisis and taking at face value the Cavalier sneer that 'never Rebell was to Arts a friend'.[4] As far as the theatres were concerned, the court stage was indeed elitist, exclusive, intimate, amateur, occasional, restricted, private in the tightest sense, but the professional theatres, both indoor and outdoor, were genuinely public – in the case of the popular theatres, fully and comprehensively so. We do not have to suppose that the collapse of the court would necessarily have spelt disaster for the theatres; rather, as a play such as *The Court Beggar* conclusively demonstrates, the sentiments which the court was failing to focus were precisely those which *were* finding vigorous and enthusiastic expression on the non-courtly stages. It is instructive to place *The Queen of Aragon* beside *The Court Beggar*, a play addressing similar issues and written and performed almost simultaneously, but which, being intended primarily for a court audience, is in every way contrasted. The differences between Habington, who wishes for some change but is still restrained and placatory, and the inflammatory Brome indicate the distance that had opened up between the courtly and the non-courtly theatres; the two were not yet antithetical but they were already in some senses opposed, and the sympathies of Brome's Phoenix audience were with the reformers, against the court.

So the distinction between courtly and non-courtly theatres is one which finally tells politically as well as culturally. Although I have demonstrated that one did not have to go out of the court to hear criticisms of royal policies, that from time to time conditions were such that a drama drawing more widely on alternative, non-courtly points of view could be presented from within the court, nevertheless it seems evident that by 1640–42 the court stage had narrowed in certain important ways and simply could not accommodate the rich, varied and unorthodox things that were being said on the non-courtly stages. This was a court that had preferred to be without Ben Jonson; it held little attraction for Milton; one hesitates to think what might have become of George Herbert had he found the court appointment he was chasing in the 1620s. These are extremely damaging charges, and they go a long way towards accounting for the isolation of Charles at the end of the decade. There had been plenty of opportunities for Charles to have built bridges with his critics in the 1630s, for him to have found an understanding with his subjects on which his government might have been safely and unshakeably established with or without parliament; but despite several near misses, and in spite of the work of men like Cartwright and Habington, in the last analysis the court over which he presided remained narrow and insular in a way which was fatal to his political credibility. Throughout the 1630s Whitehall was the only central national institution of political life, yet by 1642, as the attitudes and criticisms vociferously current on the non-courtly stages show, it had ceased to be a truly national institution. Charles's court failed finally to attract the aspirations and trust of the country at large as, say, the courts of Elizabeth and even James had managed to do. The weaknesses and limitations of the official court culture suggest how it would be possible later for many men to come to think of the court as marginal and, ultimately, to decide that it could be set aside in the name of more powerful interests altogether.

Of course the drama alone cannot explain the crisis of 1640–42, but the great voicing from the professional stages of grievances and demands which Charles was failing to conciliate or to appease does illuminate with some clarity the way that the court forfeited the confidence of the nation; certainly it suggests vividly the way that men living through these troubling circumstances could begin to entertain political alternatives, different ideas of how government, order and society ought to be, and perhaps eventually come to develop a belief in their desirability. Historians are hard put to it to chart the level of public expectation that existed at any moment that parliament might be recalled, or the extent of the pressures that Charles was under to modify the direction of his government. In the absence of any focused, formal 'opposition' to royal policies, all that survive are scanty hints such as the mention that in 1632 'Upon the King of Bohemias death some here doe suddenly expect a parlament', or that in 1635 the news of the coming of the Palatine Prince 'was received with more pleasure by those who fervently desire a parliament than by any others', or the complaint about Ship Money made by the Earl of Danby to the King in 1636, urging him to raise finance through parliament instead, or the repetition of this protest by the Earl of Warwick in 1637, or the Earl of Middlesex's admonition to Charles in the same year to give over 'these projects and extraordinary courses'.⁵ These are scattered and occasional traces of opinions unwelcome to the king, but in plays like *King John and Matilda*, *The Antipodes* and *The Wasp*, the sicknesses of the state and the possible political remedies that there might be were being openly and repeatedly discussed, while in *The Queen and Concubine* and *The Costly Whore* parliaments, of sorts, were actually being fictionally presented. As these plays entered the repertoire, were established, repeated and revived, such sentiments must have been continually before men's eyes; and at the Blackfriars, Phoenix and Salisbury Court, where the audiences regularly included country gentlemen up in town, anxious about Ship Money, lawyers concerned about the legality of Charles's prerogative schemes, great merchants and business-men whom Charles's monopolies and demands for credit had milked, representatives of the political nation who in a few years' time would be sitting again in parliament, their impact must have been immense.

As for the open-air playhouses, with their riotous audiences and unrestrained social and political comment, the distances and antagonisms between courtly and non-courtly loom larger still, and the political divergences which they mark were even more precipitous. Although the nature of the evidence is not such that we can establish the connection with complete certainty, the historical continuities of the drama of citizen heroism and aristocratic villainy do seem very strongly to be with the popular radicals of the 1640s and 50s, the Levellers, ranters and libertines whose arrogation of political, social, sexual and religious free-doms was as shocking to parliament as to the king; the political hopes and activity which the popular drama was encouraging was of a sort which Charles's propertied opponents would be less concerned to promote than to restrain. Marxist historians have familiarized us with a view of the seventeenth-century upheaval as two revolutions, the limited constitutional revolution which was achieved, and the revolt of the lower sort of people which threatened and sometimes surfaced, but which their masters managed to contain – the great plebeian questioning of traditional hierarchies, orthodoxies and conventions, of rank, property, marriage and belief. The gentlemen who wished to bring the king to terms had no desire to see the world really turned upside-down, and in the events of the Civil Wars the political fantasies of the popular drama were – by and large – prevented from becoming realities. With the return of the king in 1660 this world of teeming radical thought and freedom was ruthlessly suppressed, and so too when the playhouses reopened the popular theatres were no longer among them, the drama having been placed under a monopoly controlled by the two courtiers, Davenant and Killigrew. The disappearance of the popular playhouses is the single most important difference between the Elizabethan theatre and the new theatre of the Restoration; it is an indication of the changes that had profoundly transformed the structure of Restoration politics and society.

Finally, the very richness and variety of the charges which the professional stages were levelling against the court casts a highly suggestive light on the subsequent history of the political breakdown. In recent years some historians have been arguing that the revolution came about, as it were, by accident. In so far as this is intended to imply that there was no real crisis, it is patently false; there clearly were vast and deeply-rooted disagreements about fundamental issues in church and state without which the battles of the 1640s could not have been fought. But it is true in the sense that most of the politicians of 1640–42 were looking for solutions to their grievances and that the armed conflict only came about when the expected political understanding failed to be agreed upon. It is here that the multiplicity of the theatrical traditions is so revealing. Puritanism was one valid reason for criticizing Charles in 1640, but his subjects discovered more than one variety of puritanism and plenty of other good reasons besides. Each tradition of theatre – courtly, fashionable, popular – expressed a critical perspective on the court but each spoke for a slightly different audience, each was concerned with different grievances, each envisaged a slightly different solution and the three were ultimately incompatible. There is here a society at one in its desire for political change but deeply torn over what that change should be, in whose interest it should be made, how far it should go. The very variety of political expectation was, in terms of the political institutions which England was operating in 1642, self-confounding; once the agreed, divinely-sanctioned world-picture was thrown down, it became apparent that there were all sorts of alternative world-pictures competing for superiority which could not be fully accommodated in a supposedly simple, homogeneous society. Thus the events of the succeeding years were destined to be truly tragic – they would inevitably frustrate as much as fulfil men's expectations, expose men painfully to political choices which they had no wish to face, commit them to compromise solutions which were only partially satisfactory. These were dilemmas which could not be resolved wholly successfully except in fictions, and the very best plays of all are those which refuse to make a facile, simplifying resolution of the tensions and conflicts which they have singled out, and acknowledge the laboriousness, unlikelihood or impossibility of finding a settlement acceptable to all parties; I am thinking especially of the precarious, strained generosity which is invoked to overcome the deadlock of *The Queen of Aragon*, the pessimism and uncertainty which hang over the conclusion of *A Jovial Crew*. The 1640s would make the difficult transition from a world where the *polis* is presumed to be unanimous and government ordained by God, to a modern world where the *polis* is a collection of atoms and politics the pragmatic art of accommodation and expediency. It is a change which the drama down to 1642 is foreshadowing and helping to initiate.

Dramatic or semi-dramatic pamphlets 1641–42

The following is a list of dramatic or semi-dramatic pamphlets published in the years 1641–42, compiled mainly from a search through the Thomason tracts in the British Library. I have listed all items in which the points of view of two or more interlocutors are exchanged in dialogue. Press-marks are given for pamphlets which appear in the Thomason collection.

1641	
January	*Times Alteration*, 669f4(4).
April	*The Curate's Conference*, E208(13).
May	*The Lamentable Complaints of Nick Froth the Tapster and Rulerost the Cook*, E156(4).
	Canterbury's Will, E156(5).
	The Proctor and the Parator their Mourning, E156(13).
	A Dialogue or Accidental Discourse betwixt Mr. Alderman Abell and Richard Kilvert, E156(16).
	The Last Discourse betwixt Master Abell and Master Richard Kilvert, E156(18).
	A Description of the Passage of Thomas Late Earl of Strafford, E156 (21).
	The Discontented Conference, E157(3).
	England's Glory . . . With a Discourse betwixt Master John Calvin and a Prelatical Bishop, E157(9).
June	*The Spiritual Courts Epitomized*, E157(15).
	Sion's Charity Towards her Foes in Misery, E158(13).
	A Conference between the Two Great Monarchs of France and Spain, E160(6).
	A Dialogue betwixt Three Travellers, E160(7).
	Old News Newly Revived, E160(22).
	The Pimp's Prerogative, 669f4(18).
July	*The Bishop's Potion*, E165(1).
	The Downfall of Temporizing Poets, Unlicensed Printers, Trotting Mercuries and Bawling Hawkers, E165(5).
	A Revelation of Mr. Brightman's Revelation, E164(11).

Appendix I

August	R. Brathwaite, *Mercurius Britannicus*, E167(15) [there are four further editions of this tract].
September	L. Hewes, *Certain Grievances . . . Set Forth by Way of a Dialogue*, E171(24).
	The Stage-Players' Complaint, E172(23).
	The Sisters of the Scabberd's Holiday, E168(8).
	J. Taylor, *A Pedlar and a Romish Priest*, E168(10).
	T. Bray, *The Anatomy of Et Caetera*, E169(1).
	A Map of Mischief, E169(5).
	A Learned and Witty Conference, E172(8).
October	R. Overton(?), *A New Play Called Canterbury his Change of Diet*, E177(8).
November	*A Charitable Churchwarden*, E176(2).
	R. Overton(?), *Vox Borealis, or the Northern Discovery*, E177(5).
December	*The Countryman's Care and the Citizen's Fear*, E179(8).
	The Churchwarden's Repentance, E180(12).
Unassigned	*A Dialogue Between Sack and Six*, E146(10).
	H. Peacham, *A Dialogue Between the Cross in Cheap and Charing Cross*, E238(9).
	T. Herbert, *News Newly Discovered*, E1102(3).
	T. Herbert, *News out of Islington* (London, 1641).
	T. Herbert, *Keep Within Compass, Dick and Robin* (London, 1641).
	The Counter's Discourse, with its Varlets' Discovery (n.p., 1641).
	Read and Wonder, a War Between Two Entire Friends, The Pope and the Devil (n.p., 1641).
	J. Taylor, *The Complaint of Mr Tenterhook the Projector and Sir Thomas Dodger the Patentee* (London, 1641).
1642	
January	*A Disputation Betwixt the Devil and the Pope*, E132(8).
	A Dialogue Betwixt Roundhead and Rattlehead, E134(19).
	R. Overton, *Articles of High Treason Exhibited Against Cheapside Cross*, E134(23).
	An Antidote Against Rome's Infection, E134(34).
February	*The Friar's Last Farewell*, E136(27).
	The Arraignment of Superstition, E136(31).
	L.P., *A New Disputation Between the Two Lordly Bishops York and Canterbury*, E1113(2).
March	*A Brief Dialogue*, E140(5).
	The Organ's Funeral, or the Quirister's Lament, E141(6).
April	R.P., *A Discreet and Judicious Discourse between Wisdom and Piety*, E142(19).
	J. Taylor, *A Delicate, Dainty, Damnable Dialogue between the Devil and a Jesuit*, E142(8).
	A Purge for Pluralities, E143(5).
	J. Taylor, *A Three-fold Discourse*, E145(3).
May	H. Peacham, *Squarecaps Turned into Roundheads*, E149(1).
June	*Cornucopia, or Room for a Ramhead*, E151(6).
July	*A Conference between the Pope, the Emperor and the King of Spain*, E155(10).
August	*The Wishing Commonwealth's Men*, E114(11).

October   *A Dialogue betwixt a Courtier and a Scholar*, E122(7).
                Strange Apparitions, E123(23).
                The Last News in London, E124(11).
                A Discourse or Dialogue between Two New Potent Enemies, E240(28).
                Three Speeches, being Such Speeches as the like were Never Spoken in the City,
                E240(31).
November   *The Wicked Resolution of the Cavaliers*, E127(42).
December   *A Dialogue between a Resolved and a Doubtful Englishman*, E128(41).

Shakespeare's unprivileged playgoers
1576–1642

When this book was substantially complete, there appeared Ann
Jennalie Cook's large-scale study of the Elizabethan theatre
audiences, *The Privileged Playgoers of Shakespeare's London 1576–1642*
(Princeton, 1981), self-avowedly a rebuttal of Alfred Harbage's
classic work *Shakespeare's Audience* (1941). Professor Cook raises
two principal objections to Harbage's thesis. Firstly, she criticizes
Harbage's division of Elizabethan society into upper and lower
classes analogous to modern social anatomizations as anachro-
nistic and misleading, proposing in its place a model of society
divided into the privileged and the unprivileged, the politically
and socially free and unfree. Secondly, Harbage made little
allowance for the long working hours and breadline existence of
those citizens, labourers and unprivileged men whom he represented as constituting the major part of the Elizabethan audience.
These are valid and important correctives for which we must be
grateful to Professor Cook (though a residual doubt remains
about the rigidity with which she asserts the privileged/unprivi-
leged distinction, given that this was a time of unprecedented
social fluidity and one which saw the despairing abandonment of
official attempts to enforce explicit social demarcation through
sumptuary legislation).[1] From them proceed two conclusions:
that the theatres addressed themselves to and attracted spectators
principally from those groups which she defines as socially free
or privileged; and that this holds true for all Elizabethan
audiences, in other words that there was essentially little difference between the playgoers frequenting the cheap outdoor stages
and those who spent more lavishly at the indoor theatres. This

second conclusion, initially only hinted at, emerges with increasing force until the 'two traditions' concept is finally (p. 267) declared to be only a myth devised by Restoration commentators to explain certain features of the Elizabethan stage perceived dimly through the fog of history (Harbage may have sentimentalized his Elizabethan working man and over- and under-valued certain types of drama, but it is an interesting testimony to the coherence of his position that Cook inclines to dispute both *Shakespeare's Audience* and the basic thesis of the later *Shakespeare and the Rival Traditions*). Cook's book looks set to become a standard authority on the topic, but it is patently at odds with my arguments in chapters 6 and 8, so it is necessary to assess some of its assertions. Like all books with axes to grind, it is misleading in its emphases, in its later chapters very dangerously so.

The privileged

No one is going to deny that the privileged were in the playhouses, indoor and outdoor, in vast quantities. We all know this. Whatever the bias of Harbage's account they are there on every page, and my chapter 6 describes yet more. What is profoundly questionable is Professor Cook's implication that they were virtually, if not absolutely, the only spectators who counted.

Certainly throughout this period the numbers of the 'privileged' were growing nationally and in London: under Charles I, for example, some 1,172 London families, principally younger sons of country gentry in trade or the professions, asserted new claims to gentry status.[2] But how far can we trust Professor Cook's figure of 52,000 privileged in London in 1642, an astonishing one in six of the total London population (p. 94)? Quite correctly Cook defines her term privileged very broadly and with exactness as the socially free, the peerage, gentry, lawyers, merchants, clergy, and greater yeomanry, their wives and children (pp. 16–17), but some 200 pages later it has been simplified into 'London's gentlemen' (p. 212), a narrowing of scope which is unacknowledged but necessary to enable the varied group of 'privileged' to come to be understood as coterminous with the category 'potential playgoers'. There is an elasticity in the use of the term which is functional for Cook's argument: it tends to carry an inclusive meaning when the size of the body is in question, and an exclusive meaning when habits of playgoing are at stake.

Necessarily, Cook's discussion of theatre-going is taken up mainly with the gentry component within the privileged spectrum. She does indeed explore the opportunities for playgoing available to other privileged status groups, but the crux of the statistical underpinning which she develops for her interpretation is the depiction of London as a place of irresistible magnetism for England's gentry. Yet can we really suppose that during these decades, along with those engaged in business, law or education,

anyone with the money and freedom to pursue a life of sheer pleasure was certain to be in London much of the time. It is most likely that virtually every privileged family in the kingdom had one or more of its members in the city at any given time, and a good many families or family members lived there all the time.

(p. 93)

Every assertion here is seriously open to question. A leisured town society did indeed appear in London in these years, but as I have already argued (pp. 109–10 above) we overstate to ascribe to it the same permanence and cultural dominance as the world of fashion of later generations. The habit of visiting London in the season formed slowly and affected different sections of the privileged unevenly, while in an era of bad roads and introspective local communities a journey to the distant metropolis was for most a major expedition, not to be undertaken lightly, let alone repeatedly. Not all men who went to law at Westminster would have taken their wives with them, still fewer their households. Coaches, on Cook's own evidence (p. 81), were for the very rich; had the Knyvetts in Norfolk and the Oxindens in Kent not tended to stay at home when the gentlemen of the family occasionally went to town to do business we would have been without their fine (and entirely characteristic) series of letters from London back to the provinces. Nor too could many families afford to maintain a house in London. The Oxindens addressed their letters from the Holy Lamb in Aldersgate and the Peacock in Blackfriars; Jane Cornwallis, a Suffolk lady of some standing, lodged in London with friends or at the Stirrup near York House; the Sussex gentleman Sir Thomas Pelham was set back nearly £450 by his London visit in 1648.[3] The season was so insecurely established before the Civil War that London could be found to be void of company as well as full. In May 1617 the Countess of Bedford was complaining that this 'dull towne afords nothing worthy the wrighting, for ther is almost nobody of quality left in itt' while twenty years later Sir John North was disappointed that after the Christmas break 'few are yet come of quality, unles it be L:ds of Court, and of his Ma:ts Councell' (the following month the court and Westminster Hall had improved, but 'the rest of the towne is very empty, & almost no good families come up').[4]

Structurally, the English gentry down to the Civil War were firmly rooted to the countryside, their experience of England being predominantly one of rural rather than urban life. Cook exhibits no sense of what Lawrence Stone has called the 'persistent provincialism' of the gentry,[5] their profound attachment to their locality, and its circle of interests, kinship and commitments. The attractions of London were qualified by these ingrained allegiances and values which frequently emerged as expressions of suspicion or outright hostility to the capital. Fatigue with the expensive, uncomfortable, alien town, and anxiety to be at home again, are leitmotivs in the Knyvett and Oxinden letters. We find Sir Thomas Knyvett longing for 'a release out of this vngodlye towne' in 1626, 'as wearye of this towne as ever I was of any thinge in my life' in 1627, describing distastefully his sweaty journey to London in 1629, eager for home again in 1637, 'for I am extreame weary of the towne'.[6] So too Henry Oxinden was 'weary of the towne and stay butt for my father to releive mee' in 1639, his cousin James was 'sick of london' in 1640, to another cousin London was that 'loathed of [me] place' to which 'hardly will any thing ever draw mee thether'.[7] For Jane Cornwallis London could mean a 'journy uery tedious', her husband's letters perpetually fretted about the 'slow proceeding of or business', 'beinge so fully satisfied wth this place, that I do assure you yt is rather tedious to me than plesant', while to her brother business was 'one fetter more put upon my legge to imprison mee in London'.[8] And so on. These gentry families were not at all insular – politically conscious as they were – but their local horizons loomed larger because the texture of Tudor and Stuart provincial life was much richer, much denser than it subsequently became, and this was something which powerfully impeded London's magnetic drag. The Isle of Wight gentleman Sir John Oglander wrote in his account book for 1623, 'Hate London, as to live there, without thou hast a vocation that calleth thee to it'.[9]

These are sentiments for which Cook's description of a 'wholesale defection to London by the gentry' (p. 87) finds no place, and her 'conservative' assertion that in excess of one in five of England's gentry were in London *at any one time* (p. 94) looks rather less conservative beside the statement of the student of Caroline Somerset that only three or four of the thousand or so major Somerset gentry ever occasionally went to town,[10] or the belief of the leading modern authority on seventeenth-century provincial society that 'probably at least three provincial squires in four rarely or never visited the metropolis'.[11] The only hard evidence we have about gentry numbers in London comes from the census of 1632 (cited above, pp. 109–10) which turned up 314 houses occupied by non-indigenous gentlemen and above, including wives and widows living alone;[12] perhaps this indicates about 1,000 privileged visitors then in town. Admittedly the census was looking for those defying the recent royal proclamation against London residence, but even so it suggests another story entirely from Cook's optimistic figures. Yet even if we accept Cook's estimates, her conclusions still seem extremely incautious. The total playhouse capacity for the 1590s and 1630s appears to have been somewhere in the region of 50,000 spectators per week, in the 1610s considerably more (Cook, p. 176). This means that if they were the theatres' principal or only patrons, virtually *every single one* of Cook's 52,000 privileged in London in 1642 would have had to be going to the theatres once every week to have kept them full – or, say, a very substantial proportion two or three times a week. If, as seems a plausible guess (Cook, pp. 190–1), the theatres were regularly about half full, the devotion to theatre-going among this small, fluctuating section of the London population would still have had to be quite extraordinary for its consistency and determination. Frequent visits to the theatre do indeed seem to have been more normal in the seventeenth century than they are now (see p. 104 above), but Elizabethan London, a small city by modern standards, sustained several significantly large theatres, and the size of the ratio between population and theatre capacity seems to point very strongly in the opposite direction from Cook's conclusions, towards inclusiveness rather than exclusiveness. Cook makes an implied correlation between potential playhouse capacity and the numbers of the privileged in London (pp. 178–9), but if this was the case why could Restoration London, with its more populous *beau monde* and attestedly fashionable theatre-going circles, barely support two playhouses?[13] In fact Cook's statistical correlation – if it has any real logical force at all – also suggests opposite conclusions, for in the summer vacation, when the King's Men moved from the Blackfriars theatre to the Globe, the audience capacity rose by some 10,000 places or more per week. It would appear that more people were going to the theatres when most of the gentry were *out* of town than when they were there.

While the evidence of privileged playgoing which Cook undoubtedly supplies illustrates and supplements the orthodox picture of socially mixed theatre audiences, we do not have to assume (as Cook tends increasingly to suppose, e.g. p. 249) that it contradicts it. The statistical method has a built-in bias here: naturally the gentlemen left most written records of playhouse attendance, naturally they could best afford to go and their presence would be most frequently remarked by contemporaries. But the presence of the privileged does not logically entail the absence of the unprivileged; rather, what these records are illustrating is demonstrably only a part of the total audience. Interpreted more objectively, those testimonies which establish the existence of privileged playgoers disclose the existence of unprivileged playgoers too – indeed, they are repeatedly and persistently there even in Cook's own account.

The unprivileged

So, to use Cook's own citations, among the London audiences (principally at the popular theatres) there might also have been found 'dissolute and suspected persons' (p. 129), servingmen (pp. 129, 217, 226), butchers (pp. 137, 225), Thrift the citizen (not a country gentleman as Cook thinks (p. 138)), 'rables', applewives, chimney boys, the 'meaner sort of People' (p. 139), chambermaids (p. 160), merchants' factors (p. 203), apprentices (pp. 203, 220, 262), barbers (p. 205), tailors, tinkers, cordwainers, sailors (p. 216), 'the very scum, rascallitie, and baggage of the people', grooms, whores, porters (p. 217), yeomen and feltmakers (p. 258). This is a splendidly varied panorama of the unprivileged, and it can be amplified from other sources too, such as the complaint of the Merchant Tailors that 'everye lewd persone' was visiting the common plays in their hall, or Nashe on the 'ruder handicrafts seruants' at plays, or Joseph Hall complaining that the muses were being 'bought and sold/For every peasant's brass on each scaffold',[14] or Marston complimenting his elite theatre audience for being one that lacked 'the stench of Garlicke' and the 'barmy Jacket of a Beer-brewer', or Heywood on the actors who please 'Court and City, indeed All', 'the populous Throng/ Of Auditours', or Middleton distinguishing the 'Faire' from the 'foule' spectators,[15] or Jonson on plays of humours which please 'the Gentlemen: but the common sort they care not for't', or describing his own *Staple of News* as too fine for '*the vulgar sort/Of Nut-crackers*',[16] or the publisher of *Troilus and Cressida* saying that it had not been 'stal'd with the Stage, neuer clapped-claw'd with the palmes of the vulger'. Of course we do not now suppose that these plebeians are to be taken as the sum total of the Elizabethan audiences, but neither do they appear to have been merely an insignificant minority. They were not scattered individuals: a Red Bull prologue of 1620 pleaded with its audience to 'cease/Your dayly Tumults',[17] Henry Chettle mentions occasions when 'either

Seruingmen or Apprentises are most in number' at the theatres (Cook, p. 251), and Dekker speaks of plays which 'fill a house with Fishwiues' (p. 261). Indeed, in Dekker's repeated references to his audiences, it is plebeians who rank the largest; for him playhouse audiences were most characteristically stamped by their carmen and tinkers, gentlemen ushers and waiting women, the 'rascality', the '*Rabble*', '*Ragga-muffins*', the 'Greasie-apron *Audience*' who 'clap their *Brawny hands*', 'euery two-penny drunken *Plebeian*', and base stinkards 'whose breth is stronger then Garlicke, and able to poison all the 12. penny roomes'.[18] This the Venetian ambassador for one found to his cost in 1613 when he visited the Curtain and stood in the yard to save money 'down below among the gang of porters and carters' where he was whistled at by the people, who mistook him for a Spaniard (as the Florentine ambassador reported with some amusement). Cook suggests that low prices did not necessarily mean low audiences (p. 182), but the *politesse* of this audience argues otherwise. The Curtain, said the Florentine ambassador, was 'an infamous place in which no good citizen or gentleman would show his face'[19] – a comment which refutes Cook's position on the popular theatres decisively.

It is patently obvious, then, that the unprivileged did go to plays, in quantities, and that at least some of the time or in some theatres they constituted the principal audience. They may not have had much money, but plays were – on Cook's own evidence – a singularly inexpensive form of entertainment (the price of a loaf of bread, for example (p. 232)), and theatre-going was becoming cheaper, for although admission prices doubled in the period this increase was, as Cook says, below the general rate of inflation (p. 230). The lack of much spare cash did not prevent the unprivileged from indulging other forms of pleasure: the people killed when a bear-baiting ring collapsed in 1583 were a fellmonger, a baker, a clerk, three servants, the wife of a pewterer and the daughter of a water-bearer.[20] It is unclear why Cook allows that plebeians had other amusements but denies them the theatre; in any case, the contemporary list of plebeian pleasures which she quotes includes playgoing (pp. 269–70). The statutory working hours of artificers present a greater barrier, though it may be worth remarking that such official directives cut two ways, revealing the existence of practices to be legislated against; guild regulations and the like forbidding apprentices from attending plays, for example, may well suggest that that is just what apprentices were wont to do. The Statute of Artificers would not have constrained London's thousands of casual labourers and the attested presence of craftsmen and apprentices in theatres shows that for them too the statute could not always have been rigorously enforced, or that it must have been possible in some ways to circumvent it, and on a large scale: when 'all sorts of people . . . rich and poore, masters and servants' flocked to see Middleton's *Game at Chess* in 1624 they must have taken the whole afternoon out for it was necessary to be at the Globe 'before one a clock at the farthest to find any roome' (Cook, p. 134). Cook quotes a regulation forbidding smiths, pewterers and founders from working after 9 p.m. to suggest that working hours may have been becoming even longer than the Statute of Artificers lays down (p. 225), but the readiness of metal-workers to produce shoddy goods at unsociable hours had been a source of complaint at least since the days of Chaucer.[21] Moreover, the privileged may have been free to dispose their time at will, but that did not mean they were simply leisured; Sir Thomas Knyvett's letters repeatedly fret about the troublesomeness of business and of a city where 'a man hath scarce leysure to say his prayers'.[22]

Cook is at her most vulnerable when dealing with the complaints about the theatres made by the godly ministers and civic authorities, for here we have outside observers who were unanimous that the theatres 'draw apprentices and other seruants from their ordinary workes' and presented inflammatory matters which were stirring up disorder among 'young people of all degrees'. 'There comes to Playes of all sortes, old and younge', said Stephen Gosson, while an undistinguished, representative moralist such as Henry Crosse was adamant that plays were addressed to 'the rusticke & common sort', 'vulgar opinion', 'the rude multitude'.[23] Like the testimonies about privileged playgoing, these statements supplement, rather than contradict, the picture of a mixed audience. No doubt they contain a considerable amount of overstatement for effect (as Harbage was the first to point out)[24] and must be interpreted accordingly, but Cook simply discounts them altogether (pp. 240–9), treating them almost entirely as a fictive construct and denying them virtually any background of truth at all! This is quite unacceptable. She does not explain why the civic authorities, if they wanted the theatres to be closed, should have adopted such a roundabout way to it, devising an elaborate charade the falsity of which any contemporary would immediately have penetrated; nor even why, if the theatres really did exclude all but the privileged, the city fathers should have been so very nervous and suspicious of them on these grounds in the first place. Her comment on a civic letter of 1625, requesting that the theatres should remain closed after a plague because of the continued danger of infection among 'the meaner and lewder sorte', that the authorities' 'attitude and argument had changed very little in twenty years' (p. 254) is frankly disingenuous; their attitude had changed very little because they were justifiably convinced that 'the meaner and lewder sorte' were still supplying a principal part of the playhouse audiences. The civic language was more than a turn of phrase or a blind prejudice for it expressed perceptions which are consistently borne out everywhere in habits of speech about the theatres. The players may have been on the make (Cook, pp. 121–3) but they were still *common* players; Gosson, an ex-playwright who should have known what he was talking about, called them 'men of occupations, which they have forsaken to live by playing'. Playing was a 'base trade'; Alleyn was the son of an inn-keeper, Tarlton was once described as having been a water-bearer's apprentice (the Elizabethan equivalent, says Muriel Bradbrook, of 'articled to an ice-cream vendor').[25] Contemporaries knew perfectly well where players' origins, allegiances, interests and profits lay, making as they did 'their lyuings of the sweat of other Mens browes, much like vnto drones deuouring the sweet honie of the poore *labouring* bees'; the actor's 'wages and dependance prove him to be the servant of the people' (Cook, p. 101; my emphasis).

The rival traditions

Cook's dismissal from the playhouses of all the unprivileged except for criminals poses her with massive difficulties, not the least being an audience oddly composed solely of gentlemen on the one hand, and cutpurses and whores on the other (one wonders how the cutpurses ever escaped detection?). It leaves her at a loss to account for distinctions with which contemporaries were entirely familiar, in particular for that line which separated – not absolutely but none the less quite clearly – the fashionable indoor theatres from the less expensive and more popular outdoor playhouses, their repertoires and their clientele. That the 'two traditions' were never completely distinct has been acknowledged for some time: 'neither tradition was exclusive of features or even plays belonging to the other',[26] nor could the King's Men after 1608 have performed the same plays at the Blackfriars in the winter which they had been acting at the Globe in the summer had their two audiences been entirely dissimilar or opposed. Cook takes full advantage of testimonies that privileged spectators visited the outdoor theatres; she is less interested in pursuing the corollary that the overlapping of the two audiences could work in reverse too. As late as 1632 Jonson was still conscious of the '*Faeces*, or grounds of your people', the 'sinfull six-penny Mechanicks' who sat in 'the oblique caves and wedges' of the Blackfriars; twenty years before, he, and others, had spoken of the 'shops *Foreman*' as one among the 'many-headed *Bench*', the 'monster' who 'clapt his thousand hands,/And dround the scaene with his confused cry', the 'rout', the 'nifles', the 'common people' who had damned Fletcher's *Faithful Shepherdess* at the same theatre.[27] The references to vulgar spectators at the fashionable playhouses may be scattered, but they do not therefore fail to signify. Cook does not discuss why *The Faithful Shepherdess* and Beaumont's *Knight of the Burning Pestle* should have failed so disastrously, but it would seem that more than merely old-fashioned theatrical tastes had been at stake.

The real problem is that Cook pushes the points of contact between the two types of theatre so far as to deny the rival traditions thesis any validity at all, a position as unwise as it is insensitive. There is little point in rehearsing at length here the familiar details of the differences between the two broadly distinct theatres and their audiences, one predominantly 'privileged' at the indoor playhouses, the other much more, probably decisively 'unprivileged' at the outdoor playhouses. Suffice it to say that many varieties of evidence combine to produce them, both literary and non-literary – the theatres' differences in size, in admission price, in reputation, in repertoire, in geographical location (that the indoor theatres were built in the West End, the outdoor in less fashionable districts), even the types of violence associated with them (duels at the indoor theatres, full-scale riots at the others). Within this broad polarity there were all sorts of subtle shadings and fine tunings which have to be observed. To take the 1630s as our example, we can place the six theatres active at this time onto a rough sliding scale on which the proportion of privileged to unprivileged spectators in the audiences varies according to each theatre. On this scale, the Red Bull and Fortune, with their overwhelmingly plebeian reputations, stand as the most vulgar, and the Blackfriars, with its links with Whitehall and the court drama, as the most sophisticated. The Phoenix is plainly a fashionable theatre, though from its repertoire it would seem to have been significantly less exclusive than the Blackfriars, while the Salisbury Court is an enigma, an indoor theatre which failed to achieve either a distinctive reputation or repertoire. In the induction to *The Careless Shepherdess* of 1638 the citizen Thrift asked for his money back at the Salisbury Court and went off to an outdoor theatre instead, but during the 1630s the Salisbury Court hosted companies which at other times played both at the Fortune and the Red Bull (see p. 184 above). The blurring of elite and popular traditions at the Phoenix and Salisbury Court is highly suggestive, while the Globe presents the same problem in reverse, being an outdoor theatre where the King's Men staged plays which they knew would not take with their Blackfriars audience,[28] yet which undoubtedly attracted courtiers and other 'privileged' spectators, probably in greater quantities than did the other popular houses. These are necessary and meaningful distinctions which Cook's desire for a uniform interpretation simply overrides and annihilates. It is a peculiarly inadequate criticism to level at the two traditions thesis that it is 'too convenient' (p. 274), that it fits the facts too well.

So, for all the richness of the material on which she draws, Cook's readiness to make 'the privileged' account for every audience flattens and simplifies our understanding of the Elizabethan theatres. She also makes them account for every *part* of every audience, so distinctions within the theatres need reasserting as well as those between the theatres. As is still the case today, the hierarchy of admission prices at any one theatre was not meaningless; the playwrights knew that in different parts of the audiences they were addressing different groups of spectators. Dekker described the 'Scarcrows in the yard' who would hoot, hiss, spit, and even throw dirt;[29] another playwright distinguished the 'fooles in th'yard', the 'multitude' of 'stinckards' who hissed plays from the 'wits of gentry' who applauded (Cook, p. 260), and the prologue of a third unceremoniously spoke down to 'you in the Yard' (p. 266). The distinction between pit and galleries, with the plebeians in the pit and the gentlemen in the galleries (or the other way round at the indoor theatres),[30] was a significant, functional one. As the Venetian ambassador discovered at the Curtain, the gentlemen who paid higher prices did so because they *wanted* to separate themselves from the mob.

Distinctions such as these, then, comprehensively and continually affected the type of play which was being produced, the way that the audience was addressed, the confidences that were made or withheld, the expectations that were indulged or denied, the range of possibilities that was available or not to the dramatist to attempt and to exploit. And the most powerful rebuttal of Cook's assertions does lie in the character of the plays themselves. Cook works from the position that there was no real connection between the audiences and the plays they witnessed, that the playgoers cannot be used 'as an explanation for the plays' (p. 7), but it is surely clear that the nature of the plays is profoundly implicated in the kind of audiences which were going to see them. The stature and enduring importance of the Elizabethan drama is bound up with its eclecticism, its comprehensive assimilation, that it was straining to excite the attention and interest of as many spectators as it could reach. The roots of the Elizabethan stage were first and foremost diverse: it inherited the sophisticated experiments of the courtly and academic stages, but also a vast spectrum of types of popular performance – those festive, playful, sportive, extemporal elements of misrule and grotesquerie, nonsense, disguising, impudent parody and burlesque which are so important at all levels, and in all types of the plays which it produced. The heterogeneity of the Elizabethan audiences enabled these diverse elements to be fused within a single theatrical consensus, and necessitated the drama's quite extraordinary range of social and cultural reference, its linguistic inclusiveness and competency on which, in its turn, was founded the drama's multi-dimensional character, that it was possible for it to respect and articulate the perspective of both king and clown, and draw simultaneously on several contradictory, mutually critical points of view. In its own time it was described as 'a Gallimaufrey . . . an Hodge-podge'; Shakespeare's assimilative capacities would make him seem to a politer generation to have been 'the Plebean Driller'.[31] High tragedy and farce addressed both cultivated and unsophisticated, privileged and unprivileged, and the drama incorporated and drew its strength from these irreconcilable tensions, stubbornly counteracting and conflicting with each other around and within it. In place of Harbage's idealized working man, Cook rests her faith, somewhat improbably, in the 'cosmopolitan' qualities of the privileged spectator (pp. 95–6), but both types on their own are insufficient to have generated the complex, multifaceted plays of the Elizabethan theatre. The best introduction to the audience is still Andrew Gurr's chapter in his *The Shakespearean Stage*. *The Privileged Playgoers* contains much important information, but its usefulness is vitiated by the purposes to which it has been put.

Notes

Abbreviations used in the notes

Bentley, *JCS* G. E. Bentley, *The Jacobean and Caroline Stage* (7 vols, Oxford, 1941–68)
CSPD   Calendar of State Papers, Domestic Series
CSPV   Calendar of State Papers, Venetian Series
DNB   *Dictionary of National Biography*
ELH   *ELH*; formerly *Journal of English Literary History*
HMC   Historical Manuscripts Commission, *Report*
TLS   *Times Literary Supplement*

1. Some contentions

1. E.g. J. Dusinberre, *Shakespeare and the Nature of Women* (London, 1975); M. C. Heinemann, *Puritanism and Theatre* (Cambridge, 1980); M. C. Bradbrook, *John Webster, Citizen and Dramatist* (London, 1980); S. Shepherd, *Amazons and Warrior Women* (Brighton, 1981).

2. J. F. Danby, *Elizabethan and Jacobean Poets* (2nd edn, London, 1965), pp. 177–83.

3. P. Edwards, G. E. Bentley, K. McCluskie and L. Potter, *The Revels History of Drama in English*, IV (London, 1981), pp. 54, 63; G. Wickham, *Early English Stages*, II, pt i (London, 1963), pp. 106–7. Suggestions that hostility to the 'prerogative of maintaining players' contributed to the age's constitutional conflicts grossly exaggerate its significance.

4. A. Harbage, *Cavalier Drama* (2nd edn, New York, 1964), p. 7.

5. P. W. Thomas, 'Two cultures? Court and country under Charles I' in C. Russell (ed.), *The Origins of the English Civil War* (London, 1973), pp. 168–93.

6. G. E. Bentley, *The Jacobean and Caroline Stage* (7 vols, Oxford, 1941–68) [hereafter *JCS*], I, p. 204.

2. *Drama and the Caroline crisis*

1. In Clifford Leech, *Shakespeare's Tragedies and Other Studies* (London, 1950), pp. 159–81.
2. O. B. Hardison, 'Darwin, mutations, and the origin of medieval drama' in his *Christian Rite and Christian Drama* (Baltimore, 1965), pp. 1–34; S. Schoenbaum, 'Peut-on parler d'une "Decadence" du theatre au temps des premiers Stuart?' in J. Jacquot (ed.), *Dramaturgie et Société*, II (Paris, 1967), pp. 829-45.
3. E.g. B. O Hehir, *Harmony from Discords* (California, 1968), p. 43n (on *The Sophy*); and Edwards *et al.*, *Revels History*, p. 137 (on *Perkin Warbeck*).
4. Although I would associate myself only with those historians who deny that the seventeenth century saw a *simple* crisis of allegiance between king and parliament which would have *inevitably* produced a social and political breakdown, not with those who would argue that there was no real crisis at all.
5. E.g. D. Bevington, *Tudor Drama and Politics* (Cambridge, Mass., 1968), pp. 288, 298; cf. the comment of A. Harbage, *Sir William Davenant* (Philadelphia, 1935), p. 42–1629 'was a time for choosing sides'. The most recent general history of the period attributes to the dramatists a condition of 'self-delusion' (Edwards *et al.*, *Revels History*, p. 5).
6. G. R. Elton, *Studies in Tudor and Stuart Politics and Government*, II (Cambridge, 1974), pp. 164–82.
7. 'Cavalier' and 'Roundhead' were first exchanged as antithetical terms on 29 December 1641 (S. R. Gardiner, *History of England from the Accession of James I to the Outbreak of the Civil War*, 10 vols (London, 1883–84), X, p. 121).
8. C. Russell, *Parliaments and English Politics 1621–1629* (Oxford, 1979), pp. 404–8; J. P. Kenyon, *Stuart England* (London, 1978), p. 107. Cf. T. K. Rabb, 'The role of the commons' and D. Hirst, 'The place of principle', both in *Past and Present*, 92 (1981), 55–98.
9. Gardiner, *History*, VII, p. 224; Kenyon, *Stuart England*, pp. 32–6; J. Hexter, *The Reign of King Pym* (Cambridge, Mass., 1941), pp. 176–7, 214–16; C. Russell, 'Parliamentary history in perspective', *History*, 61 (1976), 1–27 (17–18).
10. S. D'Ewes, *Autobiography* (ed. J. Halliwell, 2 vols, London, 1845), I, p. 279.
11. Cf. Sir Edward Coke in 1628, 'It was a Wonder for him to hear that the Liberty of the Subject should be thought incompatible with the Regality of the King' (M. A. Judson, *The Crisis of the Constitution* (New Brunswick, 1949), p. 64).
12. Russell, *Parliaments and Politics*, pp. 237, 274; A. Woolrych, 'Court, country and city revisited', *History*, 65 (1980), 236–45(239).

13. Gardiner, *History*, VI, p. 83; C. Holmes, 'The county community in Stuart historiography', *Journal of British Studies*, 19 no.2 (1980), 54–73 (70).
14. Gardiner, *History*, VI, p. 128. Compare Sir Robert Phelips in K. Sharpe (ed.), *Faction and Parliament* (Oxford, 1978), p. 30.
15. D'Ewes, *Autobiography*, I, pp. 402, 407.
16. S. R. Gardiner (ed.), *Documents Relating to Proceedings against William Prynne* (London, 1877), p. 87; C. Russell, *Crisis of Parliaments* (Oxford, 1971), p. 320; Sharpe, *Faction and Parliament*, pp. 127, 131; Russell, *Parliaments and Politics*, pp. 55–6.
17. D. Gardiner (ed.), *The Oxinden Letters 1607–1642* (London, 1933), p. 173; Kenyon, *Stuart England*, pp. 111, 118–19.
18. P. Zagorin, *The Court and the Country* (Oxford, 1969), *passim*. Cf. J. S. Morrill, *The Revolt of the Provinces* (London, 1976), pp. 14–17, and D. Hirst, 'Court, country and politics before 1629' in Sharpe, *Faction and Parliament*, pp. 105–38.
19. J. Forster, *Sir John Eliot* (2 vols, London, 1864), I, p. 535; L. Hutchinson, *Memoirs of the Life of Colonel Hutchinson* (London, 1908), p. 31.
20. Wandesford, *A Book of Instructions* (ed. T. Comber, Cambridge, 1777), p. 61 (I owe this reference to S. P. Salt, 'Sir Thomas Wentworth and the parliamentary representation of Yorkshire', *Northern History*, 16 (1980), 130–68); T. G. Barnes, *Somerset 1625–1640* (London, 1961), p. 289.
21. Forster, *Eliot*, II, p. 444.
22. R. Ashton, *The City and the Court* (Cambridge, 1979), pp. 120–56.
23. J. Rushworth, *Historical Collections*, II, pt. ii (London, 1680), p. 1341.
24. B. H. G. Wormald, *Clarendon: Politics, History and Religion* (Cambridge, 1951), pp. 80–1.
25. Hexter, *Reign of King Pym*, p. 6.
26. J. Taylor, *Mad Fashions, Odd Fashions* (London, 1642), sig.A4^r.
27. B. Manning, *The English People and the English Revolution* (London, 1976), pp. 46–70.
28. J. A. R. Marriott, *The Life and Times of Lucius Cary* (London, 1907), p. 247; Morrill, *Revolt of the Provinces*, p. 41.
29. Morrill, *Revolt of the Provinces*, pp. 37, 159, 197.
30. *Parliaments and Politics*, p. 416.
31. Forster, *Eliot*, I, p. 304; W. Notestein and F. H. Relf (eds), *Commons Debates for 1629* (Minneapolis, 1921), p. 22.
32. Forster, *Eliot*, I, p. 482; II, p. 172.
33. Forster, *Eliot*, II, p. 414; Ashton, *City and Court*, p. 133; Judson, *Crisis of the Constitution*, p. 64.
34. C. Hill, 'Parliament and people in seventeenth-century England', *Past and Present*, 92 (1981), 100–24 (p. 110); Salt, 'Sir Thomas Wentworth', 159.
35. Oliver St John, *The Answer to the Rattleheads* (London, 1641), sig.A4^r; *Cobbett's Complete Collection of State Trials*, III (London, 1809), p. 1275.
36. D'Ewes, *Autobiography*, II, p. 132; W. J. Jones, *Politics and the Bench*

(London, 1975), p. 215; V. Pearl, *London and the Outbreak of the Puritan Revolution* (Oxford, 1961), p. 178.

37. S. R. Gardiner, *History*, X, p. 211; D. Gardiner, *Oxinden Letters*, p. 310; A. Fletcher, *The Outbreak of the English Civil War* (London, 1981), p. 412.

38. Judson, *Crisis of the Constitution*, p. 19.

39. Hexter, *Reign of King Pym*, pp. 214–16.

3. Court drama: the queen's circle 1632–37

1. E. Hyde, *The History of the Rebellion* (ed. W. D. Macray, 6 vols, Oxford, 1888), I, p. 242; A. Wilson, *The Inconstant Lady* (ed. P. Bliss, Oxford, 1814), p. 127.

2. E.g. Pembroke (CSPV 1636–39, p. 571) and Leicester (H. R. Trevor-Roper, *Archbishop Laud 1573–1645* (2nd edn, London, 1962), p. 375).

3. B. Manning, 'The aristocracy and the downfall of Charles I' in *idem, Politics, Religion and the English Civil War* (London, 1973), pp. 36–80. See also V. F. Snow, 'Essex and aristocratic opposition to the early Stuarts', *Journal of Modern History*, 32 (1960), 224–33.

4. L. P. Smith, *The Life and Letters of Sir Henry Wotton*, II (Oxford, 1907), p. 339; CSPD 1625–40, p. 382; M. Cavendish, *The Life of the Duke of Newcastle and Other Writings* (Dent, London, n.d.), p. 120.

5. Hyde, *History of the Rebellion*, I, p. 80; CSPD 1640, p. 278. See also B. Donagan, 'A courtier's progress: greed and consistency in the life of the Earl of Holland', *The Historical Journal*, 19 (1976), 317–53.

6. *DNB*; R. M. Smuts, 'The puritan followers of Henrietta Maria in the 1630s', *The English Historical Review*, 93 (1978), 26–45 (p. 31); J. H. Bryant, 'John Reynolds of Exeter and his canon', *The Library*, 5th ser., 15 (1960), 105–17.

7. T. Pestell, *Poems* (ed. H. Buchan, Oxford, 1940), p. 41; Smuts, 'The puritan followers', p. 26 and *passim* for this paragraph.

8. Heinemann, *Puritanism and Theatre*, pp. 214, 222; for Leicester and Salisbury, see pp. 250, 131 above.

9. Bentley, *JCS*, I, p. 37, II, pp. 684, 695; T. Randolph, *Poems* (ed. G. Thorn-Drury, London, 1929), pp. xi–xii.

10. Smuts, 'The puritan followers', p. 30; HMC 55 (various collections), vii, p. 401.

11. E. Waller, *Poems* (ed. G. Thorn-Drury, 2 vols, London, 1893), I, p. 26.

12. Bentley, *JCS*, III, p. 218.

13. W. Knowler (ed.), *The Earl of Strafford's Letters and Dispatches* (2 vols, London, 1739), I, pp. 360, 363; M. J. Havran, *Caroline Courtier* (London, 1973), p. 128; Smuts, 'The puritan followers', p. 35.

14. V. Gabrieli, 'A new Digby letter-book', *The National Library of Wales Journal*, 10 (1957), 81–106 (89).

15. CSPD 1636–37, p. 71.

16. CSPV 1632–36, p. 491. I have discussed these festivities in much greater detail in 'Entertaining the palatine prince: plays on foreign affairs 1635–37', *English Literary Renaissance*, 13 (1983), 319–44.

17. Public Record Office, S.P. 302/141; T. Heywood, *Pleasant Dialogues and Dramas* (London, 1637), pp. 250–1.

18. F. S. Boas (ed.), *The Diary of Thomas Crosfield* (London, 1935), p. 83; see my 'Entertaining the palatine prince' for a fuller discussion.

19. Knowler, *Strafford Letters*, I, p. 525.

20. Bentley, *JCS*, III, p. 219.

21. Bentley, *JCS*, V, p. 1286.

22. 'G. Chapman', *Alphonsus, Emperor of Germany* (London, 1654), p. 70.

23. Anon., *The King and Queen's Entertainment at Richmond* (Oxford, 1636), pp. 19–20.

24. CSPV 1636–39, p. 107; G. Huxley, *Endymion Porter* (London, 1959), p. 177.

25. Davenant, *The Shorter Poems* (ed. A. M. Gibbs, Oxford, 1972), p. 11. The hero of Davenant's *The Wits* (1634) is called Pallatine, and the play shows a town lady leading to victory a mock-army of gallants – perhaps another play with the queen's interests in mind?

26. John Milton, *Of Reformation Touching Church Discipline* (London, 1641), pp. 57–8.

27. Bentley, *JCS*, III, p. 85.

28. See M. Axton, *The Queen's Two Bodies* (London, 1977), pp. 38–72.

29. For the sake of convenience, I give page references to Brome's plays (here and subsequently) from the edition of J. Pearson, *The Dramatic Works of Richard Brome* (3 vols, London, 1873). I have, though, checked all quotations against the early editions.

30. Foxe, *Acts and Monuments* (4th edn, 2 vols, London, 1583), I, p. 425.

31. C. Burges, *A Sermon Preached to the Honourable House of Commons . . . November 17, 1640* (London, 1641), p. 27. See also S. Marshall, *A Sermon Preached . . . November 17, 1640* (London, 1641).

32. J. Hall, *The Works* (3 vols, London, 1647), III, p. 417; Milton, *Of Reformation*, p. 57.

33. A.-L. Scoufos, 'The mysteries in Milton's masque', *Milton Studies*, 6 (1954), 113–42.

34. Bentley, *JCS*, I, p. 299. Probably one other of these three had also been ordered by the queen (as an entertainment for the Prince Elector) – see Bentley, *JCS*, V, p. 1399 and my 'Entertaining the palatine prince'.

35. Bentley, *JCS*, V, pp. 1110–11.

36. Bentley, *JCS*, III, p. 136.

37. A. Barton, 'He that plays the king' in M. Axton and R. Williams (eds), *English Drama: Forms and Development* (Cambridge, 1977), p. 92. The play

opens with expectations of Arsamnes's impending visit to the Persian jail
– rather as Charles was just visiting Oxford?

38. I quote from G. B. Evans (ed.), *The Plays and Poems of William Cartwright* (Madison, 1951).

39. Barton, 'He that plays the king', p. 93.

40. At court, an additional spectacular scene was inserted near the end.

41. In his 'In answer of an elegiacal letter upon the death of the King of Sweden'.

42. All quotations from Massinger (here and subsequently) are taken from P. Edwards and C. Gibson (eds), *The Plays and Poems of Philip Massinger* (5 vols, Oxford, 1976).

4. *Lovers and tyrants: courtier plays 1637–42*

1. All quotations from Suckling are taken from T. Clayton and L. A. Beaurline (eds), *The Works of Sir John Suckling* (2 vols, Oxford, 1971).

2. Judson, *Crisis of the Constitution*, pp. 111–18, 136–7; R. W. K. Hinton, 'English constitutional theories from Sir John Fortescue to Sir John Eliot', *The English Historical Review*, 75 (1960), 410–25.

3. K. Thomas, *Religion and the Decline of Magic* (2nd edn, Harmondsworth, 1973), pp. 237–8; Hyde, *History of the Rebellion*, II, p. 104; C. V. Wedgwood, *The Trial of Charles I* (London, 1964), p. 32. See also Axton, *The Queen's Two Bodies*, pp. 11–37; and C. C. Weston, 'The theory of mixed monarchy under Charles I and after', *The English Historical Review*, 75 (1960), 426–43.

4. Davenant, *Shorter Poems*, pp. 139–40. See also Manning, 'The aristocracy and the downfall of Charles I', pp. 52–4.

5. A. Harbage, *Sir William Davenant, Poet Venturer* (Philadelphia, 1935), p. 85.

6. Bentley, *JCS*, V, p. 1028.

7. Bentley, *JCS*, IV, p. 522.

8. F. Beaumont and J. Fletcher, *Comedies and Tragedies* (London, 1647), sig.b3ᵛ; Bentley, *JCS*, IV, p. 521. I have profited from Douglas Sedge's discussion of Habington in 'La question de la monarchie sous le règne de Charles 1ᵉʳ' in Jacquot, *Dramaturgie et Société*, II, pp. 791–804.

9. Shepherd, *Amazons and Warrior Women*, pp. 119–25.

10. R. Tuck, '*Power* and *Authority* in seventeenth-century England', *The Historical Journal*, 17 (1974), 48–61 (50).

11. J. G. Muddiman, *The Trial of King Charles the First* (Edinburgh, n.d.), p. 119; M. Y. Hughes (ed.), *Complete Prose Works of John Milton*, III (New Haven, 1962), p. 201. See also R. E. Giesey, *If Not, Not: The Oath of the Aragonese and the Legendary Laws of Sobrarbe* (Princeton, 1968), pp. 18–101.

Some English MPs at least had been reading Spanish history in the 1620s; see Russell, *Parliaments and Politics*, p. 56.

12. M. A. Judson, 'Henry Parker and the theory of parliamentary sovereignty', in *Essays in History and Political Theory in Honor of C. H. McIlwain* (Cambridge, Mass., 1936), pp. 138–67 (p. 147). See also R. Tuck, *Natural Rights Theories* (Cambridge, 1979), pp. 99, 145–7. Parker was careful to say that this consent only operated through parliament; he did not conceive of 'the people' as having any political identity *apart* from in parliament.

13. Bentley, *JCS*, IV, p. 795.

14. Trevor-Roper, *Archbishop Laud*, p. 297.

15. See, for example, Forster, *Eliot*, II, pp. 85, 91, 122, 125, 163.

16. B. O Hehir, *Expans'd Hieroglyphics* (California, 1969), pp. 89–90. I cannot follow O Hehir in seeing Denham as simply a 'royalist' throughout 1640–42.

17. Hyde, *History of the Rebellion*, I, pp. 219, 223.

18. E. S. Cope and W. H. Coates (eds), *Proceedings of the Short Parliament* (London, 1977), pp. 140, 251; Rushworth, *Historical Collections*, II, pt ii, p. 1132.

19. Hyde, *History of the Rebellion*, I, p. 228. See also T. May, *The History of the Parliament of England* (London, 1647), pp. 60–1.

20. Cope and Coates, *Short Parliament Proceedings*, pp. 67, 75.

21. Hyde, *History of the Rebellion*, I, p. 183.

22. The 'greater Councell, which we now assemble' (III.ii.156) seems intended for the calling of the council at York in September 1640.

23. Hyde, *History of the Rebellion*, I, pp. 195–7.

24. Thomas Carew, *Poems* (ed. R. Dunlap, Oxford, 1949), p. 90 ('A New Year's gift to the King'). Howard Erskine-Hill has suggested that this couplet refers to Charles's impending campaign against the Scots in the second Bishops' War of 1640 and that the poem should be dated 1 January 1640 (*The Augustan Idea in English Literature* (London, 1983), p. 179n), but it is unlikely that Carew would have written so confidently after the disastrous English defeat at Berwick the previous year, and the poem more probably belongs to 1 January 1639, the period of preparation for the first Bishops' War of March–June 1639. I am very grateful to Dr Erskine-Hill for allowing me to read a typescript of this chapter.

25. Suckling, *Works*, I, pp. 163, 166, 165.

26. *Poetical Works* (ed. T. H. Baker, New Haven, 1928), p. 157.

27. Gardiner, *History*, VII, p. 4; see also Russell, *Parliaments and Politics*, p. 358, and C. Hill, *Intellectual Origins of the English Revolution* (Oxford, 1965), p. 151.

28. See Gardiner, *History*, IX, pp. 6, 26, 39, 98, 130, 153, 174, 177, 212, 214 (all within 18 months, 1639–40); and Pearl, *London . . . and Revolution*, pp. 96–101. This passage was toned down in the 1668 edition.

5. Puritanism and theatre

1. Gardiner, *Proceedings against Prynne*, p. 22.
2. See L. Aiken, *The Court and Times of Charles the First*, II (London, 1848), p. 222; and J. Bruce (ed.), *Letters and Papers of the Verney Family* (London, 1853), p. 158. According to Bulstrode Whitelocke the king and queen were 'exasperated' by *Histriomastix* but 'did direct nothing against [Prynne]'; instead the impetus for his prosecution came from Archbishop Laud, who already bore him a grudge for his anti-Arminian opinions and determinedly got Peter Heylin 'to peruse *Prynne's* books and to collect the scandalous points out of them' (*Memorials of the English Affairs* (London, 1682), p. 18).
3. Gardiner, *Proceedings Against Prynne*, p. 16; *The Records of the Honourable Society of Lincoln's Inn* (London, 1898), p. 317.
4. W. Prynne, *Histriomastix* (London, 1633), p. 461. See K. Wrightson, *English Society 1580–1680* (London, 1982), pp. 208–15; and K. Wrightson and D. Levine, *Poverty and Piety in an English Village* (London, 1979), pp. 154–64, 176–8.
5. Bastwick, *The Litany of John Bastwick* (4 parts, n.p., 1637), pt 2, p. 27; S. R. Gardiner, *The Constitutional Documents of the Puritan Revolution* (Oxford, 1906), p. 229.
6. Patrick Collinson, 'Towards a broader understanding of the early dissenting tradition', in R. C. Cole and M. E. Moody (eds), *The Dissenting Tradition* (Athens, Ohio, 1975), pp. 3–38 (p. 11). Out of a huge literature, see also W. Haller, *The Rise of Puritanism* (New York, 1938) and *Foxe's Book of Martyrs and the Elect Nation* (London, 1963); C. Hill, *Society and Puritanism in Pre-Revolutionary England* (London, 1964); W. Lamont, *Godly Rule* (London, 1969) and *Marginal Prynne* (London, 1963); C. H. George and C. George, *The Protestant Mind of the English Reformation* (Princeton, 1961); and two important essays in Russell, *Origins of the English Civil War*: N. Tyacke's 'Puritanism, Arminianism and counter-revolution' (pp. 119–43) and R. Clifton's 'Fear of popery' (pp. 144–67).
7. Collinson, 'The early dissenting tradition', pp. 10–11.
8. Hill, *Society and Puritanism*, p. 27. See also Tyacke, 'Puritanism, Arminianism and counter-revolution' and Clifton, 'Fear of popery', *passim*.
9. See Haller, *Foxe's Book of Martyrs, passim*; Lamont, *Godly Rule*, pp. 17–36; F. Yates, *Astraea* (Harmondsworth, 1977), pp. 38–47.
10. George and George, *The Protestant Mind*, pp. 190–3; C. Hill, *Antichrist in Seventeenth-Century England* (London, 1971), pp. 13–15.
11. Samuel Ward, *Woe to Drunkards* (London, 1624), pp. 48–9 (reprinted 1636). See Rushworth, *Historical Collections*, II, pt i, p. 301 for Ward's censure.
12. George and George, *The Protestant Mind*, p. 202.
13. Lamont, *Godly Rule*, p. 31.

14. Prynne, *Histriomastix*, pp. 826–7; Gardiner, *Proceedings against Prynne*, p. 45.

15. Lamont, *Godly Rule*, p. 46; see also *Marginal Prynne*, pp. 13–27, 41.

16. Prynne, *News from Ipswich* ('Ipswich', 1636).

17. *Idem, The Antipathy of the English Lordly Prelacy* (London, 1641), t.p.

18. Prynne, *Histriomastix*, p. 826.

19. John Bastwick, *The Litany*, pt 1, p. 2; pt 4, p. 5.

20. Bradbrook, *John Webster*, p. 182 (and see Heinemann, *Puritanism and Theatre*, pp. 280–1); G. W. Prothero, 'A Seventeenth-century account book', *English Historical Review*, 7 (1892), 88–102; William Cartwright, *The Ordinary*, ll. 1447–52.

21. Pearl, *London and . . . Revolution*, p. 166n.

22. T. C. Croker (ed.), *Autobiography of Mary Countess of Warwick* (London, 1848), p. 4.

23. *Memoirs of the Life of Colonel Hutchinson* (ed. J. Hutchinson, London, 1908), pp. 96, 43–5, 193.

24. Bentley, *JCS*, I, p. 40; R. Spalding, *The Improbable Puritan* (London, 1975), p. 186.

25. W. A. Mepham, 'Essex drama under puritanism and the commonwealth', *The Essex Review*, 58 (1949), 181–5; Bentley, *JCS*, IV, pp. 958, 841; M. E. Bohannon, 'A London bookseller's bill', *The Library*, 4th ser., 18, 223–4; HMC 7 (Lowndes MSS) i, pp. 547, 549; M. F. Keeler, *The Long Parliament* (Philadelphia, 1954), pp. 96–7.

26. R. Harris, *Abner's Funeral* (London, 1641), p. 28; J. H. Smith (ed.), *Two Latin Comedies by John Foxe the Martyrologist* (London, Ithaca, 1975), p. 5; CSPD 1633–34, pp. 47–9.

27. Zagorin, *The Court and the Country*, pp. 175–6; G. E. Aylmer, *The King's Servants* (London, 1961), pp. 377–9; CSPD 1634–35, pp. 589–92.

28. HMC 78 (Hastings MSS) i, pp. 389–90.

29. Simonds D'Ewes, *Diary* (ed. E. Bourcier, Paris, 1974), pp. 56, 170; *Autobiography*, II, p. 214. D'Ewes was also among the court audience that saw Shirley's masque *The Triumph of Peace* in 1634 (*Malone Society Collections*, XII, p. 60).

30. Bentley, *JCS*, V, p. 1157.

31. Henry Burton, *For God and the King* (London, 1636), p. 58; *England's Bondage* (London, 1641), sig.B4^r.

32. Bastwick, *The Litany*, pt 2, pp. 3–5; pt 1, p. 6. 'Souces' = 'pig's ears'.

33. H. E. Rollins, 'The Commonwealth drama', *Studies in Philology*, 20 (1923), 52–69 (54).

34. L. Salingar, J. Harrison and B. Cochrane, 'Les comédiens et leur public en Angleterre de 1520 à 1640' in Jacquot, *Dramaturgie et Société*, II, pp. 525–76 (pp. 560–73). This section is also generally indebted to Heinemann, *Puritanism and Theatre*, pp. 26–36.

35. Pearl, *London and . . . Revolution*, pp. 19–20, 23–9; Bentley, *JCS*, VI, pp. 21, 24, 27, 39.
36. See my essay, 'Two playgoers, and the closing of the London theatres, 1642', *Theatre Research International*, 9 (1983–84).
37. Gardiner, *Constitutional Documents*, p. 139.
38. Wickham, *Early English Stages*, II, i, p. 98.
39. K. Richards, 'A Sunday performance at the Caroline court', *Notes and Queries*, 222 (1977), 535; Bentley, *JCS*, VII, p. 12.
40. T. May, *The History of Parliament of England* (London, 1647), pt ii, p. 27. May was himself an ex-dramatist, but this need not invalidate his testimony. His account of the reigns of James and Charles is oriented strongly around their religious failings, and of course he wrote with parliament's official approval.
41. Prynne, *Histriomastix*, pp. 39–40, 832–5, 923.
42. John Milton, *The Reason of Church-Government Urged against Prelaty* (London, 1641), p. 40.
43. Harbage, *Sir William Davenant*, p. 126. See also Lois Potter's summary in Edwards *et al.*, *Revels History*, pp. 294–304.

6. The Caroline audience

1. Bentley, *JCS*, I, pp. 305–7; III, p. 90; *idem*, 'Randolph's *Praeludium* and the Salisbury Court theatre' in J. G. McManaway, G. E. Dawson and E. E. Willoughby, *J. Q. Adams Memorial Studies* (Washington, 1948), pp. 775–83; M. Grivelet, 'Th'Untun'd Kennell', *Etudes Anglaises*, 7 (1954), 101–6; J. Freehafer, 'Brome, Suckling and Davenant's theatre project of 1639', *Texas Studies in Literature and Language, 10* (1968), 367–83; P. Beal, 'Massinger at bay', *Yearbook of English Studies*, X (1980), pp. 190–203.
2. I take my figures from Bentley, *JCS*, I, pp. 97–100, 249, 299, 322, 336.
3. Bentley, *JCS*, I, pp. 65–6.
4. T. W. Baldwin has calculated a figure of £3365 p.a. for the King's Men in 1634 (*The Organization and Personnel of the Shakespearean Company* (Princeton, 1927), pp. 164–5, 344). The most they earned at court in one year was £300, for the 1638–39 season (compare this with £130 maximum earned by the Queen's Men in 1635–36); the average for the decade I calculate at £220 p.a. In 1635, one actor alone testified that he earned 'as hee was a Player and noe Howskeeper 180li' (*Malone Society Collections*, II, p. 372); the same year the King's Men received £250 for court performances. Besides, the court was still paying £10 a performance at a time when the Blackfriars theatre receipts averaged above £15 a performance (Bentley, *JCS*, I, p. 24).
5. M. Rawdon, *The Life* (ed. R. Davies, London, 1863), p. 25; E. M. Symonds, 'The diary of John Greene', *The English Historical Review*, 43

(1928), 285–94 (288–9); P. L. Ralph, *Sir Humphrey Mildmay* (New Brunswick, 1947), p. 43 and ch. 2 *passim*.

6. Bodleian MS North.c.4, fo.3^r; J. Cornwallis, *The Private Correspondence* (London, 1842), pp. 220–1; Gabrieli, 'Digby letter-book', pp. 128–9; E. Hyde, *The Life of Edward, Earl of Clarendon* (2 vols, Oxford, 1817), I, pp. 23–4; Suckling, *Works*, I, p. 134.

7. S. R. Gardiner (ed.), *Reports of Cases in the Courts of Star Chamber and High Commission* (London, 1886), p. 179; M. Cavendish, *A True Relation* (ed. E. Bridges, Kent, 1814), p. 9; Croker, *Autobiography of Mary Rich*, p. 4.

8. D. Mathew, *The Social Structure in Caroline England* (Oxford, 1948), pp. 97–102, 109–10.

9. *The New Inn* (London, 1631), t.p.; John Earle, *Microcosmography* (London, 1629), sig.H2^r; J. Fletcher, *The Faithful Shepherdess* (London, 1634), sig.A3^r.

10. Shirley, *Narcissus* (London, 1646), p. 44.

11. Bentley, *JCS*, II, pp. 675–9; T. N. S. Lennam, 'Sir Edward Dering's collection of play-books', *Shakespeare Quarterly*, 16 (1965), 145–53; Egerton MS. 2983, VI, fos 14^r–18^v.

12. J. Orrell, 'The London court stage in the Savoy correspondence', *Theatre Research International*, 4 (1979), 79–94 (p. 92); Shirley, *The Lady of Pleasure*, V.i.

13. Cavendish, *A True Relation*, pp. 9–10; *Life of Sir John Digby* (ed. G. Bernard, *Camden Miscellany*, 12 (London, 1910), pp. 61–149), p. 73; Symonds, 'Diary of John Greene', p. 389; Bentley, *JCS*, II, p. 679.

14. Anne Halkett, *Autobiography* (ed. J. G. Nichols, London, 1875), p. 3.

15. Bentley, *JCS*, II, pp. 693–4.

16. Waller, *Poems*, I, p.x; Gabrieli, 'Digby letter-book', p. 140; HMC (Portland MSS) ii, p. 125; CSPD 1634–35, p. 384.

17. Bentley, *JCS*, III, pp. 376, 426; R. C. Bald, *Bibliographical Studies in the Beaumont and Fletcher Folio of 1647* (Oxford, 1938), pp. 7, 110; W. W. Greg, *The Shakespeare First Folio* (Oxford, 1955), p. 153.

18. K. Weber, *Lucius Cary* (Columbia, 1940), pp. 62–3; the identity of the play in question is unclear. In James Shirley's *Poems* (1646) there is a verse letter 'to the Lady *D.S.* sent with a New Comedy' (p. 39).

19. A. Tweedie, *Hyde Park* (London, 1908), p. 69.

20. CSPD 1634–35, p. 591.

21. P. Laslett, 'Sir Robert Filmer', *The William and Mary Quarterly*, 3rd ser., 5 (1948), 523–46 (539, 541–2).

22. *Histriomastix*, sig.3A*4^r; C. C. Mish, 'Comparative popularity of early fiction and drama', *Notes and Queries*, 197 (1952), 269–70.

23. Bentley, *JCS*, VI, p. 151.

24. Ford, *'Tis pity She's a Whore*, V.v; *idem*, *The Broken Heart*, III.v; *idem*, *The Lady's Trial*, V.ii.

25. Sir Richard Baker, *Theatrum Redivivum* (London, 1661), pp. 34–5.

26. Bentley, *JCS*, II, pp. 503, 433, 461; IV, p. 491.

27. Bentley, *JCS*, I, p. 318.

28. M. W. Black, *Richard Brathwaite* (Philadelphia, 1928), p. 74; Edwards *et al.*, *Revels History*, p. 281.

29. A. C. Kirsch, 'A Caroline commentary on the drama', *Modern Philology*, 66 (1968–69), 256–61; Robert Baron, *Pocula Castalia* (London, 1650), pp. 112–14; Aston Cockayne, *A Chain of Golden Poems* (London, 1658), p. 175.

30. Tweedie, *Hyde Park*, p. 69; J. F. Bradley and J. Q. Adams (eds), *The Jonson Allusion-book* (New Haven, 1922), p. 277.

31. Bentley, *JCS*, IV, p. 693.

32. Edward Hyde, *History of the Rebellion*, IV, p. 490; I owe this reference to Lois Potter's unpublished PhD thesis, *The Fop and Related Figures in Drama from Jonson to Cibber* (Cambridge, 1965). See also Hutchinson, *Memoirs of Colonel Hutchinson*, p. 67.

33. L. Stone, 'The residential development of the West End of London in the seventeenth century' in B. C. Malament (ed.), *After the Reformation* (University of Pennsylvania Press, 1980), pp. 166–212 (p. 175); Barnes, *Somerset 1625-1640*, p. 28; A. Everitt, 'The county community' in E. W. Ives (ed.), *The English Revolution 1600–1660* (London, 1968), pp. 48–63 (p. 59). See also A. Everitt, *Change in the Provinces* (Leicester, 1969), pp. 5–35; and Mathew, *Social Structure in Caroline England*, pp. 52–5.

34. Henry Peacham, *The Art of Living in London* (London, 1642), sig.A2^r.

35. M. Neill, ' "Wits most accomplished senate": the audience of the Caroline private theatres', *Studies in English Litertature 1500–1900*, 18 (1978), 341–60 (350n).

36. Bentley, *JCS*, VI, pp. 33–4; and my forthcoming article 'Two playgoers, and the closing of the London theatres'.

37. Mathew, *Social Structure in Caroline England*, pp. 100n, 107n; HMC 14, ii (Portland MSS), p. 47.

38. A. B. Grosart, *The Lismore Papers* (2nd ser., 5 vols, London, 1887–88), IV, p. 113.

39. James Howell, *Epistolae Ho-Elianae*, I (ed. J. Jacobs, London, 1890), p. 214.

40. Cockayne, *Chain of Golden Poems*, p. 91; H. Glapthorne, *Poems* (London, 1639), pp. 29–30; Hyde, *Autobiography*, I, pp. 25–31.

41. M. Hobbs, 'Robert and Thomas Ellice, friends of Ford and Davenant', *Notes and Queries*, 219 (1974), 292–3.

42. T. Park, *Facetiae*, I (London, 1817), pp. 104, 109.

43. CSPD 1633–34, p. 86.

44. John Selden, *Table Talk* (ed. R. Milward, London, 1689), p. 43.

45. Bentley, *JCS*, II, p. 677.

46. M. Fane, *Raguaillo d'Oceano* (ed. C. Leech, Louvain, 1938), p. 13; Ralph, *Sir Humphrey Mildmay*, pp. 26–7; DNB 'Sir Francis Fane'; *Genealogical Memoranda Relating to the Family of Mildmay* (London, 1871).

47. E. P. Shirley, *Stemmata Shirleiana* (2nd edn, London, 1873), pp. 39, 235.

48. Ralph, *Sir Humphrey Mildmay*, p. 28; Bentley, *JCS*, II, p. 678; VI, p. 34; *DNB* 'William Crofts'.

49. J.B. Burke, *A Genealogical and Heraldic History of the Extinct ... Baronetcies of England* (2nd edn, London, 1846), pp. 141–2; Francis Quarles, *Sighs at the Contemporary Deaths* (London, 1640); Bentley, *JCS*, II, p. 676.

50. Edward Herbert, *The Autobiography* (ed. J. M. Shuttleworth, Oxford, 1976), p. 95; Ralph, *Sir Humphrey Mildmay*, pp. 104, 182, 212; Thomas Carew, *Poems* (ed. R. Dunlap, Oxford, 1949), p. 225.

51. Pearl, *London and ... Revolution*, pp. 93, 288–9; G. E. Cokayne, *Some Account of the Lord Mayors and Sheriffs of the City of London* (London, 1897), pp. 16–18; G. E. Cokayne, *Complete Baronetage* (5 vols, Exeter, 1900–06), II, p. 98; III, pp. 34, 55, 130; Ralph, *Sir Humphrey Mildmay*, pp. 11, 31.

52. *The Analytical Index to ... the Remembrancia* (ed. W.H. and H.C. Overall, London, 1878), p. 208n; Cokayne, *Some Account of the Lord Mayors*, pp. 65–7; E. P. Shirley, *Stemmata Shirleiana*, pp. 235, 271.

53. A. Harbage, *Sir Thomas Killigrew* (Philadelphia, 1930), pp. 30–8; Ralph, *Sir Humphrey Mildmay*, p. 135; Bentley, *JCS*, II, p. 677.

54. Ralph, *Sir Humphrey Mildmay*, p. 11; Harbage, *Thomas Killigrew*, pp. 28–30; Aurelian Townshend, *Poems and Masques* (ed. E. K. Chambers, Oxford, 1912), p.xxxvi; Bentley, *JCS*, III, pp. 33–5.

55. Rich, *Autobiography*, pp. 4–5, 21; Bentley, *JCS*, V, p. 1268.

56. Harbage, *Thomas Killigrew*, pp. 15–22; R. N. Worth, 'The family of Killigrew', *Journal of the Royal Institute of Cornwall*, 12 (April, 1871), 269–82; W. D. B. Grant, *Margaret the First* (London, 1957), pp. 27–45.

57. B. Buckler, *Stemmata Chicheleana* (Oxford, 1765), pp. 29, 123; Ralph, *Sir Humphrey Mildmay*, p. 35.

58. Ralph, *Sir Humphrey Mildmay*, pp. 31–2; C. C. Brown, 'The Chirk Castle entertainment of 1634', *Milton Quarterly*, 11 (1977), 76–86; R. J. Broadbent, 'A Masque at Knowsley', *Transactions of the Historic Society of Lancashire and Cheshire*, N.S. 41 (1925), pp. 1–16; Heinemann, *Puritanism and Theatre*, pp. 124–6, 260–4.

59. H. Peacham, *The Complete Gentleman* (ed. V. B. Heltzel, Ithaca, 1962), p. 243.

60. CSPD 1631–33, p. 529; see L. Stone, *The Crisis of the Aristocracy* (Oxford, 1965), pp. 397–8.

61. Rushworth, *Historical Collections*, II, pt i, p. 144. See also Gardiner, *Star Chamber Reports*, pp. 176–80; and L. M. Hill, 'County government in Caroline England' in Russell, *Origins of the English Civil War*, pp. 66–90.

62. E.g. A. H. Smith, *Country and Court* (Oxford, 1974), pp. 15, 99–102, 108–11.

63. See Pearl, *London and ... Revolution*, pp. 41–2; and F. J. Fisher, 'The growth of London' in Ives, *The English Revolution*, pp. 76–86.

64. B. Schofield (ed.), *The Knyvett Letters*, Norfolk Record Society, 20 (1949),

pp. 63–4; Cornwallis, *Correspondence*, p. 147; J. Bruce (ed.), *Letters and Papers of the Verney Family* (London, 1853), p. 128; Earle, *Microcosmography*, sig. D10ᵛ; I. H. C. Fraser, 'The agitation in the Commons, 2 March 1629', *Bulletin of the Institute of Historical Research*, 30 (1957), 86–95 (94).

65. HMC 55 (various), vii, p. 402; Bruce, *Verney Papers*, p. 159; HMC 55, vii, p. 409; Trevor-Roper, *Archbishop Laud*, pp. 227, 358; CSPV 1632–36, p. 466; Schofield, *Knyvett Letters*, p. 90; Bastwick, *The Litany*, pt 3, p. 16.

66. Pearl, *London and...Revolution*, pp. 41–2; Suckling, *Works*, I, p. 141; HMC 3 (House of Lords MSS) app., p. 3; Gardiner, *Oxinden Letters*, p. 163; Trevor-Roper, *Archbishop Laud*, p. 412; Schofield, *Knyvett Letters*, p. 99; W. Scott, *A Collection of Scarce and Valuable Tracts*, IV (2nd edn, London, 1810), p. 233; Hyde, *History of the Rebellion*, I, p. 392; *idem*, *Autobiography*, I, p. 68; Gardiner, *Oxinden Letters*, pp. 200, 272; Waller, *Poems*, I, p. xlviii; E. Husbands, *An Exact Collection* (London, 1642), pp. 215, 234; Pearl, *London and...Revolution*, pp. 233–4.

67. Schofield, *Knyvett Letters*, p. 31; Marriott, *Lucius Cary*, p. 153.

68. Ralph, *Sir Humphrey Mildmay*, pp. 25, 91–2, 149–50; C. Holmes, *The Eastern Association in the English Civil War* (Cambridge, 1974), p. 125; *DNB* 'Sir Walter Mildmay'.

69. Ralph, *Sir Humphrey Mildmay*, pp. 7–8; *DNB* 'Sir Henry Mildmay'; Aylmer, *The King's Servants*, pp. 353–4, 357, 384–5; C. H. Firth (ed.), *The Clarke Papers*, II (London, 1894), pp. 267–8.

70. Keeler, *The Long Parliament*, pp. 177, 126, 225–6, 250; *Harleian Society Publications*, 13 (1878), pp. 171–2, 452; Gardiner, *History*, IX, p. 224.

71. Fane, *Raguaillo d'Oceano*, pp. 13, 16, 36; R. Hutton, 'The structure of the royalist party 1642–1646', *The Historical Journal*, 24 (1981), 553–69 (561).

72. Fane, *Raguaillo d'Oceano*, p. 131.

73. J. Bramston, *Autobiography* (ed. T. W. Bramston, London, 1845), pp. 160, 103.

74. Cokayne, *Some Account of the Lord Mayors*, pp. 12–15, 73–4; Trevor-Roper, *Archbishop Laud*, p. 375.

75. *DNB* 'Sir Isaac Dorislaus'; M. H. Curtis, 'The alienated intellectuals of early Stuart England', *Past and Present*, 23 (1962), 25–43 (26–7); C. Hill, *Intellectual Origins of the English Revolution* (Oxford, 1965), p. 176.

76. D. Hirst, 'The defection of Sir Edward Dering', *The Historical Journal*, 15 (1972), 193–208; R. Ashton, *The English Civil War* (London, 1978), p. 113; L. B. Larking, *Proceedings in the County of Kent* (London, 1862), pp. xxxvi–li; Morrill, *Revolt of the Provinces*, p. 41.

77. G. W. Williams and G. B. Evans (eds), *'The History of King Henry the Fourth' as revised by Sir Edward Dering* (Charlottesville, 1974), p. viii; Lennam, 'Dering's collection of playbooks', pp. 145–53 (for the diary).

78. The account book is BL Add. MS 47787. The play, *Philander, King of Thrace*, is a Folger library manuscript which Professor J. P. Rosenblatt of Georgetown University very kindly informs me is in Dering's hand; its

terminus a quo is 1627 (J. Q. Adams, 'The author-plot of an early seventeenth-century play', *The Library*, 4th ser., 26 (1945–46), 16–27 (21)). It is interesting – and tantalizing – that Dering specifically noted that the monarchy of Thrace was elective, and that the Thracians could depose their King for misgovernment (Adams, p. 23). In other respects, this brief sketch resembles the *Queen of Aragon*. Dering also cut the reference to the swarming of playbooks out of the Kent petition against the bishops to parliament (Larking, *Proceedings in Kent*, p. 32).

79. M. F. Bond (ed.), *The Diaries and Papers of Sir Edward Dering* (London, 1976), family tree in fly-leaf; E. Hasted, *The History . . . of Kent* (4 vols, Canterbury, 1782), II, pp. 265–6; Fane, *Raguaillo d'Oceano*, p. 9; O. Barron (ed.), *Northamptonshire Families* (London, 1906), pp. 81–123.

80. M. H. Nicolson (ed.), *Conway Letters* (London, 1930), pp. 2–4; J. Webster, *The Complete Works*, II (ed. F. L. Lucas, London, 1927), p. 321.

81. *Early History of the Hobart Family* (London, n.d.); *The Visitation of Norfolk, 1664*, Norfolk Record Society, IV, p. 101; D. Brunton and D. H. Pennington, *Members of the Long Parliament* (London, 1954), pp. 99–101; J. Oglander, *The Commonplace Book* (ed. F. Bamford, London, 1936), p. 72n; Holmes, *The Eastern Association*, p. 72; Cokayne, *Complete Baronetage*, I, pp. 12–13.

82. P. Laslett, 'The gentry of Kent in 1640', *The Cambridge Historical Journal*, 9 no. 2 (1948), 148–64; *idem*, 'Sir Robert Filmer', pp. 527, 532.

83. Williams and Evans, *Dering's 'History of Henry IV'*, p. 3; *DNB* 'Edward Wotton'; G. E. Cokayne, V. Gibbs, H. A. Doubleday, D. Warrand, Howard de Walden and G. H. White, *Complete Peerage* (14 vols, London, 1910–59), XII, pt 2, pp. 866–7; *Publications of the Harleian Society*, 13, pp. 236, 437.

84. A. Everitt, *The Community of Kent and the Great Rebellion* (Leicester, 1973), p. 70; Larking, *Proceedings in Kent*, p. 14n.

85. R. Baker, *Meditations and Disquisitions on the Lord's Prayer* (ed. A. B. Grosart, London, 1882), pp. xxxiv–xxxv; Cokayne, *Complete Baronetage*, I, pp. 71–2.

86. K. Sharpe, *Sir Robert Cotton* (Oxford, 1979), pp. 212–15; P. Clark, *English Provincial Society from the Reformation to the Revolution* (Woking, 1977), p. 218; C. E. Wright, 'Sir Edward Dering', in C. Fox and B. Dickins (eds), *The Early Cultures of North-West Europe* (Cambridge, 1950), pp. 369–93; P. Styles, 'Politics and historical research in the early seventeenth century' in L. Fox (ed.), *English Historical Scholarship* (Oxford, 1956), pp. 49–72.

87. L. B. Larking, 'On the Surrenden charters', *Archaeologia Cantiana*, I (1858), pp. 50–65.

88. Bradley and Adams, *Jonson Allusion-Book*, pp. 165, 140–1; Puttick and Simpson sale catalogue, 13–15 July 1865.

89. Shirley, *Stemmata Shirleiana*, p. 61. This was the lady who had asked Falkland for the loan of a playbook (p. 106 above); her second husband, William Stafford of Blatherwyck, was a patron of Thomas Randolph

(B. H. Newdigate, 'The Constant Lovers', *TLS*, 1942, 204, 216). Sir Thomas Shirley's aunt, Theophila Coke, received dedications from Heywood (*Exemplary Lives*, 1640) and Joseph Rutter (the second part of *The Cid*, 1640).

90. W. R. Gair, 'The politics of scholarship' in D. Galloway (ed.), *The Elizabethan Theatre*, III (Ontario, 1973), pp. 100–18.

91. Ben Jonson, *The Magnetic Lady*, Induction, l.33; the Lovelace prologue is mentioned by A. J. Cook, *The Privileged Playgoers of Shakespeare's London* (Princeton, 1981), p. 265.

92. T. Cranley, *Amanda* (London, 1635), p. 35; Henry Glapthorne, *Poems* (London, 1639), p. 27. It is unclear which theatre Glapthorne's prologue belongs with. At various times between 1632 and 1639 he wrote for the King's Men, Queen's Men, King's Revels and Beeston's Boys, and the prologue could belong with any of these. However, its references to courtiers and gentry in the audience make it clear that it was intended for a 'private' theatre. 'Gests' refers to the court's summer progress into the country, or possibly to Charles's 1639 expedition against the Scots.

93. See my 'Massinger's *The City Madam* and the Caroline audience', *Renaissance Drama*, N.S. 13 (1982), 157–87 (162n). This essay explores the question of the citizen presence in the theatres at greater length than I can spare here.

94. Bentley, *JCS*, I, p. 25.

95. William Cartwright, *Comedies, Tragicomedies, with Other Poems* (London, 1651), p. 273.

96. Bentley, *JCS*, II, p. 693.

97. Bentley, *JCS*, I, pp. 22–3; HMC 9 (Salisbury MSS), xxii, pp. 267, 270.

98. P. J. Finkelpearl, *John Marston of the Middle Temple* (Cambridge, Mass., 1969), p. 14; Davenant, *Works*, sig.4A1[r].

99. N. Goodman, *Holland's Leaguer* (ed. D. S. Barnard, The Hague, 1970), p. 76.

100. In no sense do I mean to imply that the audiences of the open-air playhouses were predominantly composed of high-ranking spectators. The conclusions of A. J. Cook's *Privileged Playgoers of Shakespeare's London* (note 91 above) seem to me to be seriously misconceived and frequently contradicted by the evidence she cites. Her suggestion that there was essentially no difference between the two types of theatre runs counter to the perceptions of contemporaries (as Kathleen McLuskie notes in Edwards *et al.*, *Revels History*, p. 165). I have considered Cook's arguments in detail in Appendix II above.

101. Mathew, *Social Structure in Caroline England*, p. 53n.

102. Brunton and Penington, *Members of the Long Parliament*, pp. xiii–xvi; Hexter, *Reign of King Pym*, pp. 63–7, 75–94.

103. Laslett, 'The gentry of Kent', p. 149.

104. Keeler, *The Long Parliament*, pp. 89, 100, 108, 126, 147–8, 155–6, 171, 220, 225–6, 250, 263, 268, 272, 366–7.

105. Grimston paid for an engraved plate in Thomas Heywood's *The Hierarchy of the Blessed Angels* (1635). See also Keeler, *The Long Parliament*, p. 199.

106. BL Harleian MS 163, fo. 601^r; and see my article, 'Two playgoers, and the closing of the London theatres, 1642'.

107. L. Hotson, *The Commonwealth and Restoration Stage* (2nd edn, New York, 1962), p. 41.

108. W. Beamont, *A History of the House of Lyme* (Warrington, 1876), pp. 122–3.

109. I am grateful to Leo Salingar for pointing this out to me. See also Heinemann, *Puritanism and Theatre*, pp. 231–3.

110. Bentley, *JCS*, I, pp. 294, 277–8.

111. Bentley, *JCS*, I, p. 333.

112. See the letter from John Eliot to Secretary Coke of 22 October 1636 (CSPD 1636–37, pp. 170–1) suggesting that he should be appointed provost marshal to deal with suspicious people gathering in plague-ridden London, and referring to a gathering of people at a bull baiting.

113. Parliament's ordinances are conveniently available in facsimile in A. Freeman (ed.), *Commonwealth Tracts 1625–1650* (New York, 1974).

114. W. H. Coates, A. S. Young and V. F. Snow (eds), *Private Journals of the Long Parliament*, I (New Haven, 1982), p. 182; C. H. Hopwood (ed.), *Middle Temple Records*, II (London, 1904), p. 928.

115. *Commons Journals*, II (1640–42), pp. 749–50; *Lords Journals*, V (1642), pp. 334–7.

116. Freeman, *Commonwealth Tracts*, t.p.

117. E. K. Chambers, *The Elizabethan Stage*, IV (Oxford, 1923), p. 341. Shirley, who as an insider ought to have known what he was talking about, later claimed it was the excessive freedoms taken by the popular stages which had caused the playhouses to be closed, the magistrates 'looking at some abuses of the common theatres, which were not so happily purg'd from scurrility, and under-wit, (the onely entertainment of vulgar capacities) they have outed the more noble and ingenious actions of the eminent stages' (*The Politician* (London, 1655), sig.A2^r).

118. Coates *et al.*, *Private Journals of the Long Parliament*, I, p. 182; Freeman, *Commonwealth Tracts*, sig.A4^v; Hotson, *Commonwealth and Restoration Stage*, pp. 20, 25. See Salingar *et al.*, 'Les comédiens et leur public', pp. 572–3 for some important comments on these orders.

119. Quoted by Salingar *et al.*, 'Les comédiens et leur public', p. 573n; Hotson, *Commonwealth and Restoration Stage*, p. 40.

120. CSPD 1655–56, p. 103; CSPV 1655–56, p. 165; Rollins, 'The Commonwealth drama', p. 60.

7. *City comedies: courtiers and gentlemen*

1. Sir Philip Sidney, *The Defence of Poesie* in *The Prose Works*, III (ed. A. Feuillerat, Cambridge, 1912), pp. 1–46 (pp. 22, 41).

2. Bentley, *JCS*, III, p. 223.
3. There are suggestions of similar attitudes in another courtier play about the town, Thomas Killigrew's *The Parson's Wedding* (1640?) in which the town is a place of nonconformity and zeal, and the great ladies are not platonics but *politiques* ('Their whole endeavou[r]s are spent now in feasting, and winning close Committee-men ... that Tongue, I warrant you, which now growes hoarse with flattering the great Law breakers, once gave Law to Princes' (*Comedies and Tragedies* (London, 1664), pp. 140–1 – this may though be a later addition)).
4. J. Summerson, *Inigo Jones* (Harmondsworth, 1966), pp. 83–96; R. Webber, *Covent Garden* (London, 1969), pp. 9–21.
5. C. Trent, *The Russells* (London, 1966), pp. 117–29.
6. Webber, *Covent Garden*, p. 11; Summerson, *Inigo Jones*, p. 87. For Venice, see Brome, *Weeding of Covent Garden*, p. 1.
7. R.J. Kaufmann, *Richard Brome, Caroline playwright* (New York, 1961), pp. 69–74.
8. Kaufmann, *Richard Brome*, p. 72.
9. In his *Tottenham Court* (1633), Thomas Nabbes advances similar arguments to defend the freedom of the gentry's pleasures, and chastises two *courtiers* for their lustful intentions.
10. The t.p. of Nabbes's *Covent Garden* dates his play to February 1633, and the prologue implies that it was narrowly preceded by Brome's own Covent Garden play. But Kaufmann (*Richard Brome*, pp. 68–74) makes a good case for a slightly later date for Brome's play; perhaps Nabbes's statements are not entirely correct?
11. D'Ewes, *Autobiography*, II, p. 79.
12. Pearl, *London and ... Revolution*, p. 23.
13. *Richard Brome*, pp. 78, 85.
14. Wedgwood, *Trial of Charles I*, p. 130.
15. In my 'Massinger's *The City Madam* and the Caroline audience'.
16. I quote from the typescript of a forthcoming essay by L. G. Salingar, ' "Wit" in Jacobean comedy'.
17. Fletcher, *Works* (ed. A. Glover and A. R. Waller, 10 vols, Cambridge, 1905–12), IX, p. 119. Although probably by Middleton, this play was published as Fletcher's in 1639 and found its way into the folio of 1647.
18. See the prologue published with the third (1667) edition of his *The School of Compliments*.
19. E.g. *The Lady of Pleasure*, III.ii; *The Sparagus Garden*, IV.x.
20. Wycherley, *The Complete Plays* (ed. G. Weales, New York, 1967), p. 273.
21. Etherege, *The Dramatic Works* (ed. H. F. B. Brett-Smith, 2 vols, Oxford, 1927), III.i.4.
22. Ibid, I.ii.160, IV.iv.111. Another good instance is Aphra Behn's *The Rover* (1677) which is set among exiled royalists on the continent (ed. F. M. Link

(London, 1967), I.ii.66–7, II.ii.22, V.i.510–11). The fool is a country squire and supporter of parliament (I.ii.50–8, 293).

23. For example, Edward Howard's *The Change of Crowns* (1667) often brings Habington's *Queen of Aragon* to mind, but operates within much narrower limits. Here political difficulties dissolve easily away before the force of true love, and the 'change of crowns' is much less radical than the title might suggest – the exchange takes place within a restricted and firmly royal circle, and raises none of the questions about hierarchy and authority which Habington pursued (significantly, the disguised hero's real name is Carolo). Yet this play was deemed scandalously subversive in 1667, and was prevented from reaching print.

24. J. Dryden, *Of Dramatic Poesy and Other Essays* (ed. G. Watson, 2 vols, London, 1962), I, pp. 180–1, 252.

25. In *Dramatic Works*, I.i.123, IV.i.6. Compare Brome's Crosswill, deliberately stubborn yet, in 1633, still sympathetic.

26. See his speech of 1737 on the Licensing Bill: 'in King *Charles* IId's Time . . . when we were out of *Humour* with *Holland*, *Dryden* the Laureat wrote his Play of the *Cruelty* of the *Dutch* at *Amboyna*. When the Affair of the *Exclusion Bill* was depending, he wrote his *Duke of Guise*. When the Court took offence at the Citizens . . . the Stage was employ'd to expose them as Fools, Cheats, Usurers, and to compleat their Characters, Cuckolds. The *Cavaliers* at that Time, who were to be *flattered*, tho' the worst of Characters, were always *very worthy honest Gentlemen*; and the *Dissenters*, who were *to be abused*, were always *Scoundrels* and *quaint mischievous Fellows*' (*The Gentleman's Magazine*, 7 (1737), 410).

27. D. Underwood, *Etherege and the Seventeenth-Century Comedy of Manners* (London, 1957), pp. 138–42.

28. Gardiner, *Oxinden Letters*, p. 279.

29. My argument here has been anticipated by G. Bas, 'Titre, thèmes et structure dans *The Lady of Pleasure* de James Shirley', *Annales de la Faculté des Lettres et Sciences Humaines de Nice*, 34 (1978), 97–107. There is a revealing contrast with Fletcher's *The Noble Gentleman* (1625) which initiates a parallel debate between the thrift of the country and the wastefulness of the court which Fletcher simply does not (or cannot) resolve. In *The Lady of Pleasure* the Town provides Shirley with a third term midway between Court and Country in which the conflicting claims of each are harmonized into an acceptable mean.

30. Jones, *Politics and the Bench*, p. 214. See also Sir John Eliot's speech on grievances, 24 March 1628 (Forster, *Eliot*, II, p. 125).

31. A similar overwhelming speech in Massinger's *Believe as You List* (1631) actually is spoken by a courtesán (IV.ii.184–204).

32. L. Barkan, 'The Imperialist arts of Inigo Jones', *Renaissance Drama*, N. S. 7 (1976), 257–85, *passim*.

33. As well as in Massinger's *The Picture* (1629) and *The City Madam* (1632), and Brome's *The Sparagus Garden* (1635).
34. Bentley, *JCS*, V, p. 1077.
35. J. P. Kenyon, *The Stuart Constitution 1603–1688* (Cambridge, 1966), pp. 16–18; Wormald, *Clarendon*, pp. 11–12, 148.
36. There are recent discussions of *Hyde Park* by R. Levin, 'The triple plot of *Hyde Park*', *Modern Language Review*, 62 (1967), 17–27; and A. Wertheim, 'Games and courtship in James Shirley's *Hyde Park*', *Anglia*, 90 (1972), 71–91.
37. The country is also brought to the city in Brome's *The Sparagus Garden* and Nabbes's *Tottenham Court*. In each there is a similar association of a (cultivated) natural setting with 'country' criticism of courtiers.
38. The collocation of propriety in manners and politics (and aesthetics) is suggestively elaborated by Clarendon: 'Whatsoever is of Civility and good Manners, all that is of Art and Beauty, or of real and solid Wealth in the World, is the . . . child of beloved Propriety; and they who would strangle this Issue, desire to demolish all Buildings, eradicate all Plantations, to make the Earth barren, and man-kind to live again in Tents, and nourish his Cattle where the grass grows' (quoted in C. Hill, *Puritanism and Revolution* (London, 1958), p. 211).

8. The survival of the popular tradition

1. Salingar, 'Les comédiens et leur public', pp. 555–7.
2. Edwards *et al.*, *Revels History*, p. 117; Bentley, *JCS*, I, p. 278.
3. Bentley, *JCS*, I, pp. 318, 322; II, p. 691; VI, pp. 243, 246. The *Merry Devil of Edmonton* (1602) was also revived at the Globe at this time (*JCS*, VI, pp. 198–9).
4. Bentley, *JCS*, VI, p. 244.
5. Rowley, *A Merry and Pleasant Comedy* (London, 1638), sig. A3^v; Bentley, *JCS*, II, p. 690; VI, p. 245.
6. J. Freehafer's arguments for an earlier date ('Shakespeare's *Tempest* and *The Seven Champions*', *Studies in Philology*, 66 (1966), 87–107) seem to me to be quite unconvincing.
7. Bentley, *JCS*, V, pp. 1321–2.
8. Bentley, *JCS*, II, p. 693.
9. See especially the list of plays the company was protecting from piracy in 1639 (Bentley, *JCS*, I, pp. 330–1); and further details in *JCS*, I, pp. 337–42.
10. Bentley, *JCS*, I, pp. 254, 301.
11. See Bentley, *JCS*, I, p. 323; and F. S. Boas, *Shakespeare and the Universities* (Oxford, 1923), pp. 96–110.
12. Bentley, *JCS*, I, p. 37.

13. H. Mill, *A Night's Search* (London, 1640), sig.A2^r; A. M. Clark, *Thomas Heywood* (Oxford, 1931), p. 6.

14. T. Rawlins, *The Rebellion* (London, 1640), sig.A4^r; N. Richards, *Messallina* (London, 1640), sigs.A6^v, A7^v, A8^r, B1^v; J. Tatham, *Fancies Theatre* (London, 1640), sigs.A1^r, (*)3^v; R. Chamberlain, *Nocturnal Lucubrations* (London, 1638), sig.A3r; Mill, *Night's Search*, sigs. A1^r, A5^r; S. Marmion, *Cupid and Psyche* (London, 1638), sig.A3^v.

15. H. Mill, *Poems Occasioned by a Melancholy Vision* (London, 1639), sigs.A7^v, D8^r.

16. Ibid. sig.D8^r.

17. Thomas Heywood, *A Challenge for Beauty* (London, 1636), sig.A3^r.

18. Richards, *Messallina*, sig.A6^r.

19. R. Davenport, *The Works* (ed. A. H. Bullen, London, 1890), p. 311; Thomas Nabbes, *Microcosmus* (London, 1637), sig.A4^v.

20. Prologues to *The Antipodes* (1638) and *The Court Beggar* (1640).

21. Prologue to *The Antipodes*, l.5; Sir John Suckling, *Works*, I, pp. 345–7.

22. References are to T. Jordan, *Money is an Ass* (London, 1668).

23. Tatham, *Fancies Theatre*, sig.C7^{r-v}.

24. Richards, *Messallina* (ed. A. R. Skemp, Louvain, 1910), p. 17; T. Jordan, *Poetical Varieties* (London, 1637), sig.B1^r.

25. Davenport, *The Works*, p. 307.

26. I have discussed *Messallina* in greater detail in 'Romans in Britain' in D. Howard (ed.), *Philip Massinger: Critical Essays* (forthcoming, Cambridge, 1984).

27. Forster, *Sir John Eliot*, II, p. 471; Pearl, *London and ... Revolution*, pp. 191–2.

28. V. F. Snow, *Essex the Rebel* (Lincoln [Nebraska], 1970), pp. 185–6, 215 and *passim*; Wilson, *The Inconstant Lady*, p. 123; Clarendon, *History of the Rebellion*, I, pp. 186, 320–1; A. Collins (ed.), *Letters and Memorials of State*, II (London, 1746), p. 593; Manning, 'The aristocracy and the downfall of Charles I', p. 66. Essex appears as a great patriot and puritan hero in May's *History of Parliament*, II, p. 97; III, p. 6.

29. Bentley, *JCS*, VI, p. 6; HMC 58 (Bath MSS), v, p. 285; Bodleian MS North c.4 fo.7^r (Essex entertaining the Palatine Prince with a play, 1635). Arthur Wilson is discussed in Heinemann, *Puritanism and Theatre*, pp. 221–4.

30. R. Codrington, *The Life and Death of the Illustrious Robert Earl of Essex* (London, 1646), p. 11.

31. HMC 55 (various MSS), vii, p. 402; R. G. Trease, *Portrait of a Cavalier* (London, 1979), p. 75; HMC 77 (De L'Isle and Dudley MSS), vi, p. 157.

32. S. A. Strong, *A Catalogue of Letters* (London, 1903), p. 213.

33. Ibid., pp. 213, 210, 212, 205, 233–4, 210.

34. M. Cavendish, *The Life of William Cavendish, Duke of Newcastle* (ed. C. H. Firth, 2nd edn, London, n.d.), p.x.

35. References are to the double volume *The Country Captain and The Variety* (The Hague, 1649); the pagination of the two plays is separate.
36. Forster, *Sir John Eliot*, I, p. 493; and see A. Barton, 'Harking back to Elizabeth: Ben Jonson and Caroline nostalgia', *ELH*, 48 (1982), 706–31.
37. In addition to Anne Barton's 'Harking back to Elizabeth', see C. V. Wedgwood, *Oliver Cromwell and the Elizabethan Inheritance* (London, 1970); J. E. Neale, *Essays in Elizabethan History* (London, 1958), pp. 9–20; N. M. Fuidge, 'Queen Elizabeth I and the Petition of Right', *Bulletin of the Institute of Historical Research*, 48 (1975), pp. 45–51; G. Ziegler, 'England's Savior', *Renaissance Papers* (1980), 29–37; and see J. W. Williamson, *The Myth of the Conqueror* (New York, 1978) for parallel nostalgia for Prince Henry.
38. Forster, *Sir John Eliot*, II, p. 239; I, pp. 289, 245–6.
39. Russell, *Parliaments and English Politics*, p. 206.
40. And the popular stage too; the queen who said '*blesse ye my good people all*' at the Bull (Bentley, *JCS*, VI, p. 245) could scarcely have been any other than Elizabeth. The Foxean genre is discussed in J. D. Spikes, 'The Jacobean history play and the myth of the Elect Nation', *Renaissance Drama*, N.S. 8 (1977), pp. 117–49.
41. D'Ewes, *Autobiography*, II, p. 210; and see Harleian MS 383 fo.65^r.
42. Bentley, *JCS*, III, p. 58.
43. This King's Revels play is difficult to place exactly. Bentley (*JCS*, V, p. 997) dates it 1638–39(?), but this is too late, for the company broke up in 1636. They played for a time at the Fortune, and the play certainly reads like a popular-theatre play, but Bentley quotes lines which seem to be making fun of all three popular theatres, so it may have been designed for the Salisbury Court after all.
44. A King's Revels play. Bentley thinks it belonged to the Red Bull Revels Company of 1619–23 (*JCS*, V, p. 1313), but largely because it looks too old-fashioned for the Salisbury Court, a disparity which disappears if the Salisbury Court repertoire *was* old-fashioned.
45. Davenport, *The Works*, pp. 212–13. For a discussion, see Heinemann, *Puritanism and Theatre*, pp. 226–9.
46. Published in 1658 without any information about its auspices. For a discussion, see Barton, 'He that plays the king', pp. 88–9.
47. Davenport, *The Works*, p. 15.
48. Ibid., p. 11.
49. Citations are from the edition of J. W. Lever (Oxford, 1976).
50. The first Earl of Clare (d.1637) was involved in the political scandal around Sir Robert Cotton in 1629, and stayed away from the court until his death; his son, Denzil Holles, was an associate of Sir John Eliot, and one of the Five Members Charles attempted to impeach in 1641. Algernon Percy, Earl of Northumberland, though Charles's admiral, was, like his brother-in-law Leicester, an opponent of many of Charles's ministers and

policies. The *Wasp* manuscript is in the library of the Percy family home, Alnwick.

51. Forster, *Sir John Eliot*, II, pp. 700–1.
52. Thomas Rawlins, *The Rebellion*, sig.I2ʳ.
53. NB p. 294:
It is a property you know my Lord,
No blade, but a rich Scabbard with a Lath in't.
LETOY. So is the sword of Justice for ought he [Peregrine] knows.
54. Gardiner, *History*, VIII, p. 90.
55. J. I. Cope, *The Theater and the Dream* (Baltimore, 1973), p. 157–9.
56. George Herbert, 'The Church Militant', ll. 235–6.
57. Kaufmann, *Richard Brome*, pp. 151–68, and Freehafer, 'Brome, Suckling and Davenant's theater project of 1639', 367–83.
58. Bentley, *JCS*, I, p. 333.
59. D'Ewes, *Autobiography*, p. 171.
60. P. Burke, 'Popular culture in seventeenth-century London', *The London Journal*, 3 (1977), 143–62.
61. *Works*, p. 250.
62. Chambers, *The Elizabethan Stage*, IV, p. 232. See also M. C. Bradbrook, 'Beasts and gods', *Shakespeare Survey*, 15 (1962), 62–72; and for some pictorial examples see A. G. Dickens, *Reformation and Society in Sixteenth-Century Europe* (London, 1966), pp. 13, 39, 66, 168.
63. B. Whitelocke, *Memorials of the English Affairs* (London, 1682), p. 20.
64. [H. Burton?], *A Divine Tragedy Lately Acted* (London, 1636), p. 45.
65. This was probably an invented name, but it had been used by Dekker for a spy employed by the Earl of Lincoln in *The Shoemaker's Holiday*.
66. For example, *England and Ireland's Sad Theatre*, 1645 (BL Prints and Drawings, Political and Personal Satires No. 416).
67. According to the Spanish agent who witnessed a performance of *A Game at Chess*, the player 'who acted the Prince of Wales heartily beat and kicked the Count of Gondomar into Hell, which consisted of a great hole and hideous figures; and the white king [drove] the black king and even his queen [into Hell] almost as offensively' (Bentley, *JCS*, IV, p. 872).
68. Bentley, *JCS*, IV, p. 473; CSPD 1628–29, p. 333.
69. See S. R. Smith, 'Almost revolutionaries: the London apprentices during the Civil Wars', *The Huntington Library Quarterly*, 42 (1978–79), 313–28; and B. Manning, *The English People and the English Revolution 1640–1649* (London, 1976).
70. Bentley, *JCS*, I, p. 315.
71. G. E. Aylmer, 'Gentlemen Levellers?', *Past and Present*, 49 (1970), 120–5.
72. Bentley, *JCS*, IV, pp. 477–9; and see Heinemann, *Puritanism and Theatre*, pp. 229–31.
73. Bentley, *JCS*, I, p. 278.
74. Bentley, *JCS*, II, p. 680; V, pp. 1355–6.

75. Bentley, *JCS*, III, p. 250; G. Edmundson, *History of Holland* (Cambridge, 1922), pp. 148–9.
76. Bentley, *JCS*, V, p. 1382.
77. Bentley, *JCS*, I, p. 314.
78. Bentley, *JCS*, I, pp. 277–8, 294.
79. John Milton, *Of Reformation*, pp. 2–3.
80. J. Shirley, *The Cardinal* (London, 1652), pp. 66–7 (published as part of *Six New Plays*, 1653).
81. My discussion of these pamphlets is deeply indebted to the brilliant, pioneering chapter in Margot Heinemann's *Puritanism and Theatre*, pp. 236–57 (slightly compressed from an earlier version in M. Cornforth (ed.), *Rebels and their Causes* (London, 1978), pp. 69–92).
82. Where appropriate, I have identified these pamphlets by their reference numbers in the British Library's Thomason Collection.
83. For example, *Time's Alteration* (669f4/4), *A Description of the Passage* (E156/21), *The Discontented Conference* (E157/3), *The Friar's Last Farewell* (E136/27), *A Purge for Pluralities* (E143/5).
84. For example, *The Pimp's Prerogative* (669f4/18), *The Sisters of the Scabberd's Holiday* (E168/8).
85. C. R. Baskerville, *The Elizabethan Jig and Related Song Drama* (Chicago, 1929), p. 121. See also Bentley, *JCS*, VI, p. 171.
86. Prynne himself had made this identification on the scaffold in 1637; see W. Lamont and S. Oldfield, *Politics, Religion and Literature in the Seventeenth Century* (London, 1975), p. 52.
87. Chambers, *The Elizabethan Stage*, IV, p. 231.
88. The monopoly for soap, and the ludicrous attempt to demonstrate the superiority of royal soap, was perhaps Charles's most inglorious hour.
89. F. Quarles, *The Virgin Widow* (London, 1649), p. 62.
90. See Christopher Hill's suggestive essay 'The many-headed monster in late Tudor and early Stuart political thinking' in *Change and Continuity in Seventeenth-Century England* (London, 1974), pp. 181–204.
91. Rushworth, *Historical Collections*, III, pt i, p. 33.
92. For example, Burton, *England's Bondage*, p. 10; Parker, *Discourse Concerning Puritans*, pp. 53–4; Prynne, *An Humble Remonstrance* (London, 1641), p. 63; anon, *The Black Box of Rome Opened* (London, 1641), p. 14; Marshall, *A Sermon Preached Before the honourable House of Commons*, p. 31; and many more instances. See especially *The Frogs of Egypt, or the Caterpillars of the Commonwealth Truly Dissected* (E166/2).
93. I quote from a copy of the third, 'authorized' edition, BL pressmark 644.d.29, sig.A2^r.
94. In 'A case study in Caroline political theatre: Brathwaite's *Mercurius Britannicus* (1641)', forthcoming in *The Historical Journal*.
95. *DNB*; Sir Edward Peyton, *The Divine Catastrophe* (London, 1652), p. 61.

9. Concepts of the country in the drama

1. HMC 78 (Hastings MSS), ii, p. 68; CSPV 1632-36, p. 445.
2. Bentley, *JCS*, IV, pp. 548-50.
3. Davenant, *Shorter Poems*, p. 150.
4. Carew, *Poems*, pp.175-6.
5. I follow here the account of P. Edwards and C. Gibson in *The Plays and Poems of Philip Massinger*, IV, pp. 107-10.
6. Rushworth, *Historical Collections*, II, pt ii, p. 1351.
7. The country cast of *The Goblins* is strengthened in IV.ii by the inclusion of a depiction of a country wedding.
8. There is of course an important literary source for these plays in Fletcher's *Beggars' Bush* (1622), which has the same strong contrast between court and country, with a country monarchy placed in antithesis to the despotic government of the usurping Earl Woolfort. However, the 'country' in this play are beggars, not outlaws, and though they live free of impositions, taxes and grievances (II.i.105 – unlike, implicitly, English subjects), they do not go about to *correct* the wrongs done in orthodox society, as happens in *The Guardian* and *The Goblins*. It comes as quite a shock in the final act when three of the beggars are suddenly revealed to be discourted noblemen in disguise.
9. A. Everitt, 'Farm labourers', in J. Thirsk (ed.), *The Agrarian History of England and Wales*, IV (Cambridge, 1967), p. 411; see also C. Hill, *The World Turned Upside Down* (Harmondsworth, 1975), pp. 46-9.
10. J. Taylor, *A Swarm of Sectaries* (London, 1641), sig.B1^r, and *A Cluster of Coxcombs* (London, 1642), sig.A3^r. See also Thirsk, *Agrarian History*, IV, pp. 111-12, 462-5; C. Burrage, *The Early English Dissenters* (Cambridge, 1912), II, p. 320; and J. Chandos, *In God's Name* (London, 1971), p. 407.
11. It is unfortunate that William Holles's play *The Country Court* (Bentley, *JCS*, IV, p. 587) has been lost; Holles was a relative of the discourted Earl of Clare (see p. 328 above), and his play was unlikely to have been flattering towards the king.
12. Bentley, *JCS*, V, p. 1147. My quotations are from the text in *Six New Plays* (London, 1653).
13. I quote from the text edited by T. J. B. Spencer and S. W. Wells in *A Book of Masques in Honour of Allardyce Nicoll* (Cambridge, 1967), pp. 351-2.
14. Bentley, *JCS*, V, p. 1148; Gardiner, *History of England*, X, pp. 178, 185, 192.
15. Kaufmann, *Richard Brome*, pp. 109-30.
16. That *A Jovial Crew* is about escapism rather than escapist has already been pointed out by David Farley-Hills in *The Comic in Renaissance Comedy* (London, 1981), pp. 147-59. However, he goes on to deal with the play from a firmly *ex post facto* point of view, reading it as a hysterical expression of 'the current state of Cavalier morale' (p. 156).

17. First pointed out by Christopher Hill (*The World Turned Upside Down*, p. 48). In 1644 we find Dudley Digges defining 'native liberty' in a political tract as 'the birth-right of mankinde, and equally common to every one, as the Aire we breath in, or the Sun which sheds his beames and lustre, as comfortably upon Beggars, as upon the Kings of the Earth' (Tuck, *Natural Rights Theories*, p. 103).

10. Some conclusions

1. *The Valiant Scot* (Fortune, 1639), 5 consecutive performances; *The Whore New Vamped* (Red Bull, 1639), acted 'many days together'; *The Knave in Grain* (Fortune, > 1640), acted 'many days together'; and Jordan's *Walks of Islington and Hogsden* (Red Bull, 1641), 19 consecutive performances.
2. For further important comment in these directions, see Heinemann, *Puritanism and Theatre*, pp. 13–15; *idem*, 'Shakespearean contradictions and social change', *Science and Society*, 41 No. 1 (1977), 7–16; R. Weimann, *Shakespeare and the Popular Tradition in the Theater*, (transl. R. Schwartz, Baltimore, 1978), pp. xi–xii; and J. W. Lever's brilliant brief study *The Tragedy of State* (London, 1971), pp. vii–viii, 1–15.
3. Bentley, *JCS*, II, p. 693.
4. John Dryden, *Absalom and Achitophel*, l.873.
5. W. S. Powell, *John Pory 1572–1636* (Chapel Hill, 1977), microfiche supplement, p. 340; CSPV 1632–36, p. 469; Gardiner, *History*, VIII, pp. 201, 203; Jones, *Politics and the Bench*, p. 89. See also the quotation from the Venetian ambassador on p. 119 above.

Appendix II

1. See N. B. Harte, 'State control of dress and social change in pre-industrial England', in D. C. Coleman and A. H. John (eds), *Trade, Government and Economy in Pre-Industrial England* (London, 1976), pp. 132–65.
2. J. Grant, 'The gentry of London in the reign of Charles I', *University of Birmingham Historical Journal*, 8 No. 2 (1962), 197–202.
3. J. Cornwallis, *The Private Correspondence* (London, 1842), p. 105; A. Fletcher, *A County Community in Peace and War* (London, 1975), p. 43.
4. Cornwallis, *Correspondence*, p. 44; Bodleian MS North c.4 fos.18ʳ, 20ʳ. See also James Dillon's letter from Covent Garden to Ralph Verney in the country complaining (in 1641) 'we finde the want of you and yʳ familie' (F. P. Verney, *Memoirs of the Verney Family During the Civil War*, I (London, 1892), p. 237).
5. Stone, 'The residential development of the West End of London', p. 175. See also Everitt, 'The county community' in Ives (ed.), *The English Revolution 1600–1660*, pp. 48–63; A. Everitt, *The Community of Kent and the*

Great Rebellion (Leicester, 1973), *passim; idem, Change in the Provinces: The Seventeenth Century* (Leicester, 1969), *passim; idem,* 'The local community and the great rebellion', in K. H. D. Haley (ed.), *The Historical Association Book of the Stuarts* (London, 1973), pp. 74–101; W. B. Willcox, *Gloucestershire: A Study in Local Government* (New Haven, 1940), *passim;* and Barnes, *Somerset 1625–1640,* p. 28 and *passim.*

6. Schofield (ed.), *The Knyvett Letters,* pp. 70, 73, 75, 93.
7. Gardiner (ed.), *The Oxinden Letters,* pp. 154–5, 188, 235, 219.
8. Cornwallis, *Correspondence,* pp. 103, 98, 108, 154.
9. F. Bamford (ed.), *A Royalist's Notebook* (London, 1936), p. 229.
10. Barnes, *Somerset,* p. 28.
11. Everitt, 'The county community', p. 49. Everitt also points out that if the gentry were more numerous before the Civil War they must also have been by and large that much less well-off and that much more countrified; in 1640 'local attachments were, if anything, becoming deeper rather than more superficial' ('The local community and the great rebellion', pp. 78, 79).
12. Stone, 'The residential development of the West End', p 175.
13. I am very grateful to Peter Holland for this observation, and for several others in this appendix.
14. A. Harbage, *Shakespeare's Audience* (4th edn, New York, 1964), pp. 13, 101; *idem, Shakespeare and the Rival Traditions* (2nd edn, New York, 1968), p. 94.
15. A. Gurr, *The Shakespearean Stage 1574–1642* (2nd edn, Cambridge, 1980), pp. 199, 202, 208.
16. *The Case is Altered,* I.i.62–3; *The Staple of News,* Prologue for the Court, ll.7–8.
17. Bentley, *JCS,* III, p. 103.
18. T. Dekker, *The Non-dramatic Works* (ed. A. B. Grosart, 5 vols, London, 1884–86), II, pp. 247, 248, 250, 253; IV, pp. 55, 194; Cook, *Privileged Playgoers,* p. 261.
19. J. Orrell, 'The London stage in the Florentine correspondence, 1604–1618', *Theatre Research International,* 3 (1977–78), 157–76 (171).
20. Harbage, *Shakespeare's Audience,* p. 84.
21. See *The Miller's Tale,* ll. 3760–3 and Robinson's note. In the London of 1345 the spurriers were reported to be working at night and walking around blind drunk in the afternoons (L. F. Salzman, *English Industries of the Middle Ages* (Oxford, 1923), p. 322).
22. Schofield, *Knyvett Letters,* p. 70.
23. Harbage, *Shakespeare's Audience,* pp. 8, 90; *Malone Society Collections,* I, p. 77; H. Crosse, *Virtue's Commonwealth* (London, 1603), sig.P4^{r-v}.
24. *Shakespeare's Audience,* p. 5.
25. M. C. Bradbrook, *The Rise of the Common Player* (3rd edn, Cambridge, 1979), pp. 73, 162; Gurr, *The Shakespearean Stage,* p. 50.

26. Gurr, *The Shakespearean Stage*, p. 213. See also J. Jacquot, 'Le répertoire des compagnes d'enfants à Londres 1600–1610' in Jacquot (ed.), *Dramaturgie et Société*, II, pp. 729–82.

27. Jonson, *The Magnetic Lady*, Induction, ll. 32–4; F. Bowers (ed.), *The Dramatic Works in the Beaumont and Fletcher Canon*, III (Cambridge, 1976), pp. 490, 492, 493. Admission to the Blackfriars cost at least 6d., but at the tiny indoor theatre of Paul's in the 1580s and 1600s prices began at only 2d., and here the audiences had included tradesmen and servants; see W. R. Gair, *The Children of Paul's* (Cambridge, 1982), pp. 72–3.

28. Bentley, *JCS*, VI, pp. 193–4, 196–7.

29. Dekker, *Non-dramatic Works*, II, p. 250.

30. As statements by Lovelace (Cook, p. 265) and Jonson (*The Magnetic Lady*, Induction, ll. 32–7) indicate.

31. Weimann, *Shakespeare and the Popular Tradition*, p. 173; Brome, *Works*, III, p. 348.

Index

Index

Chamberlain, Robert, 185; *Nocturnal Lucubrations*, 191–2; *The Swaggering Damsel*, 189, 216
Chambers, E. K., 2
Chambers, Richard, 79
Chapman, George, *Bussy d'Ambois*, 107
Charles I: and the aristocracy, 25–7, 123, 147, 193–5, 286; and censorship, 72, 123, 135; and the church, 16, 86–8, 90, 198–201, 218; foreign policy of, 16, 27, 31–5, 198–9, 201–2; and his parliaments, (1620s), 11–13, 20, 22, (Short Parliament) 74–5, 227, 228, 258, 260, (Long Parliament) 16–18, 20–3, 76, 79, 81, 252–3, 282; patronage of, 42, 59, 101–2, 252; personal government of, 13–16, 49, 56–7, 58, 59, 68, 79, 118, 123, 142, 144, 148, 151, 152, 153, 156–7, 171, 209, 214, 222, 224; mentioned, 5, 6, 9, 44, 46, 100, 119, 122, 124, 129, 137, 216, 217, 218, 251, 264–5, 279, 285–6, 294
Charles II (Prince Charles), 33, 116, 124, 195–6
Charles Louis, Elector Palatine, 31–4, 42, 102, 286, 311 n. 34
Chesterfield, Philip Stanhope, 4th Earl of, 162, 325 n. 26
Chettle, Henry, 299; *The Tragedy of Hoffmann*, 184
Chicheley, Thomas, 117, 122
Christina, Queen of Sweden, 92
Clare, John Holles, 1st Earl of, 25, 208, 328 n. 50, 331 n. 11
Clarendon, Edward Hyde, Earl of, 17, 75, 103, 108, 113, 120, 134, 174–5, 326 n. 38
Clarke, Samuel, 91, 93
Cleveland, John, 181
Clifton, Gervase, 119
Cockayne, Sir Aston, 105, 108, 113; *A Masque at Brethy*, 128; *Trappolin Supposed a Prince*, 206
Cockpit playhouse, *see* Phoenix playhouse
Coke, Sir Edward, 308 n. 11
Coke, Sir John, 115, 123
Coke, Theophila, 322 n. 89
Collinson, Patrick, 85
Conway, Edward, Viscount, 26, 93, 105, 106, 112, 113, 125, 135
Conway, Anne, Viscountess, 125
Cook, Ann Jennalie, 293–306, 322 n. 100
Corneille, Pierre, 59
Cornwallis, Jane, 102, 110, 116, 296
Coryton, William, 20
Costly Whore, The, 204–5, 257, 286
Cottington, Sir Francis, 85
Cotton, Charles, 113
Cotton, Sir Robert, 128–9, 132, 328 n. 50
Counter's Discourse, The, 231
Coventry, Thomas (Lord Keeper), 103

Cranborne, Charles Cecil, Viscount, 131, 134
Crane, Sir Robert, 127, 129
Cranley, Thomas, 130
Crofts, Cecilia, 116–17
Crofts family, 115–17, 133
Crofts, William (Baron Crofts), 116, 127
Croke, Sir George, 79
Cromwell, Oliver, 63, 91, 93, 99, 135, 139
Culpepper, Sir John, 247
Curtain playhouse, 181, 300, 305
D., T., *The Bloody Banquet*, 183
Danby, Henry Danvers, Earl of, 286
Davenant, Sir William, 8, 99, 101, 111, 136, 170, 186, 220, 251, 268, 287; *Albovine*, 113; *The Fair Favourite*, 57–9, 70; *The Just Italian*, 28; *Luminalia*, 106; *Madagascar*, 34; *Salmacida Spolia*, 264; *The Temple of Love*, 29–30; *The Triumphs of the Prince d'Amour*, 32–3, 123; verse letter 'To the Queen', 58–9; *The Unfortunate Lovers*, 55; *The Wits*, 143–7, 311 n. 25
Davenport, Robert, 185, 189, 195; *A Crown for a Conqueror*, 191, 192; *King John and Matilda*, 73, 201, 206, 207, 286; *A New Trick to Cheat the Devil*, 189, 191, 206, 226, 229
Day, John, *The Blind Beggar of Bethnal Green*, 181–2, 207; *The Parliament of Bees*, 191; *The Travels of Three English Brothers*, 115
Dekker, Thomas, 113, 300, 305; *Gustavus King of Sweden*, 235; *Match Me in London*, 184; *The Shoemaker's Holiday*, 182; *The Whore of Babylon*, 41; *The Witch of Edmonton*, *see* Rowley, W.
Denham, Sir John, *Cooper's Hill*, 72–3; *The Sophy*, 79–82, 280
Denham, Sir John (judge), 79
Dering, Sir Edward, 18, 104, 117, 124–9, 134, 165, 320–1 n. 78
Desfontaines, N., *La Vraye Suite du Cid*, 59–61
D'Ewes, Simonds, 13, 21, 34, 67, 93–4, 128, 134, 152, 223
Dialogue or Accidental Discourse betwixt ... Abell and ... Kilvert, A, 238, 240
Dialogue betwixt Roundhead and Rattlehead, A, 237, 239, 241
Digby, Sir John, 104, 116
Digby, Kenelm, 30, 102, 105, 112–13, 117, 124
Digges, Sir Dudley, 14, 15, 332 n. 17
Dr Lambe and the Witches, 184
Doge and the Dragon, The, 182
Donne, John, 93
Dorislaus, Isaac, 123–4, 135
Dorset, Edward Sackville, Earl of, 26, 27, 28, 33, 59

336

Index

Index

Index